2015

D0909906

CORPORATE STATEMENTS

CORPORATE STATEMENTS

The Official Missions, Goals,
Principles and Philosophies
of Over 900 Companies

by
PAUL G. HASCHAK

McFarland & Company, Inc., Publishers
Jefferson, North Carolina, and London

British Library Cataloguing-in-Publication data are available

Library of Congress Cataloguing-in-Publication Data

Haschak, Paul G., 1948–
    Corporate statements : the official missions, goals, principles
and philosophies of over 900 companies / by Paul G. Haschak.
        p.   cm.
    Includes index.
    ISBN 0-7864-0342-X (library binding : 50# alkaline paper) ∞
    1. Mission statements.   2. Corporate culture.   I. Title.
HD30.285.H37   1998
338.7 — dc21   97-40509
                                                                CIP

Manufactured in the United States of America

McFarland & Company, Inc., Publishers
  Box 611, Jefferson, North Carolina 28640

Especially for A. Rami Hijazi

CONTENTS

PREFACE

This book brings together a varied collection of actual corporate statements for public and private companies — very large, large, medium, and emerging.

The collection includes examples of vision and mission statements, guiding beliefs, corporate values, objectives, overviews, goals, credos, mottoes, slogans, corporate philosophies, strategies, and environmental statements.

This compilation can serve a variety of purposes. It could, for example, provide an ideal starting point for a college student writing a class paper on a specific company's corporate culture. It would be a very useful resource for a college professor doing preliminary research on the missions of companies within a certain industry. It might greatly aid a job seeker preparing for his or her big job interview and wishing to get some useful background information. It should benefit investors or information specialists doing basic business research, too.

The reader should take note that nearly all of the companies in this book are located in the United States. A few companies outside the United States are included, however, because they are sufficiently prominent in their industry that their inclusion seemed important to those readers involved in industry research.

Entries for the corporations are arranged alphabetically by name. The entries include (1) name, address, and telephone number, (2) a brief description of the company, (3) examples of their corporate statement(s), and (4) their World Wide Web address (for those with Web sites). A comprehensive index includes company names, geographic references, and companies listed by industry.

As with any book, outdatedness shadows this compilation. The author has worked the last three years (1995–1997) collecting statements for this book. Chiefly, he has used publications sent directly to him from the companies themselves, as his sources of information. These publications have included annual reports, 10-K reports, and a variety of miscellaneous corporate reports, press releases, pamphlets, booklets, letters, and the like.

Change is the norm in the business world. Corporations merge. They split up. They spin off a division or divisions into a new entity. They change stock exchanges. They expand their markets. They downsize. If absolute currency is important, researchers must take precautions in using this book or any other reference tool.

When doing your research on a company, always consult other standard reference tools, including CD-ROM products and the Internet, to learn of any changes that have taken place recently. The author suggests you consult some of the following (or their equivalent):

SEC File (a collection on microfiche), published by Q-Data Corp., for annual reports.

The SEC EDGAR archives, for 10-K and variety of other SEC reports:
http://www.sec.gov/cgi-bin/srch-edgar

For articles: *ABI-INFORM* (or a similar database) is a highly useful CD-ROM product.

For financial information: *Disclosure.*

Print sources: *Hoover's Handbook of American Business* (and other Hoover titles), *Moody's Industrial Manual* (and other Moody publications), *Standard & Poor's Corporation Records, Ward's Business Directory,* and *D&B Million Dollar Directory.* Ask your librarian what sources are available locally.

You may also do as the author did and write (or phone) the company directly. Most companies are more than willing to send you a packet of information, especially if they are public companies.

The author would like to thank Ms. Gentry Lankewicz for her help in the early stages of the project.

1. Abbott Laboratories
100 Abbott Park Rd.
Abbott Park, IL 60064
Phone: (847) 937-6100
Web: http://www.abbott.com

Abbott Laboratories (NYSE; ABT) develops, manufactures, and markets nutritional, pharmaceutical, diagnostic, chemical and agricultural products, and hospital-related products. Nutritional brands include Similac, Isomil, Gain, Pedialyte, Pediasure, Ensure, Glucerna, Advera, Jevity, Flexiflo, Companion, and Quantum. Pharmaceutical products include Blaxin, Klacid, Klaricid, Erythromycin, Tosuxacin, Hytrin, Depakote, Abbokinase, Survanta, Cylert, Lupron, and Prevacid.

Slogan: "Quality Health Care Worldwide."

Mission: Abbott's mission is to improve lives worldwide by providing cost-effective health care products and services. And we do so through much more than our products. Abbott makes a difference in the community. Through programs. Through donations. Through people.

Overview: Abbott Laboratories is a diversified health care company, dedicated to improving the lives of people around the world. We are able to achieve this goal through innovations in nutritional, pharmaceutical, diagnostic and hospital-related products.

Our 50,000 employees are committed to creating cost-effective health care technologies and bringing them to market to advance health and meet customers' needs. Our ability to do this successfully has resulted in decades of consistent growth.

Today, thanks to the excellence of our science, the quality of our products and the commitment of our employees, Abbott is well positioned for continued success in the evolving global health care marketplace.

Review of Business Strategy: At Abbott, we are addressing the evolving marketplace in a steady and measured way, balancing the interests of our customers, our employees, and our shareholders. Although the major strategies that are guiding us through this rapidly changing environment have a familiar ring, there are important, if subtle, shifts in emphasis. We want to clarify these:

First, we intend to maintain a diversified portfolio of health care businesses characterized in large part, by leading market positions. The trends of our four key businesses, aided by geographic diversity, have been complementary over the years, contributing to the uniquely consistent performance that we value as a company.

Second, our growth will come primarily from new products developed internally. This will require a continued high level of investment in research and development. That investment must be focused effectively on programs offering customers cost benefit improvement and significant advances in medical practice.

We are emphasizing global product development, thereby increasing the leverage of inherently expensive and high-risk research and development programs. In several of our businesses, we are only now beginning to realize the significant benefits of global adaptability for major products. We are also increasingly addressing developing markets such as Latin America and Asia, balancing investment carefully with risk.

To augment internal discovery, we are increasing our efforts in license products, identify opportunities for alliances, and make niche acquisitions that complement our product portfolios and support our strategic focus.

Third, we are directing more effort toward capitalizing on synergies between our businesses while retaining the benefits of our traditionally strong, decentralized organizations. We must capture the kinds of opportunities that exist across product lines, across markets, and across our own organizational structure.

As a fourth strategy, we will maximize productivity throughout our company. While we are proud of our lean operating structure, we will aggressively pursue more cost effective processes, from manufacturing to research to sales and administration.

Finally, we will continue to emphasize superb execution of our plans and strategies. One of Abbott's cultural strengths is an employee base of exceptional people who operate with an expectation that we must out-execute our competitors on all fronts to meet our customers' needs and produce superior returns for our shareholders.

2. ABM Industries Inc.
50 Freemont St., 26th Fl.
San Francisco, CA 94105
Phone: (415) 597-4500
Web: http://www.abm.com

ABM Industries Inc. (NYSE; ABM) is a facility services contractor, providing air-conditioning, elevator, engineering, janitorial, lighting, parking, and security services to commercial, industrial, and institutional facilities in hundreds of cities across North America. The company is divided into the following major divisions: Janitorial (ABM Janitorial Services; Easterday Janitorial Supply), Public Service (ABM Security Services; Ampco System Parking), and Technical (Amtech Elevator Services; Amtech Engineering Services; Amtech Lighting Services; Comm-Air Mechanical Services).

Mission Statement: To excel in all that we do for our customers, stockholders and employees by expanding our Family of Services through continuous improvement in the total quality of our services, competitiveness, accident prevention and complete customer satisfaction.

Customer Focus: ABM's reputation has been built on our proactive approach to customer satisfaction.

Core Competency: All of our divisions serve commercial, industrial and institutional real estate facilities. Whether you are an owner, manager or tenant, we provide the highest level of cost-effective service.

Statement: ABM is responding to the marketplace for nationwide facility services by providing a single source for all of your maintenance, repair, parking, and security needs.

3. Acclaim Entertainment Inc.
One Acclaim Plaza
Glen Cove, NY 11542
Phone: (516) 656-5000
Web: http://www.acclaimnation.com

Acclaim Entertainment Inc. (NAS-DAQ; AKLM) is a mass market entertainment company whose principal business has been as a leading publisher of interactive entertainment software for use with interactive entertainment hardware platforms.

The Future of Entertainment: As mass market entertainment converges at the interactive world, Acclaim, as the largest entertainment software publisher worldwide, has a foothold in the future. With new businesses underway in entertainment print publishing, coin-operated amusements and entertainment technology services, and plans that stretch onto the digital highway, Acclaim is not just positioned to be a participant in the future of entertainment; we are positioned to help define that future.

4. Acme-Cleveland Corp.
30100 Chagrin Blvd.
Suite 100
Pepper Pike, OH 44124
Phone: (216) 595-9090

Acme-Cleveland Corp. manufactures and markets metalworking products and telecommunications and electronics products. These products include tools, telecommunications products, sensor devices, and computer controlled inspection equipment and systems. The company has been purchased recently by the Danaher Corp. (NYSE; DHR).

Missions and Values: Acme-Cleveland has organized its businesses into subsidiary operating units to ensure that each has the focus, flexibility, capabilities, and commitment to address the special and particular needs of its customers. Acme-Cleveland's role as a parent company is similar to that of a natural parent — to provide appropriate direction, support, and control to help promote growth, development, and realization of potential. Although the operations of each unit are diverse and different in many respects, each is guided by a common corporate mission and set of Shared Values.

Our mission as a Corporation is to be a growing manufacturer of diversified industrial products that offer exceptional value aimed at improving quality and productivity for our customers. In pursuing this mission, we are expected to both satisfy our customers' needs and increase shareholder value through improved profitability, better asset utilization, and sales growth.

Our challenge is to ensure that our individual and collective efforts all work in the same direction and are supportive of our mission. As we do so, there are certain Shared Values that each of us is expected to observe. These serve as guides and reminders as to how we should approach and handle our work tasks and relationships.

The Shared Values are few in number and easy to understand:

We will be sensitive to our environment, especially to customer needs, values, and attitudes, and will adjust our business with the changing forces in that environment.

We will act in an ethical way when dealing with customers, suppliers, fellow employees, and others.

We will base our decisions on facts, objectively considered.

We will plan our work and then work to achieve or surpass planned results.

We will continually seek to improve the way we do things.

We will evaluate and acknowledge the contribution of each employee on the basis of performance, not on personality, supposed skills, education, national origin, religion, age, or sex.

We will act with a sense of competitive urgency.

In summary, we should strive to always do the right thing, the right way, and at the right time. Occasionally, there will be demands made and pressure exerted upon us to improve the way we do things, to make deadlines, and achieve goals. No such demands or pressure should be regarded, however, as a request or excuse to abandon any of our Shared Values. If we follow these Shared Values, we will have an environment that advocates mutual respect, teamwork, and open communication.

How We Will Measure Improvements: With change and improvement being a central theme for the way we operate our business and do things, it is essential that we know where we stand and what progress is being achieved as a result of the changes being made. Financial measurements and reports do not always present a complete story as to how well we are performing or where and when additional and different efforts may be required. To meet this need, five areas of performance will be regularly measured and reported upon by each operating unit to Acme-Cleveland and you. Exceptional performance in each of these measured areas is regarded as being key to Achieving Competitive Excellence. They are:

Customer Satisfaction
Quality
Productivity
Time
Cost Improvement.

Company Initiatives: There is no single course of action or simple program that will enable us to fulfill our mission or ensure that we will be a successful organization. Our efforts to succeed in today's rapidly changing and fiercely competitive business environment must include a number of new and different approaches, actions, and programs dealing with the way we operate and conduct our business. Our initiative will include the application of new technology to manufacturing processes and products, the use of new or additional sales/distribution channels, a renewed emphasis on quality in all areas of activity, the adoption of just-in-time concepts, the installation of manufacturing cells, the realignment of organization structures to place decision-making authority and responsibility at the closest level possible to where action occurs, and the continued training and development of employees.

In summary, you can expect the implementation of a wide variety of actions and programs intended to bring about major changes and improvements in the way we do things. These changes will involve you and may alter the content and responsibilities of your present job. Your ideas for change and improvement are welcomed and needed. In short, you have an important role to play in changing and improving our company.

5. Acme Metals Inc.

13500 S. Perry Avenue
Riverdale, IL 60627
Phone: (708) 849-2500
Fax: (708) 849-4503
Web: http://www.acmemetals.com

Acme Metals Inc. (NYSE; AMI), formerly called Acme Steel, is an integrated steel producer. They manufacture strip and sheet steel, welded steel pipe, steel strapping, strapping tools, semi-finished steel, iron, and (through Universal Tool and Stamping Co.) light truck and car jacks.

Mission Statement: Acme Steel Company is committed to providing high-quality products and services which totally satisfy the needs of our customer. Customer satisfaction (both internal and external) will be achieved by implementing a continuous quality improvement process that applies to all of our business activities. Well-trained, informed, involved and committed employees, who have been provided with the necessary tools, equipment and other resources, will implement the process. Our ultimate objective is continuous improvement and perfection in all products and services delivered by Acme Steel Company.

Vision Statement: Acme Steel Company will be recognized as a provider of maximum value to its customers, shareholders, employees, suppliers, and other stakeholders.

Maximum value for our customers means products and services which:

Consistently meet or exceed their requirements.

Are unequaled by any other supplier.

Are delivered on time every time in the amount required.

Result in the optimum cost for our customer.

Maximum value for our shareholders means:

A continuous profitable company.

An opportunity for a superior return on their investment.

Affiliation with a company recognized for its integrity, pursuit of excellence and corporate citizenship.

Maximum value for our employees means:

A safe and healthy workplace.

Financial security for themselves and their families.

Opportunity for continuous professional growth and personal improvement.

Pride in the services and products made.

Maximum value for our suppliers means:

A long-term financially rewarding partnership.

The opportunity to continuously improve their own products and services.

Maximum value for Acme's other stakeholders means:

Involvement with a company that always meets it ethical, civic, environmental, financial, and legal obligations in the communities where it operates.

Affiliation with a company known for its integrity and loyal partnerships.

6. ACX Technologies Inc.
16000 Table Mountain Pkwy.
Golden, CO 80403
Phone: (303) 271-7000
Web: http://www.acxt.com

ACX Technologies Inc. (NYSE; ACX), together with its subsidiaries, is a diversified manufacturing organization. Two business segments comprise the majority of the company's results from operations: The packaging business, operated through Graphic Packaging Corp. and the ceramics business, operated through Coors Ceramics Co. In addition to the primary operating businesses, the company owns technology-based developmental businesses operated through Golden Technologies Company Inc. Golden Technologies' focus is on assembling and distributing solar electric systems, developing biodegradable plastics and marketing a health food ingredient. The electric systems business was enhanced by Golden Technologies' acquisition of a controlling interest in Photocomm Inc. (NASDAQ; PCCOM).

Visions for the Future: ACX and its subsidiary companies are totally committed to pioneering innovative, value-added customer solutions. The following vision statements capture each ACX company's unique philosophy and approach to solving customer problems.

Coors Ceramics Company: We are the premier technical ceramics company. We produce unparalleled quality, provide unprecedented service and initiate creative solutions in partnership with our customers. We excel in our chosen markets.

The values of our spirit are enthusiasm, innovation, responsibility and heart-felt commitment. Our relationships are open, honest, and trusting. We are challenged to be the best we can be and we are empowered to fulfill our potential. Our work is fun and rewarding.

Through flexibility and beneficial change, we grow, prosper and make a difference in the lives of those we touch.

Graphic Packaging Corp.: We are an organization that embraces change through continuous improvement. We strive for the highest level of performance among the competitors in our chosen target markets through an empowered organization utilizing innovative technology including superior information systems.

Golden Genesis: With the sun as our source, we convert unmet needs for electrical service into growing markets throughout the world. We embrace and foster free enterprise as the foundation for market success.

Our products and services, designed for total solutions, create and grow a strong, loyal customer base for wireless power and basic electric service — infrastructure without wires.

As the leader in all markets we serve, we provide complete technical, financing and market support for our customers. We expand our reach through improved performance in existing markets, through replication of new products and services, and through acquisition of market leaders.

Chronopol Inc.: Chronopol is an innovative technology company that engineers products to provide customer solutions. These products are designed to change the way the industry produces and uses plastics.

7. Adobe Systems Inc.
1585 Charleston Rd.
P.O. Box 7900
Mountain View, CA 94039
Phone: (415) 961-4400
Web: http://www.adobe.com

Adobe Systems Inc. (NASDAQ; ADBE) develops, markets, and supports software products and technologies (such as computer software for electronic printing and desktop publishing) that enable users to create, display, print, and communicate electronic documents. The company licenses its technology to major computer and publishing suppliers, and markets application software products and typeface products for authoring and editing visually rich documents, including digital and video output. The company distributes its products through a network of original equipment manufacturer customers, distributors and dealers, and value-added resellers and system integrators.

Aldus Corp. and Adobe Systems developed the software that launched the desktop publishing revolution, (over) ten years ago. Aldus and Adobe merged in 1994 to form one company called Adobe Systems. Adobe's product line includes Acrobat, Acrobat Capture, PostScript, Photoshop, Illustrator, Premiere, HomePublisher, Type Twister, SuperPaint, Art Explorer, Dimensions, Persuasion, After Effects, Fetch, Gallery Effects, TextureMaker, IntelliDraw, Streamline, and Page-Maker.

Slogans: PostScript — "It's Not Just Printing, It's Adobe PostScript Printing." Acrobat — "All the Benefits of Paper, Without the Chase." Acrobat Capture — "Bring Your Printed Documents Back to Life." Adobe — "Putting It All Together." "Alliances. Delivery. Authoring. Printing & Publishing."

Statement: While other major software companies deal in raw words, data and numbers, Adobe thrives on enabling visual forms of communication. We can now offer computer users everything they need to create, manage, and share content-rich information on printed and electronic media. We look forward with great excitement to bringing the Adobe and Aldus pieces together for greater product integration, larger presence in more markets worldwide, ever higher levels of customer satisfaction, and a technological impact that exceeds what either company could have achieved on its own.

The Big Picture: Ten years ago, Adobe and Aldus developed the software that launched the desktop publishing revolution and literally changed the way the world works. Today, as one company, we are uniquely positioned to make a further dramatic impact not only on how society creates information but also on how it

delivers and manages that information in the Digital Age.

The new digital world is one rich with color, movement, sound, images, text and other elements of human expression. People receive information in printed forms such as books, periodicals, brochures and reports; in projected forms such as overheads and slides; and in broadcast forms such as film and video. And because it can all be delivered electronically, the information reaches a vast, global audience in real time.

Moreover, the recipients are far from passive. They increasingly control not only what they experience, but also how, when and where they experience it. And they have access to software that enables them to create information with a level of visual sophistication once provided only by graphics professionals.

Over time, individuals and organizations will accumulate entire libraries of electronic documents and presentations, using and reusing them continuously. To satisfy this growing need to access and exchange information at will, electronic content must transcend and outlive the constraints of specific computer hardware, software, networks and operating systems now and in the future.

This communications picture is quickly coming together. And Adobe provides essential pieces for defining and shaping it. More than any other developer of personal software, we offer products that enable people to use the computer to express and share their ideas in imaginative and meaningful new ways, whether the choice of media is static, dynamic or a combination of the two.

8. Advanced Micro Devices Inc.

One AMD Place
P.O. Box 3453
Sunnydale, CA 94088
Phone: (408) 732-2400
Web: http://www.amd.com

Advanced Micro Devices Inc. (NYSE; AMD) is a manufacturer of integrated circuits — with their major focus on the personal and networked computing and communications markets. The company makes microprocessors and related peripherals, memories, programmable logic devices, and circuits for telecommunications and networking applications.

Slogan: "Run with It."

Statement: The AMD of today is an IC supplier dedicated to providing solutions in silicon that enable our customers to differentiate their products within widely accepted standards, thereby gaining an advantage in the marketplace. Our commitment to industry standards and open markets allows us to address the volume markets of the computation and communications industries. We believe in competition as the principal driving force of innovation and progress — but we do not compete with our customers.

Our vision is to become our target customers' favorite supplier of integrated circuits by the end of the decade.

We will earn our customers' favor by providing innovative products that give them a competitive advantage in their markets, by being easy to do business with, and by forging relationships built upon trust.

We are well on our way to achieving this vision.

9. Advanced Tissue Sciences Inc.
10933 North Torrey Pines Rd.
La Jolla, CA 92037
Phone: (619) 450-5730
Web: http://www.sddt.com/corpprofiles

Advanced Tissue Sciences Inc. (NASDAQ; ATIS) is engaged in the development, manufacture, and marketing of living human tissues produced through tissue engineering. Dermagraft-TC, an engineered human dermal tissue combined with a synthetic epidermal layer, is a product designed as a transitional covering for severely burned patients.

Slogan: "Redefining Transplantation Through Tissue Engineered Products."

Statements: Advanced Tissue Sciences is committed to improving the quality of human life with products developed with our tissue engineering technology. We are accomplishing this mission by:

Developing products for tissue and organ replacement that can significantly improve patients' quality of life and that can reduce the costs of medical procedures and hospitalization.

Redefining transplantation so that our products are available to people who have few, if any, viable treatment alternatives.

Conducting our activities based on our values of scientific and business integrity, a true dedication to the quality of our work, and a sense of urgency in accomplishing our mission.

Our mission and values guide our activities in the communities we serve. Dedication to these principles is the cornerstone for providing our shareholders with maximum value for their investment.

Advanced Tissue Sciences' goal is to redefine transplantation by utilizing our proprietary tissue engineering technology to develop completely human tissues and organs that address unmet therapeutic needs and offer improved, cost-effective alternatives to currently available treatments. The continued removal of synthetic products from diseases through organ transplantation, have created an increasing demand for these alternative therapies. Our technology has the potential to meet this growing demand and, through the dedicated efforts of all Advanced Tissue Sciences' associates, we believe we can realize this goal.

10. Advest Group Inc.
90 State House Sq.
Hartford, CT 06103
Phone: (860) 509-1000
Web: www.advest.com

Advest Group Inc. (NYSE; ADV), a regional investment company, is involved in investment banking, securities (brokerage and trading), lending (commercial and consumer), and other related financial services. Major subsidiaries are Advest Inc. (regional brokerage) and Advest Bank (savings bank). Other subsidiaries are Boston Security Counselors (investment management) and Billings & Company (real estate management).

Mission: Advest's mission is to be the best at helping people build wealth, primarily toward retirement, through the highest quality, most effective professionals in the industry.

Statement: Advest's goal is to become the investment firm of choice in our region and reward our shareholders with an appropriate rate of return. The strategy for achieving this goal is straightforward. We will maximize the value of our investment executives to their clients by providing superior service, state-of-the-art technology and high quality investment advice and opportunities.

11. ADVO Inc.
One Univac Lane
P.O. Box 755
Windsor, CT 06095
Phone: (860) 285-6100

ADVO Inc. (NYSE; AD) is a provider of direct mail services, primarily for retailers and service companies. ADVO specializes in effective and efficient direct mail services for the exact needs of its clients. The company wishes to be the one-stop provider of customized services to its clients' specific marketplace communications needs — to be the targeted marketing expert of choice for response-oriented retailers and other advertisers.

Slogan: "Creating Partnerships."

Statement: Our business was challenged by a soft retail economy, a substantial simultaneous rise in postal rates and paper costs, and more intense competition.

It this difficult operating environment, ADVO never wavered from its dedication to creating shareholder value by providing greater value to our clients. ADVO's associates focused steadfastly on our clear and compelling vision of being "The targeter of choice for response-oriented retailers and other advertisers." As a result, our core business continued to show solid growth and once again achieved record revenues and earnings.

12. AES Corp.
1001 North 19th St.
Arlington, VA 22209
Phone: (703) 522-1315
Web: http://www.aesc.com

The AES Corp. (NASDAQ; AESC) is a leading electric power company.

Purpose/Mission: A *Corporate community stewarding* resources and nurturing *relationships* to help meet the world's *need* for safe, clean, reliable and cost-effective electricity, while aspiring to principles of integrity, fairness, social responsibility, and fun in the workplace. In pursuing this mission we seek to be the world's leading global power company.

Relationship Philosophy: To accomplish this purpose we enter relationships. Our task is to balance, tradeoff, optimize (nurture) these relationships including AES people — shareholders — customers — suppliers — governments/communities.

Shared Principles: Our aspiration is to nurture relationships guided by shared principles:

• Integrity — wholeness, uncompartmentalized;

• Fairness — justice, not sameness;

• Social responsibility — world class performance; something extra to solve the world's other problems;

• Fun at work — design work environment around assumptions about who people are.

13. AFLAC Inc.
1932 Wynnton Rd.
Columbus, GA 21999

Phone: (706) 323-3431
Web: http://www.aflac.com

AFLAC Incorporated (NYSE; AFL), a holding company, is primarily in the supplemental health insurance business in the United States and Japan, through its subsidiary — American Family Life Assurance Company of Columbus. AFLAC sells specialty insurance products that supplement primary insurance coverage. AFLAC also owns and operates seven network-affiliated television stations.

Slogans: "Building on the Past, Focused on the Future." "Claimants Are Our Best Recommendation. They Know 'AFLAC Pays.'" "A World Leader in Supplemental Insurance." "Leave Your Worries to Us And … Just Get Better."

AFLAC Incorporated Mission and New Five-Year Objective: 1996-2000: AFLAC's mission is to be the market leader in supplemental insurance. We develop and market specialty insurance policies that effectively supplement traditional insurance coverage. These products must provide the greatest value available in the marketplace. We believe that as we focus on increasing value for customers, shareholder value will increase as well.

We'll build on our strengths — offering affordable products, investing conservatively, paying claims quickly, and providing quality customer service. Those strengths and a talented management team have served us well during the last 40 years. In addition, we'll continue adding new and enhanced supplemental products and distribution methods to prepare for the changing insurance environment of the years ahead.

Our goal is for the entire AFLAC family — our customers, sales associates, employees and shareholders — to benefit from AFLAC's success. I believe we'll achieve that success by carefully building on the past while staying focused on the future.

14. Agouron Pharmaceuticals Inc.

10350 North Torrey Pines Road
Suite 100
La Jolla, CA 92037
Phone (619) 622-3000
Web: http://www.sddt.com/corpprofiles
Web: http://www.agouron.com

Agouron Pharmaceuticals Inc. (NASDAQ; AGPH) is primarily engaged in the research and development of human pharmaceuticals utilizing protein structure-based drug design; and is pursuing the final stages of commercial development of leading products for cancer and AIDS. Product development is focused on TS Inhibitors and HIV Protease Inhibitors. Product research is centered around GART Inhibitors, MMP Inhibitors, Immunosuppressives, RhV 3C Protease Inhibitors, AICART Inhibitors, Pol Beta Inhibitors, Hepatitis C Protease Inhibitors, HSV Protease Inhibitors, and CMV Protease Inhibitors.

Statements: Agouron has built a new kind of foundation for one of the pharmaceutical industry's most elusive assets: A real product pipeline. By applying its drug design technologies to molecular targets revealed by basic research, Agouron has positioned itself to bring at least two new drugs from research into development each year.

Only a minority of new drug candidates overcome all the hurdles and obstacles of pharmaceutical development to become successfully marketed therapeutic products. Despite expanding knowledge of human biology and increasingly sophisticated systems for testing new biologically active substances, most fail to become successful drugs.

There is only one reliable strategy for beating the odds in pharmaceutical research and development. It's to have a pipeline: a flow of one solid candidate for product development after another. Not all will succeed. But to build an important pharmaceutical firm, not many have to.

For ten years, Agouron has been building a new kind of foundation for a real pharmaceutical product pipeline. We have remained leaders in an engineering technology that now permits our scientists — with unprecedented precision — to design new molecules therapeutically active against cancer, serious viral diseases, and inflammatory disease.

The resulting lineup in Agouron's product pipeline is growing clear. The first four Agouron products are well into development. Two more products should move into development over the next twelve months. And the company is positioned to sustain the yield from its pipeline with a least two new development-stage drugs every year.

15. Agway Inc.
333 Butternut Dr.
Dewitt, NY 13214
Phone: (315) 449-7061
Web: http://www.agway.com

Agway Inc. is a cooperative owned by 90,000 farmer members in 12 northeastern states — Connecticut, Delaware, Maine, Maryland, Massachusetts, New Hampshire, New Jersey, New York, Ohio, Pennsylvania, Rhode Island, and Vermont. Agway produces and markets crop needs and services, daily and livestock feeds, farm-related products, pet foods and supplies, and yard and garden products. Its subsidiaries are involved in natural food processing and marketing, energy products, lease financing, insurance, and other related ventures.

Mission: To be a customer-driven and financially successful cooperative that is highly effective in meeting the needs and interests of commercial farms and other agriculturally related markets.

Values and Beliefs: Above all, we value our customers — We are customer-driven. We know our customers and are responsive to their needs. We strive for customer confidence and are committed to exceeding their expectations. We believe that customer service and customer satisfaction are the ultimate hallmarks of an excellent company.

Employees create the image of Agway — Employees create and are responsible for relationships with our customers. We are dedicated to the development of customer-focused, productive employees. The qualities we most value are knowledge, imagination, teamwork, and integrity. We listen and respond to employees' needs and concerns. We contribute to their personal growth through job enrichment and training. Motivated and committed employees create customer satisfaction.

We are dedicated to continuous improvement — Improvement begins with open communication throughout the organization. We have a commitment to our future through continuous innovation and training. We recognize the value of research and technology that matches science to the economic needs of our customers and Agway. We believe that sustained success depends on customer-focused quality.

We honor our communities' trust and confidence — We are responsible members of our community. We recognize that the success of our business is dependent on the health, stability, and economic viability of agriculture and the other communities we serve. We support our community and encourage employee involvement in community activities.

We act responsibly to safeguard our environment — Our business conduct demonstrates our concern with the environment, today and in the future. As members of the community, we take special care to ensure the health, safety, and well being of our local environment.

We will obtain profits, the cornerstone of financial strength — We are a financially successful cooperative that generates a profit from the goods and services we market. We believe that financial success should be measured both in the long- and short-term. We believe we must responsibly invest in the future while balancing the needs of Agway, its members, employees, and investors.

Agricultural Group Mission: To be the agriculture customer's most valued partner by providing the best combination of nutritional and agronomic products, service, and technological expertise to insure our mutual, long-term success.

Customer Group Mission: To be the leader in delivering a unique blend of high quality products, superior service, and expertise to our customers and business partners, based on our rich tradition of understanding and caring for soil, plants, and animals.

Energy Group Mission: To be the leading home energy and related services company: #1 in customer service, satisfaction, and market share.

Telmart Inc. Mission: To be a successful, professional, customer service leader that meets the financing needs of agriculture and other selected markets.

Agway Insurance Mission: To be the independent agent's 'company of choice' in providing services that protect the overall financial well-being of the Northeast farm community, while meeting the financial objectives of Agway Inc.

16. Air Express International Corp.
120 Tokeneke Rd.
P.O. Box 1231
Darien, CT 06820
Phone: (203) 655-7900

Air Express International Corp. (NASDAQ; AEIC) is a diverse transportation and integrated logistics company. AEI provides air, ocean, and ground transportation, contract logistics, customs brokerage, and warehousing and distribution services worldwide.

Mission Statement: AEI will be the first choice of customers worldwide for integrated logistics services. We will grow and profit by integrating superior air, ocean and ground transportation capabilities with innovative systems to help cus-

tomers better manage the full range of their global distribution needs.

We will continue to expand the scope and quality of our services by investing internally and acquiring other companies whose people and resources will further strengthen the professionalism and performance of the entire AEI team. We will continue to focus our efforts on ensuring that each shipment is delivered to its proper destination on schedule, and that all related information is accurate.

17. Air Products and Chemicals Inc.
7201 Hamilton Blvd.
Allentown, PA 18195
Phone: (610) 481-4911
Web: http://www.airproducts.com

Air Products and Chemicals Inc. (NYSE; APD) is a supplier of industrial gases and related equipment, specialty and intermediate chemicals, and environmental and energy systems.

Slogan: "Strong Businesses for a Competitive World."

Objectives: To be the first choice of our employees and customers.

To be an industry leader in safety, health, and environmental performance.

To invest in businesses where our core skills enable us to attain leadership positions.

To globalize our business with over 50 percent of our sales outside the United States.

To achieve consistent, superior financial performance.

We are continually measuring our progress on each.

These strategic objectives reflect our aspirations for Air Products and our commitment to shareholders, employees, customers, suppliers, and the hundreds of communities around the world where we have the privilege of doing business.

Air Products' Environmental, Health, and Safety Policy: We will be an industry leader in environmental, health, and safety performance. We are committed to improvement in environmental, health, and safety performance through active participation in Responsible Care and similar initiates in the countries in which we operate. We will adhere to the following basic principles in managing our business worldwide:

We will comply with or outperform all applicable environmental laws and regulations.

We will strive for continual reduction in wastes and releases to the environment.

We will design and operate our plants and facilities in a manner that protects the environment and the health and safety of our employees and the public.

We will develop and produce products that can be manufactured, distributed, used, and recycled or disposed of in a safe and environmentally sound manner.

We are committed to open discussion of our environmental, health, and safety practices. These practices will be based on the best available scientific knowledge and expertise.

18. Airborne Freight Corp.
3101 Western Ave.
P.O. Box 662
Seattle, WA 98111
Phone: (206) 285-4600
Web: http://www.airborne-express.com

Airborne Freight Corp. (NYSE; ABF) is an air express company and air freight forwarder that expedites shipments of all sizes to destinations throughout the United States and most foreign countries. Most public presentation of the company carries the Airborne Express service mark, since this trade name more clearly communicates the primary nature of the business of the company. Airborne Express provides door-to-door express delivery of small packages and documents. ABX Air Inc., the company's principal wholly-owned subsidiary provides domestic express cargo service. The company is the sole customer of ABX for this service. ABX also offers limited charter service.

Strategy: The company's strategy is to be the low cost provider of express services for high volume corporate customers.

Competing with UPS and Federal Express:
1. Airborne competes on reliability.
2. Airborne competes on price.
3. Airborne competes on service.
4. Airborne competes on relationships.

19. Airgas Inc.
Five Radnor Corporate Center
Suite 550
100 Matsonford Rd.
Radnor, PA 19087
Phone: (610) 687-5253
Web: http://www.airgas.com

Airgas Inc. (NYSE; ARG) manufactures and markets medical and specialty gases and welding supplies.

Company Mission Statement: To serve the industrial, medical and specialty gas and welding supply markets with the most effective and progressive distribution network, one which maintains a reputation for EXCELLENCE and which earns the respect of its customers, competitors, vendors, neighbors, employees and stockholders.

To maintain courteous and professional relationships with our customers, while providing them with products and services of exceptional QUALITY.

To maintain a positive, safe and healthy work place environment in which our employees can grow personally and professionally, by stressing RESPONSIBILITY and TEAMWORK in all aspects of our business.

To provide superior returns to our stockholders over the long term.

Employee Code of Responsibility: As an Airgas employee, I accept responsibility for seeking constant improvement in my job performance and for helping facilitate the jobs of my colleagues.

As a member of the Airgas team, I accept responsibility for making an exceptional effort to achieve continuous improvement in every aspect of my company's relationships with our customers, vendors, neighbors, employees and stockholders by constantly seeking to promote safety, reduce waste, improve responsiveness, foster creativity, expand knowledge and improve communication.

By accepting these responsibilities, I am personally committing to make Airgas the industrial leader and the best that we can be.

20. AirTouch Communications Inc.

1 California St.
San Francisco, CA 94111
Phone: (415) 658-2000
Web: http://www.airtouch.com

AirTouch Communications Inc. (NYSE; ATI) is a wireless communications company, providing cellular telephones and paging services.

Our Vision: Enriching people's lives around the world through wireless communications.

Our Mission: To be consistently the best at: Anticipating and fulfilling customer needs; challenging, empowering, recognizing and rewarding employees; creating outstanding value for our owners.

Our Goals: Stay #1 in customer satisfaction in every market.

Achieve an overall score of 80 on employee satisfaction surveys company-wide by year end 1997.

Double our IPO share price by year-end 1997.

Our Values:
Unparalleled customer focus.
Innovation.
Respect for people.
Superior cost management.
Commitment to total quality.
High performance standards.

21. Akzo Nobel Inc.

Seven Livingstone Ave.
Dobbs Ferry, NY 10522

Phone: (312) 906-7500
Web: http://www.akzonobel.com

Akzo Nobel Inc., a subsidiary of Akzo Nobel N.V. (NASDAQ; AKZOY), is a diversified, chemical company. The company produces products in the following general areas: Chemicals, coatings, fibers, and health care. They are also involved in numerous joint ventures.

Slogan: "Creating the Right Chemistry."

Objective: To acquire and defend leadership positions in relevant markets, improve productivity, and enhance its commercial and financial strengths. In addition to its existing core business, the company focuses on the development of new and better products in major growth sectors that draw on the company's technological and marketing know-how.

Environmental Policy: Akzo Nobel protects the environment by preventing or reducing the environment impact of its activities and its products through appropriate design, manufacturing, distribution, use, and disposal practices.

22. Alaska Air Group Inc.

19300 Pacific Hwy. South
Seattle, WA 98188
Phone: (206) 431-7040
Web: http://www.alaska-air.com

Alaska Air Group Inc. (NYSE; ALK) is a holding company for Alaska Airlines Inc. and Horizon Air Industries Inc. Alaska serves over 60 small Alaskan communities, in addition to their scheduled air service to cities in Arizona, California, Nevada, Oregon, Washington, the six destinations in Mexico and Russia. Horizon provides air transport to destinations in Washington, Oregon, California, Idaho, Montana, Utah, and Canada.

Slogans: "Unbeatable People, Unmatched Presence." "Alaska's World."

Primary Goals: We believe the best way to achieve our two primary goals — reasonable long-term returns on investment for shareholders and job and wage security for employees — is to produce profits consistently over a period of years.

23. Albertson's Inc.

250 Parkcenter Blvd.
Boise, ID 83706
Phone: (208) 385-6200
Fax: (208) 385-6349

Albertson's Inc. (NYSE; ABS) owns and operates supermarkets and combination food/drug stores.

Slogans: "Our People Make It Your Store." "Quality & Service You Can Believe In."

Corporate Operating Philosophy: Albertson's is engaged in the business of operating retail food and drug stores with integrated distribution and manufacturing facilities to support the retail effort for the purpose of satisfying consumer needs. To fulfill this service, we must provide the customer:

(1) Distinctive quality and personalized service in all perimeter departments;

(2) Helpful friendly service throughout the store;

(3) Fast, clean, one-stop convenience;

(4) Attractive, competitive prices;

(5) Conveniently laid out, well stocked grocery and drug departments with good selection of regular and seasonal merchandise.

Albertson's is, in effect, a big store with a specialty store approach. We must be "big" in terms of low prices, convenience and wide selection of brands. We must be a "specialty" store in terms of quality, personal service, and specialized selection.

All programs, plans and actions initiated and implemented by all personnel should have the objective of satisfying the above criteria.

Albertson's Corporate Creed: Customers — Albertson's Corporate Philosophy is to give our Customers the merchandise they want at affordable prices, with friendly, efficient service in clean, attractive stores.

Employees — In support of this philosophy, we are committed to our employees' success and well-being and endeavor to provide the business climate and resources to maintain a productive, satisfied, work force that is dedicated to taking care of our Customers' needs.

Community — We endeavor to be good corporate citizens in the communities in which we operate through practicing good business ethics and through Corporate and Employee participation in civic and charitable responsibilities.

Shareholders — Our business decisions and strategic plans are predicated upon providing our shareholders with a long term and sustained return on their capital investment.

Suppliers — We recognize the extreme importance of our loyal suppliers who provide the products, goods and services that permit our continued growth and service to our Customers and work to insure a fair and mutually satisfactory business relationship.

Management — We place great importance on continuing to attract, develop and maintain the high caliber of Management required to fulfill the needs of all our above constituents.

24. Alcan Aluminium Ltd.

1188 Sherbrooke St. West
Montreal, Quebec
Canada H3A 3G2
Phone: (514) 848-8000

Alcan Aluminium Ltd. (NYSE; AL) mines, refines, manufactures, smelts, recycles, and markets aluminum and alumina.

Alcan's Purpose: Alcan's purpose is to use profitably the risk capital invested by shareholders for the production and distribution of aluminum and other related products on an international scale. In the words of its mission statement: "Alcan will be the most innovative aluminum company in the world. Through its people, Alcan will be a global, customer-oriented and environmentally responsible enterprise committed to excellence and lowest cost in its chosen aluminum and related businesses. In the 1990s, Alcan's return-on-equity target is to outperform the Standard & Poor's Industrials."

Alcan's Objectives: Alcan recognizes that the conduct and effectiveness of an organization are highly dependent upon the quality of the people who comprise it. The company's ability to fulfill its purpose and to meet its objectives requires able employees who not only place a high value on the interests of Alcan but also take into account the interests of other individuals and groups with whom they relate both inside and outside the organization. Alcan's objectives are as follows:

1. Operate at a level of profitability that will ensure our long-term economic viability by providing a return on the shareholders' investment that will enable us to attract capital adequate to support our growth.

2. Maintain an organization of able and committed individuals in the many countries in which we operate and provide opportunities for their growth and advancement both nationally and internationally.

3. Strive for a level of operating, technical, marketing and environmental excellence that will ensure a strong and continuing competitive position in the markets we serve.

4. Balance the interests of our shareholders, employees, customers and suppliers, as well as governments and the public at large, while achieving Alcan's business objectives, taking into account the differing social, economic and environmental aspirations of the communities in which we operate.

5. Demonstrate high standards of integrity in all phases of our business.

25. ALCOA—Aluminum Company of America
Alcoa Bldg.
425 Sixth Ave.
Pittsburgh, PA 15219
Phone: (412) 553-3042
Web: http://www.shareholder.com/alcoa/

Aluminum Company of America—known also as ALCOA—(NYSE; AA) is the world's leading producer of aluminum and alumina. ALCOA serves customers in the packaging, automotive, aerospace, construction, and other markets with a wide variety of products.

Mission: ALCOA's mission is to be the best aluminum company in the world, setting world standards in quality and creating value for customers, employees and shareholders through innovative technology and operational expertise.

26. Alexander & Alexander Services Inc.
1185 Avenue of the Americas
New York, NY 10036
Phone: (212) 444-4500

Alexander & Alexander Services Inc. (NYSE; AAL) is a firm involved in risk management and human resources management consulting.

Statement: Executive leadership must do whatever is necessary for A&A to be the first choice of clients, employees and shareholders. This means developing innovative services and identifying new areas of business opportunity. It means emphasizing consultative relationships and providing a level of service that is second to none.

To achieve this, it is essential to accelerate changes in how we manage our business and our employees. We are determined to foster a more open, people-oriented culture that will free our employees to devote themselves even more creatively and energetically to their clients.

27. Allegheny Ludlum Corp.
1000 Six PPG Place
Pittsburgh, PA 15222
Phone: (412) 394-2800

Allegheny Ludlum Corp. (NYSE; ALS) is engaged in the technology, production and marketing of specialty materials—

stainless steels, silicon electrical steels, tool steels and other advanced alloys.

Slogans: "A Unique Company." "A World Leader in the Technology, Production and Marketing of Specialty Materials." "Stainless Steel: The Value Option."

Strategies: To be a cost competitive producer of specialty materials.

To make major quality improvements to meet changing customer requirements while remaining cost competitive.

To find specialty niches less sensitive to competition.

To exceed our customers' expectations for on-time deliveries and service.

To seek opportunities to grow in the materials field horizontally and in related areas vertically.

To expand a profitable global presence and thereby…

To achieve a return on Capital employed which maintains and improves the financial strength of Allegheny Ludlum.

28. Allegheny Power System Inc.

12 East 49th St.
New York, NY 10017
Phone: (212) 752-2121
Web: http://www.alleghenypower.com

Allegheny Power System Inc. (NYSE; AYP) is an electric utility holding company. Principal subsidiaries are Monongahela Power Co., The Potomac Edison Co., and West Penn Power Co.

Marketing Program: The retention of existing customers and the attraction of new ones remain the key elements of our marketing program.

Protecting the Environment: Allegheny Power and nearly 100 other electric utilities entered into a unique partnership with the DOE in 1994 to identify cost-effective, voluntary ways for the companies and their customers to participate in the President's program to reduce greenhouse gas emissions to 1990 levels by the year 2000.

Cooperation of this nature is unprecedented in environmental policy making, which traditionally has been characterized by command-and-control regulations or the threat of BTU or similar energy taxes.

29. Allergan Inc.

2525 Dupont Dr.
Irvine, CA 92713
Phone: (714) 752-4500
Web: http://www.allergan.com

Allergan Inc. (NYSE; AGN) manufactures and markets pharmaceutical preparations.

Allergan Vision Statement: Partner of choice for ever better health care.

Allergan Mission Statement: Customer and Product Groups: We are a global provider of quality eye, skin and neuromuscular health care products. Our customers include consumers, patients, practitioners, health care providers, distributors and government.

How we will grow: We will develop a unique level of understanding of our customers and implement an operational strategy that will exploit that knowledge. We will translate these actions into the greatest level of value for our customers and stakeholders.

We will become the partner of choice for ever better health care through the value of our partnering skills, worldwide sales and marketing infrastructure, manufacturing capabilities, research innovation, product development and regulatory capabilities, and relationships with buyers and customers. We will use these partnerships to speed the development of new products and bring them to the marketplace worldwide.

We will maintain our commitment to using innovative technologies as a means of bringing value to the customer.

We will use acquisitions to enhance our product development or marketing capabilities.

We will use our worldwide presence to capitalize on opportunities around the globe.

Why we exist. Customers — We will provide products and services of the greatest possible value. In meeting our customer's needs, everything we do will be of the highest quality.

Employees — We value diversity in our employees and are committed to creating an environment where each person can reach their full potential. We will make our employees a partner in the success of the corporation by recognizing and rewarding individual and team achievements.

Owners — We will provide a return on investment in the top quartile of our industry peer group.

Suppliers — We will form partnerships with our suppliers that are positive for both sides and deliver the highest value to our customers.

Citizenship — We will honor our obligations to society by being an economic, intellectual and social asset to each nation and community in which we operate. We will take the environment into consideration in all our actions. We will maintain the highest ethics at all times.

Functional Policy — We will make decisions and achieve our goals through the integration of management styles, quality and shareholder value. We will encourage an entrepreneurial spirit and intelligent risk-taking. We will experiment with new ideas. We will be internally aligned and externally focused.

30. Alliance Pharmaceutical Corp.
3040 Science Park Rd.
San Diego, CA 92121
Phone: (619) 558-4300
Web: http://www.allp.com

Alliance Pharmaceutical Corp. (NASDAQ; ALLP) is devoted to the research and development related to its pharmaceutical products. Its focus is on transforming innovative scientific discoveries into novel therapeutic and diagnostic agents.

Slogan: "Responding to the New Economics of Health Care."

Partnerships: Partnership with a major pharmaceutical company provides the resources to pursue multinational regulatory approvals and achieve market penetration more rapidly and efficiently than Alliance could do on its own.

Alliance is actively seeking early-stage compounds from universities, medical centers, and other companies that may qualify for introduction into our drug development pipeline.

Three D's of Innovative Pharmaceutical Delivery:

Discovery — Universities — Breakthrough; proof of concept; patentability.

Definition — R&D Co. — Formulation; pilot manufacturing; preclinical studies; regulatory plan; phase I and II clinical studies.

Delivery — Large Pharmaceutical Co. — Phase III clinical studies; regulatory approval; commercial manufacturing; sales and marketing; reimbursement strategy.

31. AlliedSignal Inc.
101 Columbus Rd.
P.O. Box 2245
Morristown, NJ 07962
Phone: (201) 455-2000
Web: http://www.alliedsignal.com

AlliedSignal Inc. (NYSE; ALD) is a technology company involved in aerospace, automotive, and other engineered products.

Our Vision: We will be one of the world's premier companies, distinctive and successful in everything we do.

Our Commitment: We will become a Total Quality Company by continuously improving all our work processes to satisfy our internal and external customers.

Our Values: Customers — Our first priority is to satisfy customers.

Integrity — We are committed to the highest level of ethical conduct wherever we operate. We obey all laws, produce safe products, protect the environment, practice equal employment, and are socially responsible.

People — We help our fellow employees improve their skills, encourage them to take risks, treat them fairly, and recognize their accomplishments, stimulating them to approach their jobs with passion and commitment.

Teamwork — We build trust and worldwide teamwork with open, candid communications up and down and across our organization. We share technologies and best practices, and team with our suppliers and customers.

Speed — We focus on speed for competitive advantage. We simplify processes and compress cycle times.

Innovation — We accept change as the rule, not the exception, and drive it by encouraging creativity and striving for technical leadership.

Performance — We encourage high expectations, set ambitious goals, and meet our financial and other commitments. We strive to be the best in the world.

32. Allmerica Financial Corp.
440 Lincoln St.
Worcester, MA 01653
Phone: (505) 855-1000
Web: http://www.allmerica.com

Allmerica Financial (NYSE; AFC) is a group of insurance and financial services companies comprising State Mutual Life Assurance Company of America (State Mutual) and its wholly owned subsidiaries: SMA Life Assurance Company, SMA Financial Corporation and Allmerica Financial Corporation; and publicly-traded subsidiary Allmerica Property & Casualty Companies Inc. (NYSE; APY) in which State Mutual holds a majority interest. Allmerica Financial operates in four business segments: Individual financial services, employee benefit services, institutional services, and property and casualty insurance.

Slogan: "Market-Driven Strength."

Strategies in Action: Allmerica Financial's operating units share broad goals that unify them in a vision of becoming an industry-leading financial service organization. Allmerica Financial focuses on markets in which it can capitalize on competitive advantages to achieve profitable growth. In these markets, Allmerica Financial is committed to providing quality, market-driven products and services and to expanding market opportunities by distributing products and services through multiple channels. The success of business strategies is measured using established benchmarks for financial performance and returns on capital that enhance the company's financial position.

33. Allou Health & Beauty Care Inc.
50 Emjay Blvd.
Brentwood, NY 11717
Phone: (516) 273-4000

Allou Health & Beauty Care Inc. (AMEX; ALU) is a distributor of nationally advertised brand name health and beauty aid items and designer fragrances and cosmetics. Additionally, the company distributes nationally advertised non-perishable branded packaged foods, plus branded and generic prescription pharmaceuticals.

Slogan: "Expanding Our Potential, Exceeding Our Goals." "Allou Is a Goal Driven Company."

Strength: Allou's strength is in its diversity of products which are nationally recognized for their quality and value. Our achievements reflect a pattern of growth that has occurred despite economic fluctuations.

Commitment: Allou is committed to increasing stockholders value by applying sound business principles, including focusing on our core businesses and distributing only those products that enjoy consumer respect and loyalty.

34. ALLTEL Corp.
One Allied Dr.
Little Rock, AR 72202
Phone: (501) 661-8000
Web: http://www.alltel.com

ALLTEL Corp. (NYSE; AT) is an information technology company that provides wireline and wireless communications and information services.

Slogan: "Always More Than You Thought."

Statement of Purpose: Recognize our responsibilities to the shareholders for sustained profitability.

Attract and retain employees dedicated to quality performance by providing an environment which encourages teamwork, fosters creativity, and offers individual recognition and growth.

Commit ourselves to our customers' satisfaction by providing quality services and products at the best value possible.

Show pride in the communities we serve through participation and support of local activities.

Statement: As changes in technology have blurred the traditional boundaries between voice and data services, customers have increasingly come to rely on ALLTEL for a broad array of communications and information services solutions. We are in the business of applying our vast range of technological expertise and capabilities for the competitive advantage and convenience of our customers.

Corporate strategy: As changes in technology and regulation began to blur the boundaries between vice and data networks, ALLTEL started preparing for the opportunities that would arise in the newly converging communications and information services industries.

In 1990, ALLTEL embarked on a strategy of enhancing our solid base of communications operations by expanding into information services.

We have built a company that has information technology expertise and an intimate knowledge of the communications industry. These enable us not only to meet our customers' demands for advanced voice and data solutions, but also to provide technology tools that can be used within our own communications businesses to increase efficiency and enhance our marketing and customer service efforts. Because we can test these solutions within our own communications operations first, we are able to deliver superior solutions to the marketplace. This gives us a strong competitive advantage over pure information services companies or stand-alone communications providers.

As voice and data technologies have converged, customers have increasingly come to rely on ALLTEL as a technology partner capable of providing a comprehensive range of communications and information technology solutions — from local telephone and cellular to network management, client/server-based initiatives and complex systems integration projects.

35. Allwaste Environmental Services Inc.
5151 San Felipe
Suite 1500
Houston, TX 77056
Phone: (713) 623-8777

Allwaste Environmental Services Inc., a subsidiary of Allwaste Inc. (NYSE; ALW) is a diversified industrial and environmental services company with operations throughout the U.S., Canada, Mexico and Austria.

Slogans: "Quality. Safety. Allwaste." "Helping Customers Attain a Competitive Advantage in a Global Market." "Commitment to Quality." "One Team Building on Our Strengths; Expanding Our Opportunities; Shaping Our Future Together."

Mission: To be the industry leader in selected environmental service businesses by meeting or exceeding customer expectations 100 percent of the time.

Our mission is to help customers attain

a competitive advantage in a global market and our goal is to be the premier industrial services company in North America by the year 2000.

36. ALZA Corp.
950 Page Mill Rd.
Palo Alto, CA 94303
Phone: (415) 494-5000
Web: http://www.ALZA.com

ALZA Corp. (NYSE; AZA) manufactures and markets therapeutic pharmaceutical preparations.

Mission Statement: ALZA's mission is to be the world leader in the creation and commercialization of therapeutic systems for human and veterinary applications. ALZA shall provide: Significant therapeutic contributions to society, high quality products to its customers, a challenging and rewarding environment for its employees and substantial rewards to its investors.

Statement of Values: In carrying out our mission, ALZA is guided by respect for people and the environment, quality in our products and services, teamwork and sustained profitability, as essential values. Every employee has the responsibility to ensure our collective commitment to this value system, and to the Company's Guiding Principles.

Guiding Principles: Maintain quality as an essential component of all our efforts — intellectually, interpersonally, and in the products and services we provide to our colleagues and customers.

Recognize that each employee and client is unique, that diversity is an important attribute, and respect these in all our actions.

Extend ALZA's leadership in all areas of therapeutic systems through increased efficiency and productivity, growth of internal R&D and acquisitions.

Provide leadership regarding the manner in which pharmaceutical products are defined, developed, registered, and presented to their users.

Maximize ALZA's income from royalties by support of our clients at all stages in the product selection, development, and marketing processes, and commercialization of products by ALZA.

Maintain a personal and professional environment that provides for personal growth, intellectual excitement, respect and enjoyment for all members of the organization.

Strive to provide both for ourselves and society a physical environment where it is safe to work, and healthy to live.

Achieve sustained growth in corporate profitability via creativity, innovation, productivity, and hard work.

37. Amcast Industrial Corp.
7887 Washington Village Dr.
Dayton, OH 45401
Phone: (513) 291-7000
Web: http://www.amcast.com

Amcast Industrial Corp. (NYSE; AIZ) manufactures and markets metal products for the automotive and aerospace industries, and for other manufacturers of engineered products.

Mission Statement: The primary mission of Amcast Industrial Corporation is to fulfill market needs more effectively than competitors in order to provide a competitive return to shareholders through increases in the value of their shares and a consistent dividend policy.

38. America West Airlines Inc.
4000 E. Sky Harbor Blvd.
Phoenix, AZ 85034
Phone: (602) 693-0800
Web: http://www.americawest.com

America West Airlines Inc. (NYSE; AWA) is a scheduled air passenger carrier.

Slogan: "It Seems Silly to Pay More."

Mission Statement: America West will sustain and grow its market position as the low cost, full-service, nationwide airline.

We will be known for our focus on customer service and high performance culture.

We are committed to sustaining financial strength and profitability, thereby providing stability for our employees and sharehold value for our owners.

Strategic Imperatives:

Stay lowest unit cost.

Know and service our customers.

Build staying power-financial and market muscle.

Build a high-performance culture.

39. American Airlines Inc.

P.O. Box 619616
Dallas/Fort Worth Airport,
TX 75261
Phone: (817) 963-1234
Web: http://www.americanair.com

American Airlines Inc., a division of AMR Corp. (NYSE; AMR), is a major company in the scheduled air transportation industry and in related businesses.

Slogan: "Something Special in the Air."

Corporate Vision: We will be the global market leader in air transportation and related information services.

That leadership will be attained by:

Setting the industry standard for safety and security.

Providing world class customer service.

Creating an open and participative work environment which seeks positive change, rewards innovation, and provides growth, security and opportunity to all employees.

Producing consistently superior financial returns for shareholders.

40. American Bankers Insurance Group Inc.

11222 Quail Roost Dr.
Miami, FL 33157
Phone: (305) 253-2244

American Bankers Insurance Group Inc. (NASDAQ; ABIG) is a leading provider of credit-related insurance programs in the United States, Canada, and the Caribbean. The company also conducts business in Latin America and the United Kingdom. The company is an international specialty wholesaler and marketer of insurance products, services and programs to clients in markets not traditionally served by other insurance companies.

Slogans: "Focused on Solutions." "Innovations in Insurance." "Quality Is Continually Striving to Exceed Our Customers' Needs and Expectations and Taking Pride in Doing the Job Right the First Time."

Statements: Focusing on the things that are good about American Bankers, we have defined solutions that will open even more doors for the company, its clients, customers, and shareholders. Through a controlled path, the understanding of relationships, and a renewed commitment to support and technology, we are creating an environment which invites progress, seizes opportunity and promotes profitable growth.

ABIG continually seeks to develop new distribution channels and new products as variations of proven, profitable products. This ensures long-term profitability and steady growth.

What makes American Bankers different from any other organization? It's the Mission, Strategy, and Culture that have evolved and grown over the years. Some of this has happened by chance, and some of it has required careful planning and nurturing. By expressing all parts in written form, we now have a complete standard upon which each individual employee can base his business actions.

The Vision of the '90s:

The country's finest distributing insurance company with more and better channels of distribution.

Unique and innovative products for every business segment.

Competitive advantage through the use of technology.

Highly productive, motivated, disciplined personnel — achieving and being properly rewarded.

An organization where the customer is boss, where we have a relationship that generates respect and our service is perceived as best.

An excellent A, B, C (Adequate premium; Better claims handling; Common sense underwriting) profit control system.

A flexible, useful management accounting system.

Corporate Mission: To sell, through affiliated organizations, innovative and quality (a) insurance products, (b) marketing, and (c) service: To satisfy the wants and needs of the middle class market.

Corporate Strategy:

Marketing: To establish profitable insurance underwriting and service business in areas that are comparatively free of competition, where we can excel in marketing.

To segment the marketplace by type of organization and distribution network and to form strategic business units to attack those market segments.

To achieve and maintain a dominant position in each market segment, an 8% return on sales and a compounded growth rate of 15%.

To market nontraditional insurance products through nontraditional distribution networks, acting as a manufacturer and wholesaler of insurance products.

To establish a well-compensated, trained, loyal sales force, selling by uniform methods in each of our market segments.

To develop our businesses as appropriate in the United States, Canada, The United Kingdom, the Caribbean and Latin America.

Administration: To provide the staff support and service needed by our sales force, consistent with our Customer Service strategy and within the expense allowance provided by our premium rates.

To employ technology to automate administrative efforts for both the customer and ABIG.

To improve productivity through systems innovation, streamlining, value analysis and measured individual contributions.

To create continuity of management, opportunity for growth and a personal sense of accomplishment for our personnel.

To create a working environment where all employees are aware that they are each an integral part of the sales effort.

To employ and develop loyal, highly motivated and well-trained employees.

Financial: To provide the shareholders consistent annual growth and earnings per share and a return on equity above alternative investments with similar risks.

To maximize investment return, giving due regard to ultimate safety of principal with investment results in the upper industry quartile.

To maintain a favorable balance of debt to equity and other key financial ratios.

To employ control disciplines which monitor profit experience and take appropriate action.

To periodically evaluate all business segments against the corporate cost of capital and provide adequate capital as required by each affiliate.

41. American Business Information Inc.

5711 South 86th Circle
Omaha, NE 68127
Phone: (402) 593-4500
Web: http://www.abii.com

American Business Information Inc. (NASDAQ; ABII) is a provider of business-to-business marketing information which it supplies from its proprietary database containing information on approximately 10 million businesses in the United States and 1 million businesses in Canada.

Slogan: "Helping You Find New Customers and Increasing Your Sales ... Is Our Business."

Going Forward: Our number-one focus is to continue to grow our existing business, make our products better, add more value to them, expand our distribution channels, and help businesses find new customers and grow their sales. This philosophy has not changed since the inception of our company. We are also looking for more acquisition opportunities in related industries. We do not make acquisitions just for the sake of acquiring. We look for synergies and management strengths where a merger would be profitable for our shareholders.

42. American Electric Power Co. Inc.

One Riverside Plaza
Columbus, OH 43215
Phone: (614) 223-1000
Web: http://www.aep.com

American Electric Power Co. Inc. (NYSE; AEP) is a holding company that provides electric utility service.

Our Job: Our job is generating electricity and getting it to where it's used, efficiently and with respect for the environment. We're in business because it is concerned with the supply of a fundamental requirement of modern living, because it's an honorable one, because we like it, and because we want to earn a living at it.

We aim to give one kind of service to everyone ... the best that's possible. That means supplying our customers with what they want when they want it. It means being courteous at all times and maintaining attractive, easy-to-do-business-with offices.

It means doing everything we can to keep complaints from arising, and it means prompt and fair handling of those that do.

We are a citizen of each community we serve and take an active part in its affairs. Like any other citizen, we want our neighbors to think well of us. Besides, it makes good business sense. We prosper only as the community prospers; so we help it thrive in every way we can.

Such is our job as we see it. We are trying to do it well and to do it better all the time.

43. American Express Co.

American Express Tower
200 Vesey St.
New York, NY 10285
Phone: (212) 640-2000
Web: http://www.americanexpress.com

American Express Co. (NYSE; AXP) is a diversified travel and financial services company operating worldwide. American Express can be divided into three operational groups: American Express travel related services, American Express financial advisors, and American Express bank.

Slogan: "Do More."

Vision: We articulated a vision for American Express: "To become the world's most respected service brand." To grow the business, we focused on delivering superior value to customers with new products, rewards and service features targeted at attractive segments of the market.

Mission: The company's mission remains the same: To help clients achieve their financial objectives prudently and thoughtfully through a long-term relationship with a trusted and knowledgeable financial advisor.

Environmental Principles: Corporate Support — The Public Responsibility Committee of the Company's Board of Directors will oversee management's commitment to environmental policies and practices. An Environmental Protection Committee with responsibility for environmental affairs will lead corporate activities on the environment. Employee and Shareholder Right-to-Know — The company will prepare annual statements on environmental practices and make them available to shareholders and other interested persons. Employees will be periodically updated on environmental topics. The company will make the results of air monitoring and water and other hygienic testing available to employees.

Compliance with Government Regulations — The company will comply with applicable federal, state, and local laws, such as Occupational Safety and Health Administration (OSHA) guidelines. Healthy and Safe Working Conditions — Develop and promote health and safety programs. Install comprehensive fire and life-safety systems in all major office areas. Monitor air quality for formaldehyde, asbestos, radon, carbon dioxide/carbon monoxide, and other contaminants. Provide proper ventilation and air-purification systems. Adhere to clean air and smoking regulations. Carry out periodic water testing. Provide medical and/or first-aid facilities. Develop emergency evacuation contingency plans. Install security systems to minimize the risk to employees and property. Energy Conservation — Use energy-efficient materials and components in the design and construction of facilities. Design and install air-conditioning systems in new office buildings and operating centers that conserve the use of water. Design and install equipment and systems that control and reduce energy consumption, and develop programs that promote energy efficiency, such as state-of-the-art building management systems for major office buildings and operating centers; computerized on/off controls and occupancy sensors to reduce lighting; energy-saving lighting ballasts and low-wattage lamps; thermal storage for "off-hours" production of chilled water; and information and awareness among employees about saving electricity and domestic water. Reduction and Disposal of Waste — Develop and implement recycling programs. Dispose of chemicals and toxic materials in accordance with applicable federal, state, and local laws and regulations. Use qualified and experienced contractors, consultants, and technicians for work when asbestos removal, encapsulation, or other treatment is required. Carry out recycling programs for paper, metal, and other materials that can be reused or reprocessed. Sustainable Use of Natural Resources — Take appropriate measures to preserve and protect natural resources (trees, water, soil, terrain, and wildlife) when planning new facilities.

44. American Financial Group Inc.
One East Fourth St.
Cincinnati, OH 45202
Phone: (513) 579-2121
Web: http://www.amfnl.com

American Financial Group (NYSE; AFG) is a holding company which, through its subsidiaries, is engaged primarily in specialty and multi-line property and casualty insurance businesses and in the sale of tax-deferred annuities and certain life and health insurance products.

Purpose: To continue to build value for our shareholders as property/casualty insurance and annuity specialists, providing profitably priced quality products and services to our customers and offering a rewarding work environment for our employees.

The Future: Our newly combined property and casualty operations make us a major player in the insurance industry. We plan to capitalize on our strength and we look to the future with optimism knowing that our core businesses have excellent, profitable track records and a management team that is experienced, competent and respected in the industry.

Our overriding goal is to build long-term value for our shareholders. We are committed to seek growth through expansion to existing businesses, or startups of new business lines. We prefer opportunities which include additions to existing businesses, product line or geographic expansion, and niche or specialty orientations.

45. American General Corp.
2929 Allen Pkwy.
Houston, TX 77019
Phone: (713) 522-1111
Web: http://www.agc.com

American General Corp. (NYSE; AGC) is a large diversified financial services organization. It is a leading provider of retirement annuities, consumer loans, and life insurance.

Four Cornerstone Decisions: At American General Corporation, four cornerstone decisions provide the framework for the company's overall strategy — a strategy that transcends and integrates the distinct strategies of our operating companies.

Decision No. 1— The first of these decisions was to consistently build shareholder value and increase cash dividends per share.

Decision No. 2 — The second cornerstone decision was to focus on insurance and financial services. This specialization gives the company a competitive edge in serving the financial needs of households across the nation.

Decision No. 3 — The third cornerstone decision, the marketing of products and services through a company-managed distribution system, increases American General's advantage in the marketplace. Strong customer relationships, nurtured by frequent and direct customer contact, contribute significantly to the company's leadership position in all of its principal markets.

Decision No. 4 — The fourth and final cornerstone decision was the adoption of the New-Form organizational structure. New-Form is a unique blend of traditional organizational forms combined with Main Event Management (registered trademark), a system for managing an organization as a whole. Through New Form, American General's constantly growing organization can efficiently and effectively adapt to change in the dynamic business environment.

46. American Greetings Corp.
One American Rd.
Cleveland, OH 44144
Phone: (216) 252-7300
Web: http://www.amgreetings.com

American Greetings Corp. (NASDAQ; AGREA) is a creator and manufacturer of greeting cards and gift wrappings, party goods, picture frames, and candles.

Statement: In today's competitive business environment, success is measured on the bottom line.

Creativity by itself isn't enough. Successful companies smartly tap their most precious resources to grow, meet consumer needs and reward their shareholders.

At American Greetings that means leveraging creativity and applying it throughout our organization.

Our No. 1 goal is to meet the needs of each consumer every time she shops a store that features American Greetings products.

47. American Home Products Corp.
Five Giralda Farms
Madison, NJ 07940
Phone: (201) 660-5000
Web: http://www.ahp.com

American Home Products Corp. (NYSE; AHP) is a discoverer, manufacturer, and marketer of health care and agricultural products. The company has a product line of prescription drugs, vaccines, nutritionals, over-the-counter medications, and medical devices. Principal products are Lo/Ovral, Nordette, Ovral, Ovrette, Premarin, Premphase, Prempro, Stuartnatal Plus, Triphasil, Cordarone, Inderal LA, ISMO, Isordil, Maxzide, Quinidex, Sectral, Tenex, Verelan, Ziac, Ativan, Effexor, Serax, Lodine, Naprelan, Orudis, Oruvail, Micocin, Myambutol, Pipracil, Suprax, Zosyn, Advil, Anacin, Dimetapp, Dristan, Orudis KT, Robitussin, Caltrate, Centrum, Ambesol, Chap Stick, Denorex, FiberCon, Preparation H, Primatene, Chef Boyardee prepared foods, Crunch 'n Munch, Gulden's, Jiffy Pop, PAM, etc. The company has acquired American Cyanamid.

Growth Strategies: Our growth strategies are directed in large part at achieving several principal objectives: Accelerated earnings-per-share growth and increased market share in our categories; the development of innovative products that become market leaders by contributing to the well-being of people worldwide; and the strengthening of our company in ways that continue to be reflected in shareholder value.

Policy Statement of Health, Safety and Environmental Protection: It has been the policy of American Home Products Corporation and its divisions and subsidiary companies worldwide, to conduct business responsibly and in a manner designed to protect the health and safety of our employees, customers, the public and environment. It is the purpose of this statement to restate and enhance this policy so as to call these important matters to the attention of all concerned persons. As a good corporate citizen of the communities in which we operate, we must be conscious of the effects of our operations on the environment — land, water, air and sound. The corporation will continue to comply with the spirit as well as the letter of the national and local laws and regulations relating to the protection of employees, the public and the environment. American Home Products is committed to providing a safe and healthful workplace for our employees and operating our facilities in a manner that is harmonious with communities in which they are located.

48. American International Group Inc.
70 Pine St.
New York, NY 10270
Phone: (212) 770-7000
Web: http://www.aig.com

American International Group Inc. (NYSE; AIG) is an insurance and financial services organization. The company is among the nation's largest underwriters of commercial and industrial coverages. Its member companies write property, casualty, marine, life, and financial services insurance in approximately 130 countries and jurisdictions.

Slogan: "World Leaders in Insurance and Financial Services."

Statement: Our strong balance sheet, stable and diversified earnings streams, healthy cash flow and sound underwriting policies are invaluable assets which we protect and nurture. They are the tenets of our business philosophy, the foundation of our strategy, and they define our success. AIG has cultivated the ability to respond quickly to changing customer needs and marketplace conditions and opportunities. We are and strive to remain the most efficient company in our industry, as measured by the expense ratio. Our markets are global, and our people are encouraged to seek out new opportunity wherever it lies. AIG's priorities for the future include building on our strengths to remain the premier global insurance and financial services firm and the company of choice for our clients, whether they be global corporations or individuals.

49. American Medical Response Inc.
2821 South Parker Rd.
10th Floor
Aurora, CO 80014
Phone: (303) 614-8500

American Medical Response Inc., a subsidiary of Laidlaw Inc. (NYSE; LDWB), is a provider of high-quality emergency and non-emergency pre-hospital medical care and general ambulance services.

Slogan: "One Company. One Vision. One Commitment."

Statements: Through continued strategic acquisitions, consolidation and growth of existing business units and expanded service offerings, the company intends to continue its expansion while providing high quality and cost-efficient ambulance services.

Our management philosophy of fostering an entrepreneurial spirit and supporting local management with strong regional and national resources has set us apart as a clear corporate partner of choice.

Every minute of every day, American Medical Response stands ready to help the citizens of the communities it serves in their moment of need ... when every second counts.

Our Mission: Dedicated to serving our customers and employees for life.

Leadership is the shared goal of both our employees as well as our organization to empower our people and focus their vision so as to positively impact our company, our community, and our industry.

Integrity is the commitment to dealing with our customers and our people with honesty and respect.

Fiscal responsibility is the efficient use of resources with profitability being everyone's objective.

Excellence is the practice and sincere belief in high, morally correct standards for effective and compassionate care.

50. American Power Conversion Corp.

132 Fairgrounds Rd.
P.O. Box 278
West Kingston, RI 02892
Phone: (401) 789-5735
Web: http://www.apcc.com

American Power Conversion Corp. (NASDAQ; APCC) is the world leader in power protection products and services. Products offered include surge suppressers (SurgeArrest; PowerManager; Protect-Net), voltage regulators (Line-R), and uninterruptable power supplies (Back-UPS; Smart-UPS; Martix-UPS).

Slogans: "The World's Most Reliable Power Protection." "Reliability Is Everything." "What Do You Do When Your Company Already Offers the World's Most Popular UPS Protection? You Make It Better."

51. American Stores Co.

709 E. South Temple
Salt Lake City, UT 84102
Phone: (801) 539-0112
Web: http://www.americandrugstores.com

American Stores Co. (NYSE; ASC) is a major retailer, operating food and drug stores in the U.S. Food operations operate under the names Lucky, Jewel, Jewel Osco, Acme, and Super Saver. Drug operations operate under the names Osco and Savon. Consumers' durable medical equipment needs are met by Osco Home Health Care stores. Their pharmacy benefit management company is RxAmerica.

Slogans: "One Well-Oiled Machine." "We're Saving America." "Rest Assured, We're There When You Need Us!" "Now You Can Feed the Whole Club Without Joining One."

Statements: Our businesses meet customers' food and drug needs every day. Bringing the highest quality products at some of the very best values around.

We have to be a retail organization that is able to give customers what they want in multiple formats and to change quickly when their needs and tastes change — and those changes are coming faster and faster.

52. Ameritech Corp.

30 South Wacker Dr.
Chicago, IL 60606
Phone: (312) 750-5000
Web: http://www.ameritech.com

Ameritech Corp. (NYSE; AIT) is a regional Bell Company operating in Illinois, Indiana, Michigan, Ohio, and Wisconsin. The company is getting involved in foreign investments.

Slogan: Your Link to Better Communication."

Our Vision: Ameritech will be the world's premier provider of full-service communications for people at work, at home or on the move. Our goal will be to improve the quality of life for individuals and to increase the competitive effectiveness of the businesses we serve.

As we move and manage information for our customers, we will set standards for value and quality.

Ameritech's competence will reach worldwide, building on our strength in America's vibrant upper Midwest. Customers can be assured that we will assume no task we cannot do exceedingly well.

The opening paragraph of the vision statement dictates the first major component of Ameritech's strategy: We will serve the customer within the profile of today's business. Over the years we've built an excellent business by meeting customer needs with a variety of products and services. We intend to continue doing so. And by intensifying our response to the customer, we'll make the most of the significant opportunities that lie here.

Strategies:

1. Speed growth in our core communications business.

2. Introduce new services for customers.

3. Connect customers around the world.

53. AMETEK Inc.

Station Sq.
Paoli, PA 19301
Phone: (610) 647-2121
Web: http://www.ametek.com

AMETEK Inc. (NYSE; AME) is a manufacturer of electronic, electrical, and electro-mechanical products. Products are sold worldwide through three operating groups: Electro-mechanical, Precision Instruments, and Industrial Materials. Products include electric motors and blowers; precision instruments for aerospace, the process industry and heavy vehicles; and specialty materials and water filtration products.

Slogan: "Committed to Total Quality."

Mission: Enhance long-term shareholder value with a strong operating company serving niche markets. Achieve long-term, double-digit growth in per share earnings and cash flow. Earn a superior return on total capital.

Vision: AMETEK seeks to be an internationally recognized and respected company that produces the highest value products and services for the markets it serves while:

Investors actively seek the company for investment.

Customer and suppliers delight in doing business with the company.

The company's employees actively participate and flourish in their work.

Communities welcome the company openly.

Values: To accomplish AMETEK's mission, values are ascribed to:

Providing our investors with a superior return on their investment.

Providing customers with world-class products and services at competitive prices.

Providing suppliers with financial opportunity though partnership.

Treating our employees fairly and giving them an opportunity to contribute and grow.

Being responsible citizens in the communities where we live, maintaining high ethical standards of business and environmental responsibility.

Strategies: To achieve the mission, AMETEK will:

Develop a strategic plan for each business.

Focus on continuous improvements in customer satisfaction (both internal and external); all business processes and procedures; growth; asset utilization and profitability.

Actively encourage and foster an environment for employee growth and development through proper communications, training, employee participation and recognition.

Never knowingly create an undesirable environment or safety condition for our employees, our customers or our neighbors.

Develop the means to measure and be accountable for the various steps required to achieve our Mission.

Recognize TQM as the process AME-
TEK is committed to use to achieve our
Vision and Mission.

Business Relationships.
Progress.

56. AMP Inc.
P.O. Box 3608
Harrisburg, PA 17105
Phone: (717) 564-0100
Web: http://www.amp.com

54. Amgen Inc.
1840 DeHavilland Dr.
Thousand Oaks, CA 91320
Phone: (805) 447-1000
Web: http://www.amgen.com

Amgen Inc. (NASDAQ; AMGN) develops and markets therapeutic products.

Mission: To be the world leader in the
developing and delivering of important,
cost-effective therapeutics based on advances in cellular and molecular biology.

55. Amoco Corp.
200 East Randolph Dr.
Chicago, IL 60601
Phone: (312) 856-6111
Web: http://www.amoco.com

Amoco Corp. (NYSE: AN) is a worldwide integrated petroleum and chemical
company.

Our Mission: We find and develop petroleum resources and provide quality
products and services for our customers.
We conduct our business responsibly to
achieve a superior financial return, balanced with long-term growth, to benefit
shareholders and fulfill our commitment
to the community and the environment.

Our Vision: Amoco will be a global
business enterprise, recognized throughout the world as preeminent by employees, customers, competitors, investors and
the public. We will be the standard by
which other businesses measure their performance. Our hallmarks will be the innovation, initiative and teamwork of our
people, and our ability to anticipate and
effectively respond to change, and to create opportunity.

Our Values:
Integrity.
People.
Technology.
Environment, Health, and Safety.

AMP Inc. (NYSE; AMP) is in the business of designing, manufacturing, marketing and selling interconnection components, subassemblies, and services for
electrical, electronic and optical applications. These are supplied both direct to
the customers and through distributors
and subcontractors.

Slogan: "We Are AMP People Working
Together to Satisfy Our Customers."

Our Mission: AMP's business is customer driven, technology-influenced and
engineering-oriented, coupled with world-
class manufacturing.

In order to achieve the core company
goals, various business units have been
created. These business units consist of
sectors, groups, divisions, departments,
companies and strategic alliances, which
have the responsibility for developing cohesive mission, quantifiable objectives and
comprehensive strategies through adopt-
ing the guiding principles within the following key result areas:
Total customer satisfaction.
Continuous quality improvement.
Human resource excellence.
Growth.
Profitability.
Cost reduction.
Innovation/technical leadership.
Public responsibility/corporate citizenship.

Our Vision: We share a vision of AMP
Incorporated as a worldwide team of people who are motivated to pursue the path
to excellence through continuous improvement in all that we do. Empowered
to think globally and act locally as we address the true needs of our markets. Inspired to provide our customers with

products and services so outstanding that we will be the supplier of choice.

Our Values: At AMP we believe in...

Earning our leadership position in the interconnection industry by continuing to develop innovative products and services and by meeting and surpassing our customers' expectations.

Maintaining steadfast commitment to excellence in every product and every service we provide as a means of earning the confidence and loyalty of our customers.

Serving our customers' global needs by offering them our foundation of worldwide support.

Encouraging personal and team ownership of problem identification, prevention, and solution.

Creating a climate of trust and respect that empowers our people to develop to the fullest, while sharing the responsibilities of success and the rewards of achievement.

Keeping each individual and function informed about AMP, its customers, suppliers, and competitors.

Forming lasting, mutually beneficial relationships with our customers and suppliers, based on fairness and integrity.

Achieving the growth and profit that guarantee our financial stability and competitive strength to maximize the long-term return to shareholders.

Fulfilling our responsibilities as a good corporate citizen by being a positive, powerful force in our communities worldwide and helping conserve our natural environment.

57. AMR Corp.

4333 Amon Carter Blvd.
Fort Worth, TX 76155
Phone: (817) 963-1234
Web: http://www.amr.com

AMR Corp. (NYSE; AMR) is the parent company of American Airlines Inc.

Corporate Vision: We will be the global market leader in air transportation and related information services.

That leadership will be attained by:

Setting the industry standard for safety and security.

Providing world class customer service.

Creating an open and participative work environment which seeks positive change, rewards innovation, and provides growth, security and opportunity to all employees.

Producing consistently superior financial returns for shareholders.

58. AmSouth Bancorporation

AmSouth Sonat Tower
1900 Fifth Ave. North
Birmingham, AL 35203
Phone: (205) 320-7151
Web: http://www.amsouth.com

AmSouth Bancorporation (NYSE; ASO) is a bank holding company, primarily operating in Alabama, Florida, Tennessee, and Georgia.

Slogans: "Creating the Vision for Continued Success." "The Relationship People."

Statement: Do more than is expected. Make a difference. Make time for people. If something's wrong make it right. Improve someone's life. Do the right thing. The ripple effect. It is what motivates us at AmSouth to live each day by these six very basic values. Each value is like a pebble on still waters. A simple beginning with far-reaching impact, in banking, as well as in everyday life, the benefits are endless.

Vision: As a preeminent midsouth financial institution, AmSouth is committed to:

Exceeding the expectations of our customers by delivering the finest quality of financial services.

We do this through well-trained and highly motivated employees.

The results of which produce consistently, over time, a superior total rate of return for our shareholders.

Mission ('95): Our corporate mission is to achieve, over time, a superior return for our shareholders by delivering the finest quality financial services, by managing our balance sheet and capital aggressively, and by controlling our costs of doing business. To achieve our goals, we will continue the transition away from our thrift-like loan mix and emphasize the competitive but profitable pricing of our deposit products. We will seek additional cost efficiencies by continuously re-engineering our processes, further consolidating our operations and applying enhanced technology company wide.

Mission Statement ('96): As a preeminent midsouth financial institution, Am-South is committed to:

Exceeding the expectations of our customers by delivering the finest quality of financial services.

We do this through well-trained and highly-motivated employees.

The results of which produce consistently, over time, a superior total rate of return for our shareholders.

59. Amway Corp.
7575 Fulton St. East
Ada, MI 49355
Phone: (616) 676-6000
Web: http://www.amway.com

Amway Corp. is a privately held company engaged in direct selling. Amway products and services are marketed by independent distributors in the U.S. and more than 70 other countries and territories. Amway's products and services fall into the following categories: Home care, health and fitness, personal care, hometech, education and entertainment, and business to business categories, such as laundry, janitorial, food service, agricultural, and business services.

Amway's Environmental Mission Statement: Amway Corporation believes that the proper use and management of the world's limited resources and the environment are the responsibilities of industry and individuals alike. As a leading manufacturer of consumer goods with a direct sales network of more than two million independent distributors worldwide, Amway recognizes its responsibility and role in both fostering and promoting sound environmental stewardship.

60. Analog Devices Inc.
One Technology Way
P.O. Box 9106
Norwood, MA 02062
Phone: (617) 329-4700
Web: http://www.analog.com

Analog Devices Inc. (NYSE; ADI) designs, manufactures, and markets a broad line of high-performance linear, mixed signal, and digital integrated circuits (ICs). The company's principal products include special-purpose linear and mixed signal ICs, digital signal processing ICs, and general-purpose, standard-function linear and mixed signal ICs. The company also manufactures and markets devices using assembled product technology, the largest of which are hybrid ICs which combine unpackaged IC chips and other chip-level components in a single package.

Trends: Analog has long been a leader in the development, production, and marketing of linear and mixed signal ICs, particularly technology-driven, high-performance, general purpose, standard-function ICs. Building on its core technology competencies, Analog believes that it is a leading worldwide supplier of data converters and operational amplifiers.

Over the past four years, Analog has been engaged in a transition from being primarily a supplier of SLICs serving a very fragmented market to a company whose strategy is to balance its traditional stable, profitable SLIC business with the growth opportunities available for SPLICs and DSP ICs.

Outlook: Looking further out, we have mapped out a strategy for Analog Devices to become a much larger company over the next few years by capitalizing on the tremendous opportunities available to us in real-world signal processing. We have really just begun to benefit from the investments we have made over the past several years to create new core competencies; to reposition the company in fast-growing markets; and to streamline, realign and generally upgrade our organization.

61. Analogic Corp.
8 Centennial Dr.
Peabody, MA 01960
Phone: (508) 977-3000

Analogic Corp. (NASDAQ; ALOG) manufactures and markets voltage converters, high-speed digital signal processors, image processing equipment, and other devices.

Slogan: "The World Resource for Precision Signal Technology."

Vision: It is Analogic Corporation's intention, policy, and strategy to offer the highest quality, state-of-the-art products at economically attractive prices... to provide solutions to our customers' problems through a broad, multi-disciplined technical capability, in concert with a reliability-oriented, highly efficient, dedicated manufacturing organization.

Mission: Analogic Corporation is engaged in the design, manufacture and marketing of advanced precision data conversion and computer-based signal processing instruments and equipment... which are used to acquire, condition, translate, compute, interpret, store, transmit, or display critical data in modern industrial, scientific, medical, communications, and other system applications.

62. Anchor Gaming
815 Pilot Rd.
Suite G
Las Vegas, NV 89119
Phone: (702) 896-7568

Anchor Gaming (NASDAQ; SLOT) is a diversified gaming company that concentrates on the operation of gaming machines. Anchor Gaming operates two casinos in Colorado and one of the largest gaming machine routes in Nevada. The company also develops and distributes unique proprietary games.

Statements: Anchor Gaming seeks to capitalize on its experience as an operator of gaming machines to explore and develop gaming machine oriented businesses, particularly in emerging markets.

Company management continues to actively evaluate gaming oriented business opportunities. Our strong balance sheet, the quality of our current earnings, our positive cash flow, the support from the banking and investment communities and our responsive management style all combine to give us the tools we need to expand our business. The stage has been set for Anchor Gaming to become a major participant in the emerging gaming market.

63. Anheuser-Busch Companies Inc.
One Busch Place
St. Louis, MO 63118
Phone: (314) 577-2000
Web: http://www.budweiser.com

Anheuser-Busch Companies Inc. (NYSE; BUD) is a holding company parent of Anheuser-Busch Inc. (ABI), the world's largest brewer of beer. The company is also the parent corporation to a number of subsidiaries that conduct various other business operations, including those related to the brewing of beer, the manufacture of metal beverage containers, the recycling of metal and glass beverage containers, the production and sale of food and food-related products, and the operation of theme parks.

The company's principal product is beer, produced and distributed by its subsidiary ABI under the brand names Budweiser, Bud Light, Bud Dry, Bud Ice, Michelob, Michelob Light, Michelob Classic Dark, Busch, Busch Light, Natural Light, Natural Pilsner, King Cobra, and O'Doul's (a non alcohol malt beverage). Additionally, ABI imports Carlsberg and Carlsberg Light beers and Elephant Malt Liquor in U.S. markets.

The company's wholly owned Eagle Snacks produces and distributes a line of salted snacks, nut items, and cookies. Another wholly owned subsidiary, Busch Entertainment Corp. operates Busch Gardens and Sea World theme parks.

The company also owns the St. Louis Cardinals major league baseball team.

Slogans: "This Bud's for You." "Nothing Beats a Bud." "Proud to Be Your Bud." "Gimme a Light." "Why Ask Why? Try Bud Dry." "Some Days Are Made for Michelob." "Fresh Beer Tastes Better." Bud Ice — "Beware the Penguins." "Brewing Solutions for a Better Environment."

A Mission Statement: This mission statement clarifies the direction and general goals of Anheuser-Busch Companies, enabling employees at all levels to better understand their company and the role they play in its success. Additionally, by looking beyond any one product or operating company, this statement provides a reference point from which specific business strategies can be assessed and progress can be measured.

In the broadest sense, our field of competition is the leisure industry. Our place in that industry is clear... Beer is our core business and always will be.

Other businesses complementary to beer will be needed over the long-term to maintain our status as a growth company.

(1) Beer — Our goals are to:

Maintain our reputation for the highest quality products and services in the brewing industry.

Market our products aggressively, successfully, and responsibly. At no time will we encourage the abusive consumption of our products, or their consumption by minors.

Sustain and enhance our competitive position within the United States through continued market share growth.

Increase our share of global brewing industry sales through our historic emphasis on quality products, and by adapting

our marketing and distribution expertise to meet the cultural demands of a local marketplace.

(2) Diversification efforts — Our goals are to:

Broaden the business base of our company and maintain its strong growth trends by successfully developing opportunities in the entertainment, packaging, and food products industries.

Focus on businesses that permit us to earn a premium on our investment by providing superior products and services; that have substantial room for financial and market share growth; that complement our beer business; and that are compatible with our existing corporate culture.

Rely on technical expertise, investment spending and careful management to achieve and maintain the position of low-cost producer in commodity businesses which we have entered to support our brewing operations.

Provide approximately one-third of our company's earnings, including financial contributions from international brewing, by the end of this century.

(3) Stakeholders — In discharging our responsibility to the various stakeholders we serve, Anheuser-Busch must translate its business strategies to more specific objectives. Our goals are to provide:

Our employees at all levels with satisfying and financially rewarding work, and with continuing opportunities for personal development and advancement.

Our shareholders with a superior return on their investment in our company.

Our consumers with premium quality products and services that have the highest value-to-cost ratio in their category.

Our wholesalers with a commitment to our ongoing and mutually beneficial relationship, including opportunities for profitable growth, supporting services, and financing.

Our suppliers with an exemplary demonstration of corporate social responsibility and good citizenship in all areas, but with particular attention to the reduction of alcohol abuse through research and education, the protection of our environment, and the full integration of all peoples into the life of our nation.

Guiding Beliefs: In working together to achieve our mission, the men and women of Anheuser-Busch are guided by a set of shared beliefs that make progress possible. Our task is to strive for constant improvement in making these beliefs a reality.

(1) Our products and people — We believe in:

A commitment to quality as the cornerstone of our success.

Maintaining the highest standards of personal and business integrity.

Earned pride in our company at all levels... in its products and services, its marketing activities, its community responsibility, and in its progressive approach to social and environmental issues.

(2) Our work methods — We believe in:

A sense of urgency and commitment that aggressively seeks to develop every opportunity open to our company.

Teamwork... involving people with a diversity of disciplines to reach decisions that are right, and benefit the entire company.

Long-range planning that is based on conclusive analysis of problems at all levels, including sensitivity and dialectic problem analysis.

Innovation and creativity in all aspects of our business.

Learning from today's mistakes to build tomorrow's successes.

Full debate; then all close ranks behind decisions.

(3) Our working conditions — We believe in:

Encouraging all employees to work at their maximum potential.

Motivating our employees through meaningful work that involves them in appropriate problem-solving and decision-making activities.

Caring for and standing behind our employees.

Honesty and the forthright expression of opinions at all levels.

64. APL Ltd.

111 Broadway
Oakland, CA 94607
Phone: (510) 272-8000
Web: http://www.apl.com

APL Ltd., formerly American President Companies Ltd., (NYSE; APL) provides container transportation and related services in Asia, the Americas, Europe, and the Middle East through an intermodal system combining ocean, rail, and truck transportation.

Vision: Our vision is to be one of the very best containerized surface transportation companies in the world. Our goal is to satisfy:

Our customers by providing high-value services on a global basis that meet their needs and surpass their expectations;

Our shareholders by efficiently utilizing capital and producing an attractive return; and

Ourselves by achieving this vision and by operating with integrity in all of our relationships.

65. Apogee Enterprises Inc.

7900 Xerxes Ave. South
Suite 1800
Minneapolis, MN 55431
Phone: (612) 835-1874

Apogee Enterprises Inc. (NYSE; APOG) manufactures and markets glass, windows, and related products.

Mission: The fundamental mission of Apogee Enterprises Inc. is to achieve profitable growth through leadership in development, manufacture, and worldwide marketing, primarily of glass, windows, and related products and services for automotive, architectural, and construction markets.

Vision for the Future: To be described by our customers, employees, suppliers, communities and shareholders as an excellent company and an ethical company.

To build strong partnerships with employees, customers, and suppliers based on mutual respect, trust, and concern for the success of our partners.

To be perceived by our customers as a quality leader.

To be a dominant player in the niches we serve.

To expand our core businesses and to acquire or start up new operations that link up with technologies, expertise or markets that we understand.

66. Apple Computer Inc.
One Infinite Loop
Cupertino, CA 95014
Phone: (408) 996-1010
Web: http://www.apple.com

Apple Computer Inc. (NASDAQ; AAP) is a leading manufacturer of personal computers and software.

Mission for Apple: Help people transform the way they work, learn, and communicate by providing exceptional personal computing products and innovative customer services.

Vision: To change the world by empowering individuals through personal computing technology.

Apple's Business Goal: Our goal is to enhance our position as the innovator and premiere manufacturer of personal computers — the value leader, not the price leader. We intend to continue our strong sales growth worldwide. We will do this by concentrating on two strengths: Human engineering and customer service.

67. ARAMARK Corp.
ARAMARK Tower
1101 Market St.
Philadelphia, PA 19107
Phone: (215) 238-3000
Web: http://www.ARAMARK.com

ARAMARK Corp., a private company, is involved in food service, health care, child care, uniform services, and periodicals distribution.

Slogan: "Managed Services, Managed Better."

Our Vision: A company where the best people want to work.

Customers who recommend us to others because we constantly exceed their expectations.

Success measured in the growth of our company, its earning and ourselves.

The world leader in managed services.

Our Guiding Principles: Because we value our relationship, we treat customers as long-term partners, and each other with candor and respect.

Because we succeed through performance, we encourage the entrepreneur in each of us, and work always to improve our service.

Because we thrive on growth, we seek new markets and new opportunities, and we innovate to get and keep customers.

And because we're ARAMARK, we do everything with integrity.

68. Arbor Drugs Inc.
3331 W. Big Beaver Rd.
Troy, MI 48007
Phone: (810) 643-9420
Web: http://www.arbordrugs.com

Arbor Drugs Inc. (NASDAQ; ARBR) is a growing retailer operating full-service drugstores.

Statement: With the support of our employees, suppliers, and investors, we will continue our proven plan of success. By maintaining our edge in technological enhancements and cost controls, Arbor will remain the premier drugstore provider in the markets we serve. We will not stray into diversification or over-leverage our outstanding balance sheet. I believe these efforts will provide continued growth in market share, earnings and most importantly, the value of your investment in Arbor Drugs.

69. Arby's Inc.
1000 Corporate Dr.
Ft. Lauderdale, FL 33334
Phone: (305) 351-5100

Arby's Inc., a subsidiary of Triarc Companies Inc. (NYSE; TRY), is a quick service restaurant chain. Arby's restaurants feature sandwiches with a variety of slow-roasted meats, including beef, chicken, ham and turkey, and accompanied by a variety of side items, including salads and curly fries. A breakfast menu, which consists of croissants with a variety of fillings, is also available at some Arby's restaurants. The name Arby's is derived from the initials of the Raffel brothers, who founded the chain. In a test, over a dozen restaurants in the chain offer menu items from other restaurants, such as Green Burrito, Mrs. Winner's Chicken, and Sbarro's. The majority of units are franchisees; currently the company owns approximately 10% of the units in the system.

Slogans: "Different Is Good." "Crave Reviews." "Escape from Boring Burgers." "Taste the Arby's Difference." "Go West. It's Better Out Here."

Vision: Top tier is the next frontier. We have a good brand that has the potential to become a great brand. The company wants to ride into the top five in the U.S. quick service restaurant industry, in the next several years — by both adding units and increasing volume.

Business Strategy: Arby's business strategy is designed to increase the total number of restaurants in the Arby's system and to improve the revenues and profitability of the restaurants. The key elements of this strategy include: (1) an accelerated store opening program; (2) a remodeling program; (3) expanding the franchise network; (4) increasing operating efficiency; (5) more focused retail-oriented marketing; (6) international expansion; and (7) dual branding.

70. Archer-Daniels-Midland Co.
4666 Faries Pkwy.
Decatur, IL 62526
Phone: (217) 424-5200
Web: http://www.admworld.com

Archer-Daniels-Midland Co (NYSE; ADM) is a leading agricultural processor, with manufacturing plants, sales offices, and distribution facilities on five continents. Every day, ADM processes five million bushels of the farmer's crops into food, vitamins, feed, and fuel products.

Slogan: "Supermarket to the World."

Environmental Responsibility: ADM spends significant resources for environmental improvement and pollution control. Part of this commitment is evident in the growth of our internal environment staff.

We're constantly seeking ways to live up to our environmental responsibility: Leaving little to waste, conserving energy, preventing pollution, and manufacturing products that have their own ecological benefits.

The reason is simple; preserving the world begins here.

71. ARCO Chemical Co.
3801 West Chester Pike
Newton Square, PA 19073
Phone: (215) 359-2000
Web: http://www.arcochem.com

ARCO Chemical Co. (NYSE; RCM) manufactures and markets chemicals and specialty products.

Statement: We do desire to be a profitable leader in our industry and a responsible corporate citizen.

We focus on quality assets, low-cost resources and competitive differentiation. We continue to evaluate the capital markets for opportunities to utilize those markets effectively. We maintain financial leverage appropriate to our company's circumstances and long-range plans.

These strategies have served as the foundation for our success and have been the driving force in terms of investment in our core businesses. At the same time, they give us the flexibility required in a business where the job of finding resources and turning them into producible assets is quite challenging. Most important, however, they provide the framework necessary to keep our actions focused on financial and operational strength and on returns to stockholders for the long term.

72. Arctco Inc.
600 Brooks Ave.
Thief River Falls, MN 56701
Phone: (218) 681-8558

Arctco Inc. (NASDAQ; ACAT) designs, engineers, manufactures, and markets snowmobiles under the Arctic Cat registered brand name, and personal watercraft under the Tigershark registered brand name.

Statement: We credit our success... to the sound business strategy that has guided us for more than a decade; responding to the demands of our customers, a commitment to building the best products on the market, holding the line on prices and supporting our dealers, while continuing our efforts to cut costs and maintain margins.

73. Armco Inc.
One Oxford Centre
301 Grant St.
Pittsburgh, PA 15219
Phone: (412) 255-9800
Web: http://www.armco.com

Armco Inc. (NYSE; AS) is a major domestic producer of flat-rolled stainless and electrical steels. The company also produces other steel and fabricated products and has an interest in an oil field equipment and supply joint venture. Markets for specialty flat-rolled steel include automotive emission control, automotive trim, appliances, cookware, cutlery, industrial machinery, power generation and distribution, electric motors, generators, and lighting.

Slogan: "That's Armco."

Statements: Our focus on specialty flat-rolled steels is a return to what Armco does best — making the highest quality stainless and electrical steels in the industry. This strategic focus has led to the continued divestment of numerous businesses and investments.

We are rebuilding shareholder value on our specialty flat-rolled steel business. Earnings for these operations are the foundation. All of us at Armco are focused on this as our primary goal.

Armco's long-range goal is to be the premier domestic specialty steel producer. This has meant focusing on our specialty steel business, divesting non-core, non-performing businesses and making our cost structure more competitive.

74. Armstrong World Industries Inc.
P. O. Box 3001
313 West Liberty St.
Lancaster, PA 17604
Phone: (717) 397-0611
Web: http://www.armstrong.com

Armstrong World Industries Inc. (NYSE; ACK) manufactures and markets building products, floor coverings, and other specialty products.

Vision: To be the leader in our chosen flooring markets

Mission: Delight our customers and create new customers by providing quality products and services while achieving our long-term financial objectives.

Strategy: Apply the quality process in everything we do.

Expand our market opportunities worldwide.

Continually improve our existing products and services.

Develop new products and services driven by market need.

Continually improve all processes to serve the expectations and needs of: Customers; employees; the environment.

Provide the opportunity for employees to reach their full potential.

Must Do's:

Increase sales.

Manage assets.

Control costs and expenses.

Continuous learning.

Stretch Goals:
Developed by the business units.
Increase customer satisfaction with our products.
Add value to the business.

75. Artisoft Inc.
575 E. River St.
Tucson, AZ 857045
Phone: (602) 670-7100
Web: http://www.artisoft.com

Artisoft Inc. (NASDAQ; ASFT) develops and markets computer networking solutions, including software, hardware and support. Registered trade name products include LANtastic, CorStream, Simply LANtastic, and NodeRunner.

Statements: Our principal goal is to enable people in computing workgroups to be as productive as possible by allowing them to easily access all resources connected to the network — without concern for the underlying technology.

Our corporate objective: Becoming the leading provider of work-group connectivity solutions.

76. Arvin Industries Inc.
One Noblitt Plaza
Box No. 3000
Columbus, IN 47202
Phone: (812) 379-3000
Web: http://www.arvin.com

Arvin Industries Inc. (NYSE; ARV) manufactures mufflers, shock absorbers, struts, and ride control systems.

Strategy: The strategy of a business organization is the single most important ingredient to success. It must be founded on a realistic evaluation of market strengths and weaknesses and developed with knowledge of competitors' strategies. Once in place, corporate strategy drives marketing tactics, manufacturing investments, product development, personnel policies, labor relations, etc., etc. Since it affects all aspects of the business, it is necessary to communicate the strategy to all employees so that their efforts are more productively directed to the company's success.

There is no single department that is most important in a business. All departments must contribute to the strategic planning process and support the direction determined best for the business.

Also fundamental to successful business strategy is the consideration of society's needs. By aligning the company's focus and direction so that it fulfills basic societal needs, the likelihood of long-term success for the enterprise is made more certain.

Environment: Arvin's environmental stewardship policy commits the company to use resources in a manner that will help assure a clean environment for future generations and to comply fully with the laws protecting the environment. And that stewardship charges every Arvin employee with responsibility for compliance with the letter as well as the spirit of those laws and for understanding the legal and moral implications of his or her actions with respect to the environment.

Arvin's commitment to the environment is as import to our reputation as the quality of our products and, therefore, must be a part of the day-to-day management of our business.

Ethics: Arvin always has placed a premium on the quality of individual judgment and integrity. Rather than specific prescriptions for ethical behavior in business situations, Arvin expects all employees to be guided by their highest personal moral and ethical conduct.

No employee should ever violate such ethical standards in the belief that the company will benefit.

Throughout Arvin everyone should understand that to maintain and enhance the confidence of customers, suppliers, shareholders, and the public, trust and integrity cannot be compromised.

Although the company can accommodate inadvertent error and honest difference of opinion, it never can condone deceit or subordination of principle.

Adherence to the highest ethical standards is the Arvin criterion which all business transactions must meet.

77. ASARCO Inc.
180 Maiden Lane
New York, NY 10038
Phone: (212) 510-2000
Web: http://www.asarco.com

ASARCO Inc. is a leading producer of nonferrous metals, principally copper, lead, zinc, silver and molybdenum. The company also produces specialty chemicals and aggregates.

Environment: ASARCO recognizes and believes that all operations and activities of the company should be conducted responsibly and in a manner designed to protect the health and safety of its employees, its customers, the public, and the environment. ASARCO's operations interact with the environment daily. The company is committed to the responsible management of natural resources.

78. Ashland Coal Inc.
P.O. Box 6300
Huntington, WV 25771
Phone: (304) 526-3333
Web: http://invest.quest.columbus.oh.us/
InvestQuest/a/aci

Ashland Coal under its new name Arch Coal Inc. (NYSE; ACI) mines, processes, and markets low-sulfur bituminous coal.

Mission and Strategies: Ashland Coal has pursued a single mission: To create value for its owners by positioning itself to profit from the increasing demand for environmentally acceptable low-sulfur coal. Three strategies guide the company's progress toward this end:

To seek out innovative ways to increase productivity and reduce mining costs.

To pursue selective acquisitions that expand both its low-sulfur reserve base and its market penetration.

To capitalize on a strong reserve position by adding new, low-cost production.

79. Ashland Inc.
1000 Ashland Dr.
Russell, KY 41169
Phone: (606) 329-3333
Web: http://www.ashland.com

Ashland Inc. (NYSE; ASH) is a worldwide energy and chemical company. Ashland provides a wide array of products for both industry and the retail customer. Ashland is one of the nation's largest independent refiners (Ashland Petroleum); a leading independent crude oil gatherer and marketer; a regional retail marketer of gasoline and merchandise (SuperAmerica); and a top U.S. motor oil (Valvoline) and automotive chemical marketer (Zerex, Pyroil performance products, NAPA and various other private label brands). Additionally, Ashland is the largest distributor of chemicals and plastics in North America (Ashland Chemical); a leading supplier of specialty chemicals worldwide; the nation's largest highway contractor (APAC construction group); and a producer of natural gas and crude oil. Also, Ashland has equity positions in two large coal companies (Ashland Coal and Arch Mineral).

Slogan: Valvoline — "#1 Choice of Top Mechanics." Valvoline — "People Who Know Use Valvoline."

Statement: Leveraging traditional strengths for profitable growth: Technological leadership; marketing and distribution; and customer service.

Our Strategy is Working: Since 1982, we have pursued a dual strategy aimed at maintaining a strong competitive position in petroleum refining and wholesale marketing while pursuing growth in our related energy and chemical businesses.

While the refining industry offers tremendous upside potential when refinery margins are attractive, volatility in commodity markets is often reflected in these margins. Consequently, we have sought to balance that risk with an increasingly important portfolio of related energy and chemical businesses so we can offer our shareholders a stronger and more consistent return.

Sources of Value Creation: Along with our refining operations, our related energy and chemical businesses allow us to capitalize upon our traditional strengths in technology, marketing and distribution, and superior customer service. These strengths, in fact are the hallmarks of all our businesses and will serve in large part as the basis for future capital investment as we seek further value creation and profit growth.

Ashland Outlook: As we move forward through the '90s, we will continue to emphasize the themes we have stressed in recent years — increasing earning from related energy and chemical businesses, maintaining a strong competitive position in refining and further improving the balance sheet.

We look forward to pursuing opportunities to create value and increase profits.

Environmental Protection: As a responsible corporate citizen, Ashland realizes the importance of environmental considerations regarding its current and future operations and recognizes its responsibility to protect and maintain the quality of the environment. The company continues to commit the personnel and financial resources necessary to meet these goals. It also participates in many voluntary initiatives.

80. AST Research Inc.
16215 Alton Pkwy.
Irvine, CA 92718
Phone: (714) 727-4141
Web: http://www.ast.com

AST Research Inc. (NASDAQ; ASTA) designs, manufactures, markets, services, and supports a broad line of personal computers including desktop, notebook and server computer systems marketed under the following registered brand names: Advantage!, Bravo, Premmia, Ascentia, and Manhattan SMP.

Slogan: "Working for Your Business."

Statement: Moving forward, we intend to become first to market with the latest PC technologies to capitalize on early momentum, maintain short and flexible supply lines and establish best-of-class service and support for our resellers. We plan to maintain our valued reseller relationships and strive to become the brand of choice among multi-national companies throughout the world in order to foster growth and leverage our worldwide strengths.

AST management is focused on both the challenges and opportunities that lie ahead. The key success factors have been identified and are being addressed.

81. AT&T Corp.
32 Avenue of the Americas
New York, NY 10013
Phone: (212) 387-5400
Web: http://www.att.com

AT&T Corp. (NYSE; T) is a participant in two industries: The global information movement and management industry and the financial services and leasing industry. On September 20, 1995, AT&T announced a plan to separate into three publicly-held stand-alone companies that will each be focused on serving certain core businesses: Communication services (to be carried on by the new AT&T, communications systems and technology (to be carried on by the newly formed Lucent Technologies Inc.), and transaction-intensive computing (to be carried on by NCR Corporation.

Slogans: "Your True Choice." "It's All Within Your Reach."

Mission: We are dedicated to being the world's best at bringing people together — giving them easy access to each other and to the information and services they want and need — anytime, anywhere.

The New AT&T: Our future is a long distance from long distance. We're moving to a full menu of communications and information services including local and wireless calling, credit cards, on-line services, consulting and electronic commerce.

We aspire to be the most admired and

valuable company in the world. Our goal is to improve the lives of our customers by bringing to market exciting and useful communications services, building shareowners' value in the process.

Environment: We will sustain the successes and significant gains we've already made against our goals in CGC elimination, manufacturing waste disposal reduction and reportable air emission reduction, as we add new operations and as we grow globally.

In addition, by the year 2000:

We will put in place internationally recognized E&S management systems for at least 95 percent of our products, services, operations and facilities; we will ensure that at least 95 percent of our services, operation and facilities meet the rigorous criteria of AT&T's model safety program; we will develop and apply design for environment (DRE) criteria that provides competitive, environmentally preferable products and services; we will improve the energy efficiency of our operations, avoiding what would otherwise be the emission of at least 500,000 metric tons of greenhouse gases; we will recycle at least 70% of our wastepaper.

Why AT&T Is Restructuring: This restructuring is a bold strategic move that will realign AT&T's current businesses to take full advantage of changes in the fast growing global information industry. We undertake this restructuring from a position of strength. AT&T has never been stronger.

The restructuring will improve each business's current exceptional capabilities and better enable it to create long-term value for shareowners.

Each new business will have a sharper focus on its individual market and clearer strategic intent.

The restructuring will eliminate strategic conflict between businesses (e.g., simultaneously selling to and competing with service providers). This will not only remove complications from sales to existing markets (e.g., the RBOC's), it will open new markets (e.g., competitors of AT&T's current service and equipment businesses).

It will accelerate decision making by greatly simplifying our corporate structure.

It will give each business unit financial flexibility appropriate to its market and opportunities (e.g., capital structure and cost structure).

This restructuring resolves thorny public policy issues which limit our business flexibility.

Throughout the transition and beyond, AT&T and these new companies will meet all existing commitments. We will not miss a beat in serving customers. We will communicate openly and honestly with employees. We will always act in the best interests of AT&T's current shareowners.

Our Common Bond: We commit to these values to guide our decisions and behavior: Respect for individuals; dedication to helping customers; highest standards of integrity; innovation; teamwork.

By leaving these values, AT&T aspires to set a standard of excellence worldwide that will reward our shareowners, our customers, and all AT&T people.

82. Atmel Corp.
2125 O'Neil Dr.
San Jose, CA 95131
Phone: (408) 441-0311
Web: http://www.atmel.com

Atmel Corp. (NASDAQ; ATML) develops and manufactures a broad line of complex integrated circuits. Atmel serves the manufacturers of communications equipment, computers and computer peripherals as well as sectors within the instrumentation, consumer, automotive, military and industrial markets.

Strategy: Atmel's strategy is to focus on specialized areas within each of its selected markets and to provide components with performance improvements or other special features for its circuits that can provide higher-than-average per-unit selling prices.

The key to Atmel's strategy is growth. The company focuses its design attention on specialized areas within each of several billion-dollar-market opportunities.

83. Atmos Energy Corp.
P.O. Box 650205
Dallas, TX 75265
Phone: (972) 934-9227
Web: http://www.atmosenergy.com

Atmos Energy Corp. (NYSE; ATO) provides natural gas service to customers in Texas, Colorado, Kansas, Missouri, Louisiana, and Kentucky through its operating companies — Energas Company, Greeley Gas Company, Trans Louisiana Gas Company and Western Kentucky Gas Company.

Slogan: "The First Time — Every Time."

Statement: Atmos will continue with its long-standing growth plan of expanding geographically through acquisitions. This allows the company to diversify its exposure to weather patterns, markets, economic conditions, and regulatory climates.

84. Austin Co.
3650 Mayfield Rd.
Cleveland, OH 44121
Phone: (216) 382-6600

Austin Co., a private company, provides consulting, design, engineering, and construction services.

Mission Statement: Mission: The Austin Company is committed to world leadership as the premier complete-service engineering/construction firm. Through profitability, growth, and enterprise, Austin will constantly strive to set the standard for the construction industry.

Goals: To accomplish this mission, Austin will provide consulting, design, engineering, and construction services of the highest possible quality.

Austin will focus on those markets characterized by projects that are large, complex, and logistically difficult to implement.

Austin will strive to develop unique capabilities and qualifications to give the company a significant competitive advantage in those markets in which it competes.

Austin services will be organized and delivered so as to be fully responsible to the needs of clients and prospects.

Particular emphasis will be placed on cost-effectiveness, so that clients always receive full value for their facility investments.

The company will strive to increase productivity by stimulating and encouraging innovation, as well as through the application of advanced technologies.

Austin will encourage excellent and enthusiastic performance by employees through appropriate company policies governing compensation, incentives, promotion, benefits and challenging assignments.

Objectives: To fulfill Austin's mission and to achieve the company's goals, the following objectives will guide corporate decisions:

Continuous improvement in the quality of services; highly skilled and totally motivated work force; capable, competent and committed management; technical superiority; financial strength; commitment to integrity.

85. Autocam Corp.
4070 East Paris Ave.
Kentwood, MI 49512
Phone: (616) 698-0707
Web: http://www.autocam.com

Autocam Corp. (NASDAQ; ACAM), manufactures and markets specialty metal alloy components.

Autocam Mission Statement: Our mission is to be a worldwide leader in the manufacture of precision components for customers with whom we develop long term business relationships. Our mission will only be met by focusing on continually improving our processes, thereby improving our products and services to meet and exceed our customer's expectations.

Values and Principles: We will all strive to meet our mission while keeping certain values and principles in mind: These values and principles will help us achieve our mission.

(1) Worldwide leadership will be achieved by providing the highest quality products and services. We improve these by continually reducing variation in all of our organization's processes.

(2) We believe results from continuous improvement are best achieved in a context of meaningful employment. Our employees will be treated equitably and continually provided with opportunity for personal growth. Our success will come through the efforts of all employees working together. Every employee will participate as equal contributors to this team and all team members will treat each other with trust and respect.

(3) We will strive to conserve, reuse, and recycle all materials with the objective of having zero impact on the environment.

(4) Our customers and suppliers will be partners in our process.

(5) Employees, suppliers, and customers will all share in the benefits derived from continuous improvement efforts.

86. Automatic Data Processing Inc.
One ADP Blvd.
Roseland, NJ 07068
Phone: (201) 994-5000
Web: http://www.adp.com

Automatic Data Processing Inc.(NYSE; AUD) is the largest payroll processing company in the U.S.

Mission: ADP's mission is to help an ever-increasing number of businesses improve their performance by regularly applying ADP's solutions to their ongoing needs for record keeping, data communications, information services, and automation. We seek to establish and maintain our competitive edge through product and service differentiation. We want to be the primary, most innovative vendor of each service that we offer, with a reputation for: (1) superior, responsive people, (2) the highest quality and value, and (3) cost effective, modern technology.

87. Avery Dennison Corp.
150 North Orange Grove Blvd.
Pasadena, CA 91103
Phone: (818) 304-2000
Web: http://www.averydennison.com

Avery Dennison Corp. (NYSE; AVY) is a worldwide manufacturer of pressure-sensitive adhesives and materials, office products and converted products, serving a broad consumer and industrial base. The company's major markets are in office products, retail, industrial tapes, durable goods, apparel, food, transportation, health care, and data processing.

Vision: Our vision is to become the global leader in self-adhesive base materials and self-adhesive office products through technological innovation and leadership in adhesives and materials combinations. This vision remains fundamental to our operating strategies and is at the heart of every business decision we make. Every program we put in place is designed to increase shareholder wealth and is based on achieving this vision.

Our vision for growth is predicated on three dynamic external factors, pervasive in global markets, which consistently drive our actions:

The ever-expanding use of computers and variable-information and non-impact printing systems for information management and the fact that office automation consumes billions of square feet of pressure-sensitive labels and self-adhesive materials each year.

The proliferation of graphics on packaging and consumer goods, particularly labeling on clear plastic and glass containers, creates demand for high-quality pressure-sensitive labels for eye-catching product identification.

The growth of new markets in Asia,

Latin America and Eastern Europe, with their enormous consumer buying potential, offers tremendous opportunity for Avery Dennison products.

Statement: We have a consistent and clear vision. We create innovative products with high growth potential in expanding economies and in any market. We have advanced technology which is largely proprietary, to support our core businesses. And we have invested more than four decades in two powerful brand names — Avery and Fasson — that are recognized and respected in consumer and industrial markets worldwide. Our two operating sectors, pressure-sensitive adhesives and materials, and consumer and converted products, provide the solid structure for sustained and vigorous growth.

88. Avid Technology Inc.

Metropolitan Technology Park
One Park West
Tewksbury, MA 01876
Phone: (508) 640-6789
Web: http://www.avid.com

Avid Technology Inc. (NASDAQ; AVID) provides film studios, television networks, and recording studios with integrated digital production services.

Charter: Avid is committed to providing customers with integrated digital production environments capable of handling all phases of media production — recording, logging, editing, playback, mastering, distribution, and archiving. Its goal is to continue to provide the most feature-rich production and post-production tools available, and tie them together with high-speed, advanced network technology and central media servers. By delivering solutions that are compatible, networkable and share an industry-standard data format, Avid's customers will realize significant benefits in terms of increased speed, reduced production costs and higher-quality end products.

89. Avis Rent A Car System Inc.

900 Old Country Rd.
Garden City, NY 11530
Phone: (516) 222-3000
Web: http://www.avis.com

Avis Rent A Car System Inc., a private employee-owned company, is a major company in the rental car business. The holdings of Avis include: U.S. Rent A Car Division; International Division; and WizCom International LTD. The Avis system covers over 140 nations, with about 4,800 locations.

Slogan: "We Try Harder." "The World Around Us Is Changing — and So Is Avis."

The Avis Quest For Excellence: At Avis Rent A Car, our business is renting cars; our mission is total customer satisfaction.

Our goal is to provide the best quality customer service: To treat each customer the way we ourselves want to be treated. To exceed our customers' expectations.

We believe that only by maximizing our service and our productivity can we maximize our employee equity and our profits.

We are dedicated to a vigorous program of self-evaluation and improvement.

We continually strive to provide better and innovative services to enhance the travel experience for our customers. We work to strengthen our bonds with all active participants in the delivery of our service: Our customers, our suppliers, and our co-workers in all areas.

We know that total customer service and satisfaction require the team effort of all employees, at all times.

"We try harder."

The Avis Vision: Avis will be recognized as the preeminent company in the rent a car industry in the areas of customer service and satisfaction, employee participation, and return to shareholders.

90. Avnet Inc.

80 Cutter Mill Rd.
Great Neck, NY 11021

Phone: (516) 466-7000
Web: http://www.avnet.com

Avnet Inc. (NYSE; AVT) is a large distributor of electronic components and computer products for industrial and military customers.

Statement: Why then this strategy of acquisitions, enhancement of line cards and broadening of value-added services? It is driven by a multitude of factors. Among the most important are the many suppliers have found it beneficial to do business with only a few well financed, technically competent distributors. Of equal importance, customers are looking to outsource more of their value-added requirements to distributors who can perform these functions more reliably and cost effectively than they, themselves, can.

In addition, the growing preference for quality certified distributors on the part of suppliers and customers requires distributors to make total commitments to quality. Moreover, the presence of growing numbers of global customers demands a global presence by the few truly effective, well-capitalized distributors who can provide these benefits. As these capabilities are perceived and acknowledged by its suppliers and customers, the role of the distributor will continue to broaden.

Many suppliers have steadily reduced their roster of distributors, retaining those with the technical and financial strength not only to make those commitments but also to implement them. Because of these franchise reductions and the consolidation among suppliers and distributors in recent years, the largest distributors have significantly increased their share of the total available distribution market. Avnet has been a prime beneficiary of this migration to fewer and larger distributors.

By leveraging the management, technical talent and unique value-added capabilities we possess, improving our roster of top suppliers and broadening our geographic coverage on both continents, we have become increasingly valuable to our global suppliers and customers. The commitments we have made and will continue to make are clearly enhancing our growth prospects. Accordingly, Avnet will continue to invest, to acquire, to broaden our ability to serve our customers and to be invaluable to our suppliers.

91. Avon Products Inc.

9 W. 57th St.
New York, NY 10019
Phone: (212) 546-6015
Web: http://www.avon.com

Avon Products Inc. (NYSE; AVP) markets cosmetics and other beauty products directly to the consumer.

Our Vision: To be the company that best understands and satisfies the product, service and self-fulfillment needs of women — globally.

Our Mission: Avon will be the global leader in offering women the most convenient and enjoyable direct buying opportunities. We will achieve this leadership position by understanding and responding to the aspirations and unique needs of women and their families.

We are committed to being a world leader in beauty. Developing, manufacturing, and selling beauty products will be the centerpiece of our business. We will build Avon into the beauty brand women turn to worldwide.

We will also leverage our unique marketing channels to offer women the broad range of complementary products they need to beautify and enhance their faces.

Our competitive advantage will come from providing our Customers personalized service — when, where and how they want it.

Avon Representatives will continue to be the spirit and driving force of the company. They are the foundation of our uniqueness, and the focus for delivering our services to our Customers. We are committed to providing the training, support, motivation and earnings opportunities that will attract them and help them be successful.

We will strive to be an employer of

choice. Because we know our Associates are critical to our future, we will attract, develop and reward excellence worldwide.

Fulfilling this Mission will produce profitable global growth and create increasing prosperity for our Shareholders, our Representatives, our Associates and the communities in which we work and live.

92. Aztar Corp.
2390 E. CamelBack Rd.
Suite 400
Phoenix, AZ 85016
Phone: (602) 381-4100

Aztar Corp. (NYSE; AZR) operates casino hotels in Atlantic City, New Jersey, and in Las Vegas and Laughlin, Nevada, and is developing riverboat casinos in Caruthersville, Missouri, and Evansville, Indiana.

Product Concept: Our product concept is "the creation of fun, fantasy, excitement, and entertainment" in a casino gaming environment. While we market to the full spectrum of casino players, our focus is on the high end of the middle market. Each of our land-based casinos is designed and themed for the unique demographics of its particular market. Our riverboat casinos share a common theme and brand. Our staff is dedicated to the principles of friendliness and service. Our goal is to enhance through operating excellence the value of the shareholders' investment in our company while maintaining a prudent financial position.

93. Bacardi-Martini USA Inc.
2100 Biscayne Blvd.
Miami, FL 33137
Phone: (305) 573-8511
Web: http://www.bacardi.com

Bacardi-Martini USA Inc., formerly Bacardi Imports, is a private company owned by Bacardi Limited. It manufactures and sells alcoholic spirits, including Bacardi Rum and Martini Brand Vermouth.

Slogan: "Just Add Bacardi."

Mission: By the year 2000, Bacardi Limited will be one of the top five spirits in the world. We will emulate the spirit and achievements of the 1960's by doubling sales of 1992 margin-equivalent cases, and by improving our world dominance of all rum-based products.

We will become a global company by allocating our talents and resources to the products and markets with the highest potential for profits and growth, and without regard to provincial interest.

We will be recognized as the most socially responsible beverage alcohol company in the world.

Values:
Accountability: Keep your promises.
Total quality: Think, act and be number 1.
Creativity: If it ain't broke, break it.
High energy: Do it now, because you can.
Longterm vision: Invest today thinking of tomorrow.
Teamwork: Help others without taking the credit.
Productivity: All the dollars to invest, not a penny to spend.
Family values: Treat others as you would have them treat you.

Vision: Our vision is: The most creative, energetic and innovative leader in the beverage industry reflected by our people, our products and the way we do business.

Where change is viewed as an opportunity and not as a threat.

Where "risk taking" is a way to creativity and innovation.

Where we are truly empowered and accountable to each other.

Where learning is valued and we proactively seek the sharing of knowledge and information.

Where personal growth is achieved through trust and continuous feedback.

Where we achieve even more than the strategic business objectives by fulfilling our own aspirations.

We have fun in everything we do fueled by a passion for success.

94. (J.) Baker Inc.
555 Turnpike St.
Canton, MA 02021
Phone: (617) 828-9300

J. Baker, Inc. (NASDAQ; JBAK) is a diversified retailer of footware and apparel, operating over 2,600 retail locations.

Statement: J. Baker enters fiscal year 1996 with the goal of producing earnings growth more in line with the company's historical performance and our expectations. Our efforts will be supported by the company's strong financial condition, highlighted by growth in shareholders' equity. To reach our goal, we will focus on running each of our businesses more effectively in the changing retail marketplace.

95. Baker Hughes Inc.
3900 Essex Lane, Suite 1200
P.O. Box 4740
Houston, TX 77210
Phone: (713) 439-8600
Web: http://www.bhi-net.com

Baker Hughes Inc. (NYSE; BHI) was founded with the merger of two oil field equipment and service companies, Baker International Corporation and Hughes Tool Company. Each company has been a pioneer in oilfield technology since the early 1900s. Baker Hughes has established itself as one of the industry's major oilfield service companies. Recent organizational changes have included acquisitions of Eastman Christensen and Teleco Oilfield Services; the combination of Baker Service Tools, TriState Oil Tools, and Baker Oil Tools divisions into a single unit bearing the Baker Oil Tools name; and the formation of Baker Hughes INTEQ from five oilfield service divisions.

Slogan: "The Technology Leader — Then and Now."

Statement: The evolution of these organizations is a continuous improvement process that allows our focus to remain the same: Provide our customers with the best products, services and solutions in the drilling, completion, and production of oil and gas wells.

Environmental Policy: Baker Hughes Incorporated recognizes its responsibility to maintain the compatibility of its operations with the environment while supplying high quality products and services to the customers it serves. The company firmly and seriously accepts its social responsibility to work with the public, the government and others to develop and |use natural resources in an environmentally sound manner while protecting the health and safety of our employees and the public. To meet these responsibilities, the company and its subsidiaries commit to the following operational principles:

To recognize community concerns about the methods in which we use our raw materials, products, and operations.

To make safety, health, and environmental considerations a priority in our planning and development of new products and processes.

To operate our plants and facilities and to handle our raw materials and products in a manner which is consistent with prudent environmental, health, and safety practice.

To commit to reduce overall emissions and waste generation.

To participate with government and others in creating responsible laws, regulations and standards to safeguard the community work place and environment.

96. Baldor Electric Co.
P.O. Box 2400
Fort Smith, AR 72902
Phone: (501) 646-4711

Baldor Electric Co. (NYSE; BEZ) markets and manufactures electric motors and drives.

Mission: Our mission is: To be the best (as determined by our customers) marketers, designers and manufacturers of electric motors and drives.

To achieve this, we must:

Provide better value to our customers than any of our competitors.

Attract and retain competent employees dedicated to reaching our goals and objectives.

Produce good, long-term results for our shareholders.

97. Baldwin Technology Co. Inc.

65 Rowayton Ave.
Rowayton, CT 06853
Phone: (203) 838-7470
Web: http://www.baldwintech.com

Baldwin Technology Co. Inc. (AMEX; BLD) manufactures and markets products and services for publishers and printers. Printers and printing equipment manufacturers the world over rely on Baldwin "technology" to improve quality and profitability in innovative ways. Baldwin's material handling, accessory, control and pre-press equipment performs many tasks, among them providing sliced rolls of paper to the press; maintaining the best print chemistries; automatically cleaning key areas of the press; keeping paper webs perfectly aligned; folding, cutting, and gluing material as fast as it comes off the press; and counting stacking, inserting and bundling finished products.

Slogan: "Where There's Printing, There's Baldwin."

Fundamental Beliefs: Integrity — We conduct all business affairs with integrity. To ensure our customers of satisfaction, the final measure of success. To provide our employees with opportunities to grow and develop. To serve the printing industry and our community locations around the world.

Innovation — We listen to printers. To develop patentable products through technical innovation. To maintain a growing portfolio of proprietary products.

Income — We set high profit goals. To support investment in R&D. To enter new fields. To remain independent.

Internationalism — We position our-

selves in all major printing machinery and print markets. To provide maximum opportunity for growth. To service our products in each of our markets. To bring new products from one market to another.

Business Concepts: Our customers are our driving force. Our business is to seek out the productivity, safety, quality and environmental needs of publishers and printers worldwide. We will grow profitably by satisfying those needs with superior auxiliary, control, and material handling products and related supplies.

Areas of Excellence: Customer satisfaction — We must excel at surpassing our customers' expectations.

Marketing — We must excel at coordinating our marketing, sales and service capabilities in order to leverage these into worldwide opportunities.

Market research — We must excel at understanding printers' and publishers' operational needs and problems to proactively identify new product opportunities.

Product Development — We must excel at the analysis, development, acquisition, and adequate testing of products that provide superior performance and meet customer requirements.

98. Ball Corp.

P.O. Box 2407
Muncie, IN 47307
Phone: (317) 747-6100
Web: http://www.ball.com

Ball Corp. (NYSE; BLL) produces metal and glass packaging products, primarily for foods and beverages, and provides aerospace and communications products and services to government and commercial customers.

Slogan: "When Was the Last Time You Had a Ball in the Kitchen?"

Mission: To provide consistent customer value through competitive levels of technology, quality and service, while maintaining high standards of integrity, ethical conduct and social responsibility.

Our Objective: To maximize shareholder value.

99. Bally Entertainment Corp.
8700 W. Bryn Mawr
Chicago, IL 60631
Phone: (312) 399-1300
Web: http://www.ballys.com

Bally Entertainment Corp. (NYSE; BLY) is engaged in the operation of casinos, some with adjacent hotels, and fitness centers. Hilton Hotels has purchased majority interest.

Statement: We are holding to our plans to increase stockholder value by improving operating performance and selectively developing opportunities in emerging gaming markets. I believe the greatest opportunities in the gaming industry today continue to be in the mature markets, Atlantic City and Las Vegas.

100. Banc One Corp.
100 East Broad St.
Columbus, OH 43271
Phone: (614) 248-5944
Web: http://www.bankone.com

Banc One Corp. (NYSE; ONE) is a banking institution with branches in 13 states.

Mission Statement: We believe…Enterprise and the opportunities crested by individual choice are cornerstones of our "Uncommon Partnership." They provide the greatest value for the customer and the greatest stimulant to business. Those core values provide the best plan for delivering true satisfaction for every customer and the most desirable return for inventors.

Precepts… Based on this belief, the Board of Directors of Banc One Corporation adopted these precepts as the official guideline for the commitment and performance of our people.

One — We believe in creating an atmosphere in which our people working together: Care about what they do; utilize their own abilities to make the right decisions; focus on customers and uncover innovative ways to service their changing financial needs; promptly respond to problems and customers' concerns in a professional sensitive manner.

Two — We believe in conducting our business: With uncompromising honesty, fairness, and integrity; to achieve superior financial performance for our shareholders; to identify, develop, retain, and provide equal opportunity for all people who demonstrate the willingness and ability to perform and grow; and with an unflinching focus on providing a quality of services that ensures customer satisfaction.

Three — We believe management should base decisions on: Maintaining a balance between the needs of our customers, employees and shareholders; the need to support the social, cultural and economical programs which enhance the quality of life in our communities; providing creative leadership to the direction and success of the financial industry; expanding the geographic influence and customer service opportunities of the organization as enterprise and prudence permits.

We believe commitment to performance and a focus on the quality of customer service are essential to success. We believe in the everlasting process of building a great bank.

101. Bandag Inc.
2905 N. Hwy. 61
Muscatine, IA 52761
Phone: (319) 262-1400
Web: http://www.bandag.com

Bandag Inc. (NYSE; BDG) is an international company selling rubber products and services.

Mission Statement: Our mission is to be the market leader in every market served by offering our customers clearly outstanding and unique products and services. As the market leader, we are dedicated to constantly and forever improving quality, service and customer satisfaction. We believe that continually improving the system of production and delivery of services and products will improve quality and reduce costs. This ultimately will enhance our competitive position, resulting in outstanding long-term growth and profitability.

We believe the key to the success of this mission is the cooperative effort of highly motivated and dedicated people. It is the responsibility of leadership to ensure that the system allows people to achieve quality and pride in their work.

This requires:

The establishment of teams in which each team member respects the individuality of others and values the critical role of every team member.

The development of an environment where all team members have the maximum opportunity to continually improve and enrich their work experience, skills and careers through training, educational opportunities and career growth.

The creation of a work environment of open communication where all members are encouraged to contribute to our mutual success.

Maintaining an outstanding pay and benefit package.

Promoting an environment of dignity, trust and mutual respect free of coercion and fear.

That well-informed team members take responsibility for and be committed to accomplishing our mission.

Conducting our business at the highest ethical standard and be outstanding citizens and obey the laws of our host markets.

Vision: We are dedicated to being the world's best provider of tire and wheel management systems.

10-Year Vision:

1. A company with global perspective committed to providing the support necessary to increase our retread sales mix.

2. An organization of trust, empowerment, and commitment based upon open communications, the development of people and teamwork.

3. The innovative leader in retread process technology, product, and services.

4. Serving a diverse group of profitable dealers delivering to the end user, outstanding services and a product comparable to new tires.

5. A quality based culture that systematically reduces waste and variation and improves processes.

Quality: Quality is the never-ending improvement of our processes.

Our quality goal is to delight our customers, both external and internal, by providing products and services that not only meet but exceed their needs and expectations.

The pursuit of our quality goal is never-ending, more a journey than a destination. By using tools and concepts such as Employee Involvement, Statistical Process Control, and database decision making, we will constantly improve the systems and processes to accomplish our mission.

Guiding Principles:

Honesty and Integrity.
Accountability and Responsibility.
View Change as Opportunity.
Learning, Growth and Transfer of Knowledge.
Openness and Respect.
Being of Service.
Collaboration.
Customer Orientation.
Innovation and Risk Taking.
Alignment.
Continuous Improvement.
Spirit and Optimism.

102. Bank of Boston Corp.

100 Federal St.
Boston, MA 02110
Phone: (617) 434-2200
Web: http://www.bkb.com

Bank of Boston Corp. (NYSE; BKB) is a bank holding company. Most recently it acquired BayBanks.

Our Commitment: We will build lasting relationships with our customers by understanding their goals and exceeding their expectations.

We will meet this commitment by demonstrating teamwork, candor, and capability, and by delivering excellent service with efficiency and with integrity.

103. BankAmerica Corp.

Box 37000
San Francisco, CA 94137
Phone: (415) 622-3530
Web: http://www.bankamerica.com

BankAmerica Corp. (NYSE; BAC) and its consolidated subsidiaries provide diverse financial products and services to individuals, businesses, government agencies, and financial institutions throughout the world. BankAmerica's principal banking subsidiaries operate full-service branches in California, Washington, Texas, Arizona, Oregon, Nevada, New Mexico, Hawaii, Idaho, and Alaska, as well as corporate banking and business credit offices in major U.S. cities, and branches, corporate offices, and representative offices in 36 countries.

Corporate Strategy: Our corporate strategy, briefly stated, has three components. We want to: Be as important to our customers as they are to us. We believe in the "importance of being important" to our customers, sometimes called "relationship banking." We apply the principle in both wholesale and retail financial services markets.

Achieve excellence in certain core capabilities, or competencies, that will make us the most important provider for key customer segments.

Invest our shareholders' capital only in those businesses in which we can create value for our shareholders by earning more than our cost of capital.

Environmental Program: Guiding all of our activities is the goal of achieving a dynamic balance between economic growth and environmental protection. We are more convinced than ever that as a business committed to long-term growth and shareholder value, we simply cannot sacrifice environmental resources in favor of short-term growth. Nor can we afford to let environmental regulations unnecessarily distort or suppress vital economic development. There is a balance that must be struck — one that is selected in new initiates such as water marketing and conservation banking.

As our program matures, we will focus on two areas: Expanding employee awareness and participation, and increasing our involvement in public policy issues which we can play a constructive role in building bridges between the business and environment communities.

104. Bankers Trust New York Corp.

One Bankers Trust Plaza
130 Liberty St.
New York, NY 10006
Phone: (212) 250-2500
Web: http://www.bankerstrust.com

Bankers Trust New York Corp. (NYSE; BT) is a large bank holding company.

Mission for the 90's: Our mission in the 90's is to become the leader in global finance.

We will achieve this by evolving into the world's premier manager of risk for our own account and those of our clients. This generic definition of our business accurately describes Bankers Trust as a firm devoted to adding value through intermediation/arbitrage of financial, information, and processing flows.

We will become the leader because our singularity of business purpose will be matched by an equally singular commitment to attract and retain the best people.

The result: By the end of the 1990's, Bankers Trust can become the leader in global finance. We have the potential to build an intermediary organization not seen before, which can, in many respects, represent the new standards for conducting the business of financial intermediation. Bankers Trust will become a universal institution, not just an institution focusing on the institutional markets. This universal coverage of the customer markets will help resolve the earnings diversification issue. Product innovation, now extending over the full banking, securities, and fiduciary franchise, utilizing financial technology to create high value products, can solve the other side of the earnings diversification question. Increasing global expansion of customer relationships and product marketing will be a feature of this qualitative improvement in our revenue.

We should move toward full disclosure of our earnings profile, and we must succeed in fully liquefying the loan account so that all assets will be reflected on the books at marked-to-market values. The size and quality of these earnings, and the quality and liquidity of the assets, will eliminate the current discount on the stock multiple and we will receive the premium valuation that our competitive position will warrant.

Bankers Trust will be deemed large enough to be described as a leader. By the end of the decade size and critical mass will be viewed differently. These concepts will no longer be defined solely by notations of absolute, direct balance sheet totals and market value. Size will be replaced by more appropriate criteria. These will include business turnover, market share in particular businesses, and total values managed or controlled consisting of direct, off-balance sheet and fiduciary assets managed, as well as market-to-book relationships and price/earnings rations.

We will have enough capital to support our business; if we have a temporary need for more capital, we will satisfy that need through arrangements with firms with which we will create alliances appropriate to the task at hand. Our technology and information infrastructures, our people (their competence, knowledge and experience), as well as our market dominance in several businesses, also can represent non-replicable assets and barriers to entry for our competition.

The origination function must be developed to world-class status. When we succeed, Bankers Trust will become a valued advisor to its clients and a leadership institution in their terms.

105. (C. R.) Bard Inc.
730 Central Ave.
Murray Hill, NJ 07974
Phone: (908) 277-8000

C. R. Bard Inc. (NYSE; BCR) is a manufacturer and distributor of urological, cardiovascular and surgical products.

Mission: Bard's mission to advance the delivery of health care by profitably developing, manufacturing and marketing value-driven products which meet the quality, integrity and service expectations of our customers while providing opportunities for employees. As a result we will optimize shareholder value and be a respected worldwide health care company.

106. Barnes Group Inc.
123 Main St.
P.O. Box 489
Bristol, CT 06011
Phone: (860) 583-7070

Barnes Group Inc. (NYSE; B) manufactures and distributes springs and custom metal parts.

Guiding Philosophy: Barnes Group is a diversified public company consisting of three businesses dedicated to providing superior quality products and services to selected industrial markets. We believe that:

We exist to serve our customers.

We must focus on those customers who recognize and reward superior quality and service.

We must focus on manufacturing and distributing products and services where we have or can gain a competitive advantage.

People are our most important resource. We will foster a decentralized, entrepreneurial environment where each person is respected as in individual who can make significant contributions to the success of the company. We will provide an atmosphere of participation and partnership which encourages open communication, individual creativity, and a continuing search for better ways to conduct our business. We expect superior performance and will pay for it.

Our vendors are business partners. We intend to develop long-term relationships at fair prices with vendors who help us attain competitive advantage through quality, innovation and on-time delivery.

We are a responsible corporate citizen. We will conduct our business in accord with the highest ethical standards, and be responsive to the concerns of the countries and communities in which we operate.

Superior financial results will follow as a natural outcome of our efforts.

Our actions as a corporation will be fully consistent with these beliefs enabling Barnes Group and its stockholders to continue to prosper in an ever changing world.

107. Barnett Banks Inc.
50 N. Laura St.
Jacksonville, FL 32202
Phone: (904) 791-7720
Web: http://www.barnett.com

Barnett Banks Inc. (NYSE; BBI) operates in the banking and financial services industries.

Mission Statement: The mission of Barnett is to create value for its owners, customers and employees as a major services provider in the United States.

We will strengthen our position in existing markets by providing a full range of financial services, by acquiring other financial institutions, and by capitalizing on our market knowledge and our commitment to entrepreneurial market ownership.

Our focus will be on satisfying our customers' total financial needs by offering differentiated benefits driven by a sales and

service process that solidifies and expands the total customer relationship.

Barnett will aggressively pursue diversified income opportunities which include internal initiatives, acquisitions, and alliances in attractive markets throughout the country which complement, leverage, and expand our core capabilities.

By the year 2000, Barnett will be a fully diversified financial services organization with the acknowledged leadership position in the evolving banking business in its markets and with a diversified group of other financial businesses throughout the nation.

108. BASF Corp.
3000 Continental Dr. — North
Mount Olive, NJ 07828
Phone: (201) 426-2600
Web: http://www.basf.com
or: http://www.basf.de

BASF Corp, a subsidiary of BASF AG (ADR; BASFY) is a multinational chemical company. Operations extend from oil and gas to high-tech chemical products and consumer goods.

Our Vision & Values: BASF Corporation is the North American representative of the BASF Group. That means we are part of a transnational chemical company. And we are bound by the BASF Group's vision for the year 2010 — that our customers view us as their partner of choice in the global chemical market. To achieve this goal in the NAFTA region, BASF Corporation is committed to the following mission, vision, and values:

Our Mission — BASF Corporation is a North American chemical company dedicated to providing products which make our customers' products better.

Our Vision — We consistently meet the expectations of our customers, our employees, the BASF Group, and the general public by:

Being a preferred supplier to our targeted markets, as indicated by measures of customer satisfaction.

Nurturing partnerships with our customers and suppliers for mutual benefit.

Providing a work environment that fosters teamwork, accountability, personal growth and job enjoyment, free of bureaucratic and organizational barriers.

Recognizing and rewarding the contributions of our employees.

Achieving a return on assets consistent with the global strategy of the BASF Group.

Being recognized as responsible corporate citizens in the communities in which we work and live.

Our Values — Our actions are driven by customer and business needs.

Integrity, honesty and trust are fundamental to success.

We treat all people with dignity, respect and fairness.

Effective teamwork and open communications are essential.

We seek and accept change as necessary for success.

We value innovation and encourage responsible risk taking.

We operate in a safe and environmentally responsible manner.

We provide only those products we believe to be safe.

Long-term results are the ultimate measure of our success.

We continuously strive for improvement.

109. Bassett Furniture Industries Inc.

Two Main St.
Bassett, VA 24055
Phone: (540) 629-6000
Web: http://www.bassettfurniture.com

Bassett Furniture Industries Inc. (NASDAQ; BSET) makes and markets fine furniture.

Mission Statement: At Bassett Furniture Industries, we strive to be the preeminent furniture maker/marketer by being productive and innovative employees, who provide quality products and services as measured by our customers' satisfaction, our company's reputation and profitability.

Values: How we accomplish our mission is as important as the mission itself. Fundamental to success for the company are these basic values.

People: Our people are the source of our strength. They provide our corporate intelligence and determine our reputation and vitality. Involvement and teamwork are our core human values.

Products: Our products are the end result of our efforts and they should be the best in serving customers nationwide. As our products are viewed, so are we.

Profits: Profits are the ultimate measure of how efficiently we provide customers with the best products for their needs. Profits are required to survive and grow.

Guiding Principles:

Quality comes first.

Customers are the focus of everything we do.

Continuous improvement is essential to our success.

Employee involvement is our way of life.

Dealers and suppliers are our partners.

110. Battle Mountain Gold Co.

Forty Second Fl.
333 Clay St.
Houston, TX 77002
Phone: (713) 650-6400
Web: http://www.bmgold.com

Battle Mountain Gold Co. (NYSE; BMG) explores for, mines, and processes gold and associated metals.

Mission Statement: Battle Mountain Gold Company is an international gold mining company. Using our skills and technologies, we will seek to enhance shareholder value through growth and industry leadership. We will succeed by exploring for and acquiring reserves, constructing and operating profitable mines, and providing challenging opportunities for our employees.

We will apply our resources to the fundamental obligations that we have to our shareholders, employees, communities, and the environment, while capitalizing upon opportunities worldwide.

111. Baxter Healthcare Corp.
1 Baxter Pkwy.
Deerfield, IL 60015
Phone: (847) 948-2000
Web: http://www.baxter.com

Baxter Healthcare Corporation is a subsidiary of Baxter International Inc. (NYSE; BAX), a producer, developer, and distributor of medical products and technologies for use in hospitals and other health-care settings. The company operates in two industry segments: Medical specialties and medical/laboratory products and distribution.

Mission: We will be the leading health-care company by providing the best products and services for customers around the world, consistently emphasizing innovation, operational excellence and the highest quality in everything we do.

Strategy: Service: Provide the undisputed best service to customers in both distributing and manufacturing. Technological innovation: Bring to market a stream of innovative new products in selected areas of medical technology, through internal development and external partnerships. International expansion: Increase global market penetration.

Values: Respect: We will treat all individuals with dignity and respect and be honest, open and ethical in all our dealings with customers, with shareholders and with each other. Responsiveness: We will strive continually to understand and meet the changing requirements of our customers through teamwork, empowerment and innovation. Results: We will consistently keep our commitment to provide value to our customers, to shareholders and to one another.

112. Bay Networks Inc.
4401 Great America Parkway
P.O. Box 58185
Santa Clara, CA 95052
Phone: (408) 988-2400
Web: http://www.baynetworks.com

Bay Networks Inc. (NYSE, BAY), a leading network vendor of hubs routers, switches, and network management, is the merged company of SynOptics and Wellfleet.

Vision: With the merger behind us and the internetworking market going strong, what is in the future for Bay Networks? Given the consolidation of the market and the growing customer requirement for total solutions, we believe that the conditions are favorable for a diversified, fast-moving company to increase its market share.

In the long view, it is the aim of Bay Networks to provide ongoing market leadership by "future proofing" our customers' networks with well-engineered products that are unified by the comprehensive BaySIS architecture for reliable, high-performance communication systems. This strategy should allow us to continue to meet the needs of our large base of customer partners throughout the world.

Philosophy: The Bay Networks philosophy is simple: Help you migrate to the switched internetwork of the future, at your own pace, while extending the life of existing investments.

A Corporate Overview: Helping you evolve to the future of switched internetworking.

113. Bayer Corp.
One Mellon Center
500 Grant St.
Pittsburgh, PA 15219
Phone: (412) 394-5500
Web: http://www.bayer.de

Bayer Corporation (formerly Miles Inc.), a research-based company with major businesses in chemicals, health care, consumer care, and imaging technologies, is a subsidiary of Bayer AG (ADR; BAYZY). Consumer products include licensed brand names Alka-Seltzer, Phillips Milk of Magnesia, Bayer Aspirin, One-A-Day vitamins, Mycelex-7, Haley's MO, Bactine, CamphoPhenique, Stridex, and Midol.

Slogans: "We Cure More Headaches Than You Think." "Powerful Pain Relief and So Much More."

Environment: We also are committed to environmental protection and to the health and safety of our employees, customers, and the communities where we operate. These commitments are among the core principles upon which we at Bayer Corporation base our business operations. We take on these responsibilities willingly. Not only are they the right things to do, they help ensure our company's present-day and future strength.

114. Bearings Inc.
3600 Euclid Ave.
Cleveland, OH 44101
Phone: (216) 881-8900

Bearings Inc. (NYSE; BER) is focused on the distribution of industrial component technologies to the Maintenance Repair Operation (MRO) and Original Equipment Manufacturing (OEM) markets throughout North America.

Strategic Objective: Our strategic objective is to become the leading distributor of industrial component technologies to the MRO and OEM markets throughout North America.

Mission: Our mission is to create jubilant customers by distributing world-class products and providing services in our selected technologies and by providing innovative solutions that keep North American industry operating competitively.

Vision: Our vision is to be an open, energizing organization known for its integrity, creativity and "award winning" service, and where:

Highly qualified associates are enabled to achieve their potential while enthusiastically fulfilling the Bearings, Inc. mission.

115. BEC Group Inc.
555 Theodore Fremd Ave.
Suite B302
Rye, NY 10580
Phone: (914) 967-9400
Web: http://www.becgroup.com

BEC Group Inc. (NYSE; EYE), formerly Benson Eyecare, has two core businesses: The optical technologies group, which manufactures and markets lighting, electronic and electroformed products, and Bolle America, the exclusive marketer and distributor of Bolle premium sunglasses, sport shields and goggles in the United States, Mexico, and Costa Rica.

Statement: A consistent global marketing strategy and integrated, worldwide distributorship structure will enable Bolle to expand its share in the higher margin, premium segment on the sunglass, ski goggle, and safety eyewear markets.

116. Bechtel Group Inc.
50 Beale St.
San Francisco, CA 94105
Phone: (415) 768-1234
Web: http://www.bechtel.com

Bechtel Group Inc., a private company, is in the engineering-construction industry.

Purpose: Bechtel provides premier technical, management, and directly related services to develop, manage, engineer, build, and operate installations for our customers worldwide.

Mission: We will be the engineer-constructor of choice for customers, employees, and key suppliers in every industry market we serve by: Delivering value to our customers; earning a fair return on our delivered value; and working closely with our customers, key suppliers, and communities to help improve the standard of living and quality of life.

Core Principles: We bring to work: A proud heritage of accomplishment, integrity, excellence, and commitment to our customers' interests; and a willingness to appropriately adapt ourselves to change while maintaining our fundamental values and constancy of purpose.

117. Beckman Instruments Inc.
2500 Harbor Blvd.
Box 3100
Fullerton, CA 92634
Phone: (714) 871-4848
Web: http://www.beckman.com

Beckman Instruments Inc. (NYSE; BEC) is a manufacturer in the medical supplies industry. The company's products are used in laboratories for biological analysis in all phases of the battle against disease, from pioneering medical research through drug discovery to clinical diagnosis.

Slogan: "Focused on the Chemistry of Life."

Vision: Our business is the chemistry of life, and we seek to be the world's acknowledged leader in providing laboratory systems that advance scientific discovery and speed the diagnosis of disease. In so doing, we will help science improve the quality of life.

Mission: Our mission is to profitably gain and retain customers by providing quality products and services that simplify and automate chemical analysis across the continuum from academic bioresearch to applications in the bioindustrial and diagnostic laboratory.

Our affairs will be conducted at the highest level of excellence, so as to create lasting customer partnerships, provide growth and opportunity for employees, and return superior value to our investors.

Values: There is no satisfactory substitute for excellence.

Integrity is the virtue that guides Beckman business.

We have a dedication to customers.

Our outlook is global.

Innovation is essential to our progress.

Individuals make Beckman's success possible.

118. Becton, Dickinson and Co.
1 Becton Dr.
Franklin Lakes, NJ 07417
Phone: (201) 847-6800

Becton, Dickinson and Co. (NYSE; BDX) manufactures and markets medical devices and diagnostic equipment.

Mission: Our mission as a company is to provide the many markets we serve with products of consistently superior quality at price levels that are fair and competitive. Achieving this mission is a responsibility we all share and is necessary to meet the expectations of our customers, ourselves, and our shareholders. With this uncompromising dedication to superior quality, we have a focus for our actions that unifies us, adds value to our work, and enriches our lives.

119. Bell & Howell Co.
5215 Old Orchard Rd.
Skokie, IL 60077
Phone: (847) 470-7668
http://www.bellhowell.com

Bell & Howell Co. (NYSE; BHW) is involved in microfilm information systems (UMI), publications, information management, and mail-processing.

Mission Statement: Bell & Howell will be the acknowledged world-wide leader in providing effective information management solutions for mail processing, document management, and published information.

We will strive to establish a partnership with each of our customers, consistently emphasizing innovation, operational excellence and speed in everything we do.

Guiding Principles: At Bell & Howell, we: Believe that customer satisfaction is created and sustained by employees who have a passion for their work. Believe that people make a difference. Believe that everyone is capable of continuous growth, within an environment that fosters personal development. Recognize people who can and will initiate change, and demonstrate a high tolerance for any honest resulting failures. Take prompt action on opportunities, problems and conflict. Appreciate effective team-building. Share information widely and openly. Believe that work should be enjoyable. Behave with a high level of trust, honesty, fairness and mutual respect. Reward those who achieve results while practicing these principles.

120. Bell Atlantic Corp.

1717 Arch St., 29th Fl.
Philadelphia, PA 19103
Phone: (215) 963-6000
Web: http://www.ba.com

Bell Atlantic Corp. (NYSE; BEL) is a diversified telecommunications company. They are involved in the communications, entertainment, and information industry. Bell Atlantic Corp. and NYNEX have been joined together through a recent merger.

Slogan: "The Heart of Communication."

Vision: Bell Atlantic will be the world's best communications, information, and entertainment company.

121. Bell Industries Inc.

11812 San Vicente Blvd.
Los Angeles, CA 90049
Phone: (310) 826-2355
Web: http://www.bellind.com

Bell Industries Inc. (BI; NYSE) is a national distributor of electronic components. Additionally, Bell distributes graphic imaging and recreational-related products.

Statement: We continually refine our focus on what we do best — provide value-added solutions in distributing electronic

components and electronic imaging technology.

122. BellSouth Corp.

1155 Peachtree St.
Atlanta, GA 30367
Phone: (404) 249-2000
Web: http://www.bellsouth.com

BellSouth Corp. (NYSE; BLS) is a telecommunications holding company. BellSouth is the largest of the seven holding companies formed at divestiture.

Slogans: "Keeping you Ahead of the Game." "Start with the One You Know." "It's All Here." "Nobody Knows a Neighbor Like a Neighbor."

Mission Statement: BellSouth intends to be a preeminent global provider of voice, data, imaging services in the telecommunications and information industry.

BellSouth provides information services in local exchange and exchange access markets in its nine state franchised territory. It also provides communications services and products such as advertising and publishing, mobile cellular telephone service, paging, and telecommunications and computer systems through its entities, both in the nine state region as well as in other major U.S. and international markets.

Management Philosophy: The management structure for the BellSouth companies is based on a team approach. Management responsibility for BellSouth Corporation is vested in its senior corporate officers who, among other duties, establish financial goals and provide financial management and long-range corporate planning for the total enterprise.

Goals: In support of its mission statement to become a preeminent global provider of voice, data, and imaging services in the telecommunications and information industry, BellSouth has established the following goals:

To be a leader among industry peers in total shareholder return.

To maintain the vitality of its telephone company operations.

To grow profitable wireless businesses, domestic, and international.

To invest in related high growth areas.

To positively shape our industry.

To demonstrate total commitment to the BellSouth Corporate and Excellence Through Quality: Customer First; Pursuit of Excellence; Community Mindedness; Positive Response to Change; Respect for the Individual.

Statement: BellSouth has a simple formula. We focus on our customers. We invest in powerful technologies and make them easy for people to use. We leverage our financial strength. I am convinced this formula will make BellSouth continue to win.

123. Ben & Jerry's Homemade Inc.
P.O. Box 240
Waterbury, VT 05676
Phone: (802) 244-6957
Web: http://www.benjerry.com

Ben & Jerry's Homemade Inc. (NASDAQ; BJICA) makes and distributes ice cream and frozen yogurt products.

Slogan: "Vermont's Finest Ice Cream & Frozen Yogurt."

Mission Statement: Ben & Jerry's is dedicated to the creation and demonstration of a new corporate concept of linked prosperity. Our Mission consists of three parts:

Product Mission: To make, distribute, and sell the finest quality, all-natural ice cream and related products in a wide variety of innovative flavors made from Vermont dairy products.

Social Mission: To operate the company in a way that actively recognizes the central role that business plays in the structure of society by initiating innovative ways to improve the quality of life of a broad community — local, national, and international.

Economic Mission: To operate the

company on a sound financial basis of profitable growth, increasing value for our shareholders, and creating career opportunities and financial rewards for our employees.

Underlying the mission of Ben & Jerry's is the determination to seek new and creative ways of addressing all three parts, while holding a deep respect for the individuals, inside and outside the company, and for the communities of which they are a part.

124. Beneficial Corp.
301 North Walnut St.
Wilmington, DE 19801
Phone: (302) 425-2500
Web: http://www.beneficial.com

Beneficial Corp. (NYSE; BNL) was formed through the consolidation of three companies which had been operating under the same management. The company is a holding company, subsidiaries of which are engaged principally in the consumer finance and credit-related insurance businesses.

Statement: Our strategic focus on our consumer financial services niche will remain sharp. We will continue to concentrate on serving our middle-income customers, providing them with credit and related insurance products they need and desire. In so doing we expect to continue to improve our profitability ratios, as well as significantly increase our earnings and dividends per share.

125. Berkshire Hathaway Inc.
1440 Kiewit Plaza
Omaha, NE 68131
Phone: (402) 346-1400
Web: http://www.berkshirehathaway.com

Berkshire Hathaway Inc. (NYSE; BRKA) is a holding company owning subsidiaries engaged in a number of diverse business activities. The most important of these is the property and casualty insurance business conducted on both a direct and reinsurance basis through a number of subsidiaries collectively referred to as the Berkshire Hathaway Insurance Group. Additionally, Berkshire Hathaway Inc. publishes the *Buffalo News*. Other business activities conducted by non-insurance subsidiaries include publication and distribution of encyclopedias and related educational and instructional material (*World Book* and *Childcraft* products), manufacture and marketing of home cleaning systems and related accessories (sold primarily under the *Kirby* name), manufacture and sale of boxed chocolates and other confectionery products (*See's Candies*), retailing of home furnishings (*Nebraska Furniture Mart*), manufacture and distribution of footwear (*H. H. Brown Shoe Company, Lowell Shoe Inc.*, and *Dexter Shoe Company*) and manufacture and distribution of air compressors, air tools and painting systems (*Campbell Hausfeld* products). Plus other businesses.

Statement: Our long-term economic goal is to maximize the average annual rate of gain in intrinsic business value on a per-share basis. We do not measure the economic significance or performance of Berkshire by its size; we measure by per-share progress. We are certain that the rate of per-share progress will diminish in the future — a greatly enlarged capital base will see to that. But we will be disappointed if our rate does not exceed that of the average large American corporation.

126. Bertucci's Inc.

14 Audubon Rd.
Wakefield, MA 01880
Phone: (617) 246-6700

Bertucci's Inc. (NASDAQ; BERT) runs a chain of full-service pizza restaurants.

Mission Statement: Bertucci's is committed to serving our customers as guests in an atmosphere that reflects the traditional welcome, warmth, and abundance of an Italian Home.

To this we add value, quality, and service as the restaurant cornerstones upon

which we have built and will continue to build our futures.

We are dedicated to provide the best experience for our guests so that our entire family of team members, stockholders, suppliers and, in addition, our communities benefit.

127. Bethlehem Steel Corp.

1170 8th Ave.
Bethlehem, PA 18016
Phone: (610) 694-2424
http://www.bethsteel.com

Bethlehem Steel Corp. (NYSE; BS) is a producer and supplier of steel products.

Objectives: To be a customer-driven, premier producer and supplier of quality products.

To generate sustained profitability and enhance long-term value for our stockholders.

To have a sound financial base for meeting the challenges and opportunities of the future.

Strategy: We will manage our resources to make our businesses competitive and profitable on a long-term basis and to improve our financial base.

We will continually restructure our businesses, as appropriate, to support our Corporate objectives.

We will pursue business opportunities that provide increased value to Bethlehem and our constituents.

Tactics: Design processes where customers come first.

Have employees focus on continuous improvement.

Measure progress against quantifiable goals.

Focus on teamwork.

Guiding Principles: Customers: We know our ability to meet our objectives depends on anticipating and satisfying our customers' needs. To be a premier supplier, we will continually focus our efforts on improving product quality and customer service and reducing costs.

We will invest new technologies and

facilities that are required to maintain our competitiveness and support our objectives.

Stockholders: We intend to enhance our long-term value for our stockholders through the accomplishment of our Objectives by following our Strategy and Guiding Principles.

128. Betz Dearborn Inc.
4636 Somerton Rd.
Trevose, PA 19053
Phone: (215) 355-3300

Betz Dearborn Inc. (NYSE; BTL), formerly Betz Laboratories Inc., produces chemical treatment products for water and wastewater systems.

Betz Mission Statement: Core Values: We value high performance, hard work, honesty and teamwork. We will hold ourselves accountable to the highest standards of ethics, trust and quality. We will respect and always strive to do what is right for our customers, employees, suppliers, and the community.

Purpose: Our purpose is to help our customers be more successful by reducing their operating costs and by achieving their environmental objectives through our superior technology and service.

Mission: Transform Betz into an integrated global organization... while expanding our leadership position in the United States.

129. Beverly Enterprises Inc.
P. O. Box 3324
Fort Smith, AR 72913
Phone: (501) 452-6712

Beverly Enterprises Inc. (NYSE; BEV) is in the medical services industry, operating nursing and retirement homes.

Mission Statement: Its mission is to deliver high quality health care that exceeds the expectations of each of its customers and to be the provider and employer of choice in each of the communities served.

130. BIC Corp.
500 BIC Dr.
Milford, CT 06460
Phone: (203) 783-2000

BIC Corp., (delisted from the NYSE; it is no longer a public company) a subsidiary of Societe Bic S. A., manufactures and sells ballpoint pens, felt tip pens, disposable cigarette lighters, sailboards, correction fluids, and disposable shavers.

Slogans: "Maximum Service. Minimum Fair Price." "Worth Every Penny!"

BIC and the Environment: Our mission is to be a global leader in providing our customers with the highest quality convenience products they demand at a fair value. One of our responsibilities is to minimize the impact of our products and operations on the environment. To achieve this goal, we must continuously challenge ourselves, our suppliers, our customers, and consumers to work together toward beneficial solutions.

131. Biogen Inc.
14 Cambridge Ctr.
Cambridge, MA 02142
Phone: (617) 679-2000

Biogen Inc. (NASDAQ; BGEN) is a biopharmaceutical company principally engaged in the business of developing and manufacturing drugs for human health care through genetic engineering.

Vision: The developments in modern biology in the last three decades have caused a major discontinuity in the rate of change in life science research that establishes for the first time in 35 years the opportunity for major new companies to be built in the pharmaceutical industry. These companies will be based upon new products and therapies that dramatically improve the practice of medicine and the quality of life for patients. Biogen was created to be a corporate and scientific leader in this new opportunity environment.

Mission: To build a global based pharmaceutical company based on leadership in creating fundamental change in new drug discovery and development to create, make, and market pharmaceuticals.

As We Pursue This Mission, We Will: Staff the organization with people possessing both excellence in professional skills and strong values.

Create an organizational culture that is sensitive to people without compromising excellence in performance standards.

Lead the company with policies that give equal importance to the needs of our customers, employees and shareholders and conduct ourselves in this endeavor by the benefits actually created by our products in the market.

Values Statement: Biogen's success is based on its people. Everyone here is a leader. The core of leadership is integrity and courage — characteristics we seek in every Biogen employee. These shared values describe how we aspire to lead and work together. They promote the most important organizational behavior patterns critical in building a successful company and should be viewed in the context of what is best for Biogen:

Hire only the highest quality talent... Encourage each person's development... Recognize differences in people and look for the diverse ways they can contribute to our success... Treat each individual with respect and dignity.

Communicate and then obtain alignment to our strategy and goals... Vigorously pursue the interdependent goals of world-class science and commercial success... Set aggressive, ever-increasing performance standards and hold people accountable for meeting them.

Tell the truth, even when it appears to be discouraged, and expect nothing less in others.

Face the facts, admit mistakes, accept criticism, learn from it and improve... Admit you don't have all the answers and learn from anyone, anyplace. Be intolerant of arrogance.

Build teams... Play whatever role in your team is necessary to get the job done... Share information openly, up, down, and across the company to help others... Help others succeed even at some cost to yourself.

Forcefully resist adding layers, procedures, and bureaucracy... Keep the matrix alive and fluid. Trust people with wide latitude and discretion.

Assume your position responsibilities are a starting point, not a limitation... Take the initiative and have the self-confidence required to reach your goals... Strive for speed and quality in all that you do.

Weigh the risks carefully but do not hesitate to innovate or to encourage and reward innovation and initiative... Accept that innovative approaches do not always succeed... Don't shrink from unpopular positions if you have passion for them.

See change as an opportunity, not a threat... Recognize the need for flexibility... Be comfortable with ambiguity... Shift focus and priority with unwavering intensity and commitment.

Serve and defend with equal energy our customers', our employees' and our shareholders' interests... The primary measure of our success as an organization is the value we create with our products.

132. Birkenstock Footprint Sandals, Inc.

8171 Redwood Blvd.
P. O. Box 6140
Novato, CA 94948
Phone: (415) 892-4200
Web: http://www.birkenstock.com

Birkenstock Footprint Sandals Inc., a private company, manufactures and markets footwear.

Statements: Birkenstock shoes have no form without function, no feature without purpose, no apology. They are made with materials that are durable, repairable, and nothing but significantly beneficial.

All Birkenstock shores are made in Birkenstock factories. So precise is the design of the footwear, from the depth of the heel cup to the contour of the arch, that, no matter how great the product demand, Birkenstock will not manufacture its shoes through a second source.

Shoe manufacturing is the art of bringing design to life and combining foot function with aesthetics.

133. Birmingham Steel Corp.
1000 Urban Center Pkwy.
Suite 300
Birmingham, AL 35242
Phone: (205) 970-1200

Birmingham Steel Corp. (NYSE; BIR) is one of the largest U.S. steelmakers.

Mission: It is the mission of Birmingham Steel Corporation:

To be the preferred supplier through a commitment to meet or exceed customer expectations in quality, value and service.

To be the lowest cost, highest quality manufacturer of steel products in the markets served.

To aggressively pursue opportunities for growth within the steel industry.

To treat employees with fairness and respect, developing a competent, motivated and involved workforce enabling each of us to reach our highest potential.

To provide a safe workplace and an environmentally responsible organization.

To be a process driven organization through discipline, continuous improvement and the latest proven technology.

To build a financially sound and profitable organization which provides a superior return to shareholders and creates value for our stakeholders.

The underlying principle of this mission statement is to conduct business with the highest level of integrity and ethical conduct.

Goal: Birmingham Steel Corporation's goal is to be the supplier of choice in the long products steel market. To reach that objective, the company is committed to having the most modern and efficient steel production facilities in its industry. It is also striving to deliver an exceptional level of customer service, an equally important step on the way to meeting its goal.

134. BISYS Group Inc.
Overlook at Great Notch
150 Clove Rd.
Little Falls, NJ 07424
Phone: (201) 812-8600
Web: http://www.bisys.com

BISYS Group Inc. (NASDAQ; BSYS) provides outsourcing solutions to and through financial organizations. BISYS Information Services Group provides the financial industry with advanced outsourcing solutions for account and item processing, loan servicing, and competitive product pricing support. BISYS Investment Services Group designs, administers and distributes proprietary mutual funds, and provides 401 (k) administration services in partnership with some of the nation's leading investment management companies.

BISYS Mission: To be a major provider of outsourcing solutions that improve the performance, profitability and competitive position of all types of financial organizations, and to increase shareholder value by growing revenues and earnings through a combination of internal growth, direct new client sales, and strategic acquisitions.

135. BJ Services Co.
5500 N.W. Central Dr.
P.O. Box 4442
Houston, TX 77210
Phone: (713) 462-4239

BJ Services Co. (NYSE: BJS) provides oilfield services.

Mission Statement: We strive to serve our customer's needs with high quality, value added products and services.

We will attract and retain the best people and foster an environment throughout our organization of openness and trust which empowers all of us to contribute to our full potential.

We are committed to operate our business as a valued neighbor in the communities in which we reside.

We believe that integrity and honesty

are essential and we will not compromise them in our business.

We will continually improve everything we do more efficiently and better than our competitors.

We strive to achieve superior return on equity and superior earnings growth for our stockholders, both short term and long term.

136. Black and Decker Corp.
701 E. Joppa Ave.
Towson, MD 21204
Phone: (410) 716-3900
Web: http://www.blackanddecker.com

Black and Decker Corp. (NYSE; BDK) manufactures and markets home and commercial appliances and electronics.

Slogans: "How Things Get Done." "Very Clever."

Mission Statement: A global marketer and manufacturer of high-quality, innovative products that are used in and around the home and in commercial applications and that command leading market shares, first or second, in their respective markets.

Goal: Black & Decker's goal is to put into the hands of people around the world quality products that fulfill our commitment to innovation, research, design, and customer satisfaction. We are committed to meet or exceed the needs of those who depend on our products on the job, in the home, or at play.

137. (H. & R.) Block Inc.
4410 Main St.
Kansas City, MO 64111
Phone: (816) 753-6900
Web: http://www.handrblock.com

H. & R. Block (NYSE; HRB) is in the tax and financial services businesses.

Tax Services' Mission Statement: Our mission statement presents the values on which Block's Tax Services, Inc. rests. It states our purpose for being in business and is the foundation for the objectives we intend to accomplish. All the tasks we

undertake lead us toward the fulfillment of our mission. All of us have a stake in supporting the statement. The mission it describes sustains us in business.

This is Tax Services' mission statement:

To provide quality tax preparation and related services that: Anticipate and satisfy our clients' needs; while providing a challenging and rewarding environment for our employees and franchisees and; maintaining a level of earnings to support growth and sustain the confidence of those who invest in us.

138. Blockbuster Entertainment Group
One Blockbuster Plaza
Fort Lauderdale, FL 33301
Phone: (954) 832-3000
Web: http://www.blockbuster.com

Blockbuster Entertainment Group, a division of Viacom Inc. (AMEX; VIAB), is a holding company that owns and franchises an international chain of prerecorded videocassette retail stores.

Slogan: "Make It a Blockbuster Night."

Mission Statement: The mission of Blockbuster Entertainment Corporation is to be the best provider of entertainment options that meet consumer needs. We will accomplish this by:

1. Understanding the entertainment interests of the consumer better than anyone else.

2. Delivering unique products with the highest level of consumer service.

Our resolve to consistently provide the best customer entertainment experience will result in exciting opportunities for our employees and an exceptional return for our investors.

139. Blue Cross and Blue Shield Association
676 St. Clair St.
Chicago, IL 60611
Phone: (312) 440-6000
Web: http://www.bluecares.com

Blue Cross and Blue Shield Association is not a single company, but rather a network of independent, locally operated companies called Plans or Blues.

Statement: The Blues will continue to focus on "adapting" to local markets and provider conditions.

140. BMC Software Inc.
2101 CityWest Blvd.
Houston, TX 77042
Phone: (713) 918-8800
Web: http://www.bmc.com

BMC Software Inc. (NASDAQ; BMCS) is a supplier of computer software.

BMC Mission Statement: BMC Software, driven by global markets and in partnership with its customers and employees, will be the preferred supplier of software solutions that meet our customers' changing needs. We will be Best of Class in developing, marketing, and supporting these solutions worldwide.

BMC's defining characteristic is its commitment to its customers, employees, and shareholders. BMC shall maintain this commitment:

To it customers: By providing software solutions and support of the highest quality with capabilities that enable critical business processing.

To its employees: By providing a superior environment with opportunity for personal and professional growth.

To its shareholders: By maximizing shareholder value through consistent revenue and earnings growth.

141. Boeing Corp.
7755 E. Marginal Way S.
Seattle, WA 98108
Phone: (206) 655-2121
Web: http://www.boeing.com

Boeing Corp. (NYSE; BA) is a major aerospace and defense contractor.

Long-Range Mission: To be the number one aerospace company in the world among the premier industrial concerns in terms of quality, profitability, and growth.

Fundamental Goals: Quality as measured by: Customer, employee, and community satisfaction.

Profitability as measured against our ability to achieve and then maintain: 20 percent average annual return on stockholders' equity.

Growth over the long term as measured against a goal to achieve: Greater than 5 percent average annual real sales growth than 1988 base.

Objectives: To achieve the above goals and fulfill Boeing's mission, the following objectives will guide company actions:

Continuous improvement in quality of products and processes.

A highly skilled and motivated work force.

Capable and focused management.

Technical excellence.

Financial strength.

Commitment to integrity.

142. Boise Cascade Corp.
1111 W. Jefferson St.
Boise, ID 83728
Phone: (208) 384-6161
Web: http://www.bc.com

Boise Cascade Corp. (NYSE; BCC) is in the paper and paper products, office products, and building products businesses.

Our Mission: To continuously improve the company's long-term value to customers, employees, shareholders, and society.

Our Total Quality Commitment: To continuously make improvements that will enable us to anticipate, understand, and fulfill both internal and external customer expectations so that the company becomes the preferred supplier of each of our customers.

What We Value: Safety, health, caring, innovation, teamwork, trust, integrity, respect, responsibility, citizenship.

Our Strategy: We will pursue

efficiency, distinctive competence, and focused growth in the paper and paper products, office products, and building products businesses, while applying the principles of Total Quality.

143. Bombardier Inc.
800 Rene-Levesque Blvd. West
Montreal, Canada PQ H3B 1Y8
Phone: (514) 861-9481
Web: http://www.bombardier.com

Bombardier Inc. (Toronto Exchange) is a large aerospace company. It makes Learjet commuter aircraft, Canadair military aircraft, missile systems, and consumer products such as Ski Doo and Lynx snowmobiles.

Mission: Bombardier's mission is to be the leader in all markets in which it operates. This objective will be achieved through excellence in design, manufacturing, and marketing in the fields of transportation equipment, aerospace, motorized consumer products and services related to its core competencies.

144. Boston Beer Co. Inc.
75 Arlington St.
Boston, MA 02116
Phone: (617) 368-5000
Web: http://www.samadams.com

Boston Beer Co. Inc. (NYSE; SAM), a large microbrewer, is in the business of brewing beer, both year-round and seasonal.

Slogan: Samuel Adams — "Do You Love Beer?"

Company Philosophy: We are the Boston Beer Company. We make the best beer in America. We treat others as we would like to be treated ourselves. We sell our beer with enthusiasm, energy for our jobs, and respect for our customers.

As a company, we seek to add value to our customers, by providing them with a superior product at a favorable price; to our employees, by providing them with employment which encourages personal growth and pride at favorable compensations; to our investors, by providing a superior return on their investment and to our communities, by providing taxes, charitable contributions, and community support.

Because we represent the company at all times, we act in a manner which increases the respect of others for the Boston Beer Company and its people.

We constantly seek ways to improve our own skills and how we do our jobs.

We are committed to making Samuel Adams the largest and most respected craft or import beer in the United States before 2006.

145. Boston Chicken Inc.
14103 Denver West Pkwy.
Golden, CO 80401
Phone: (303) 278-9500

Boston Chicken Inc. (NASDAQ; BOST) operates and franchises food service stores that specialize in fresh convenient meals featuring home style entrees, fresh vegetable, salads, and other side dishes.

Mission: To broaden our leadership position in the home meal replacement category through fresh convenient meals. To provide our customers with continuous improving products and services that are responsive to their needs. To maintain an environment where responsible employees and area developers can achieve their objectives. To allocate and focus corporate resources for maximization of long-term stockholder value. To respect, study and learn from our competition.

Philosophy: To act with integrity, respect and understanding. To satisfy the customer at all costs. To keep it simple and direct. To lead by example. To value information and communicate it openly. To add value and cut waste. To take risks and accept new mistakes. To work together, aggressively accomplish goals and have fun.

146. Boston Edison Co.

800 Boylston St.
Boston, MA 02199
Phone: (617) 424-2000
Web: http://www.bostonedison.com

Boston Edison Co. (NYSE; BSE) is a public utility engaged principally in the generation, purchase, transmission, and distribution and sale of electric energy.

Mission Statement: Energy and energy services are the reasons we are in business. To establish and maintain the lasting confidence of all the publics we serve, our mission must be to provide energy and energy services in a safe, environmentally sound, competitively priced and reliable manner. Rising standards of excellence will guide us in achieving our mission.

147. Boston Scientific Corp.

One Boston Scientific Pl.
Natick, MA 01760
Phone: (508) 650-8000

Boston Scientific Corp. (NYSE; BSX) is a worldwide developer, manufacturer and marketer of medical devices.

Mission Statement: Since its origin in the late 1960's, Boston Scientific Corporation's mission has been to improve the quality of patient care and the productivity of healthcare delivery through the development and advocacy of less invasive medical devices and procedures. This is accomplished through the continuing refinement of existing products and procedures and the investigation and development of new technologies which can reduce risk, trauma, cost, procedure time, and the need for aftercare.

148. BP America Inc.

200 Public Sq.
Cleveland, OH 44114
Phone: (216) 586-4141
Web: http://www.bp.com

BP America Inc., a subsidiary of British Petroleum Co. PLC (NYSE; BP), discovers, refines, and sells petroleum products.

Statement: For us, size by itself is not important. What matters more is the challenge we set ourselves to give the best possible return to all BP's stakeholders; Our shareholders, our customers, our employees, our suppliers, and our neighbors.

BP is a performance-oriented company. Our goal is continuous improvement.

149. BRE Properties Inc.

One Montgomery St.
Suite 2500
Telesis Tower
San Francisco, CA 94104
Phone: (415) 445-6530
Web: http://www.breproperties.com

BRE Properties Inc. (NYSE; BRE) is a self-administered equity real estate investment trust which primarily opens and operates apartment communities in the Western United States.

Corporate Objective: BRE's corporate objective is to become the preeminent multifamily real estate investment trust in the Western United States. The purpose of the objective is to increase shareholder value. Our four-point business plan for meeting the objective is:

Focus on acquisition of multifamily properties.

Continue the orderly disposition of non-core assets.

Internalize property management.

Increase access to capital markets.

150. Breed Technologies Inc.

5300 Old Tampa Hwy.
Lakeland, FL 33807
Phone: (941) 668-6000
Web: http://www.breedtech.com

Breed Technologies Inc. (NYSE; BDT) manufactures and markets automobile crash sensors and airbag systems.

Slogan: "Advanced Technology for Occupant Safety Systems."

The Future: Increase airbag customer base worldwide.

New airbag products and technologies.

Expand product line.

Strategic investments/acquisitions.

High quality/low cost producer.

151. Briggs & Stratton Corp.
12301 W. Wirth St.
Wauwatosa, WI 53222
Phone: (414) 259-5333

Briggs & Stratton Corp. (NYSE; BGG) produces air cooled gasoline engines for the outdoor power equipment industry.

Statement: We at Briggs & Stratton are committed to creating value for our shareholders. We have implemented economic value based performance measures and incentive compensation that we believe align the interests of management and shareholders. We also believe that to create long term value for shareholders we must also create value in our relationships with customers, employees, suppliers, and the communities in which we operate.

A basic element of economic value creation is an effective corporate strategy. We think that an effective corporate strategy is one that identifies an appropriate competitive position and then focuses virtually all the corporation's resources on attaining and holding that position. The competitive position we have identified is the leader in high volume, high value, low cost air cooled engines and related products and services. That is our traditional position and it is the one we are best equipped to maintain through skill and experience.

152. Brinker International Inc.
6820 LBJ Freeway
Dallas, TX 75240
Phone: (214) 980-9917

Brinker International Inc. is in the restaurant business. Restaurants the company runs include Chili's Grill, Romano's Macaroni Grill, Grady's American Grill, Spageddies Italian Kitchen, On the Border Cafes, and Cozymel's.

Statement: Our objective is to expand the company at a pace that will drive us toward $3 billion in annual system-wide sales by the end of the decade. As we continue our rapid expansion, our goal is to maintain a lean organizational structure with the power and strength of a large company combined with the speed, ability and flexibility of a small company.

153. Bristol-Myers Squibb Co.
345 Park Ave.
New York, NY 10154
Phone: (212) 546-4000
Web: http://www.bms.com

Bristol-Myers Squibb Co. (NYSE; BMY) is a large pharmaceuticals company also involved in consumer personal care products, nutritionals, and medical devices.

Mission: The Mission of Bristol-Myers Squibb is to extend and enhance human life by providing the highest quality health and personal care products. Our aim is to be the preeminent global diversified health and personal care company. We have three priorities: Growth, productivity, and a dynamic operating culture.

Goals: Leadership in each product category and in each geographic market in which we compete. We aim to achieve number one or number two position with increasing market shares.

Superior customer satisfaction by providing the highest quality products and services to our customers. We will strive to be rated number one or two with continuous improvement as measured by our customers.

Superior steady shareholder returns as measured by number one or two competitive position in economic performance within our industries.

An organization which is committed to

winning through teamwork, empowerment, customer focus, and open communications.

154. British Steel PLC
9 Albert Embankment
London, England SE 1 7SN, UK
Phone: 44 (01) 71-735-76
Web: http://www.britishsteel.co.uk

British Steel PLC (NYSE; BST) manufactures and markets a wide range of steel products.

Aims: British Steel aims to:

Provide its customers with quality products, competitively priced, on time, and to specifications.

Maintain its internationally competitive cost base.

Provide its shareholders with a proper return on their investment.

Continue investing in research and development, new technology, processes and products either independently or through joint ventures or mergers and acquisitions.

Meet the training needs of all employees and provide them with fair rewards, job satisfaction and opportunities for career and personal development.

Respond effectively to public concerns over environmental issues and changing legislative requirements particularly with regard to communities local to its steel-making and processing plants.

Environmental Policy: Appropriate attention to protection of the environment is an integral part of the activities of the British Steel Group of Companies, and it is British Steel's policy to develop an environmentally-aware workforce and to manage its activities so as to avoid causing unnecessary or unacceptable risk to its employees, contractors, customers, members of the public, and the environment.

It follows that British Steel will conduct its operation so as to comply with all relevant environmental legislation in the countries where it operates, and to minimize the risk of all forms of pollution of water, air and land, and nuisance due to odor and noise.

In pursuit of these objectives, British Steel aims to minimize energy consumption and the use of materials harmful to the environment; to promote further the recycling of its products and byproducts; to introduce cleaner technologies and to encourage suppliers and customers to adopt sound environmental practices.

155. Brooke Group Ltd.
100 SE Second St.
Miami, FL 33131
Phone: (305) 579-8000

Brooke Group Ltd. (NYSE; BGL) is principally engaged in the manufacture and sale of cigarettes, through its Liggett Group Inc., subsidiary. Registered brand names include L&M, Chesterfield, Lark, and Eve.

Business Strategy: Liggett's near-term business strategy is to further reduce certain of its operating and selling costs so as to maintain or increase the profitability of both its full-price and price/value products as their current unit sales value and, further, to reduce its investment in working capital.

Liggett's long-term business strategy in the full-price branded segment of the market is to maintain its share of that segment of the market by consistently offering promotional programs with the objective of maximizing the profitability of its full-price brands. Liggett's long-term business strategy in the price/value segment of the market is to maintain its market share and increase its profitability by providing consistently high quality products and services at prices and terms comparable to those available elsewhere in the market.

156. Brown Group Inc.
8300 Maryland Ave.
St. Louis, MO 63166
Phone: (314) 854-4000
Web: http://www.browngroup.com

Brown Group Inc. (NYSE; BG) is a retailer of footwear for men, women and children.

Priorities: To develop and invest in our successful growth businesses aggressively, recognizing that this is the best proven way to build long-term value for shareholders.

To manage changing operations with intensity, either to "turn them around" or to withdraw investment from them.

To protect the balance sheet and the company's ability to finance our businesses, maintaining debt at prudent levels.

To return capital to the shareholders through dividends, recognizing that this supports shareholders' total return importantly.

157. Brown-Forman Corp.

P.O. Box 1080
Louisville, KY 40201
Phone: (502) 585-1100
Web: http://www.brown-forman.com

Brown-Forman Corp. (NYSE; BFB) is a diversified producer, marketer and exporter of such registered brand name products as Jack Daniel's Tennessee Whiskey, Canadian Mist Canadian Whisky, Southern Comfort, Early Times Old Style Kentucky Whisky, Jack Daniel's Country Cocktails, Fetzer Vineyards California Wines, Korbel California Champagnes (brand marketed by BF worldwide by agency agreement), Bolla Italian Wines (brand marketed by BF in the U.S. and other select markets by agency agreement), Lenox China and Crystal, Dansk International Designs, Gorham Silver, Crystal and China, and Hartmann Luggage and Business Cases.

Slogan: Southern Comfort — "Take It Easy."

American Heritage: Brown-Forman believes it has an ideal opportunity to take advantage of the increasing demand for American consumer products. With ownership of some of the largest brands with strong North American heritage, Brown-Forman is uniquely positioned to become the world's premier producer, marketer, and exporter of premium North American spirits, wines, and consumer durables.

In addition to having the right brands, Brown-Forman also has an appropriate legacy to build upon the concept of exporting "Americana" to world markets. The company was founded in 1870 in Louisville, Kentucky, by George Garvin Brown, whose trademark was a dedication to excellence in quality. Mr. Brown built his company on the idea that providing consumers with consistently high quality whisky would result in success. As Brown-Forman has expanded its business over the past 125 years, we have been resolute in preserving this philosophy of excellence as our guiding principle. The result is a company known today for the quality of its brands and its employees, and for a continuing commitment to long-term growth.

Growth Initiatives: At home and in countries around the world, products such as Jack Daniel's, Southern Comfort, Fetzer, Lenox, Gorham, and Hartmann are highly valued because of the American heritage and quality craftsmanship they represent. These brands have been the foundation of our company's success, and will be the cornerstone for our future.

In defining Brown-Forman's future, we have set a course to accelerate the company's growth by pursuing three specific initiatives:

Expanding our international business, creating successful new beverage products, and realizing the full potential of our Lenox group of companies.

Strategy for Growth (BF's Sales and Marketing Divisions):

North American Group — Has the mission of developing the company's regional, specialty, and agency spirits brands.

Core Market Group — This group's charge is to continue building the company's brands, while also introducing into the markets additional products from the company's portfolio.

Advancing Markets Group — Is laying

the groundwork to provide the brands that these emerging middle class populations are seeking.

Wine Group — Mission is to become, over time, the premier global producer and marketer of premium wines.

Statement on Drinking: The enjoyment of wine and spirits is a legal right exercised by more than 100 million Americans, the vast majority of whom do so responsibly and without adverse effect to themselves, their families, or society.

Brown-Forman has always been concerned about the dangers of irresponsible and illegal drinking and the problems caused by a small percentage of drinkers who misuse these products. As a founder of the Distilled Spirits Council of the United States (DISCUS), we have for many years underwritten public education programs on responsible drinking and funded ongoing research on the causes of alcoholism and alcohol abuse.

Brown-Forman also is a founding member of the Century Council, a national nonprofit organization created in 1991 by concerned distillers, vintners, and brewers. The Century Council's objective is to combat alcohol abuse and misuse, and the founding companies initially have committed $40 million toward that goal. The first priorities of this effort are to reduce drunk driving and eliminate underage drinking problems in our society. Working in partnership with many other organizations, the Century Council already has implemented several programs designed to address drunk driving and underage drinking problems in communities all across the country. The formation of the Century Council represents the first time that distillers, vintners, and brewers have united in their efforts to fight alcohol abuse in the United States.

There are some people in our society who are trying to equate any alcohol use with alcohol abuse and thereby seek to remove moderate drinking from the mainstream of contemporary social behavior. We oppose those efforts. The use of wine and spirits is one of life's most ancient and enjoyable pleasures and we support the right of all people of legal drinking age to use and enjoy our products responsibly.

158. Browning-Ferris Industries
757 N. Eldridge
Houston, TX 77253
Phone: (713) 870-8100

Browning-Ferris Industries (NYSE; BFI) is in the waste services industry.

The Mission: Our mission is to provide the highest quality waste collection, transportation, processing, disposal and related services to both public and private customers worldwide. We will carry out our mission efficiently, safely, and in an environmentally responsible manner with respect for the role of government in protecting the public interest.

Our financial goal is to achieve consistently superior results that maintain BFI as a premier growth organization and maximize shareholder value.

159. Bruno's Inc.
800 Lakeshore Pkwy.
Birmingham, AL 35201
Phone: (205) 940-9400

Bruno's Inc. (OTC; BRNO) operates a regional supermarket chain.

Mission Statement: Bruno's Inc. is a leading southeastern supermarket chain that utilizes multiple store formats to cater to all consumers. We will always offer our customers the best possible values. Our perishable departments will be superior, offering the freshest and highest quality products unmatched by any competitor. We will treat our family of employees fairly, and we will be customer and community minded. We will use selected technology to enhance our efficiencies and to support our future growth. Through these means we will continue to provide added value to our customers, our shareholders, our employees, and our communities.

160. Brunswick Corp.
1 N. Field Ct.
Lake Forest, IL 60045
Phone: (708) 735-4700

Brunswick Corp. (NYSE; BC) is in the recreation/ leisure industry. They manufacture and market marine engines, boats, fishing tackle and bowling products.

Mission: The mission of Brunswick Corporation is to be a world class, diversified recreation/leisure company with a strong commitment to its values of quality, serving customers, and people. To achieve this goal, the company has a wealth of core strengths which include: Strong brand names, excellent distribution, high quality/value products and services, strength in international markets, particularly in marine engines and bowling, technology leadership in marine engines, boats, fishing tackle and bowling, seasoned executives, a strong balance sheet, credibility, and market leadership.

161. Brush Wellman Inc.
17876 St. Clair. Ave.
Cleveland, OH 44110
Phone: (216) 486-4200

Brush Wellman Inc. (NYSE; BW) is a supplier of high performance engineered materials, with a concentration of its operations on the advancement of beryllium-based materials.

Vision: As the world leader in beryllium and related high-performance materials, Brush Wellman will be recognized as a highly-focused and aggressive organization, which is consistently expanding the worldwide market for our products and services by demonstrating that they are safe, cost-effective solutions for a wide variety of current and emerging market needs.

Mission:

1. Our core business is the manufacture and sale of beryllium-containing materials. Our objective is to be the leading supplier of all forms of beryllium in each market we serve on a worldwide basis. We will exert great effort to expand the safe usage of beryllium worldwide.

2. We will accomplish our share and market growth objectives through continuous improvement of our products and processes and through product line extensions, utilizing innovative techniques of manufacturing, marketing and distribution.

3. We will be viewed as a market-driven, responsive organization aimed at meeting the needs of our customers with cost effective solutions while continuously improving our traditional high product quality.

4. Diversification opportunities must build on our existing strengths and hold the potential for near-term profitability. Profit — not volume — will be our creed. Unless we can see a measurable benefit to our shareholders, we will not diversify. Rather, we will operate our basic business profitably for the shareholders.

5. We will create an environment which encourages innovation and prudent risk-taking. We will ensure that recognition and rewards will be based on performance. Feedback to employees regarding performance will be provided on a timely basis. We will foster a spirit of teamwork throughout the organization, and remain committed to equality of opportunity and to the development of the full potential of all our employees.

Environmental Policy: Brush Wellman Inc. considers environmental, health and safety as integral parts of our business strategy and necessary for our success. It is the policy of Brush Wellman to design, manufacture, and distribute all products and to manage and dispose of all materials in a safe, environmentally sound manner. We are committed to utilizing our resources and technical capabilities to their fullest extent to protect the health and safety of our employees, our customers, the general public, and the environment.

162. Buffets Inc.
10260 Viking Dr.
Eden Prairie, MN 55344
Phone: (612) 942-9760

Buffets Inc. (NASDAQ; BOCB) is in the restaurant business.

Mission Statement: A new mission statement has been developed: Our food quality, friendly service and cleanliness will exceed your expectations.

163. Burlington Coat Factory Warehouse Corp.
1830 Route 130 North
Burlington, NJ 08016
Phone: (609) 387-7800

Burlington Coat Factory Warehouse Corp. (NYSE; BCF) owns and operates seven divisions, specializing in merchandising: Burlington Coat Factory, Cohoes Fashions, Decelle, Luxury Linens, Totally 4 Kids, Baby Depot, and Fit for Men.

Slogan: "We're More Than Great Coats."

Statements: Burlington Coat Factory, known nationally for its selection of coats and outerwear, has taken the initiative to build on its marketing strength and diversify its product line. Through diversification, the company will seek to continue to grow and maintain a position of market leadership.

Our long-term initiatives for continuing growth and market leadership: Increase profitability, expand market share, enhance customer focus, achieve greater operating efficiency.

Our strategy has been and continues to be to offer a broad range of first quality, current brand name and designer merchandise for the whole family at prices substantially below department and specialty stores.

Profitability: To seek long-term profitability which allows for steady growth while providing the sound financial basis required to attain our corporate objectives. This commitment of superior profitability is an essential condition for our growth and continuing development as a company.

Customer satisfaction: To offer our customers an extensive selection of high quality merchandise at the lowest prices possible in stores that are modern, clean, conveniently located, and staffed by well-trained and courteous personnel.

Stockholder return: To sustain value for our stockholders is best done over time. We manage the company for long-term earnings with a commitment to earning an attractive return for our stockholders.

164. Burlington Industries Inc.
3330 W. Friendly Ave.
Greensboro, NC 27410
Phone: (910) 379-2000
Web: http://www.burlington-ind.com

Burlington Industries Inc. (NYSE; BUR) is a textile company.

Guiding Principles: Our customers come first. We must emphasize responsiveness and total customer satisfaction, striving daily not simply to meet our customers' needs but to exceed their expectations.

We dedicate ourselves to innovation and continuous improvement. We recognize that our customers' needs are always changing. To be the market leader we must always innovate and improve the products and services we provide.

We are an "open" company. We encourage the sharing of ideas and information, welcome discussion and involvement at all levels, and provide opportunities for advancement and betterment to everyone.

We accept our responsibilities. We are committed to safety in our workplace, the quality of our environment, and the support of our communities.

Integrity is the heart of our company. We expect everyone to maintain high ethical standards and to base their working relationships on honesty and trust.

Our goal is to be the best. We take pride in our history and the great company that we have today. To be the best, we recognize that we must set high standards for ourselves and be committed to excellence in everything we do.

165. Burlington Northern Santa Fe Corp.

3800 Continental Plaza
777 Main St.
Ft. Worth, TX 76102
Phone: (817) 333-2000
Web: http://www.bnsf.com

Burlington Northern Santa Fe Corp. (NYSE; BNI) is in the rail and transportation services industry.

Mission: Our goal is to provide high-quality transportation and information services that exceed customers' expectations, maximize our return to shareholders, and offer all BN people growth and opportunity in an injury-free workplace.

166. Burlington Resources Inc.

5051 Westheimer
Suite 1400
Houston, TX 77056
Phone: (713) 624-9500

Burlington Resources Inc. (NYSE; BR) is a holding company engaged, through its principal subsidiary, Burlington Resources Oil & Gas Company (formerly known as Meridian Oil Inc.) and its affiliated companies, in the exploration, development, production and marketing of oil and gas.

Statement: The company's objective is to build long-term shareholder value through value-added growth and effective cost management by increasing production, reserves, earnings, and cash flow. The company intends to achieve this objective primarily by increasing its focus on high potential, high margin exploration and development projects. The company will continue to pursue acquisitions that complement its core area focus and provide future growth potential.

167. Cabletron Systems Inc.

35 Industrial Way
Rochester, NH 03867
Phone: (603) 332-9400
Web: http://www.cabletron.com

Cabletron Systems Inc. (NYSE; CS) develops, manufactures, markets, installs, and supports a broad range of standards-based local area network (LAN) and wide area network (WAN) connectivity hardware and software. The company's operations are grouped into three product line areas: Network interconnection products, cable assemblies and various cables, and test equipment.

Slogan: "The Complete Networking Solution."

Statement: Cabletron's commitment to its customers has fueled the corporation's success as the world's leading developer and manufacturer of intelligent wiring hubs and network management software for LANs. With a no-frills corporate philosophy, Cabletron is able to offer the industry's broadest line of products at lower costs, allowing customers to tailor their networks to fit individual needs.

Statement: The company continues to grow as we build the next generation of network infrastructures. Our Research and Development effort is guided by listening to our customers and delivering what we promise. This simple philosophy is one we've used since the founding of Cabletron, and is what helped us become the billion-dollar company we are today.

168. Cadbury Schweppes PLC

25 Berkeley Sq.
London W1X 6HT
Phone: 44 (01) 71-409-13
Web: http://www.cadbury.co.uk

Cadbury Schweppes PLC (NYSE; CSG) is a major global company in the beverage and confectionery industries. Registered brand names in the beverage group include Schweppes, Canada Dry, Crush, Sunkist, A&W Root Beer, Hires, Squirt, Dr Pepper, Seven-Up, Mott's apple brand, and Clamato juices. Confectionary brand names include Cadbury, Fry, Poulain, Bouquet d'Or, Trebor,

Bassett, Pascall, Barratt, Maynards, Sharps, Stani, and Dulciora.

Slogans: Cadbury's — "The Chocolate. The Taste." Diet Dr Pepper — "The Taste You've Been Looking For." Dr Pepper — "This Is the Taste." 7-Up — "It's an Up Thing."

Statements: Our task is to build on our traditions of quality and value to provide brands, products, financial results and management performance that meet the interests of our shareholders, consumers, employees, customers, suppliers and the communities in which we operate.

One of Cadbury Schweppes' key goals is to be the largest and most successful brand owner operating in the non-cola sector of the worldwide soft drinks business. The acquisition of Dr Pepper/Seven-Up helps us reach this goal. It is a major strategic milestone for the Group.

The Group's strategy is to grow profitability, brand strength and volume on a global basis by the development of its two product streams, Beverages and Confectionery, through a combination of internal growth, targeted acquisitions and joint ventures where there are appropriate opportunities. Capital and marketing expenditure, to maintain and enhance the Group's position as a low cost producer and to ensure the continuing strength and earning potential of the Group's brands, are also priorities.

169. Calgon Carbon Corp.
P.O. Box 717
Pittsburgh, PA 15230
Phone: (412) 787-6700
Web: http://www.calgon.com

Calgon Carbon Corp. (NYSE; CCC) is engaged in the production and marketing of activated carbons and related services and systems throughout the world. The company's activities consist of our integrally related areas: (1) activated carbons; (2) services; (3) systems; and (4) charcoal.

Strategy: New strategic initiatives were adopted in 1994 to return Calgon Carbon

to its historical levels of growth and profitability. Collectively, they will broaden the company's technological base, widen its scope of operations, reduce cost, improve quality, and increase customer satisfaction. Each was carefully designed to support a fresh vision of Calgon Carbon as the world's leading producer, supplier, and designer of innovative technologies, value-added products and services, specifically developed for the purification, separation, and concentration of liquids and gases. They are the cornerstone of Calgon Carbon's future, and the keys to increased value for its shareholders.

170. Callaway Golf Co.
2285 Rutherford Rd.
Carlsbad, CA 92008
Phone: (619) 931-1771
Web: http://www.callawaygolf.com

Callaway Golf Co. (NYSE; ELY) designs, develops, manufactures, and markets high-quality golf clubs. Registered trade names include Big Bertha and War Bird.

Statements: The company believes that the introduction of new, innovative golf clubs will be crucial to its future success.

The company's basic objective is to design and manufacture its clubs in such a way that they are demonstrably superior to, and pleasingly different from, competitors' golf clubs. The company's golf clubs are sold at premium prices to both average and skilled golfers on the basis of performance, ease of use and appearance.

171. CalMat Co.
3200 San Fernando Rd.
Los Angeles, CA 90065
Phone: (213) 258-2777

CalMat Co. (NYSE; CZM) mines, processes, and markets aggregates — rock, sand and gravel — as a basic, irreplaceable material in the construction business.

Slogan: "Pavement Never Ends."

Mission Statement: CalMat will be the most successful construction materials company in its peer industry group within the U.S. by being stockholder-oriented, customer-focused, quality-conscious, employee-sensitive, locally involved, environmentally aware, and the provider of a safe work place.

Environmental Investment: CalMat is committed to working with our neighbors and local governmental agencies to protect the environment and ongoing productive use of the land. Mining, after all, is an interim activity, and we strongly believe in assuming responsibility for ensuring the land can be reused after mining has ceased.

At the start of every project, we define the sequence of mining, short-term concurrent land uses and a post-mining reclamation plan. Concurrent uses include developed buffer areas adjacent to mining sites, raw land leased for agriculture or other uses until needed, and self-storage facilities. Our reclamation program provides for a habitat restoration, water conservation, and commercial, residential and industrial development.

172. Cambior Inc.
800 Rene-Levesque Ouest
Bureau 850
Montreal (Quebec)
Canada H3B 1X9
Phone: (514) 878-3166

Cambior Inc. (AMEX; CBJ) is a Canadian gold mining company.

Growth Strategy: For over nine years now, the company has pursued a growth strategy that has enabled it to consolidate its operations in Canada, and stake out a presence in the United States, Mexico and South America. Its interests in nine mines and numerous development projects and exploration properties provide Cambior and its shareholders with a solid foundation for a promising future.

173. Canadian Pacific Ltd.
P.O. Box 6042
Station Centre-Ville
Montreal, Quebec
Canada H3C 3E4
Phone: (514) 395-5151
Web: http://www.cprailway.com

Canadian Pacific Ltd. (NYSE; CP) businesses include CP Rail System, CP Ships, PanCanadian Petroleum, Fording Coal, Marathon Realty and Canadian Pacific Hotels.

Slogan: "Delivering Value."

Looking Ahead: We see a railway with growing margins benefiting from the full effects of cost-cutting initiatives; continued profitable growth in our energy businesses, provided commodity prices do not fall significantly; solid performances from our container shipping and hotel businesses; and a more focused real estate company.

174. Canandaigua Wine Co. Inc.
116 Buffalo St.
Canandaigua, NY 14424
Phone: (716) 394-7900

Canandaigua Wine Co. Inc. (NASDAQ; WINEA and WINEB) operates in the alcohol industry, and is a producer and supplier of wine, an importer and producer of beer and supplier of grape juice concentrate in the U.S.

Statement: At Canandaigua Wine Company, increasing shareholder value is our major objective.

Four-Fold Strategy:
Immediate — Benefit from recent acquisitions.
Short-term — Cost synergies.
Long-term — Strengthen relationships.
Long-term — Sales Growth.

175. Cannondale Corp.
9 Brookside Place
Georgetown, CT 06829

Phone: (203) 544-9800
Web: http://www.cannondale.com

Cannondale Corp. (NASDAQ; BIKE) engineers and markets bicycle frames and components.

Cannondale Philosophy: To our customers: As Cannondale celebrates its 25th anniversary, I'd like to express my appreciation to all of you for your support over the years. It is only fitting that the success you've given us now allows us to give more back to you, in the form of increasingly innovative, high-performance cycling products.

Our passion is to be the best cycling company in the world. We will succeed because:

1. We care about our customers, suppliers and each other.

2. We design and deliver a stream of innovative products.

3. We continuously improve.

4. We concentrate on detail.

5. We limit our distribution to the best bicycle retailers in the world.

6. We govern our every deed by what is just and right.

176. Capital Cities/ABC Inc.
77 W. 66th St.
New York, NY 10023
Phone: (212) 456-7777
Web: http://www.abctelevision.com
Parent's Web: http://www.disney.com

Capital Cities/ABC Inc., a subsidiary of Walt Disney Co. (NYSE; DIS), operates the ABC television network.

Slogan: "ABC — The Action Broadcasting Company."

Statement: Decentralization is the cornerstone of our management philosophy. Our goal is to hire the best people we can find and give them the responsibility and authority they need to perform their jobs. Decisions are made at the local level, consistent with the basic responsibilities of corporate management. Budgets, which are set yearly and reviewed quarterly, originate with the operating units that are responsible for them. We expect a great deal from our managers. We expect them to be forever cost-conscious and to recognize and exploit sales potential. But above all, we expect them to manage their operations as good citizens and use their facilities to further the community welfare.

177. Capsure Holdings Corp.
Two North Riverside Plaza
Chicago, IL 60606
Phone: (312) 879-1900

Capsure Holdings Corp. (NYSE; CSH) and its subsidiaries are engaged in the property and casualty insurance business. Capsure's principal property and casualty insurance entities are Western Surety Co., United Capitol Insurance Co., and Universal Surety of America.

Strategies: The company's business strategy with respect to its existing insurance operations is to emphasize the underwriting of risks where reasonable expectations of underwriting profits exist.

The company's primary growth strategy is to expand its operations in the specialty insurance and financial services industries by capitalizing on Western Surety's licenses, distribution system, and A-plus rating.

Statement: Since its beginning, Capsure Holdings has embraced the essence of transition. At Capsure, we steer clear of a static herd mentality; we continually look at things just a little differently, take advantage of opportunities, are willing to change. Is that good? We think so. It's how Capsure transformed a struggling oil and gas concern into a profitable insurance company. It's how we achieve a combined ratio about 20 points better than the industry average. It's why our acquisitions have had outstanding results from day one. It's how we do business. It's how we succeed.

178. Carlson Companies Inc.
12755 State Highway 55
Minneapolis, MN 55441

Phone: (612) 540-5000
Web: http://www.carlson.com

Carlson Companies Inc., a private company, is the parent corporation of a diversified, worldwide group of service corporations operating primarily in the businesses of marketing, hospitality, and travel.

Statement: The strategic objective for each of its Operating Groups and subsidiaries is to be the market leader in every business in which it competes. These Groups and its companies are customer and market driven and dedicated to excellence of performance in carrying out their business mission throughout the world.

The Personal Business Philosophy of Curtis L. Carlson: The philosophy which governs my actions and decisions in the business world has been shaped by my experience as an entrepreneur. It is composed of very definite guidelines which I feel are necessary for corporate success. These guidelines are a result more from the experience I have acquired in the day-to-day decision-making process of business rather than a conscious effort to define specific rules of success.

Fundamental to my business philosophy is a firm belief in the free enterprise system. To effectively thrive within this system, a successful business must produce a profit. Therefore, I consider profit to be an honorable and essential ingredient of the free enterprise system.

For example, a profitable company contributes immeasurably to a community's or a nation's social, cultural and economic growth and stability by providing jobs, good salaries plus opportunities for advancement and education. All of these factors are essential for the dignity of employees and their self respect, particularly in the eyes of their families and society.

Conversely, the company which operates with limited or no profit is a parasite which gnaws away at the free enterprise system, preying upon the welfare of the individuals by precipitating low salaries, reduced opportunities for advancement,

few employee fringe benefits and possible loss of jobs. These kinds of conditions tend to generate unrest and discontent in a society along with a feeling of bitterness toward business.

The tempo of change is increasing at a rapid pace. Every change in the state of the art or the unusual conduct of our economy presents an opportunity to fulfill new needs. If one does so effectively he has then developed the potential of a profitable business. In order to grow, a company must develop a fountainhead of capital which can generate the necessary funds to assure expansion and permit diversification. When this fountainhead is firmly established, soundly managed and tightly controlled, a company can further guarantee its success through diversification by expanding into varied fields.

Through diversification a businessman reduces the risk of capital losses. Diversification then becomes a tremendous tool for continued success. Allocating capital into different areas of endeavor permits the dilution of one business without sacrificing the strength of other viable thriving parts of the total company.

Diversification, however, carries with it some risks because, with every new endeavor, the possibility of failure looms on the horizon. This is a great concern for the president of any company and personally I find the mental stress about the great risks we take in expansion and diversification the most difficult part of my job.

Yet I firmly believe that there is no place in the business world for the status quo — remaining constant or standing still — since there are always others moving rapidly behind who will accelerate quickly and pass you by if your momentum is reduced. I have always maintained that you will stay even with your competitor by working five days a week but you can get ahead of your competition by working six days. The old saying is still true, "The harder I work, the luckier I get."

A successful business should always be ready for change and maintain enough flexibility to move quickly and adapt readily to fluctuating economic conditions.

To produce a good product and generate the momentum necessary for success, a business must have the support and enthusiasm of its employees. The officers of a company can set priorities and chart the course of business but the employees must carry out the programs and ideas to make them work. The management of a company can build an organization but it is the organization which builds the company. Therefore, employees are the most important part of a business. The employees make a company move forward and, without their loyalty and dedication, the best business programs and ideas in the world are worthless.

The task of commanding employees' loyalty and dedication is a difficult one which requires the company to create a stimulating business climate and provide meaningful motivation for its employees. I have learned that the best means of motivating is the proper use of goals — specific, measurable, reasonable goals — that are tied to a definite time frame. They must be simple enough so that both the employee and the supervisors understand them clearly. A monthly published list of the current standing against the quota is a must. The bonus must be worthwhile and commensurate with the quota.

The employee with a definite career goal makes a positive contribution to the company by directing his or her daily actions toward this specific objective. This system worked for me personally. When I started into business I wrote the next goal which I hoped to attain on a piece of paper, folded it carefully and carried it with me in my billfold.

When I reached that goal, I removed the piece of paper and threw it away. But I set a new goal and wrote it on another piece of paper and carried it with me until that goal was reached. As our organization grew in size, my goals were transferred from personal ones into company objectives.

Originally, we set our sites on doubling our revenues every four years. Obviously, we gained some measure of success as we had an average sales increase of 33% compounded stretching over 42 years. Our capital base has mushroomed to such an extent that now we only look for a 15% annual increase which results in doubling our volume every five years.

An aside here may be in order. Setting any goal is meaningless unless your earnings plus your borrowing capacity is such that it can be financed. Adding more stores, more salesmen and saleswomen, and more inventory costs money. This must be provided for in your analysis, before setting your goals.

In addition to establishing proper goals, a successful company must also display and create a climate of creativity and imagination among its employees if it is to recognize and properly satisfy consumer needs. Innovations that add value greater than your competitors is essential to continued growth.

An imaginative company is one which can recognize a public need, properly analyze that need, develop the ideas which meet that need and then carry these ideas to their successful fruition.

A creative company must have the foresight to see all aspects of a consumer problem and work with the long-range profit goal in mind rather than the near-term advantage of a quick profit.

To attain the long range view necessary for stable and steady growth, a company must rely heavily on its executives and top employees for the in-depth thought which goes into business planning. An imaginative and creative executive, who has a history of job stability and is deeply involved in his job, will instill these same qualities in the employees who work for him or her. Together they will spark the company to move forward in meaningful and forceful directions which will capture the attention of the consumer.

Operating a successful business is in many respects similar to running a successful political campaign except a businessman does not have as much time to prove a program viable as a politician. In the world of business, the public votes with its dollars. Only as long as a company can produce a desired, worthwhile and needed product or service, and can command public respect, will it receive the public dollar and succeed.

While I believe firmly in goals and in employee motivation to meet specified goals, I believe with equal conviction that a businessman or woman must never content himself or herself with having reached a goal. I consider a goal as a marker on a journey rather than a final destination. Along the route new opportunities develop, new directions are possible and new and exciting goals can be set.

179. Carmike Cinemas Inc.
1301 First Ave.
Columbus, GA 31901
Phone: (706) 576-3400
Web: http://www.carmike.com

Carmike Cinemas Inc. (NYSE; CKE) is the second largest operator of motion picture screens in the U.S. Through the operation of motion picture theatres, revenues are generated principally through admissions and concession sales.

Statement: The management of Carmike is optimistic about the future of the industry and about continuing Carmike's strategy of growth through acquisition and construction of new screens.

180. Carnival Corp.
3655 N.W. 87th Ave.
Miami, FL 33178
Phone: (305) 599-2600
Web: http://www.carnival.com

Carnival Corp. (NYSE; CCL) and its subsidiaries operate three separate cruise lines under the names Carnival Cruise Lines, Holland America Line, and Windstar Cruises and a tour business, Holland America Westours. Additionally, the company has investments in other cruise operations.

Slogans: "The Most Popular Cruise Line in the World." "Ain't We Got Fun."

Statement: We remain very bullish on the future of the cruise industry and this is the primary reason we have been so aggressive with our ship building program. We believe that improvements in our financial performance will continue to be largely driven by capacity additions.

We believe that the construction of new, modern ships will become increasingly important as we enter the last half of the 1990s. In addition to the competitive advantages and economies of scale derived from the larger, newer and more efficient vessels, the cruise industry faces more stringent safety standards set by the International Maritime Organization starting in 1997.

181. Carolina Power & Light Co.
411 Fayetteville St.
Raleigh, NC 27601
Phone: (919) 546-6111
Web: http://www.cplc.com

Carolina Power & Light Co. (NYSE; CPL) generates and distributes electricity to residents in South and North Carolina.

The Next Five Years — 1995-1999: CP&L's strategic planning process was initiated in 1989 as the company emerged from a lengthy program of new plant construction. The Strategic Plan focused on performance and has resulted in significant improvement of company operations. The Plan has been successful in guiding the company to meet the needs of our customers and shareholders. As the industry prepares for increased competition and uncertainty, our updated strategies will ensure continued success in the future. These strategies focus on continuing to improve operations and achieving significant reductions in costs. CP&L will continue to take aggressive steps to prosper in a competitive world. We will be one of the industry's premier electric utilities.

Vision: CP&L will be a leader in the

electric utility industry measured in terms of the cost, reliability and quality of operations, service to customers and returns to our investors.

Values: We conduct our business with integrity.

We perform to the highest standard of excellence.

We deliver superior value for our customers.

We create shareholder value.

We are committed to the safety of employees and the public.

We maintain respect, trust and fairness among our employees.

We support the communities that we serve.

We are stewards of the environment.

Strategies: We will aggressively lower costs while emphasizing high levels of performance, safety and environmental stewardship.

We will aggressively market electricity to significantly increase profitable sales.

We will create superior value for our shareholders.

We will control our destiny by defining our industry.

We will emphasize a performance-oriented culture.

Strategic Goals: To achieve our vision we have set specific goals which provide long-range minimum targets to guide annual planning activities. These goals will be achieved by implementing our strategies in ways that are consistent with our values.

Total cost of operations will be among the lowest 25% of the Eastern utilities peer group.

Nuclear safety performance will be in the top 25% of U.S. nuclear plants.

Growth rate in kilowatt hour sales will be in the top 25% of the eastern utilities peer group.

We will be a leader in customer satisfaction.

Total shareholder return will be in the top 25% of the S&P Utilities.

Corporate culture will be performance-oriented and will reflect an empowered and successful work force.

Environmental Policy: At Carolina Power & Light Company we will conduct all aspects of our business in an environmentally conscious manner. Environmental factors will be an integral part of planning, design, construction, and operational decisions. We acknowledge our responsibilities to be good stewards of the natural resources entrusted to our management. Further we shall:

Comply with applicable environmental laws and regulations.

Maintain an ongoing assessment of our activities to assure compliance with applicable environmental laws and regulations.

Participate directly as well as jointly with other business and industry organizations to develop effective and reasonable environmental regulations.

Be vigilant in our efforts to prevent damage to the environment. We will also be prepared to act effectively and in a timely fashion in the event of an environmental emergency.

Ensure proper handling, treatment, and disposal of all wastes and emissions while taking steps to control their generation and encourage recycling and development of markets for our wastes.

Provide support for research and development of science and technologies that mitigate the environmental effects of our operations.

Ensure that our employees support the implementation of this policy.

Promote cost-effective conservation and wise use of energy by customers.

Participate with government and private organizations in cooperative efforts to protect and enhance the natural resources of our service area.

182. Carpenter Technology Corp.
101 W. Bern St.
Reading, PA 19601
Phone: (610) 208-2000
Web: http://www.cartech.com

Carpenter Technology Corp. (NYSE; CRS) manufactures and markets specialty steels, with end-user applications that include the following product markets: Airplanes, automobiles, daily life, home, and medical.

Slogans: "Moving to a Higher Level of Performance." "More Than a Steel Company."

Strategy: A growth strategy built on leveraging core strengths: Five years after establishing a corporate development program, Carpenter is progressing accordingly to plan in its strategy to expand the company beyond its successful core Steel Division.

Key steps include creating a global capability in specialty steels to take advantage of higher growth rates elsewhere in the world, building on the company's expertise in advanced materials by adding high-growth product lines and fully utilizing Carpenter's powerful distribution operation and knowledge of customers' needs to sell more products to its customer base.

In creating a critical mass quickly, the company is following a partnering and acquisition path.

Three Components of the Strategic Plan: All our attention is focused on making the company stronger and, at the same time, growing strategically. We believe our excellent financial numbers are a direct result of the diligence being applied to carrying our Carpenter's sound strategic plan. It has three prime pieces:

1. To be recognized as the premier specialty steel provider in the world, based on products delivering high value to customers, ongoing product development and efficiency in manufacturing operations.

2. To bring our core products into faster-growing world markets to substantially increase sales and earnings. International sales of products made at our domestic mill are rising according to plan, aided by marketing from our joint venture company in Taiwan and our recently-acquired distributor in Mexico.

3. To expand our role in advanced materials through structural ceramics, a fast-growing industry serving applications akin to Carpenter specialty steels.

Our Vision: To be a major, profitable and growing international producer and distributor of specialty alloys, materials, and components by providing specialty materials and service solutions for our customers by integrating our growing knowledge of materials science, customer needs, user-industries and engineering applications.

183. Casino America Inc.
711 Washington Loop
Biloxi, MS 39530
Phone: (601) 436-7000

Casino America Inc. (NASDAQ; CSNO) is one of the nation's pioneers in riverboat and dockside gaming, currently operating in Mississippi and Louisiana, and exploring additional locations throughout the U.S. The casinos operate under the name "Isle of Capri Casino."

Slogan: "We've Got It All!"

Our Mission: Casino America's mission is to continue to be a leader in new venue gaming by:

Continuing the development and quality enhancement of our Isle of Capri's Caribbean-themed hospitality and entertainment product;

Providing a fun, exciting, fresh and full-range casino environment which provides the best game rules for our players;

Providing our guests with a friendly, superior, service-oriented experience that exceeds their expectations, is viewed as the best among our local competitors and results in loyal and frequent visitations;

Providing our employees an enjoyable and rewarding work experience which results in high levels of job satisfaction and staff retention;

Building and maintaining strong community involvement and commitment in our local markets;

Aggressively seeking growth in generally non-overlapping jurisdictions where we can be the first, or among the first, to operate;

Maintaining an ethical, open and honest approach in all relationships with employees, guests, partners, vendors, regulators, communities, and our shareholders.

184. Casino Data Systems Inc.
3300 Birtcherr Dr.
Las Vegas, NV 89118
Phone: (702) 269-5000

Casino Data Systems Inc. (NASDAQ; CSDS) is a designer, manufacturer, and distributor of computer based technology for the gaming industry.

Mission: Casino Data Systems is a creator of high-technology products and we are dedicated to providing Quality, Innovation, and Excellence to our customers, our employees, and our shareholders.

At CDS, our mission is to produce state-of-the-art computer products for our customers.

We will excite our customers with the promise of new technology; delight them with the fulfillment of that promise; and deliver the best service to them.

We will accomplish our objectives by utilizing our knowledge and skill, our innovation and creativity, and our constant attention to the needs of our customers.

We pledge to treat our product like silver and our customers like gold.

In new technologies, rather than follow, we will lead.

As employees, we will unite and work together and, as a team, we will provide each other with a quality work place, the opportunity to be creative, and the opportunity to succeed and grow.

With continued focus and dedication to our customers, our products, and our team, we will provide long term value and opportunity to our shareholders.

"CDC's mission is to create additional innovative and unique applications of progressive and interactive technology which expand the industry and offer great

excitement for the casino patron," according to Steven A. Weiss, Chairman of the Board. "We believe that casino operators will welcome new and innovative link technology products which serve to make generating greater success for the casino."

185. Catalina Marketing Corp.
11300 9th St. North
St. Petersburg, FL 33716
Phone: (813) 579-5000
Web: http://www.catalinamktg.com

Catalina Marketing Corp. (NYSE; POS) is a leading provider of in-store electronic marketing services. Through its proprietary network, Catalina Marketing provides consumer products manufacturers and retailers with cost-effective methods of delivering promotional incentives and advertising messages directly to consumers based on their purchasing behavior.

Slogans: "Creating Value Through the Power of the Network." "The New In-Store Medium That Knows Who Needs Your Product. And When." "Only By Knowing Someone's Intimate Secrets Can You Really Change Their Shopping Behavior." "Introducing Checkout Message. The New No-Waste Ad Medium That Only Reaches the People You Want."

Building on Our Momentum: When Catalina Marketing was established eleven years ago, our goal was to become the leading provider of in-store electronic marketing services. Having achieved that goal, we are now committed to building further on our leadership.

To that end we continue to invest in upgrades to our existing network, as well as the development of new marketing tools and network applications. As a pioneer in our industry, we are working closely with manufacturers, retailers, and marketing professionals on a variety of industrywide issues.

186. Caterpillar Inc.

100 N.E. Adams St.
Peoria, IL 61629
Phone: (309) 675-1000
Web: http://www.caterpillar.com

Caterpillar Inc. (NYSE; CAT) makes earthmoving equipment.

Four Phrases Spell Out Caterpillar's Mission: Chairman George Schaefer recently released a mission statement that defines what Caterpillar is trying to accomplish as a corporation. The statement was formulated by the Strategic Planning Committee, group of 10 of the company's senior managers, including Schaefer, who are examining strategic issues important to Caterpillar's future. Here it is:

Provide differentiated products and services of recognized superior value to discriminating customers worldwide.

Pursue businesses in which we can be a leader based on one or more of our strengths.

Build and maintain a productive work environment in which high levels of personal satisfaction can be achieved while conforming to our Code of Worldwide Business Conduct and Operation Principles.

Achieve growth and above average returns for stockholders, resulting from both management of ongoing businesses and a studied awareness and development of new opportunities.

"Four key phrases stand out in those statements — provide differentiated products and services, be a leader, productive work environment, and growth and above average returns," Schaefer said. "This is a very brief and simple message which should serve as a constant reminder of what we are trying to accomplish as an ongoing business institution."

187. CEL-SCI Corp.

66 Canal Center Plaza
Suite 510
Alexandria, VA 22314
Phone: (703) 549-5293
Web: http://www.cel-sci.com

CEL-SCI Corp. (NASDAQ; CELI) is a biotechnology company. Registered trade name products are Multikine and HGP-30. Viral Technologies Inc., a 50% owned subsidiary of CEL-SCI, is involved in the development of new peptide technology that could be commercially useful in the development of vaccines and reagents for the prevention and diagnosis of HIV infection and for the treatment of AIDS.

Slogan: "Pioneers in Natural Immunotherapy."

Mission: CEL-SCI Corporation, founded in 1983, is a biotechnology company developing products for the treatment of diseases which affect the immune system.

188. Centerior Energy Corp.

6200 Oak Tree Blvd.
Independence, OH 44131
Phone: (216) 447-3100
Web: http://www.centerior.com

Centerior Energy Corp. (NYSE; CX) owns and operates the Cleveland Electric Illuminating Company and Toledo Edison.

Mission: Our mission is to provide competitively-priced electricity and related services to retail and wholesale customers.

We will accomplish this by generating, transmitting, and distributing our products safely, reliably, and profitably.

Vision: We will be a competitive, market-driven, customer-focused company providing excellent customer service and increasing share owner value.

At the heart of our vision is a winning team of employees with continuous improvement the responsibility of every member of the organization. Every employee will demonstrate teamwork and accountability, and will receive appropriate direction, training, resources, recognition, and rewards. Every employee brings unique qualities and skills that are valued by the total organization. Every employee, every customer and every community we serve can rely on us to provide a safe, healthy environment.

189. Centex Corp.

3333 Lee Pkwy.
P.O. Box 19000
Dallas, TX 75219
Phone: (214) 559-6500
Web: http://www.centex.com

Centex Corp. (NYSE; CTX), through its subsidiaries, is among the nation's premier home building, financial services, and contracting and construction services companies.

Slogan: "Measuring Up."

Focusing on Quality Not Quantity: The economic variables for the home building industry over the next few years are difficult to access. Our strategy in this environment will be to increase the quality and profitability of each home we build, rather than adding volume. Concentrating on improvement at each step in the home building process is, we believe, the way to raise the returns on our home building investments. Being the best home builder has been and will continue to be more important to us than being the largest.

190. Centocor Inc.

200 Great Valley Pkwy.
Malvern, PA 19355
Phone: (610) 651-6000

Centocor Inc. (NASDAQ; CNTO) is a biotechnology company which develops biopharamaceutical therapeutics and diagnostic products for cardiovascular, inflammatory, and infectious diseases, and cancer. The company concentrates on research, development, and manufacturing, with a technological focus on monoclonal antibodies, peptides, and nucleic acids. Centocor collaborates with academic institutions and selected biotechnology companies, which provide candidates for product development. The company's

products are marketed by major health-care companies worldwide.

Statement: Our key competitive strength is the ability to assess the promise of breakthroughs in biotechnology before they are widely understood, then to develop them into innovative products. Our technological expertise is in the fields of monoclonal antibodies, peptides, and nucleic acids. Our scientific strengths are in immunology, molecular and cell biology, biochemistry and chemistry.

To pursue product leads, we collaborate with research institutions and emerging biotechnology firms. The products we develop and manufacture are marketed by established pharmaceutical companies, a strategy that allows us to focus on what we do best: Product development.

We are working to improve our operating efficiency, increase the return on our research and development investment, and shorten product-development time while maintaining the high quality of our scientific efforts. By meeting these challenges and sharpening our strategic focus, we plan to make Centocor one of the most innovative product development companies in the pharmaceutical industry, a sound and profitable business, and an important contributor to the advancement of healthcare for patients worldwide.

191. Central Louisiana Electric Co. Inc.

2030 Donahue Ferry Rd.
Pineville, LA 71360
Phone: (318) 484-7400

Central Louisiana Electric Co. Inc. (NYSE; CNL) generates and distributes electric energy to residential, commercial, and industrial customers.

Vision: We will be recognized by our customers, investors, and regulators as an agile utility that sets the standard for quality customer service and superior performance in an increasingly competitive industry.

Mission: We are in the business to provide our customers with quality electric services at competitive prices, our shareholders with an attractive return on investment, and ourselves with a safe and challenging work environment.

192. Cephalon Inc.

145 Brandywide Pkwy.
West Chester, PA 19380
Phone: (610) 344-0200

Cephalon Inc. (NASDAQ; CEPH) discovers, develops and markets products to treat neurologic disorders. The company is addressing unmet medical needs through proprietary research programs and by acquiring promising products for clinical development and commercial sale. In collaboration with Bristol-Myers Squibb, Cephalon's markets butorphanol tartrate under the registered brand name of Standol NS. Cephalon has two drug candidates in late-stage clinical research: Myotrophin and modafinil.

Slogan: "Bringing Innovative Therapies to Neurology."

An Inside Perspective: Since its inception, Cephalon has followed a clearly focused corporate strategy, one that has differentiated the company from the rest of the biotechnology industry. In today's rapidly changing pharmaceutical environment, the value of the company's strategic focus is more important than ever.

"The new pharmaceutical marketplace demands innovative products that alter the course of disease and positively impact disease management," said Frank Baldino, Jr., Ph.D., Cephalon's founder and CEO. "However, such innovation implies an assumption of risk which must be managed carefully. Our strategy of effectively balancing risk inherent in pharmaceutical research distinguishes Cephalon from other companies. Perhaps the best example of this strategy is modafinil, which we licensed for development in the United States as a treatment for narcolepsy, based upon its efficacy in French clinical trials and approval in France. Modafinil is the first new drug being developed to treat this disease in more than thirty-five years, and represents the kind of innovative therapy we hope to deliver to neurologists and their patients.

"We believe our disease focus and proven technologies will provide a wide range of solutions to a severely underserved marketplace. We're not involved in a wide-ranging and costly search for products to serve non-neurological markets. The result is we are now developing brand new molecules that, if successful, will actually alter the course of neurodegenerative diseases for the first time."

193. Cerner Corp.

2800 Rockcreek Pkwy.
Kansas City, MO 64117
Phone: (816) 212-1024
Web: http://www.cerner.com

Cerner Corp. (NASDAQ; CERN) is a leading developer of clinical and management information systems that support evolving relationships between providers, purchasers, payers, and consumers of health services.

Mission: To automate the process of managing health.

Vision: Cerner believes that in order to effectively manage the health status of a defined population, a health organization's information infrastructure must be centered around the human life and designed to enhance the quality and efficiency of caring for the individual's health needs. Cerner is dedicated to providing products and services that are focused on automating the process of managing health.

194. CF MotorFreight

3240 Hillview Ave.
Palo Alto, CA 94304
Phone: (650) 494-2900
Web: http://www.cnf.com

CF MotorFreight, a subsidiary of CNF Transportation Inc. (NYSE, CNF), is a long-haul motor carrier.

Mission: CF MotorFreight will continue to distinguish itself as the premier long-haul LTL motor carrier in North America. The company will maintain this position by embracing a no-compromise philosophy to customer satisfaction. Evidence of our success is the marketplace perception that CF MotorFreight is a preferred service company with which to do business.

195. Champion International Corp.
One Champion Plaza
Stamford, CT 06921
Phone: (203) 358-7000
Web: http://
www.championinternational.com

Champion International Corp. (NYSE; CHA) is a leading manufacturer of paper and wood products. The company's paper is used for business communications, commercial printing, publications, and newspapers. The company also manufactures pulp, as well as lumber, plywood, studs, and specialty wood products.

The Champion Way Statement: Champion's objective is leadership in American industry. Profitable growth is fundamental to the achievement of that goal and will benefit all to whom we are responsible: Shareholders, customers, employees, communities, and society at large.

Champion's way of achieving profitable growth requires the active participation of all employees increasing productivity, reducing costs, improving quality, and strengthening customer service.

Champion wants to be known for the excellence of its products and service and the integrity of its dealings.

Champion wants to be known as an excellent place to work. This means jobs in facilities that are clean and safe, where a spirit of cooperation and mutual respect prevails, where all feel free to make suggestions, and where all can take pride in working for Champion.

Champion wants to be known for its fair and thoughtful treatment of employees. We are committed to providing equality of opportunity for all people, regardless of race, national origin, sex, age, or religion. We actively seek a talented, diverse, enthusiastic workforce. We believe in the individual worth of each employee and seek to foster opportunities for personal development.

Champion wants to be known for its interest in and support of the communities in which employees live and work. We encourage all employees to take an active part in the affairs of their communities, and we will support their volunteer efforts.

Champion wants to be known as a public-spirited corporation, mindful of its need to assist — through volunteer efforts and donated funds — non-profit educational, civic, cultural, and social welfare organizations which contribute uniquely to our national life.

Champion wants to be known as an open, truthful company. We are committed to the highest standards of business conduct in our relationships with customers, suppliers, employees, communities, and shareholders. In all our pursuits we are unequivocal in our support of the laws of the land, and acts of questionable legality will not be tolerated.

Champion wants to be known as a company which strives to conserve resources, to reduce waste, and to use and dispose of materials with scrupulous regard for safety and health. We take particular pride in this company's record of compliance with the spirit as well as the letter of all environmental regulations.

Champion believes that only through the individual actions of all employees — guided by a company-wide commitment to excellence — will our long-term economic success and leadership position be ensured.

Pledge: For our part, we pledge:

To manage our forests wisely so that they can continue to provide wood for our mills, healthy habitats for a wide variety of plants and animals, and recreation for the public.

To monitor air and water quality at all of our manufacturing sites to ensure full compliance with federal, state, and local regulations.

To search for ways to reduce the impact of our operations on our communities and the environment to the lowest level possible.

To conserve resources wherever possible through source reduction, reuse, and recycling.

To respond to customer demands for recycled-content paper.

To eliminate all significant risks to the health and safety of our employees and our communities.

We are all stewards of this earth. It is imperative that all of us — business, people, educators, scientists, legislators, government officials, environmentalists, and others — work as partners to make sure our society functions in harmony with nature, not in opposition to it.

At Champion, we are committed to preserving and protecting the world in which we live, while continuing to produce the high-quality products our customers demand. That is both our challenge and our pledge.

196. Chase Manhattan Corp.

270 Park Ave.
Suite 220
New York, NY 10017
Phone: (212) 270-6000
Web: http://www.chase.com

Chase Manhattan Corp. (NYSE; CMB) is the name given to the single banking entity created after Chemical Banking Corp. merged with Chase Manhattan Bank.

The Chase Manhattan Vision: We provide financial services that enhance the well-being and success of individuals, industries, communities, and countries around the world.

Through our shared commitment to those we serve, we will be the best financial services company in the world.

Customers will choose us first because we deliver the highest quality service and performance.

People will be proud and eager to work here.

Investors will buy our stock as a superior long-term investment.

Values: To be the best for our customers, we are team players who show respect for our colleagues and commit to the highest standards of quality and professionalism.

Customer focus.

Respect for each other.

Teamwork.

Quality.

Professionalism.

Goals: As we enter the 21st century, Chase Manhattan will be positioned as a financial services company that is: World class, balanced, financially strong, big.

197. Chesapeake Corp.

1021 E. Cary St.
Richmond, VA 23218
Phone: (804) 697-1000

Chesapeake Corp. (NYSE; CSK) is a diversified packaging and paper company whose primary businesses are packaging and tissue.

Statement: Chesapeake's strategic goals include achieving $2 billion in sales by the year 2000 with a 15% average return on equity through the business cycle. The company plans to grow its packaging business to $1 billion and its tissue business to $600 million by the year 2000 through internal growth initiatives and acquisitions.

198. Chesebrough-Pond's USA Co.

32 Benedict Place
Box 6000
Greenwich, CT 06836
Phone: (203) 661-2000
Parent's Web: http://www.unilever.com

Chesebrough-Pond's USA Co., a subsidiary of Ulilever PLC (NYSE; UL), is in the following businesses: Cosmetics, toiletries, proprietary, and specialty fields. Registered trade name products include Vaseline Petroleum Jelly, Q-tips, Faberge, Cutex, Pond's creams and powders, Dermasil, and Mentadent toothpaste and mouthwash.

Slogans: Q-tips — "Packaged for Purity." Mentadent — "The Ingredients Dentists Recommend Most for the Care of Teeth and Gums." Vaseline — "Pure Petroleum Jelly."

Growth: The growth of Chesebrough-Pond's was made possible by:

Maintaining the popularity of sales of established products.

Developing new products inside the company.

Adding new products and moving into new fields.

Improving profit margins by expanding sales domestically and internationally.

Increasing efficiency in production and marketing.

Achieving operating economies from integration and consolidation.

Formation and development of a young professional management team.

Employment of the most modern production, packaging, and marketing techniques.

Goal: The company's goal and its international plan of operations and marketing are clear and consistent. The plan is designed to deliver the proper combination of high quality products, developed to sell in the moderate price range, and to support them with aggressive advertising, marketing, and merchandising. This activity is especially programmed for the rapidly expanding purchasing power in the principal countries of the world. The goal is to enable the company to achieve its fair share of these expanding markets and to continue the growth pattern in the international field which Chesebrough-Pond's has shown for so many years.

The Future: As a result of all the energetic work both in the United States and throughout the world and the studious attention to business detail and the corporate blueprint for growth, Chesebrough-Pond's Inc. has emerged as the international leader in less than ten years from the time of the merger of the two companies with similar aims and aspirations.

Chesebrough-Pond's customers all over the world are now more certain than ever to finding their favorite cosmetics, beauty aid, toiletry, specialty, or proprietary medicine wherever they may be.

Chesebrough-Pond's is well positioned financially and competitively, both in the international market place and in the United States, for a growing and profitable future. The continued success of its present products coupled with the response to new ones in the United States and throughout the world lend encouragement to the company's optimism for the future.

199. Cheyenne Software Inc.

3 Expressway Plaza
Roslyn Heights, NY 11577
Phone: (516) 484-5110
Web: http://www.cheyenne.com

Cheyenne Software Inc. (AMEX; CYE) develops and sells sophisticated local area network (LAN) management software products.

Slogan: "Making Our Mark Around the World."

Philosophy: From inception to completion, Cheyenne products have been revolutionizing the industry on a global basis. For over ten years Cheyenne has been devoted to solving the problems associated with data and network management. This philosophy has also been extended to the support given to Cheyenne's network of channel partners and customers. Focusing on the future, while fully aware of the needs of today, has allowed Cheyenne to build solid relationships with leading original equipment manufacturers, distributors, resellers, and customers throughout the world.

Mission: At Cheyenne, our mission is to provide problem-solving software that eases the pressures of network management. We address more than the current needs of our customers; we anticipate future needs and build products to meet them.

200. Chick-fil-A Inc.
5200 Buffington Rd.
Atlanta, GA 30349
Phone: (404) 765-8000

Chick-fil-A Inc., a private company, is America's third largest quick-service chicken restaurant. The company is a pioneer in mall-based fast-food. Registered trademark products include the original Chick-fil-A Chicken Sandwich, Chicken Nuggets, Chick-n-Strips, Grilled 'n Lites, Chargrilled Chicken Sandwich, plus additional entree selections.

Slogans: "If It's Not Chick-fil-A, It's a Joke." "Together … We Will Be America's Best."

Mission: Be America's best quick-service restaurant at satisfying every customer.

Our Purpose: To glorify God by being a faithful steward of all that is entrusted to us. To have a positive influence on all who come in contact with Chick-fil-A.

Statements: The warm, family atmosphere upon which Chick-fil-A was founded and built was no accident. It grew from deeply-held, Biblically-based beliefs about servanthood and stewardship. It has continued to grow because those who have joined the family share those beliefs. As long as we value these principles and conduct our business based on them, Chick-fil-A will remain strong.

Through the years, we have learned from our experiences. Now, as we confront a more complex business climate than ever before, it is comforting to know that the core principles of our business will never change.

At Chick-fil-A, our vision is a composite of three things: Our purpose, our mission, and our principles.

Our best days are ahead. We are embarking on a course which has exciting possibilities for every member of the Chick-fil-A family. Whatever changes we make, Chick-fil-A will be known as:

People with vision … People who know who they are and where they are going.

Highly-motivated, extremely effective, and innovative people working together in teams.

An industry leader at satisfying customers.

An organization that is steadily increasing its sales and brand reputation.

An organization that produces good financial return for its people.

Our Principles: We are people who have strong beliefs about how business should be conducted. We gladly state these beliefs … not with any claim of perfection … but as principles toward which we continually strive:

Customers first — Our customers are the focus of everything we do. We do whatever it takes to satisfy their needs. When it comes to serving customers, we are flexible … both as individuals and as an organization.

Working together — Teamwork is essential to meeting the needs of our customers. Our Operators, team members, and staff work together as an interdependent team to achieve success.

Continuous improvement — Continuous improvement and innovation lead to success. Whatever the innovation is in products — the original boneless breast of chicken sandwich — or in the services — our original mall restaurants — we are dedicated to continuous improvement.

Personal excellence — We strive for excellence in all that we do. Our behavior must be honest, upright, and sincere. Personal excellence means doing what you say you will do, when you say you will do it, as you say it will be done … doing things right the first time every time.

Stewardship — We strive to be good stewards of all that is entrusted in us … our time, talents, treasures, and natural resources. We believe the best decisions are made with a long-term perspective.

201. Chipcom Corp.

118 Turnpike Rd.
Southborough, MA 01772
Phone: (508) 460-8900
Web: http://www.chipcom.com

Chipcom Corp. (NASDAQ; CHPM) is a designer, manufacturer, marketer, and servicer of intelligent switching systems, including a broad range of hub, internetworking and network management products. These products are used by networking professionals in various industries worldwide to build intelligent, or smart, networks.

Slogan: "From Smart Hubs to Smart Networks."

Mission Statement: Chipcom is a customer-focused company dedicated to being the trailblazer in providing the most robust, reliable, long-lasting network foundations for progressive organizations around the world.

Values Statement: Chipcom's values, enumerated below, are based on the cornerstones of pride, quality, respect, and sound business practices:

We, the people of Chipcom, are proud of our company, our fellow employees, ourselves, the job we do for all our customers and the reputation we earn by doing so.

We strive to set the highest standards for delivering quality products and services by knowing our customers and valuing their needs. Our success in the marketplace is directly related to the quality of our products and services.

We show respect for our customers, our business partners, and each other by being ethical, open, honest, and fair.

We manage our business conservatively to ensure Chipcom's financial strength. We make decisions based on facts and reality. We do what we say we will do. We take responsibility for Chipcom's success at every level of the company. We value each other's essential contributions to the company's success, and we recognize our need for meaningful and rewarding careers.

202. Chiquita Brands International

250 East Fifth St.
Cincinnati, OH 45202
Phone: (513) 784-8011
Web: http://www.chiquita.com

Chiquita Brands International (NYSE; CQB) is a marketer, distributor, and producer of fresh fruit and vegetables and a leading marker and producer of value-added processed foods.

Slogan: "Quite Possibly, the World's Most Perfect Food."

Mission: Chiquita'a mission is to deliver long-term growth in shareholder value as a global leader in premium branded foods.

Long-Term Programs: The company's long-term programs include:

Completion of a multi-year investment spending program to replace "rented" infrastructure used in the banana business with higher quality, lower cost "owned" transportation and production assets;

Realignment of marketing operations, transportation assets and production resources to further integrate and simplify operations; and

Reorganization of management structure and aggressive cost reduction commensurate with the new realities in the industry.

These programs have been at the core of our management team's dedication to delivering superior quality and value to customers at the lowest possible long-term cost. On a parallel track, we have successfully enhanced Chiquita's position as the premium priced industry leader with the largest overall share of the world's principle banana markets: Europe and North America.

203. Chiron Corp.

4560 Horton St.
Emeryville, CA 94608
Phone: (510) 655-8730
Web: http://www.chiron.com

Chiron Corp. (NASDAQ; CHIR) is a

human healthcare company, applying biotechnology and other techniques of modern biology and chemistry to develop, produce, and sell products intended to improve the quality of life by diagnosing, preventing and treating human disease. Chiron participates in the global healthcare industry in four markets: Diagnostic, therapeutics, vaccines, and ophthalmic surgical products.

Mission Statement: Our mission is to be the premier biotechnology company by creating products that will transform the practice of medicine.

We aim to improve human health and extend healthy life, while lowering the cost of healthcare. We will accomplish our mission through technological leadership, product-oriented research, rapid development, superior manufacturing, and commercial strategies that will create and reshape markets. We commit to our investors a superior return, and to all our constituencies the highest standards of financial and operational performance.

Purpose: Our purpose is to end human suffering caused by disease. We have a sense of urgency about achieving this as we know disease will not wait for solutions. To this end our environment at Chiron will be intense, challenging, focused on creating value for those who use our products and result in sustained profitable growth for the company, its people and its investors.

204. Chrysler Corp.
12000 Chrysler Dr.
Highland Park, MI 48288
Phone: (313) 956-5252
Web: http://www.chryslercorp.com

Chrysler Corp. (NYSE; C) is the third leading U.S. car maker, following General Motors and Ford Motors. Major subsidiaries include Dollar Rent A Car Inc., Snappy Car Rental Inc., Thrifty Rent-A-Car Inc., Chrysler Financial Corp., and Automobili Lamborghini SpA.

Slogans: "What's New in Your World?"

Dodge—"This Changes Everything." Chrysler—"The Rules Have Changed." Dodge and Plymouth—"The Minivan Company." Jeep—"There's Only One Jeep." Concorde—"An Elegant Expression of Form Following Function." Intrepid—"We're Changing Everything." Town & Country—"The Ultimate." Plymouth—"One Clever Idea After Another." Dodge—"America's Truck Stop." Chrysler/Plymouth—"We Want What You Want."

Our Purpose: To produce cars and trucks that people will want to buy, will enjoy driving, and will want to buy again.

205. Ciba-Geigy Corp.
540 White Plains Rd.
P.O. Box 2005
Tarrytown, NY 10591
Phone: (914) 785-2000
Web: http://www.ciba.com

Ciba-Geigy Corp., now a part of Novartis AG (OTC; NVTSY)—a company formed with the merger of Ciba-Geigy and Sandoz—is a worldwide biological and chemical company, serving the needs of healthcare (pharmaceuticals, drugs for self-medication), agriculture (herbicides, fungicides, seeds), and industry (dyestuffs, chemicals, additives, pigments, adhesives, polymers, composites).

Positioning Statement: We strive to achieve sustainable growth by balancing our economic, social, and environmental responsibilities. Empowered employees and a flexible organization support our commitment to excellence.

Environmental Goals: Ciba works to produce high-quality products without subjecting human beings and the environment to unnecessary risks.

1. We strive to make products that are environmentally sound.

2. We develop safe production processes using the lowest possible quantities of harmful substances.

3. We carry out exhaustive analysis of production processes, which allows us to

identify risks and weak points early and to take the necessary safety precautions.

4. We ensure that technical steps are taken to treat unavoidable waste and dispose of it without harming the environment.

Business Strategy: Ciba's business strategy is guided by a set of principles known as Vision 2000. This is a policy aimed at steering the company into the 21st century and guaranteeing our long-term future.

The basis of Vision 2000 is the sincere belief that our business has three areas of responsibility. We believe that we must face all of these with commitment in order to survive in our business, which is to provide products that improve the quality of life in all our markets.

These three areas of responsibility are separate but interlinked. The first is economic. This means that we aim to serve our stakeholders — employees, business partners, investors, and the public — in the way that we know best; by remaining a market leader where we choose to do business. In doing this, we keep our sights firmly fixed on the long-term future. We will generate appropriate financial results through sustainable growth and the constant renewal of a balanced business structure. We will not put our long-term future at risk by taking short-term profits.

Our second responsibility is towards society. We look to generate informed trust by being open in our dealings with society. This means that we communicate honestly. We manufacture products that add to the quality of life — whether they are pharmaceuticals, agriculture products, high performance plastics or life-enriching dyestuffs. We recognize our responsibilities when turning new discoveries in science and technology into commercial reality; we carefully evaluate the benefits and risks of all our activities, processes, and products, and welcome debate in areas of public interest.

The final area of responsibility ... is our environmental responsibility. Respect for the environment is part of everything we do. We design products and processes to fulfill their purpose as safely and with as little environmental impact as possible. We use natural resources and energy in the most efficient way and reduce waste in all forms. It is our duty to dispose of all unavoidable waste as safely as possible using the latest advances in technology.

206. CIDCO Inc.
105-H Cochrane Circle
Morgan Hill, CA 95037
Phone: (408) 779-1162
Web: http://www.cidco.com

CIDCO Inc. (NASDAQ; CDCO) manufactures and markets caller ID products.

Slogan: "The Caller ID Company."

Mission Statement: To provide the best in quality and on-time delivery of subscriber equipment for intelligent telephone network services that exceed customer expectations.

207. CIGNA Corp.
One Liberty Place
Philadelphia, PA 19192
Phone: (215) 761-1000
Web: http://www.cigna.com

CIGNA Corp. (NYSE; CI) is in the insurance and financial services businesses.

Slogan: "A Business of Caring."

Vision Statement: At CIGNA, we intend to be the best at helping our customers enhance and extend their lives, and protect their financial security. Satisfying customers is the key to being able to meet employee needs and shareholder expectations, and will enable CIGNA to build on our reputation as a financially strong and highly respected company.

We believe:

Providing the customer with products and services they value more than those of our competitors is critical to our success;

Talented, well-trained, committed and mutually supportive people — working to the highest standards of performance and integrity — are what make success possible;

The profitable growth of our businesses makes career opportunities and personal growth possible; and,

Profitability is the ultimate measure of our success.

208. CILCORP Inc.
300 Hamilton Blvd.
Suite 300
Peoria, IL 61602
Phone: (309) 675-8850
Web: http://www.cilco.com

CILCORP Inc. (NYSE; CER) is a holding company with five first-tier subsidiaries: Central Illinois Light Co., CILCORP Investment Management Inc., QST Enterprises Inc., CILCORP Ventures Inc., and Environmental Science & Engineering Inc.

Preparing for the Future: No one can control the weather. No one can control the future. But through honing internal strengths and outward actions, one can achieve the drive and resiliency to meet the future as an ally on the doorstep.

CILCORP Inc. is helping redesign the regulatory blueprint. We are leading the effort to hammer out new rules in the legislative halls, craft new markets, and restructure operations to accommodate an evolving utility industry.

Change is at the center of subsidiaries' growth, and our management of it will be a source of shareholder confidence.

We will stay on top of the job, making decisions, taking action, producing results and building shareholder value. It is an exciting time of renewal.

Environmental Statement: Central Illinois Light Company (CILCO) is committed to producing energy for our customers in concert with our environment. We are proud of the technological advances and proactive practices we have adopted to reduce our impact upon our natural resources. Our corporate policies to prevent pollutants, conserve raw materials, recycle and reuse waste by-products, promote the wise use of energy, safeguard our customers and employees, and comply fully with all applicable environmental regulations have established us as a leader in addressing Illinois and national environmental concerns. Our role as a responsible steward of the environment is an ongoing commitment and a pledge we make to the larger community — our earth.

209. Cincinnati Milacron Inc.
4701 Marburg Ave.
Cincinnati, OH 45209
Phone: (513) 841-8100
Web: http://www.milacron.com

Cincinnati Milacron Inc. (NYSE; CMZ) is a world leader in advanced manufacturing technologies for the plastics processing and metalworking industries. Their products include plastics machinery, machine tools, composites processing systems, computer controls, software, flexible manufacturing cells, metalcutting tools, metalworking fluids, and precision grinding wheels.

Slogan: "We Build Productivity."

Statement: We believe Milacron is now positioned as a worldclass company with worldclass products, distribution, and service. And while going through several years of building a strong base for long-term growth and profitability, we have enjoyed solid support, not only from our employees, but also from our customers, our suppliers, and from our shareholders.

Building on Our Strengths: Strong global presence.

Broad customer base.

Balanced product mix.

Shaping a Strong Future: Developing new products.

Investing for greater productivity.

Focusing on large markets.

Expanding throughout the world.

Creating and exploiting synergies.

210. Cineplex Odeon Corp.

1303 Yonge St.
Toronto, Ontario
Canada M4T 2Y9
Phone: (416) 323-6600
Web: http://www.cineplexodeon.com

Cineplex Odeon Corp. (NYSE; CPX) is an entertainment corporation which owns and operates motion picture theatres and related food service concessions in 14 U.S. states, the District of Columbia, and 6 Canadian provinces.

Looking Forward: We are confident that the rise in the key moviegoing population segments, the availability of enticing motion picture product and the continued increase in international audiences for mainstream movies, among other factors, will stimulate further industry expansion. We believe that the inimitable, exciting and enduring entertainment experience of moviegoing will generate growth potential for the Corporation well into the future. We will not merely be the passive beneficiary of these favorable trends, but will continually seek to explore new opportunities, expand our market presence and pursue quality in our product and operational performance.

211. CIPSCO Inc.

607 East Adams St.
Springfield, IL 62739
Phone: (217) 523-3600
Web: http://www.cipsco.com

CIPSCO Inc. (NYSE; CIP), is a subsidiary of Union Electric Company. It supplies electricity and natural gas services to central and southern Illinois. Through its subsidiary, CIPSCO Investment Company (CIC), it directs the company's non-utility investments, including leases, securities, and energy projects.

CIPS Corporate Mission: Our business purpose is to produce and supply electric energy; to supply natural gas; to be the provider of choice for our customers in the areas we serve; and meet the needs our customers value most. We will fulfill this mission by continuing to improve the quality of our services. We will provide the energy that makes it possible for customers to improve the quality of their lives and for businesses in our region to have the ability to maximize their potential.

CIPS Corporate Vision: Central Illinois Public Service Company will be a leader in a changing business environment and will compete effectively in the energy marketplace. This goal is established on the basis of specific industry and market changes expected to occur by 2004.

212. Circle K Corp.

3003 N. Central Ave.
Suite 1600
Phoenix, AZ 85072
Phone: (602) 530-5001

Circle K Corp., a division of TOSCO Corp. (NYSE; TOS), is a large convenience store chain.

Principles: Grow the people, grow the business and grow the trademark.

Vision: By the year 2000, we want to be renowned as the leading convenience store chain worldwide by being famous for great people, great products, and great prices. That vision is our goal.

On the Way to the 21st Century: Since its humble beginning in 1951, Circle K has become a cultural phenomenon and a symbol of success.

Born from a simple idea to offer customers value and convenience — a mix of ingenuity and the ability to adapt to market demands created a corporate culture that still drives Circle K today.

For more than four decades, the company has been a leader in the convenience store industry. But Circle K has never been content to stand still in the status quo.

A new management team has redesigned the company to meet the challenges of the 1990's. Today, Circle K is more efficient in its productivity, more progressive in its marketing, and more sensitive than ever to the needs of its customers.

The company utilizes a sound strategy to maximize potential, and it reinvests in the things that keep customers coming back.

213. Circuit City Stores Inc.
9950 Mayland Dr.
Richmond, VA 23233
Phone: (804) 527-4000
Web: http://www.circuitcity.com

Circuit City Stores Inc. (NYSE; CC) is a leading retailer of brand-name consumer electronics and major appliances.

Slogan: "Price. Selection. Service."

Future: The future is bright for Circuit City. By continuing to deliver exceptional service and value to the consumer, the company can build market share in existing markets, sustain a successful expansion program and further extend its stable financial record.

People: Our Most Valuable Resource: I believe that the true difference between Circuit City and the competition is our Associates. The individuals who compose the Circuit City team are challenged by a dynamic industry and a fast-paced, high-growth environment. By setting new standards for customer service they help ensure that Circuit City stands apart — in the marketplace and in financial performance.

Our goal is to maintain an environment that attracts leaders — an environment that respects hard work and rewards outstanding achievement. A strong team of Associates is the best way to maintain Circuit City's winning record.

A Winning Combination: At Circuit City, our commitment to Associates translates into a commitment to customers and stockholders. Circuit City Associates are proud to be on a winning team. They recognize that the customer is the most important ingredient in our success formula. They join forces every day to set the pace for customer service, not just in our segment, but in all of retailing. The final result is continuously superior perfor-

mance — for customers and ultimately, for stockholders.

214. Circus Circus Enterprises Inc.
2880 Las Vegas Blvd. South
Las Vegas, NV 89109
Phone: (702) 734-0410

Circus Circus Enterprises Inc. (NYSE; CIR) is a gaming company that operates eight properties and is a major presence in each of its three Nevada markets — Las Vegas, Reno, and Laughlin. In addition, the company operates a riverboat casino in Tunica County, Mississippi and is a partner in a joint venture casino project in Windsor, Canada.

Marketing Policies: The company's marketing policies emphasize an exceptional price-to-entertainment value for its customers exemplified by liberal paybacks on slot machines, courteous service, and moderately priced rooms and food. Circus Circus believes that its repeat customer rate is the highest in the industry.

Statement: Circus has been dedicated to achieving superior financial performance, maximizing long-term returns for shareowners and delivering outstanding quality and value to our customers. While some things may change, these core commitments will not. We fully intend to be a growing force in this dynamic industry and look forward with anticipation to a "new day" and the next chapter in the Circus success story.

215. Cisco Systems Inc.
170 West Tasman Dr.
San Jose, CA 95134
Phone: (408) 526-4000
Web: http://www.cisco.com

Cisco Systems Inc. (NASDAQ; CSCO) is a leading supplier of high-performance, multimedia, multiprotocol internet-working solutions. Cisco products include a wide range of software-based routers, bridges, workgroup systems, ATM switches, access servers, and router management applications.

Cisco Mission: Be the supplier of choice by leading all competitors in customer satisfaction, product leadership, market share, and profitability.

216. CITGO Petroleum Corp.
P.O. Box 3758
Tulsa, OK 74102
Phone: (918) 495-4000

CITGO Petroleum Corp. is a manufacturer, marketer, and transporter of gasoline, jet turbine fuel, diesel fuel, heating oils, lubricants, refined waxes, petrochemicals, asphalt, and other petroleum based industrial products. The company is owned by PDV America Inc., an indirect, wholly-owned subsidiary of Petroleos de Venezuela, S.A. (PDVSA), the national oil company of Venezuela.

Environmental Slogan: "Sharing the Earth with Responsibility."

Slogans: "CITGO Says Go." "The Sign of Quality." "Power Up America, CITGO Power Is All You Need."

Priorities: Foremost among CITGO's priorities are safe worksites for its employees, environmental stewardship and a commitment to long-term financial health through strategic growth and business diversity.

Statement of Values: CITGO Petroleum Corp. is a market-driven, customer-focused refiner, marketer and transporter of high quality transportation fuels, lubricants, waxes, petrochemicals, asphalt, and industrial products. Our vision is to be the best refining, marketing and transportation company in the U.S. petroleum industry. To achieve that objective, we adhere to the following values:

Corporate responsibility — To manufacture, transport and market high quality CITGO products while protecting the environment and the health and safety of employees, contractors and the general public; to take active leadership roles in the communities served; and to conduct all aspects of CITGO's business ethically, legally and with uncompromising honesty, reliability and integrity.

Profitable growth — To provide long-term stability of earnings by remaining true to proven corporate strategies, remaining focused on meeting customer needs, avoiding complacency while remaining flexible and innovative, and creating new opportunities while controlling costs through continuous improvement.

217. Citicorp
399 Park Ave.
New York, NY 10043
Phone: (212) 559-4822
Web: http://www.citicorp.com

Citicorp (NYSE; CCI) has three major businesses: Its worldwide consumer business, its local and regional banking business, and its role as a provider of global products and services geared to major corporate and institutional customers.

Slogans: "The Citi Never Sleeps." "Around the World, Around the Clock ... The Citi Never Sleeps."

Statement: We will endeavor to manage the company to achieve better results and greater value, and have established a set of business objectives to support these goals:

We will continue to work the "basics."

We will run Citicorp for performance, emphasizing value, balance, and predictability.

We will focus on our existing franchises.

We will build our worldwide consumer business.

We will build on our unique set of local and regional banking businesses in the emerging markets, while being conservative in accepting cross-border exposure.

We will build our banking business in North America, Europe and Japan, but shift emphasis to those customers, products, and capital market activities that are global rather than domestic in their fundamental orientation.

We will work to reduce existing concentration of risk, volatility and those activities that are not "core."

218. Citizens Utilities
High Ridge Park
Stamford, CT 06905
Phone: (203) 329-8800
Web: http://www.czn.net

Citizens Utilities (NYSE; CZNA and CZNB — series A and B, respectively) is a diversified service company providing telecommunications, natural gas transmission and distribution, electric distribution, and water and wastewater treatment services to customers in 18 states.

Our Mission: To be a preeminent world-class growth company. As a business organization, we endeavor to provide our employees with an enriching and rewarding work experience and environment. As a public-service company, we strive to exceed the expectations of our customers and the communities we serve. And, as a publicly held company, we manage the operations and growth of our resources to maximize corporate value and return for our shareholders.

Our Values: In the pursuit of our corporate goals, we will strive to: Treat one another with respect. Be scrupulously ethical in all of our dealings. Always take the initiative. Be an outstanding citizen in each of the communities we serve. Preserve and protect our environment. Take pride in our work and pleasure in what we do.

219. Clark Equipment Co.
100 N. Michigan St.
South Bend, IN 46634
Phone: (219) 239-0100

Clark Equipment Co., a subsidiary of Ingersoll-Rand (NYSE; IR) is a manufacturer of skid-steer loaders, transmissions for trucks, and axles and transmissions for off-road equipment.

Mission: The mission of Clark Equip-ment Company is to design, manufacture and market the finest equipment in the world for our customers, to provide the most satisfying career for our employees, and to earn high returns and growth for our stockholders.

We seek to become a great company. On the path to greatness, we must:

Develop the best design engineering skills.

Develop the best manufacturing operations.

Develop the best marketing and sales capability.

Integrate these abilities into the best products and services.

Our Guiding Principles: The principles of the company are to conduct itself with honesty and integrity, provide value to its customers, treat all employees with fairness, behave responsibly with respect to the environment and with respect to the safety of its employees and the users of its products, and operate at all times ethically and well within the laws of all the countries of the world.

220. Clayton Homes Inc.
623 Market St.
Knoxville, TN 37902
Phone: (423) 970-7200

Clayton Homes Inc. (NYSE, CMH) is a manufacturer, retailer, financier and insurer of homes, concentrated in the prime mobile home states in the Southeast, South, and Southwest.

Focus: Our focus is squarely on customer satisfaction and providing the customer with the best housing value available.

Corporate Philosophy: Happy people — select caring, team-oriented people, and provide growth and development opportunities in a stimulating environment.

Happy customers — Provide quality, affordable housing; always exceeding customer expectations.

Happy shareholders — Consistently increase the value of our shareholder's investment.

Statement: Clayton people are dedicated to deliver quality homes at affordable prices.

221. Clorox Co.
1221 Broadway
Oakland, CA 94612
Phone: (510) 271-7000
Web: http://www.clorox.com

Clorox Co. (NYSE; CLX) develops, manufactures, and markets consumer products. Registered brand names include Clorox bleach, Pine-Sol, S.O.S. products, Kingsford products, Combat, Hidden Valley Ranch salad dressings, Tilex, Brita water filtration systems, K.C. Masterpiece barbecue sauce and (co-branded with Lay's) K.C. Masterpiece barbecue-flavored potato chips.

Slogans: Clorox Bleach — "There's Only One Clorox Bleach." Clorox 2 — "It's Love at First Sniff."

Priorities: Portfolio, People, Face. Performance, and Public Responsibility.

Performance Focus: Our focus is to generate a superior return for our shareholders.

Statement: We're working on clarifying our values and the kind of culture we'd like to have. We want to facilitate the growth and development of our people so they can add value to our company. Even more important, we're working on identifying the ways in which we think we must change, and are outlining action plans to make those changes.

Our objective is to come up with plans to respond to the changes in our business environment and our people's need for the new skills that are demanded today. We're working on an integrated program of people development and training, and we're fielding our first broad-based employee survey to be sure that we know how our people are feeling.

We will continue our efforts against our three improvement initiatives: Work simplification, the Customer Interface Redesign Project, and our People Strategy.

222. CML Group Inc.
524 Main St.
Acton, MA 01720
Phone: (508) 242-4155
Web: http://www.shareholder.com/cml

CML Group Inc. (NYSE; CML) creates and markets products that enhance people's health, understanding of the natural world, and sense of well-being. The company operates specialty marketing companies in the fitness, nature-appreciation, and gardening markets. It sells to consumers under the registered trade names NordicTrack, The Nature Company, and Smith & Hawken.

Marketing Strategy: CML in many ways is the retailer of the future. The company controls nearly all aspects of the marketing process, from the manufacture and/or sourcing of the products to its retail sale through 260 company-owned retail stores, kiosks, direct response, and via catalog. This strategy enables the company to keep in constant touch with its customers in order to identify their needs as well as obtain timely feedback.

223. Coachmen Industries Inc.
P.O. Box 3300
601 E. Beardsley
Elkhart, IN 46515
Phone: (219) 262-0123

Coachmen Industries Inc. (NYSE; COA) is a manufacturer of recreational vehicles, manufactured homes, specialty vehicles, and related products.

Motto: "Dedicated to the Enrichment of Your Life."

Mission: Our mission is to design, market and continually advance our products to be the value leader in the industries we serve. This, in turn, allows us to prosper as a business and to offer opportunities to our employees as well as provide a reasonable return to our shareholders.

Principles: How we accomplish our mission is as important as the mission itself. Fundamental to success for the company are those basic values which have guided our progress since our founding.

Our corporate motto is "Dedicated to the Enrichment of Your Life." this means we will do our best to provide quality products and services which will improve the lifestyle of our users.

Our word is our bond. Our dealers and suppliers are our partners. We endeavor to practice the Golden Rule in all of our relations with others.

Quality is our first priority. We must achieve customer satisfaction by building quality products. This will allow us to compete effectively in the marketplace. We will always remember: No sale is a good sale for Coachmen unless it fulfills our customers' expectations.

Customers are the focus of everything we do. As a company we must never lose light of the commitment we make to those who buy our products. Our deep-seated philosophy is that "Business goes where it is invited and stays where it is well cared for."

Integrity is our commitment. The conduct of our company's affairs must be pursued in a manner that commands respect for its honesty and integrity.

Profits are required for the company to grow and flourish. Profits are our report card of how well we provide customers with the best products for their needs.

Statement: Our doors are always open to men and women who can contribute to our fulfillment of these goals.

224. Coastal Corp.
Coastal Tower
Nine Greenway Plaza
Houston, TX 77046
Phone: (713) 877-6821

Coastal Corp. (NYSE; CGP) operates in natural gas marketing, transmission, storage, gathering and processing; oil and gas exploration and production; petroleum refining, marketing and distribution and chemicals; independent power production; and coal.

Slogan: "The Energy People."

Statement: The company's diverse segments aim to create value for its stockholders by growing consistently and taking advantage of new opportunities in an ever-changing global energy market.

Summary: Our objective has always been, and remains, to enhance long-term value of our stock, nearly 20 percent of which is owned by company directors and employees.

We have repositioned refining, marketing and chemicals so that it is now competitive even in adverse market conditions.

We have sustained the earnings and cash flow contributions from our large regulated natural gas business during a time of unprecedented regulatory change and are competing successfully in the new, less regulated business environment.

We are rapidly expanding Coastal's higher growth businesses, especially those related to exploration and production and international power production.

And we have built a strong foundation for future growth through debt paydown and improvements in our balance sheet, a process accelerated by the successful sale of our Utah coal subsidiaries in 1996.

225. Coca-Cola Co.
1 Coca-Cola Plaza N.W.
Atlanta, GA 30313
Phone: (404) 676-2121
Web: http://www.cocacola.com

Coca-Cola Co. (NYSE, KO) is the largest manufacturer, marketer, and distributor of carbonated soft drinks, concentrates, and syrups in the world. Registered trade name products include Coca-Cola, Coca-Cola Classic, Diet Coke, Cherry Coke, Sprite, Diet Sprite, Mr. PiBB, Mello Yello, Fanta brand soft drinks, Tab, and Fresca. The company also manufactures, produces, markets, and distributes juice and juice drink products. Coca-Cola Foods, a division of the company, is the world's largest marketer and distributor of juice and juice drink products. Trade name products include Minute Maid juices, Five Alive, Bright and Early beverages, Fruitopia juices, and Hi-C brand fruit juices. The company produces and distributes PowerAde, a sports drink. Also, the company has a 50% joint venture with Nestle, producing ready to drink teas and coffees.

Slogans: (Coke) "Always Delicious. Always Coca-Cola." "Always the Original. Always Coca-Cola." "Coke Is It." "Coca-Cola Just Went One Better." "The Pause That Refreshes." "It's the Real Thing." "Always New, Always Real, Always You, Always Coke." (Diet Coke) "The Move Is On to Diet Coke." "Just for the Taste of It." (Sprite) "I Like the Sprite in You." "Image Is Nothing. Thirst Is Everything. Obey Your Thirst." (Cherry Coke) "Ch...Ch...Ch...Cherry Coke. Outrageous."

Our Opportunity: Bring refreshment to a thirsty world is a unique opportunity for our company ... and for all of our Coca-Cola associates ... to create shareholder value. Ours is the only production and distribution business system capable of realizing the opportunity on a global scale. And we are committed to realizing it.

Our Goal: With Coca-Cola as the centerpiece, ours is a worldwide system of superior brands and services through which we, our franchisees and other business partners deliver satisfaction and value to customers and consumers. By doing so, we enhance brand equity on a global basis. As a result, we increase shareholder wealth over time.

Our goal for the 1990s sounds deceptively simple. It is to expand our global business system, reaching increasing numbers of consumers who will enjoy our brands and products more and more often.

Our Challenge: The 1990s promise to be a paradoxical time for our business. Distribution channels will continue to consolidate while new ones will emerge ... yet, customers will demand more choices, as well as customized service and marketing programs at the lowest possible cost. Consumers in developed countries will grow in age and affluence but not in number ... while strong population growth in lesser developed countries means the vitality of these young consumer markets will depend on job creation and expanding economies. To succeed in this environment we will make effective use of our fundamental resources: Brands, systems, capital, and most important, people.

Because these resources are already available, one might assume we need only to draw on them for achieving our goal. Nothing could be more wrong. The challenge of the 1990s will be not only to use these resources, but to expand them ... to adapt them ... to reconfigure them in constantly changing ways in order to bring about an ever renewed relationship between the Coca-Cola system and the consumers of the world ... to make the best even better.

Our Shared Vision: The Coca-Cola system is indeed a special business. One hundred and three years of dedicated effort by literally millions of individuals have combined to create in Coca-Cola a remarkable trademark presence and economic value unchallenged since the dawn of commercial history.

However, any edge we have is fragile. Our journey to the year 2000 requires that our brands, systems, capital and people grow and change to meet our goal and thus realize our opportunity. To borrow a recent popular phrase, we see six billion points of light in a thirsty world — six billion customers in the world of the year 2000 — all being refreshed as never before by the Coca-Cola system.

That is a wonderful goal we all can share and strive for as we more together — toward 2000.

226. Coeur d'Alene Mines Corp.
505 Front Ave.
P.O. Box 1
Coeur d'Alene, ID 83816
Phone: (208) 667-3511
Web: http://www.couer.com

Coeur d'Alene Mines Corp. (NYSE; CDE) mines for gold and silver.

Slogan: "The Precious Metals Company."

Statement: As planned, we are emerging as the nation's leading primary silver producer, at a time when many of our traditional competitors have either left the business or are in decline. We will remain focused on our long-term objectives: To continue building Coeur's gold and silver production capacity, as well as its reserves, revenues, cash flow and earnings, as the developing and increasingly dynamic economies of the world continue to demand our products at ever increasing levels.

227. Cognex Corp.
One Vision Dr.
Natick, MA 01760
Phone: (508) 650-3000
Web: http://www.cognex.com

Cognex Corp. (NASDAQ; CGNX) designs, develops, manufactures, and markets a family of machine vision systems that are used to replace human vision in a wide range of manufacturing processes. These high-level systems consist of sophisticated image analysis software and high-speed, special-purpose computers (vision engines) which, when connected to a video camera, interpret video images and generate information about them.

Slogan: "Vision for Industry."

Strategy: Cognex's strategy is to develop and sell — worldwide — standard products which require minimal customization and support by the company. Its customers for those products are OEMs and system integrators who can configure their own complete vision solutions.

228. Coherent Inc.
5100 Patrick Henry Dr.
P.O. Box 54980
Santa Clara, CA 95056
Phone: (408) 764-4000
Web: http://www.cohr.com

Coherent Inc. (NASDAQ; COHR) designs, manufactures, and sells the components that go into lasers, systems, and delivery devices. Markets for these products include the following areas: Scientific, ophthalmic, surgical, commercial, and optics.

Slogan: "Laser Excellence and Innovation Since 1966."

Statements: Customer satisfaction is our most important measure of quality. Custom application development, product training, and customer education are services that we consider integral parts of our products.

Our broad technical expertise, longevity, and strong financial condition assure that our long-term commitment to customers will be supported — now and in the future.

229. Colgate-Palmolive Co.
300 Park Ave.
New York, NY 10022
Phone: (212) 310-2000
Web: http://www.colgate.com

Colgate-Palmolive Co. (NYSE; CL) manufacturers and markets consumer products. Registered brand names include Ajax cleaning preparations, Colgate toothpastes and mouthwashes, Fab detergents, Irish Spring soap, Murphy's Oil Soap, to name a few.

Slogan: (Colgate Baking Soda & Peroxide Toothpaste) "The Colgate Deep Clean."

Statement: Great ideas stimulate continued profitability growth.

Colgate's profitable growth worldwide is based on its results-oriented approach. Stay focused on the business fundamentals ... Set global priorities ... implement them strategically. With this philosophy, Colgate people around the world work together to bring great ideas to profitable reality.

230. Colonial Gas Co.
40 Market St.
P.O. Box 3064
Lowell, MA 01853
Phone: (508) 458-3171

Colonial Gas Co. (NASDAQ; CGES) is primarily a regulated natural gas distribution utility. The company serves utility customers in 24 municipalities located northwest of Boston and on Cape Cod. Through its wholly-owned energy trucking subsidiary, Transgas Inc., the company also provides over-the-road transportation of liquefied natural gas, propane, and other commodities.

Competitive Success: Organizational efficiency; innovative problem-solving; advanced technology solutions; customer service excellence; Real-world experience indicates that the newly deregulated businesses which most effectively pursue these goals are the most likely to outperform their competition and emerge as industry leaders.

Modeling itself on these industry winners, Colonial believes that it is prepared to succeed in its more competitive, deregulated environment and to continually meet its market's emerging requirements. Through re-engineering, we are raising our organizational efficiency to new heights and creating a culture of individual empowerment which rewards innovation. By harnessing the power of advanced technologies, we are optimizing our newfound efficiencies and working smarter than ever before. And through a customer satisfaction strategy that keeps us focused on meeting our customers' current and future needs for the most affordable, reliable natural gas services in our territories, we are continuing to attract new business while increasing the loyalty of our existing customer base.

All of which adds up to a single fact: While the rules may be different, Colonial is ready to extend its past success far into the future — delivering enhanced shareholder value by sustaining its exceptional growth rate in the face of new competition.

231. Columbia Gas System Inc.

20 Montchanin Rd.
Wilmington, DE 19807

Phone: (302) 429-5000
Web: http://www.columbiaenergy.com

Columbia Gas System Inc. (NYSE; CG) is a holding company in the natural gas industry.

Mission Statement: The Columbia Gas System Inc., through its subsidiaries, is active in pursuing opportunities in all segments of the natural gas industry and in related energy resource development. Exemplified by Columbia's three-star logo, these separately managed companies strive to benefit: System shareholders — through enhancing the value of their investment; customers — through efficient, safe, reliable service; and employees — through challenging and rewarding careers.

232. Columbia/HCA Health Care Corp.

One Park Plaza
P.O. Box 550
Nashville, TN 37202
Phone: (615) 327-9551
Web: http://www.columbia.net

Columbia/HCA Health Care Corp. (NYSE; COL), the nation's largest healthcare services provider, owning and operating 340 hospitals and 125 outpatient surgery centers and other healthcare facilities, hopes to sell off its home health care unit and some hospitals.

Slogans: "A New Commitment to Healthcare ... Together." "Healthcare Has Never Worked Like This Before."

Our Mission: The mission of Columbia is to work with our employees, physicians and volunteers to provide a continuum of quality health care cost-effectively for the people in the communities we serve.

Our Vision: Our vision is for Columbia to work with employees and physicians to build a company that is focused on the well-being of people, that is patient oriented, that offers the most advanced technology and information systems, that is financially sound, and that is synonymous with quality, cost-effective healthcare.

233. Comcast Corp.
1500 Market St.
Philadelphia, PA 19102
Phone: (215) 665-1700
Web: http://www.comcast.com

Comcast Corp. (NASDAQ; CMCSK) is a provider of communications (cable and sound), entertainment, and information services worldwide.

Our Vision: Comcast Corp. ... is committed to its customers, employees and shareholders. Comcast will continue growing through its entrepreneurial and operating skills and its strong commitment to fiscal responsibility.

Achieving Our Vision: Our Values: Comcast is committed to growth in our existing businesses and will pursue opportunities for expansion in related fields worldwide. We will continue as a leading company in cable and sound communications and as a major participant in the cellular telephone industry.

As a quality provider, we will be the company of choice for our customers and employees and for the communities in which we do business. Comcast will be a customer service oriented organization which cares about providing quality and valued services. We will be concerned with our employees' welfare, career development and ability to share in the company's success. We will be socially conscious and responsive to community needs.

Comcast also will be the company of choice for investors. Comcast will strive to maintain the support of the financial community through superior operating and financial performance. Shareholder value will be increased by our dedication to continued responsible growth.

We will be a spirited team of diverse views and backgrounds possessing a strong entrepreneurial bent, the highest technical skills, and the drive and ability to successfully adjust to changing business environments. We will seek to optimize cash flow and increase revenues for both the long and the short term. We will be willing to take risks to achieve our goals and will adhere to the highest standards of integrity and morality.

We believe that the interests of all who have a stake in Comcast will best be served by our being an independent company, with all of our employees working together efficiently, dedicated to excellence and unified by the desire to realize our vision.

Comcast — Growth ... Quality ... Commitment.

234. Comerica Inc.
P.O. Box 75000
Detroit, MI 48275
Phone: (313) 370-5000
Web: http://www.comerica.com

Comerica Inc. (NYSE; CMA) is a bank holding company headquartered in Detroit that operates banking affiliates in Michigan, Texas, California, Illinois, and Florida. Comerica is a diversified financial services provider, offering a whole range of financial products and services for businesses and individuals.

Slogan: "All Banks Understand Banking. We Also Understand People."

Our Mission: To forge a cohesive team dedicated to being the standard for exceptional customer service.

Our Purpose: We are in business to enrich people's lives.

Our Business Vision: We define ourselves as a relationship-driven organization.

Our customers are our first priority.

Our board of directors are the shareholders' representatives; we are accountable to them.

We shall strive to consistently produce outstanding earnings.

We shall strive to be leaders in the communities we serve.

Our employees are our most valuable resource; we will invest in them.

Our employees will be known for their teamwork and will be faithful to our core values and beliefs.

We will be known for our outstanding management processes.

235. Community Psychiatric Centers

6600 W. Charleston Blvd.
Las Vegas, NV 89102
Phone: (702) 259-3600

Community Psychiatric Centers (NYSE; CMY) is a provider of psychiatric services for adults, adolescents, and children with acute psychiatric, emotional, substance abuse, and behavioral disorders. The company offers a broad spectrum of inpatient, partial hospitalization, outpatient, and residential treatment programs in 15 states, Puerto Rico, and the United Kingdom.

Statement: The mission of Community Psychiatric Centers is to deliver consistently superior care and service for the benefit of our patients, payors, clinicians, and other referral sources, our own employees, and our investors.

236. Compaq Computer Corp.

20555 State Hwy. 249
Houston, TX 77070
Phone: (713) 370-0670
Web: http://www.compaq.com

Compaq Computer Corp. (NYSE; CPQ) designs, develops, manufactures, and markets personal computers, PC systems, and related products for business, home, government, and education customers. The company is one of the world's largest suppliers of personal computers.

Motto: "When It Says Compaq on the Outside, You Don't Need to Worry About What's on the Inside."

Slogans: "Just Because You Learned the Hard Way Doesn't Mean Your Kid Has To." "We've Just Created Thousands of Reasons Why It's a Great Time to Buy a Compaq Desktop."

Vision Statements: In the future the company plans to capitalize on its leadership position in integrating hardware and software to furnish the building blocks of personal and corporate computing while participating in software and communi-

cations markets either directly or through business alliances. Through this strategy, the company expects to become a leading provider of enterprise-wide solutions for business as well as information appliances for the home by offering the products and services that customers need to easily access and manage information. The company believes its key to success is leveraging the company's engineering talent, purchasing power, manufacturing capabilities, distribution strengths, and brand name to bring to market high-quality cost-competitive products with different features in different price ranges.

Experience has shown us that with better quality, lower costs, and operational excellence, you can capture the market. And that's why quality and reengineering have become the No. 1 and No. 2 all-consuming priorities for every one of our employees worldwide.

I see Compaq as a new breed of full-range computer company. Think of us as the ultimate, multipurpose platform provider. Not just PCs. Not just servers. Not just hardware. But a provider of enterprise servers worldwide.

Responding to today's needs while preparing for tomorrow's by striving to find the future first. We know no better way to build world leadership.

The Environment: Designing new tools for the information age is a forward-looking process. We try to access not only the future needs of our customers, but also the future impact of our products on the environment. That means designing products that, for their entire life cycle, result in a safer and cleaner world. It means progressively reducing the amount of energy our PCs consume and the byproducts our factories produce. It means building our products with an even higher percentage of recyclable materials. And it means conducting worldwide audits to ensure compliance with the spirit and not just the letter of environmental regulations.

Goal: Our goal is to create the digital equivalent of a Swiss Army Knife—a compact, easy-to-use, rugged, and affordable tool that incorporates numerous functions and performs flawlessly.

237. Compression Labs Inc.
350 E. Plumeria
San Jose, CA 95134
Phone: (408) 435-3000

Compression Labs Inc. (NASDAQ; CLIX) manufactures and markets video-conferencing systems.

CLI Mission Statement: To make video communications an integral part of everyday life ... in business and the home.

CLI Values: Customer satisfaction — Customers are the lifeblood of our company. Customer needs will be considered in all that we do. We continually seek ways to exceed our customer's expectations.

People empowerment — People are CLI's greatest strength. We value our diversity and treat each other with the utmost respect. We are committed to continual personal improvement and to always doing our best.

Product & Service Excellence — We use our creativity and innovative technology to provide industry leading products and services that will fulfill real customers needs now and in the future. We are committed to excellence in quality and continuous improvement in our products, processes, and relationships.

Profitability & Growth — Profits are the key to our growth and economic stability. We seek a fair return, consistent with our other values, to enable the growth of our company. We will use our resources to increase our value to our customers, our people, and our shareholders.

Commitment & Teamwork — We will make and keep personal commitments. We encourage initiative and performance. We measure our success, however, through the attainment of team goals.

Ethics & Community — Integrity and trust are the foundation of our relationships with our customers, suppliers, and each other. We will act responsibly and be contributors to our community.

CLI Quality Statement: Do the right thing right the first time ... do it better the next time.

238. CompuCom Systems Inc.
10100 North Central Expressway
Dallas, TX 75231
Phone: (214) 265-3600
Web: http://www.compucom.com

CompuCom Systems Inc. (NASDAQ; CMPC), together with its subsidiaries, is a leading personal computer services integration company that provides services to large and medium sized businesses throughout the United States.

Slogan: "Mastering the Art of Customer Satisfaction."

Customer Strategy: What's CompuCom's strategy for mastering the art of customer satisfaction? First, listen to customers. Then, respond by bringing the voice of the customer into the heart of your operations. What's why the customer is at the top of CompuCom's organization chart.

239. Computer Discount Warehouse
1020 E. Lake Cook Rd.
Buffalo Grove, IL 60089
Phone: (847) 465-6000
Web: http://www.cdw.com

Computer Discount Warehouse (NASDAQ; CDWC) is one of the fastest growing computer direct marketers in the nation. CDW is a direct marketer of brand name microcomputer products at discount prices.

Slogan: "Why Pay Retail? CDW Sells for Less."

Motto: "Success Means Never Being Satisfied."

Statements: Above all, CDW remains dedicated to its mission: "To be one of the nation's highest volume computer resellers selling brand name products; providing a 'fun' and challenging work environment, and above-average earnings; give the customer competitive prices and excellence in service; and maintain a high net profit by running a lean, highly automated systems-oriented company."

Our success comes from staying focused on what we do best and continuously improving how we do it. Our objective is to create a WIN/WIN relationship with our customers, vendors, and employees, whereby we all prosper together and achieve high levels of satisfaction.

CDW plans to build on its core strengths to help drive continued growth and profitability. These strengths include:

Superior customer service based on the premise "People do business with people they like."

Flexible structure that allows for adaptive strategies, quick response and individual initiatives.

Adherence to the philosophy "Success means never being satisfied."

Applying technology to improve effectiveness and efficiency.

Motivated employees with a shared commitment for growth.

Continuous training through "CDW University" to ensure account executives are knowledgeable and provide quality customer service.

240. Computer Sciences Inc.
2100 E. Grand Ave.
El Segundo, CA 90245
Phone: (310) 615-0311
Web: http://www.csc.com/index.html

Computer Sciences Corp. (NYSE; CSC) provides management consulting in the strategic use of information technology and develops and implements complete information systems.

Goal: Be the leader in bringing radically new ideas to companies looking to make breakthrough gains in their mar-

kets. Also continue to play a leading role in helping companies revamp business processes to stay competitive.

241. COMSAT Corp.
22300 COMSAT Dr.
Clarksburg, MD 20871
Phone: (301) 428-4000
Web: http://www.comsat.com

COMSAT Corp. (NYSE; CQ) is a leading telecommunications and entertainment provider in the U.S.

COMSAT Vision: COMSAT is dedicated to serving the growing communications and entertainment needs of the global marketplace.

COMSAT Mission: To take advantage of the strengths and synergies in all our businesses.

To achieve a rate of return of 15 percent or greater.

To foster a working environment of great diversity where exceptional performance is encouraged, recognized, and rewarded.

242. Cone Mills Corp.
1201 Maple St.
Greensboro, NC 27405
Phone: (910) 379-6220

Cone Mills Corp. (NYSE; COE) operates in two business segments: Apparel fabrics (denims, yarn-dyed and chamois flannel shirtings, prints, and sportswear fabrics) and home furnishings products (commission printing and finishing services, decorative fabrics used for upholstery, draperies and bedspreads, polyurethane and bonded fiber products and furniture cushions).

Vision: The company's mission: Meet consumer needs; add value for customers; appropriate return; responsible environment; position Cone for Year 2000.

243. Conseco Inc.

11825 N. Pennsylvania St.
P.O. Box 1911
Carmel, IN 46032
Phone: (317) 817-6100
Web: http://www.conseco.com

Conseco Inc. (NYSE; CNC) is a financial services holding company. The company operates life insurance companies; provides investment management, administrative and other services to affiliates and nonaffiliates for fees; and acquires and restructures life insurance companies in partnership with other investors.

Statement: Our operating strategy is to consolidate and streamline the administrative function of acquired companies, to improve their investment yields through active asset management by a centralized investment operation, to expand their profitability products and distribution channels, and to eliminate those products and distribution channels that are unprofitable. Ultimately, we seek to realize the increase in value that our management brings to such companies through sale or restructuring.

Conseco is dedicated to leading the process of change in the financial services industry by setting new standards for operating efficiency, product innovation, product profitability and active investment management. We believe strongly that this process assures the best products and services for our customers, the highest value for our shareholders, and the most rewarding careers for our employees.

244. Consolidated Edison Co. of New York Inc.

4 Irving Pl.
New York, NY 10003
Phone: (212) 460-4600
Web: http://www.coned.com

Consolidated Edison Co. of New York Inc. (NYSE; ED) is a provider of energy (electricity, gas, steam) services.

Mission Statement: To provide energy services to our customers safely, reliably, and efficiently; to provide a workplace that allows employees to realize their full potential; to provide a fair return to our investors, and to improve the quality of life in the community we serve.

Corporate Values: Service: We will provide the best possible energy service. We will never forget that what we do, and the way we do it, vitally affects the millions of New Yorkers who depend on our service.

Honesty: We will conduct our business with honesty and integrity.

Concern: We will show concern for the welfare of our customers, our fellow employees, and the men and women who invest their savings in our company. We will protect the environment in which we live.

Courtesy: We will be courteous to our customers, to each other, and to all those whose lives we touch.

Excellence: We will strive for excellence in all that we do. We will never be satisfied with less than the highest standards of performance.

Teamwork: We will work in harmony as a team, combining our best thinking and efforts to make our company the finest utility in the nation.

Environmental Policy: Con Edison's policy is to demonstrate leadership and excellence in environmental protection. Our commitment to environmental excellence must be evident in all company operations. It should be known and understood by the company's employees, customers, and shareholders, and continuously reinforced by our actions within and outside the company.

Every Con Edison employee has a personal obligation to meet the fundamental workplace requirements established by law and by regulation, and to reach beyond these basic requirements to realize a higher level of achievement.

245. Consolidated Freightways Inc.

3240 Hillview Ave.

Palo Alto, CA 94304
Phone: (415) 494-2900
Web: http://www.cnf.com

Consolidated Freightways Inc. (NYSE; CNF), now called CNF Transportation Inc., is in the freight business.

Statement: We provide much more than just freight transportation services. We design a complete package of customized solutions for business problems.

246. Consolidated Rail Corp.
2001 Market St.
Philadelphia, PA 19101
Phone: (215) 209-4000
Web: http://www.conrail.com

Consolidated Rail Corp. — Conrail — (NYSE; CRR) operates a railroad route network dedicated exclusively to freight transportation service.

Statement: We, the employees of Conrail, are dedicated to making our company the carrier of choice in every transportation market we serve. We promise safe, reliable and innovative services that meet or exceed customers' expectations. We are committed to continuous quality improvement as a means of providing superior service to our customers, developing and recognizing excellence in one another, enhancing value for our shareholders and being worthy of the public's trust.

Goals: To be the safest carrier.

To provide total customer satisfaction as measured by the customer.

To develop employees to fully responsibly meet the changing needs of our customers and shareholders.

To achieve growth that will support our investments.

To achieve an operating ratio and asset utilization that provides a superior return on assets.

A Corporate Commitment: We are committed to protecting the environment. The rail mode is inherently more kind to the environment than its trucking competitors; our locomotives contribute fewer emissions and our trains haul hazardous

materials more safely. Through a corporate-wide environmental program and the independent efforts of many employee groups and individuals, we are striving to become even more environmentally friendly. Our environmental efforts have concentrated on making our operations cleaner, furthering safety improvements in hazardous commodities handling, using safer cleaning compounds, and recycling more materials used in both the operation and business sides of the railroad.

247. Continental Airlines Inc.
2929 Allen Pkwy.
Houston, TX 77019
Phone: (713) 834-5000
Web: http://www.flycontinental.com

Continental Airlines Inc. (NYSE; CAIA and CAIB) is in the scheduled air transportation industry.

Slogan: "More Airline for Your Money."

The Go Forward Plan: Continental Airlines implemented its Go Forward Plan in early 1995 to guide the company through significant changes it must make to become profitable and ensure its long-term competitiveness.

The plan is being used to all levels within each area of the company to help prioritize and assign responsibilities that support the overall strategy.

All of the major initiative and decisions that Continental undertakes are carried out in relation to one or more of the plan's four primary elements:

Fly to Win — Capitalize on the company's strengths; eliminate unprofitable flying; price our product to maximize revenues; listen to our customers.

Fund the Future — Monetize non-strategic assets; conserve cash to ensure a stable financial future; improve the debt amortization schedule.

Make Reliability a Reality — Keep our promise to our customers by achieving higher on-time performance, completion rates, and baggage delivery standards. Produce a product that the customer wants.

Working Together — Encourage and reward cooperation; let people do the job they know without a lot of interference; treat each other with dignity and respect.

248. Continental Cablevision Inc.
The Pilot House
Lewis Wharf
Boston, MA 02110
Phone: (617) 742-9500
Web: http://www.continental.com

The company, now under MediaOne, a subsidiary of U.S. West Inc. (NYSE; UMG), is a leader in the telecommunications industry: In the development of high-capacity, broadband communications networks, the delivery of top-quality, multi-channel video services, and the deployment of new technology.

Statement: Our commitment to excellent customer service, decentralized management, and advanced technology has given Continental a distinct competitive advantage.

Strategy for Growth: Our mission is simple: To acquire and retain customers that will subscribe to a broad spectrum of multimedia and telecommunications services.

We envision that one day, in the not-too-distant future, our customers will receive all of their multimedia and telecommunications needs — enhanced video, high-speed Internet access, local and long-distance telephone service, wireless communications, and more — from one source, Continental Cablevision.

249. Continuum Co. Inc.
9500 Arboretum Blvd.
Austin, TX 78759
Phone: (512) 345-5700

Continuum Co. Inc. (NYSE; CNU) is a leading international supplier of software solutions and related services to the insurance industry.

Slogan: "Solutions to Insurance Challenges Through Technology and Partnership."

Statements: The company's objective is to be the leading business partner for the provision of superior quality technology-based solutions to meet the needs of the global insurance industry.

Continuum's rapid growth over the last two years is part of an ongoing strategy to expand the company's capabilities and market presence as appropriate opportunities are identified. In pursuing these opportunities, Continuum has retained its focus on the insurance industry and complementary markets.

Long-term vision: Building on Success.

Continuum's long-term vision has enabled the company to build on its success, strengthen its industry leadership and extend new capabilities to its customers.

Continuum will continue to develop and promote a vision of the future of technology in insurance. Drawing on its industry and technical expertise, the company will help its customers exploit technology to continually redefine and improve their companies.

250. Con-Way Transportation Services Inc.
2882 Sand Hill Rd.
Menlo Park, CA 94025
Phone: (415) 854-7500

Con-Way Transportation Services Inc., a subsidiary of Consolidated Freightways Inc. (NYSE; CNF), is involved in regional trucking and international shipping.

Mission Statement: The Con-Way Transportation Services mission is to expand and diversify its transportation and support services, including LTL regional trucking, full truckload transportation, and international shipping.

Con-Way Transportation Services will balance short and long range objectives, optimize profitability, and develop dominant market position through product leadership and effective integration of human, capital and material resources.

Key Elements: People; service; capacity; technology; CFI support.

251. Cooper Industries Inc.
600 Travis
Suite 5800
Houston, TX 77210
Phone: (713) 739-5400
Web: http://www.cooperindustries.com

Cooper Industries Inc. (NYSE; CBE) is a manufacturing company. It makes automotive parts, electrical products, and hardware. Registered brand names include Champion spark plugs and Anco windshield wipers.

Our Fundamental Objectives: We remain committed to the following fundamental objectives:

To provide the best value delivered to our customers; to provide our shareholders with a superior investment over the long term; and, to do both of these things while performing as a responsible employer and good corporate citizen.

Our Basic Strategies: Among the basic strategies for accomplishing these objectives, we have identified the following:

Put customer satisfaction above all other criteria as the measure of manufacturing and product success; progressively improve return on investment through a carefully designed program of diversification, cost reduction and cash flow management; treat employees with fairness and respect; and, strive to be the kind of corporate citizen that people want to have in their communities.

252. Cooper Tire and Rubber Co.
701 Lima Ave.
Findlay, OH 45840
Phone: (419) 423-1321
Web: http://www.coopertire.com

Cooper Tire and Rubber Co. (NYSE; CTB) manufactures and markets rubber products, including radial tires.

Slogans: "Drive On." "Performance at Every Turn." "Your Next Set of Tires."

Creed: It was in 1926 that I. J. Cooper expressed our company's Business Creed with these words:

"It wouldn't be called a plan or a policy by a high powered modern business expert because it is not complicated enough. In fact, it is very simple. Our platform of business conduct has only three planks in it: Good merchandise, fair play, and a square deal.

"Good merchandise because it doesn't pay to make, sell or use an inferior article. Fair prices that satisfy the user, leave the dealer a profit and the maker with a margin to cover his labor, thought and investment. And a square deal to everyone, every time, because you can't beat a natural law and still progress and prosper."

253. (Adolph) Coors Brewing Co.
12th and Ford Sts.
Golden, CO 80401
Phone: (303) 279-6565

Adolph Coors Brewing Co. (NASDAQ; ACCOB) is the third largest brewer of beer in the U.S.—behind Anheuser-Busch and Miller Brewing. Coors product line include the following registered trade name: (Premium category) Original Coors, Coors Light, Coors Extra Gold, Coors Dry, Coors Cutter (non-alcohol), Coors Arctic Ice, Coors Arctic Ice Light, Coors Special Lager, Coors Red Light; (Popular category) Keystone, Keystone Light, Keystone Dry, Keystone Ice, Keystone Amber Light; (Economy/Value-Added) Shulers Lager, Shulers Light; (Specialty/Seasonal) Winterfest; (Specialty/ Import) Killian's Irish Red, Killian's Irish Brown Ale, Castlemaine XXXX, Steinlager, Cass Fresh.

Slogans: "Tap the Rockies." "Family of Fine Beers." "Keep It Movin'" "It's the Right Beer Now." "Beer Is Back." "The Last Real Beer." Zima—"A Few Degrees Cooler."

Responsible Serving and Hosting: Coors supports and promotes the sensible consumption of beer in appropriate settings and situations. Toward this end, Coors makes available point-of-sale materials that reinforce safe and healthy decisions. These responsible serving and hosting practices include verifying legal age of purchase, having adequate amounts of food available, serving both alcohol and non-alcohol beverages, promoting moderate consumption, encouraging designated drivers and offering alternative transportation to anyone who is impaired.

At Coors, we built our reputation by making the finest quality products. We pride ourselves on the care and attention we put into every malt beverage we brew.

We're also proud that our reputation for quality extends to how we advertise and sell our products, and the programs and policies we support to fight alcohol abuse. More than 80 million adult Americans drink beer. We're pleased that the vast majority do so responsibly. We also care about the small minority who don't.

Coors is recognized as a leader in the creation and support of educational programs that promote healthy lifestyles and prevent alcohol abuse.

Our Values: Our corporate philosophy can be summed up by the statement, "Quality in all we are and all we do." This statement reflects our total commitment to quality relationships with customers, suppliers, community, stockholders and each other. Quality relationships are honorable, just, truthful, genuine, unselfish, and reputable.

We are committed first to our customers for whom we must provide products and services of recognizably superior quality. Our customers are essential to our existence. Every effort must be made to provide them with the highest quality products and services at fair and competitive prices.

We are committed to build quality relationships with suppliers because we require the highest quality goods and services. Contracts and prices should be mutually beneficial to the company and the supplier and be honorably adhered to by both.

We are committed to improve the quality of life within our community. Our policy is to comply strictly with all local, state, and federal laws, with our Corporate Code of Conduct and to promote the responsible use of our products. We strive to conserve our natural resources and minimize our impact on the environment. We pay our fair tax share and contribute resources to enhance community life. We boldly and visibly support the free enterprise system and individual freedom within a framework which also promotes personal responsibility and caring for others.

We are committed to the long-term financial success of our stockholders through consistent dividends and appreciation in the value of the capital they have put at risk, Reinvestment in facilities, research and development, marketing and new business opportunities which provide long-term earnings growth take precedence over short-term financial optimization.

These values can only be fulfilled by quality people dedicated to quality relationships within our company. We are committed to provide fair compensation and a quality work environment that is safe and friendly. We value personal dignity. We recognize individual accomplishment and the success of the team. Quality relationships are built upon mutual respect, compassion and open communication among all employees. We foster personal and professional growth and development without bias or prejudice and encourage wellness in body, mind, and spirit for all employees.

Be Truly Customer Focused: To be successful in the beer industry today, Coors must be as good at selling beer as we are at making it. To do that, we are focusing on serving our customers, with a renewed emphasis on the retailers who sell our products and the consumers who buy them. It is essential that we get closer to our customers so that we anticipate their needs and act quickly to meet them.

Financial Review: Coors' overall financial goal is to achieve consistent growth in profitability and shareholder value. The key to reaching this goal is better management of our resources, which includes building stronger, appropriate financial processes and disciplines.

Priorities: Do great beer, be truly customer focused and make money.

254. COR Therapeutics Inc.
256 E. Grand Ave.
South San Francisco, CA 94080
Phone: (415) 244-6800

COR Therapeutics Inc. (NASDAQ, CORR) is a company focused on the discovery, development, and commercialization of novel products that address severe diseases of the heart and circulatory system.

Statements: Our research has focused on advancing the basic understanding of the molecular and cellular mechanisms underlying the development of cardiovascular diseases. This targeted scientific strategy, when combined with the company's multidisciplinary approach to drug discovery and design, has resulted in the identification of novel molecules with the potential to treat a range of cardiovascular disorders, including complications associated with coronary angioplasty, unstable angina, acute myocardial infarction, stroke, and deep vein thrombosis.

We have moved closer to our ultimate goal: Leadership in the research, development, and marketing of novel cardiovascular therapeutics.

255. CoreStates Financial Corp.
PNB Bldg.
Broad & Chestnut Sts.
Philadelphia, PA 19107
Phone: (215) 973-3827
Web: http://www.corestates.com

CoreStates Financial Corp. (NYSE; CFL) is involved in banking, consumer financial services, and investment management.

Mission Statement: Our mission is to create long-term value for our stakeholders — shareholders, customers, employees, and the communities in which we operate. CoreStates creates value by designing and delivering quality products and services that are responsive to our customers' requirements. We emphasize business lines that generate high returns on equity and strong income growth. Our employees are our most valued strategic advantage. Our employees are crucial to the development and effective delivery of high quality customer-driven products. We follow strict standards of financial integrity, manage within prudent risk parameters, and operate under the highest ethical and moral principles. The corporation has a deep commitment to the communities in which we operate. We support and encourage our employees who share that commitment to give of themselves in the communities where they live and work.

256. Corning Inc.
One Riverfront Plaza
Houghton Park
Corning, NY 14831
Phone: (607) 974-9000
Web: http://www.corning.com

Corning Inc. (NYSE; GLW) manufactures and markets glass and glass products, including optical fiber.

Statement: Our values, quality, people … these must come first. Performance follows — it is a result of putting our customers and employees first.

Our Purpose: Our purpose is to deliver superior, long-range economic benefits to our customers, our employees, our shareholders, and the communities in which we operate. We accomplish this by living our corporate values.

Our Strategy: Corning is an evolving network of wholly owned and jointly owned businesses which owes its continued existence to shared values, core competence in science and technology, and an unending spirit of innovation in all aspects of our corporate life.

Corning will focus on four strategies that will enable the corporation to reach its long-term financial goals:

Growth markets: Invest aggressively in growing markets in which we are or expect to be #1 or #2 and in which we are the high-quality, low-cost supplier. These markets are: Communications, environment, life sciences.

Traditional businesses: Manage our traditional businesses for cash to support these growth investments.

Core science and technology: Nurture our science and technology so that it drives our growth markets and also creates as-yet undefined future opportunities.

Corporate investments: Hold our investments in Dow Corning and Pittsburgh Corning for optimal growth and cash generation over time.

Our corporate network adds value to its component parts through our company's name and reputation, a common dedication to our core values, a coherent overall strategy, and shared financial and human resources.

Our Values: We have a set of enduring beliefs that are ingrained in the way we think and act. These values guide our choices, defining for us the right courses of action, the clearest directions, the preferred responses. Consistent with these values we set our objectives, formulate our strategies, and judge our results. By living these values we will achieve our purpose.

Quality: Total quality is the guiding principle of Corning's business life. It requires each of us, individually and in teams, to understand, anticipate, and surpass the expectations of our customers. Total quality demands continuous improvement in all our processes, products, and services. Our success depends on our ability to learn from experience, to embrace change, and to achieve the full involvement of all our employees.

Integrity: Integrity is the foundation of Corning's reputation. We have earned the respect the trust of people around the world through more than a century of behavior that is honest, decent, and fair. Such behavior must continue to characterize all our relationships, both inside and outside the Corning network.

Performance: Providing Corning shareholders a superior long-term return on their investment is a business imperative. This requires that we allocate our resources to ensure profitable growth, maintain an effective balance between today and tomorrow, deliver what we promise, and tie our own rewards directly to our performance.

Leadership: Corning is a leader, not a follower. Our history and our culture impel us to seek a leadership role in our markets, our multiple technologies, our manufacturing processes, our management practices, and our financial performance. The goods and services we produce are never merely ordinary and must always be truly useful.

Innovation: Corning leads primarily by technical innovation and shares a deep belief in the power of technology. The company has a history of great contributions in science and technology, and it is the same spirit of innovation that has enabled us to create new products and new markets, to introduce new forms of corporate organization, and to seek new levels of employee participation. We embrace the opportunities inherent in change, and we are confident of our ability to help shape the future.

Independence: Corning cherishes — and will defend — its corporate freedom. That independence is our historic foundation. It fosters the innovation and initiative that has made our company great, and will continue to provide inspiration and energy to all parts of our network in the future.

The Individual: We know that in the end the commitment and contribution of all our employees will determine our success. Corning believes in the fundamental dignity of the individual. Our network consists of a rich mixture of people of diverse nationality, race, gender, and opinion, and this diversity will continue to be a source of our strength. We value the unique ability of each individual to contribute fully, to grow professionally, and to develop to his or her highest potential.

Performance Goals: We will be consistently in the top 25 percent of the Fortune 500 in financial performance as measured by return on equity and long-term growth in earnings per share.

257. Cott Corp.

207 Queen's Quay W.
Toronto, Ontario
Canada M5J 1A7
Phone: (416) 203-3898

Cott Corp. (NASDAQ; COTTF) is a leading supplier of retailer-branded beverages in the soft drink and water industry.

Beliefs and Guiding Principles: Cott's over-arching goal is to build a people-sensitive, energized organization with a capability for sustained high performance. The following beliefs are the basis on which the company has developed and will continue to grow.

Partnership: Cott is committed to a philosophy of partnership and to sharing the benefits of success with those who help Cott grow. These two ideas guide strategic decisions as well as day-to-day interaction with customers, suppliers, business partners, and shareholders.

Innovation and flexibility: We see innovation and flexibility as integral parts of the manufacturing and marketing process, critical to Cott's vitality. We will work collaboratively with our customers and suppliers to develop truly valued products and services, and constantly encourage employees to search for new and better ways to achieve our goals.

People: Our strength and ability for sustained growth are based on the idea that people are our single most important

asset. We will seek out the best, and work to create a culture which is high performance, developmental and caring about the aspirations, needs, and well being of each one of our employees.

Providing customers and consumers with more for less: We believe we will be successful as long as we can do more for our customers and consumers than competing national brands. As such, we will be relentless in our efforts to provide value-priced products and services which delight shoppers and enhance retailer profitability.

Community support: We have a responsibility to contribute to communities in which we operate by creating quality employment, by protecting the environment, and by doing our share to support community service organizations.

258. Countrywide Credit Industries Inc.

155 North Lake Ave.
Pasadena, CA 91101
Phone: (818) 304-8400
Web: http://www.countrywide.com

Countrywide Credit Industries Inc. (NYSE; CCR) is the nation's leading residential mortgage lender and servicer. A variety of complementary financial products and services augments the company's mortgage lending and servicing operations.

Slogan: "Easy. Really."

Statements: Countrywide has achieved industry leadership by continually streamlining the mortgage process. The goal is to provide consumers with better service and their lowest cost loan alternative. Streamlining mortgage transactions involves eliminating unnecessary "friction" in the process. This friction is principally caused by unneeded intermediaries that drive consumer costs up and erode service levels.

Countrywide intends to be the consumers' lender of choice. Providing consumers with the best service and their lowest cost loan alternative will earn their business.

The company's strategy is concentrated on three components of its business: Loan production, loan servicing, and businesses ancillary to mortgage lending. The company intends to continue its efforts to increase its market share of, and realize increased income from, its loan production. In addition, the company is engaged in building its loan servicing portfolio because of the returns it can earn from such investment. Finally, the company is involved in business activities complementary to its mortgage banking business, such as acting as agent in the sale of homeowners, fire, flood, earthquake, mortgage life, and disability insurance to its mortgagors, brokering servicing rights and selling odd-lot and other mortgage-backed securities.

259. Cox Enterprises Inc.
1400 Lake Hearn Dr.
Atlanta, GA 30319
Phone: (404) 843-5000
Web: http://www.cimedia.com/coxsites.html

Cox Enterprises Inc., a private company, is in the newspaper (Cox Newspapers), TV and radio broadcasting (Cox Broadcasting), cable television (Cox Communications), and auction (Manheim Auctions) businesses. Cox and The Times Mirror Company merged their cable operations on February 1, 1995, creating a new public company, Cox Communications (NYSE; COX). Cox Enterprises maintains approximately 80% ownership of the company.

Statement: Cox is rooted firmly in our core businesses and committed to offering customers a new world of services. By harnessing years of expertise and maintaining the pioneering spirit of our founder, we're building a bright future on a firm foundation.

Company Values: Cox Enterprises is positioned to meet the challenges of the future with an operating philosophy based on these principles. Our employees are the company's most important resource. We encourage individual initiative and entrepreneurship at every level. We value and reward achievement. Our customers are the company's lifeblood. We are dedicated to building lasting relationships with them and to meeting their needs with high-quality service beyond their expectations. We embrace new technology to give our customers the variety and quality of services they demand. We invest in new business opportunities, with a mixture of caution and initiative, to enhance our growth. We believe it's good business to be good citizens of the communities we serve through volunteerism and financial support. We are committed to helping shape a better world. We do this by using our media to educate the public about important issues, such as the environment, and through responsible company and individual actions.

260. CPI Corp.
1706 Washington Ave.
St. Louis, MO 63103
Phone: (314) 231-1575
Web: http://www.cpicorp.com

CPI Corp. (NYSE; CPY) is a leader in two segments of the photography industry — preschool portrait photography and one-hour photofinishing. Other business segments include the sale of value-priced posters, prints, and frames, and a chain of high-tech copy stores offering a range of electronic imaging services.

Philosophy: Over CPI's retailing history of more than 50 years, a focused management philosophy has evolved consisting of: Pursuit of market leadership; innovative marketing programs; partnering with leaders in retailing and technology; performance incentives for top managers; and reinvestment of cash flows to support growth initiates.

Business Philosophy: The depth of experience and leadership skills of senior management are focused on producing long-term results for CPI. Although the company has seen profits decline over the past three years, actions were taken in the context of maintaining market leadership and improving its competitive advantage — both aimed at generating sustainable growth in earnings per share. Strong cash flows continue to be a cornerstone of CPI's program to produce higher returns to shareholders through a combination of expansion and acquisitions.

Statement: CPI will continue to pursue new avenues of growth in high-margin consumer businesses which are: Responsible to promotional marketing; expandable on a broad geographic scale; operated as small retail units; controllable with system-wide monitoring; and focused on high value-added services.

261. Cracker Barrel Old Country Store Inc.

P.O. Box 787
Hartman Dr.
Lebanon, TN 37088
Phone: (615) 444-5533

Cracker Barrel Old Country Store Inc. (NASDAQ; CBRL) operates restaurants primarily near interstate interchanges in Tennessee, Georgia, Indiana, Kentucky, Florida, North Carolina, Ohio, Illinois, South Carolina, Alabama, Virginia, Missouri, Michigan, Mississippi, West Virginia, Wisconsin, Louisiana, Texas, Iowa, Oklahoma, Kansas, Minnesota, and Pennsylvania. The stores feature down-home atmosphere and country cooking. Gift shops have been a part of each store, featuring American reproductions of products and old fashioned candies, jellies, and foods.

Philosophy: 100% guest satisfaction.

Statement: As we look toward the future, we are mindful of what has brought us this far — offering our guests an enjoyable dining experience at a reasonable price. As it has been since our beginning, our attempt is to preserve a part of our past by serving good food characteristic of rural America, at reasonable prices, in friendly environments. This is what we

will continue to provide at the Cracker Barrel.

262. Crane Plastics Co. LP

2141 Fairwood Ave.
P.O. Box 1047
Columbus, OH 43207
Phone: (614) 443-4891

Crane Plastics Co., LP, a private company, manufactures plastic products.

Our Philosophy: Our customers and suppliers: We believe that our first responsibility is to provide state-of-the-art plastic extruded products which exceed our customers' quality expectations at competitive prices, delivered on time, every time. We will explore new technologies to anticipate and satisfy customer needs. Customers' orders will be serviced promptly and accurately. We will constantly strive to reduce costs and eliminate waste. We will treat our suppliers and distributors openly and fairly, and encourage them to join us as partners in business.

Our communities: We are responsible to the communities in which we live and work. We will actively contribute to the economic and social well-being of our community. We believe it is important to encourage civic improvements and better health and education. We will maintain in good order the property we use and recognize our duty to operate as an environmentally responsible citizen.

Our company: Our final responsibility is to make a fair profit. We will experiment with new ideas and develop new products and innovative programs. We will maintain the quality and condition of our equipment and facilities and, where necessary, additional equipment and facilities will be provided. We will exercise financial responsibility to provide for adverse times. We believe adhering to these principles will allow the owners, employees, and the community to share in the company's success.

263. Crestar Financial Corp.

Crestar Center
919 E. Main St.
Richmond, VA 23219
Phone: (804) 782-5000

Crestar Financial Corp. (NYSE; CF) is a holding company for three bank subsidiaries operating in Virginia, the District of Columbia, and Maryland, plus mortgage banking, insurance, investment management, and securities-related subsidiaries.

Our Vision: The name Crestar Financial Corporation should call to mind a financial services organization that consistently performs on a par with the best institutions in the nation.

Our Mission: The mission of Crestar Financial Corporation is to provide a broad array of financial products and services at a price that represents the best value for our customers' money, and, by doing so, to provide a superior return for our shareholders.

Our Strategy: To pursue our vision and carry out our mission Crestar Financial Corporation will:

Use our organizational strength — our strong branch network, superb technology and deep pool of talented and skilled people, willing and able to work together — to tap opportunities within our markets.

Offer the best products — products that meet and exceed the expectations of our customers and are better than those offered by our competitors.

Provide the best service quality — characterized by convenience, speed and an upbeat attitude.

Ensure that our customers are getting the best price for value and work hard to keep it that way.

Keep our cost structure low to provide our customers with superior price for value and our shareholders with the best possible return on their investments.

Statement: Central to Crestar's business approach is a concerted emphasis on service quality and a commitment to contribute to the economic vitality of the communities in which it operates.

264. Crompton & Knowles Corp.

One Station Place
Metro Center
Stamford, CT 06902
Phone: (203) 353-5400

Crompton & Knowles Corp. (NYSE; CNK) is a producer and marketer of specialty chemicals and equipment. The company is a major producer and marketer of dyes and specialty food and pharmaceutical ingredients, extrusion systems, industrial blow molding equipment, and related electronic controls for the plastics industry.

Statements: Crompton & Knowles has gained leadership positions in its chosen markets by providing quality products, technical service and performance know-how to solve problems and add value to customers' products.

In the final analysis, our fundamental objectives have not changed. We remain committed to managing the corporation for the enhancement of shareholder value. We have accomplished a great deal this year to assure above-average growth for the future. Our confidence is supported by the continuing commitment of our employees to deliver superior services, technology, and performance to our customers.

265. (A. T.) Cross Co.

One Albion Rd.
Lincoln, RI 02865
Phone: (401) 333-1200

A. T. Cross Co. (AMEX; ATXA) manufactures and markets fine writing instruments.

Vision Statement: At A. T. Cross we are committed to achievement at all levels, insisting that our products and services be of the highest quality and encouraging active participation by all employees and suppliers in achieving our objectives. Through this steadfast commitment, and inspired by our unique heritage, we will be able to succeed by any standard. We are committed to the continuing growth of market share and profitability worldwide. These goals can only be achieved by reaching the highest levels of customer satisfaction and by creating an atmosphere where both teamwork and personal growth can flourish.

266. Crown Cork & Seal Co. Inc.
9300 Ashton Rd.
Philadelphia, PA 19136
Phone: (215) 698-5100

Crown Cork & Seal Co. Inc. (NYSE; CCK) manufactures and sells metal and plastic containers, crowns, aluminum and plastic closures and the building of filling, packaging and handling machinery.

Statements: Our dedication to improving productivity and return on investment will ensure the most favorable results possible as we confront the challenges ahead.

The company's Code of Ethics continues to demand the highest standards from employees. Our employees, worldwide, have continued to actively embrace total-quality management and the results of this, along with the continued development of statistical process control in our manufacturing systems, has been favorably commented on by our customers.

267. CSX Corp.
901 E. Cary St.
Richmond, VA 23219
Phone: (804) 782-1400
Web: http://www.csx.com

CSX Corp. (NYSE; CSX) is a transportation company.

Mission Statement: CSX is a transportation company committed to being a leader in railroad, inland water, and containerized distribution markets.

To attract the human and financial resources necessary to achieve this leadership position, CSX will support our three major constituencies:

For our customers, we will work as a partner to provide excellent service by meeting all agreed-upon commitments.

For our employees, we will create a work environment that motivates and allows them to grow and develop and perform their jobs to the maximum of their capacity.

For our shareholders, we will meet our goals to provide them with sustainable superior returns.

CSX Values Statement: The primary responsibility of every CSX employee is to serve customers in the spirit of partnership in order to understand and satisfy their needs.

We must provide quality execution on a consistent basis over the long-term through:

An organization that values its employees and respects their dignity.

A commitment to teamwork, openness, and candor.

A commitment to increased quality and continuous improvement.

Increased empowerment and personal accountability.

A commitment to ethical conduct.

A willingness to innovate and change in well-planned ways that yield a competitive advantage.

A sense of urgency and bias for action.

Only by carrying out these values will CSX be able to fulfill our ultimate responsibility to provide satisfactory returns to our shareholders.

Criteria for Success: CSX believes that the corporation's success is tied directly to the success of our employees. Therefore, it is important that every employee of CSX function as a member of the CSX team to:

Serve our customers with concern and commitment.

Support and execute the company's mission.

Personally practice the CSX values.

Be knowledgeable about the industries in which we operate and use that knowledge to anticipate changes that CSX must make to provide a high level of excellent service by meeting all agreed-upon commitments.

Value company assets as one's own.

Demonstrate an ability and willingness to go beyond planned requirements.

Take personal responsibility to act in the company's best interests.

268. Cubic Corp.

9333 Balboa Ave.
P.O. Box 85587
San Diego, CA 92186
Phone: (619) 277-6780
Web: http://www.cubic.com

Cubic Corp. (AMEX; CUB) was founded as an electronics firm. Today it is the parent company to two major segments: The Cubic Automatic Revenue Collection Group and the Cubic Defense Group. The Cubic Automatic Revenue Collection Group designs and manufactures automatic revenue collection systems for public mass transit projects throughout the world including rail, buses, bridges, tunnels, toll roads, and parking lots.

The Cubic Defense Group provides instumented training systems for the U.S. Army, Air Force, and Navy, as well as avionics, data links, aerospace systems, and product logistical support. This group also provides battle command training, radio communication systems, and field service operation and maintenance.

Mission Statement: Provide state of the art customized combat training systems and electronic products to customers worldwide, while actively insuring customer satisfaction and the highest possible system and product quality.

Values: Fulfillment of our Mission requires development and cultivation of these basic values:

People: Our most valuable asset and our competitive edge.

Quality: Our first priority in everything we do.

Customers: Our goal is to create satisfied customers inside as well as outside Cubic Defense Systems.

Ethics: Our actions will evidence CDS's high standards of personal and professional integrity to foster truth in what we say and trust in what we promise.

Teamwork: Our greatest accomplishments are possible only when we work together.

Vision: The best today, may not be the best tomorrow ... therefore we must continuously refocus our vision. We all must:

Understand that people are our most valuable asset.

Continuously seek to improve quality, reduce cost, meet commitments.

Apply the principles of management by planning, continuous process improvement, new quality technology, empowerment.

269. CUC International Inc.

P.O. Box 10049
707 Summer St.
Stamford, CT 06904
Phone: (203) 324-9261
Web: http://www.cuc.com

CUC International Inc. (NYSE; CU) is a provider of membership-based discount services.

Goal: Our goal is to make our products and services even more accessible to a broad range of consumers through both global expansion and our support of newest delivery technologies.

Statements: We founded this company to create value by bringing products and services directly from the manufacturer and distributor to the consumer.

Today, our vision of technology-driven retailing is coming true.

270. Culp Inc.

101 S. Main St.
High Point, NC 27261
Phone: (910) 889-5161

Culp Inc. (NASDAQ; CULP) is a supplier to the upholstery fabric, mattress ticking, and specialty fabric markets.

Corporate Mission Statement: By utilizing our resources as effectively as possible, our mission at Culp is to be the leading supplier to the upholstery fabric, mattress ticking, and specialty fabric markets. We dedicate ourselves to these fundamental principles:

To promote an environment of mutual trust and to recognize the value that each associate contributes to our success.

To understand the needs of our customers and the markets that we serve.

To design, manufacture and market products which consistently meet our customers' requirements.

To fulfill Culp's role as a corporate citizen.

To produce a reasonable profit which provides growth and job security.

271. Cummins Engine Co. Inc.

500 Jackson St.
Columbus, IN 47201
Phone: (812) 377-5000
Web: http://www.cummins.com

Cummins Engine Co. Inc. (NYSE; CUM) is a designer and manufacturer of diesel engines — ranging from 76 to 2,000 horsepower. Key markets include heavy-duty trucks, midrange trucks, power generators, bus and light commercial vehicles, industrial products, etc. Additionally, the company produces strategic components and subsystems critical to the engine, including filters, turbochargers and electronic control systems.

Statements: Our customer-led Quality program with the objective of being known by everyone who comes in contact with Cummins as the leader in "quality," "innovation," and "integrity." These traits made us successful in the past and will ensure that we meet the challenges and capitalize on the opportunities of the future.

We are committed to providing our customers with a comparative advantage in each of our markets worldwide, measured in product performance, economic value to the customer and all aspects of customer support. Comparative advantage is a customer term. The customer compares the value received from Cummins with that from other potential suppliers. Achieving a comparative advantage requires that we be proactive in understanding our customers' needs, involve all our people in seeking out and using best practices and pursue continuous improvement for each customer.

The key to our success is helping our customers be successful, not simply supplying them with quality engines. Increasingly, the value we bring to customers can be described as smart power, which is a value-added package of products, information systems and support services that provides improved performance and business solutions for our customers. The electronic and computing capabilities of our engines are what permit us to step up value to our customers.

The second goal of Customer-led Quality is to achieve a 15-percent average return on equity over each business cycle.

We are committed to providing a superior return to our shareholders. Meeting our return-on-equity objective will require that we grow, on average, in double digit percentages. There are several facets to our growth strategy.

First we continue to expand our current business base through internal growth, strategic alliances and acquisitions. Second, we continue to seek opportunities to broaden our engine product line into both lower and higher horsepower engines. Third, as global emissions standards become increasingly more stringent, we have an opportunity to work with integrated original equipment manufacturers to provide them with Cummins engines.

272. Curtiss-Wright Corp.

1200 Wall St. West — Suite 501
Lyndhurst, NJ 07071
Phone: (201) 896-8400

Curtiss-Wright Corp. (NYSE; CW) is a manufacturing company in the aerospace, industrial, and marine markets.

Strategic Intent: The growth objective of Curtiss-Wright goes beyond the realization of higher sales and profitability levels. Our growth objective includes the expansion of our technologies and core competencies to new markets. Our success will be dependent on the organization's ability to identify and seize the "Wright" opportunities, when and where they occur. This will be accomplished by focusing on those key factors which we have identified as most crucial.

We must strive for recognition by our customers as the technological leader and innovator in our chosen markets based upon the core competencies that we have developed. This must be done in combination with the establishment of "partnership" relationships with our customers to be in a position to effectively provide the solutions to their needs. We must realize that their problems are also our problems and their successes in becoming more competitive have a direct relationship to the long-term successes of Curtiss-Wright.

Curtiss-Wright's achievements can only be the result of the dedication and involvement of our people. To foster and encourage such involvement, it is necessary that the company provides its people with opportunities for growth and that there be a commonly-held view that our objectives can be best realized through the efforts of the team. The team concept can succeed only in an atmosphere of mutual trust and cooperation among the people of Curtiss-Wright and the company and through the realization that as one team member benefits, all benefit. Curtiss-Wright must insure that such an atmosphere exists and that recognition of its people is a commitment of the company.

273. Cygne Designs Inc.
1372 Broadway
New York, NY 10018
Phone: (212) 354-6474

Cygne Designs Inc. (NASDAQ; CYDS) is a private label designer, merchandiser and manufacturer of women's and men's apparel.

Statement: The company believes it has developed a strong reputation for its ability to identify, gauge and respond to changing consumer demands and fashion trends in fabrics and style. Cygne has conceived a customer-dedicated team strategy which, it believes, best addresses its customers' needs by combining an intimate knowledge of each customer's distinctive culture with creativity and marketing aggressiveness of an outside resource. Cygne believes that its primary point of competitive differentiation is its broad design and merchandising expertise combined with its ability to manufacture with short lead times, thus affording customers the flexibility to respond to shifts in consumer buying patterns. In the company's view, this combination, supported by strong technical and sample-making capabilities, sets Cygne apart from most private label manufacturers, which primarily only arrange for the production of styles specified by customers.

274. Cygnus Inc.
400 Penobscot Dr.
Redwood City, CA 94063
Phone: (415) 369-4300

Cygnus Inc. (NASDAQ; CYGN) researches, develops and manufactures delivery systems for drug, consumer and diagnostic products that improve therapies and health care.

Purpose: Our expertise is in applying physical, biological and engineering disciplines to create innovative, high quality, cost effective products in the shortest time possible.

Our passion is to improve health care and help reduce its cost, thereby improving the quality of life and well-being for people throughout the world.

Our mission is to develop and produce products that meet or exceed customer expectations by working closely with them to rapidly create products of uncompromised quality.

Our goal is to become the acknowledged worldwide leader in drug delivery markets in which we compete.

275. Cyprus Amax Minerals Co.
9100 East Mineral Circle
Englewood, CO 80155
Phone: (303) 643-5000

Cyprus Amax Minerals Co. (NYSE; CYM) is in the mining industry.

Slogan: "Passion Defines the Difference Between Mediocrity and Brilliance."

Vision: Cyprus Amax Minerals seeks to be the most admired company in the mining industry.

We will be one of the lowest cost, largest volume, highest quality finders and producers of target mineral and metal products.

We will utilize unusual and creative marketing, financial, managerial, and technological practices.

Results will create exceptional benefits and rewards for customers, shareholders, and employees.

We break down boundaries, we do it differently, quicker and better and we have more fun doing it!

276. Cyrix Corp.
2703 N. Central Expwy.
Richardson, TX 75080
Phone: (214) 968-8388
Web: http://www.cyrix.com

Cyrix Corp. (NASDAQ; CYRX) designs and markets high-performance processors for the personal computer industry.

Slogan: "Advancing the Standards."

Mission: The company's mission is to become the leading supplier of products that continually advance the standards of technology.

Cyrix has a singular mission — to build x86 microprocessors that deliver the speed and performance our customers need to run today's business and consumer software faster. With our rapid design approach and our "get it right the first time" attitude, Cyrix aggressively competes at the leading edge of microprocessor technology.

Goal: Cyrix has one goal — to enhance our customers' effectiveness in the marketplace.

277. CYTOGEN Corp.
600 College Road East CN 5308
Princeton, NJ 08540
Phone: (609) 987-8200
Web: http://www.cytogen.com

CYTOGEN Corp. (NASDAQ; CYTO) provides pharmaceutical products, technologies, and services that benefit cancer patients and others.

Slogans: "Setting New Standards in Cancer Care." "Looking Cancer in the Eye with Better Products to Diagnose and Treat Disease."

Mission Statement: We will deliver value and earn trust by providing quality pharmaceutical products, technologies, and services that benefit patients with cancer and other diseases.

278. Dain Bosworth Inc.
60 South 6th St.
Minneapolis, MN 55402
Phone: (612) 371-2711

Dain Bosworth Inc., a subsidiary of Inter-Regional Financial Group Inc. (NYSE; IFG), is a full-service brokerage and investment banking firm.

Mission: The mission of Dain Bosworth is to understand and achieve the investment and capital formation objectives of its clients.

Vision for the '90s: The people who comprise Dain Bosworth are committed to being the finest regional brokerage and investment banking firm in America. Our commitment to our goals and guiding beliefs will earn clients' trust and confidence, employees' pride, communities' respect, and increased shareholder value.

Special focus on unique markets within our region will allow us to align ourselves closely with the differing needs of each client. We will concentrate on our core businesses, providing appropriate investments to our individual and institutional clients, and investment banking services to our corporate and governmental clients.

Each client will do business with a firm that constantly seeks to understand his or her differing and changing objectives. Our clients are entitled to the very best we have to offer. Our products will be carefully selected and properly sold. Our high ethical standards will not be compromised for expedience or profit. We will be noted for professionalism, innovation, quality, competitiveness and fairness. We will earn each client's trust through performance and service.

Exceptional teamwork, driven by individual talent, will result from a single mind. We will work together to achieve each client's goals and to make each other successful. We will have fun being our best in a demanding and dynamic industry.

Employees will represent diverse skills, disciplines and ethnic backgrounds. We will treat each other with respect and will remain dedicated to providing each employee the opportunity to reach his or her potential, selecting tomorrow's leadership from our own ranks. To do so, we will maintain the finest training and development programs of any regional firm in our industry.

Communities will benefit from our financial support and from our employees volunteering time, energy and leadership to community efforts. It will be Dain Bosworth's way of saying thank you, as well as helping to develop the quality of life in the communities where we and our families live and work.

Our future will be founded in our regional firm philosophy. We will remain entrepreneurial and opportunistic within

strategic, financial and human resource parameters. We will seek benefit from the collective financial strength of our parent, Inter-Regional Financial Group, and our sister companies. Our broad employees ownership will ensure a tireless quest for shareholder value.

Shareholders will benefit from our growth, our outstanding performance and the value and reputation which Dain Bosworth has achieved.

We will relentlessly pursue this vision for our clients, each other, and ourselves.

279. Dana Corp.
P.O. Box 1000
Toledo, Ohio 43697
Phone: (419) 535-4500
Web: http://www.dana.com

Dana Corp. (NYSE; DCN) manufactures parts and systems for automobiles and trucks.

Slogan: "People Finding a Better Way."

Our Philosophy: People are our most important assist.

Our Purposes: The purpose of the Dana Corporation is to earn money for its shareholders and to increase the value of their investment. We believe the best way to do this is to earn an acceptable return by properly utilizing our assets and controlling our cash.

Growth: We believe in steady growth to protect our assets against inflation. We will grow in our selected markets by implementing our product and service strategies.

280. Danaher Corp.
1250 24th St., NW
Suite 800
Washington, DC 20037
Phone: (202) 828-0850

Danaher Corp. (NYSE; DHR) designs, manufactures and markets industrial and consumer products in two principle businesses: Tools and components and process/environmental controls.

Statement: The Danaher Business System, our operating philosophy, keeps re-validating itself. Our operating philosophy seeks to achieve world-class excellence in customer satisfaction. Our system begins with the voice of the customer and continually strives to improve quality, service, and cost.

281. Danka Business Systems PLC

11201 Danka Circle North
St. Petersburg, FL 33716
Phone: (813) 576-6003
Web: http://www.danka.com

Danka Business Systems PLC (NAS-DAQ; DANKY) is a large automated office equipment supplier in North America and the United Kingdom.

Statement: The company's strength lies in its deep commitment to service, backed by intensive training of its personnel. An outstanding service reputation has been a major factor in its phenomenal growth and has led to a level of customer loyalty that is among the highest in the industry.

282. Danmark International Inc.

7101 Winnetka Ave. North
Minneapolis, MN 55428
Phone: (612) 531-0066

Danmark International Inc. (NAS-DAQ; DMRK) is a membership-driven information-based national direct marketer of brand name and other general merchandise.

Slogan: "The Great Deal Company."

Goals and Strategies: Continued expansion of club membership through aggressive catalog mailings.

Expand the benefits of club membership through partnership growth.

Development of non-traditional sources of new club members.

Continued investment in systems and infrastructure.

Consistent and predictable results while achieving sales and earnings growth.

283. Data General Corp.

4400 Computer Dr.
Westboro, MA 01580
Phone: (508) 898-5000
Web: http://www.dg.com

Data General Corp. (NYSE; DGN) designs advanced systems, builds software alliances, and provides comprehensive integration services to design, implement, and support total computing solutions.

Slogan: "Bring Common Sense to Computing."

Statement: We focused on what we do best — hardware and systems software development — and leveraged our core technological strengths.

284. Dayton Hudson Corp.

777 N. Collet Mall
Minneapolis, MN 55402
Phone: (612) 370-6948
Web: http://www.shop-at.com

Dayton Hudson Corp. is in the retail merchandising industry.

Statement: We are committed to: Serving customers better than the competition, being a lower-cost distributor of merchandise, innovating to make continuous improvements, achieving consistent earnings growth, building strong partnerships with vendors and providing leadership through corporate giving and employee volunteerism in the communities we serve. As we fulfill these commitments, we provide shareholders with attractive returns.

285. Dean Foods Co.

3600 River Rd.
Franklin Park, IL 60131
Phone: (847) 678-1680
Web: http://www.birdseye.com

Dean Foods Co. (NYSE; DF) is a dairy and specialty foods processor.

Statements: Provide our customers with the highest quality products and service possible at a competitive price.

Reinvest in our plants and fleets to improve productivity and lower costs.

Treat our employees, suppliers and customers with respect, honesty and integrity.

Conduct our day-to-day operations on a decentralized basis with management decisions placed in the hands of local management wherever possible.

Stress teamwork, stable employment and hard work — the work ethic of our employees is one of our most valuable assets.

Communicate with local management through our profit planning system, the basis of our decentralized organization.

Maintain a balanced growth approach that welcomes newly acquired companies, but does not overlook internal growth opportunities.

Maintain a friendly, informal atmosphere where everyone's job is important and rewarding.

286. Dean Witter, Discover & Co.
2 World Trade Center
New York, NY 10048
Phone: (212) 392-2222
Web: http://www.
deanwitterdiscover.com

Dean Witter, Discover & Co. (NYSE; DWD) is a diversified financial services organization that provides a broad range of nationally marketed credit and investment products.

Slogan: "It Pays to Discover."

Statement: Our clients expect quality. For us, quality begins with the selection and training of the people who serve our clients. We work hard to instill the Dean Witter culture of always putting our clients' interests first.

287. (Edward J.) Debartolo Corp.
7620 Market St.
Youngstown, OH 44513
Phone: (303) 965-2072

Edward J. DeBartolo Corp. is a private company in the real estate business.

Fundamental Strategy: To realize the outstanding growth opportunities imbedded in its existing portfolio of properties. In conjunction with this primary focus, new development and acquisitions will be pursued on a selective basis.

288. Deere & Co.
John Deere Rd.
Moline, IL 61265
Phone: (309) 765-8000
Web: http://www.deere.com

Deere & Co. (NYSE; DE) manufactures farm and lawn care equipment.

Slogan: "Nothing Runs Like a Deere."

Business Conduct: Customer satisfaction: Our business exists because we provide products, either goods or services, that customers want to buy. This means that our products must respond to important customer needs, must represent superior value to the user, must be reliable, and must be supported by appropriate service.

Quality: Through our history, John Deere has earned a reputation for high quality in everything we do, and this has been an asset of incalculable value. We intend to continue to earn that reputation through the products and services we provide, our facilities, and our relationships with employees and people outside Deere.

Business relationships: Our relationships must be based on the concept of mutual advantage — that is, the relationship has to be a good one both for the other party and for the company.

Profits and focus: To survive, the company must maintain the profitability needed to ensure investor confidence and attract future equity capital. Profits are a measure of how efficiently we are doing our job, how well we are meeting the needs of our customers, and how wisely we are directing our effort and investment. We intend to focus our business on the things we do best, choosing and developing products and business where we have, or can create, a sustainable competitive advantage.

289. DEKALB Genetics Corp.
3100 Sycamore Rd.
DeKalb, IL 6115
Phone: (815) 758-3461
Web: http://www.dekalb.com

DEKALB Genetics Corp. (NASDAQ; SEEDB) develops hybrid seeds for farmers, including seed corn.

Mission: To provide our customers with quality products and services that will increase their productivity and profitability.

290. Delchamps Inc.
305 Delchamps Dr.
Mobile, AL 36602
Phone: (334) 433-0431

Delchamps Inc. (NASDAQ; DLCH) operates a chain of supermarkets.

Slogans: "Still the Low Price Leader Overall." "Your Super Market."

Statement: The management focus at Delchamps is to increase sales and profit. To accomplish our task, we will continue to emphasize the absolute need to win in the areas our customers deem most important: Low prices, fresh top quality perishables, improved variety, improved check-out service, and dependability.

291. Deluxe Corp.
3680 Victoria St. North
Shoreview, MN 55126
Phone: (612) 483-7111
Web: http://www.deluxe.com

Deluxe Corp. (NYSE; DLX) prints checks and related products, provides electronic funds transfer processing ser-

vices and software, and offers ATM card services, account verification services, and sales development services.

Our Corporate Goals: Our corporate goals consist of: Satisfying the needs of our customers; providing meaningful work for our employees; producing a quality return to our shareholders; and preserving the health of our business.

Our Mission: Our mission is to serve our customers as the best supplier of products and services in the markets we serve.

292. Dexter Corp.
One Elm St.
Windsor Locks, CT 06096
Phone: (860) 627-9051

Dexter Corp. (NYSE; DEX) is a world class manufacturer.

Our Vision: The Dexter Corporation will be the technological leader and supplier of choice in each of our served markets and will be a $2 billion company in the year 2000.

Our Mission: The Dexter Corporation is a unique specialty materials company that uses proprietary technology to succeed in defined segments of five strategic global markets. We are committed to operating excellence and continuous improvement to provide customers with responsible, innovative and cost-effective solutions to their specialty material needs and will leverage our resources throughout the corporation to do so. We will be recognized as an environmentally pro-active corporation that rewards talented and dedicated employees and satisfied shareholder expectations for earnings growth.

Our Beliefs: We are all employed to serve our customers.

We are focused on markets which recognize and reward superior quality of products and services.

Our company is composed of strong people, skilled in their work who treat each other with dignity and respect.

We recognize and reward distinguished performance.

We will communicate openly without fear or threat.

We are a decentralized organization that encourages an entrepreneurial attitude and technical innovation.

We are committed to total quality in everything we do.

We differentiate ourselves on the basis of proprietary technology and prompt, superior technical service.

We compete in global markets that require world class manufacturing processes.

We seek partnerships with suppliers and reward those that meet our quality standards.

We strive for continuous improvement in the safety of our operations.

We will work to safeguard the environment.

We will conduct our business with the highest standard of ethical behavior.

We will work to create steady growth in shareholder value.

We will be involved citizens in the communities in which we work and the world at large.

293. Diagnostic Products Corp.
5700 West 96th St.
Los Angeles, CA 90045
Phone: (213) 776-0180
Web: http://www.dpcweb.com

Diagnostic Products Corp. (NYSE; DP) is dedicated to immunodiagnostics and the manufacture of immunodiagnostic kits.

Statement: While DPC looks confidently toward a future of continuing growth and adaptation to the evolving world immunodiagnostics market, it also remains committed to offering a wide menu of the highest quality assays and technologies — the company's policy at its inception 25 years ago, and still its guiding principle.

294. Dial Corp.
1850 North Central Ave.
Phoenix, AZ 85004
Phone: (602) 207-2800

Dial Corp. (NYSE; DL) makes and markets consumer products, such as Dial soap, Breck shampoo, Purex detergent, Renuzit air fresheners, Brillo, and Armour Star food products.

Slogan: "Aren't You Glad You Use Dial? Don't You Wish Everybody Did?"

Mission: The Dial Corp. will strengthen stockholder value by providing high-quality consumer products and services that offer a superior price/value relationship to consumers.

295. Diebold Inc.
5995 Mayfair Rd.
North Canton, OH 44720
Phone: (330) 490-4000
Web: http://www.diebold.com

Diebold Inc. (NYSE; DBD) makes and markets ATM's and security and surveillance systems.

Mission Statement: Diebold and its associates have a common goal to meet customer requirements and to exceed their expectations in the markets we serve.

We provide quality security, self-service payment transactions and information solutions through state-of-the-art products, software, systems and service.

296. Digital Equipment Corp.
146 Main St.
Maynard, MA 01754
Phone: (508) 493-5111
Web: http://www.dec.com

Digital Equipment Corp. (NYSE; DEC) manufactures and markets computers, computer components, and software. The company is a leader in open client/server solutions from personal computers to integrated worldwide information systems.

Slogans: "Whatever It Takes." "Beyond the Box." "Don't Let Your Box Box You In." "Judge a Book by Its Coverage."

Statement: Digital has built strategic alliances with customers, other computer companies, systems integrators, and vendors to address the needs of a rapidly changing marketplace. Digital is fully invested in and clearly focused on understanding and responding to customer needs in every industry where it can add significant value and where it can offer services and products that help customers succeed.

297. Dillard Department Stores Inc.
1600 Cantrell Rd.
Little Rock, AR 72201
Phone: (501) 376-5200
Web: http://www.azstarnet.com/dillards

Dillard Department Stores Inc. (NYSE; DDS) operates a regional group of traditional department stores.

Statements: The corporation's philosophy continues to embrace an ambitious program of expansion and remodeling as well as aggressive responses to industry trends in merchandise and pricing.

Our goal is to increase our ability to solve problems before they become advantages for our competitors and to take advantage of opportunities before they become opportunities for someone else.

298. DiMon Inc.
512 Bridge St.
Danville, VA 24543
Phone: (804) 792-7511

DiMon Inc. (NYSE; DMN) is engaged in two businesses — purchasing, processing, packing, and storing tobacco and importing and distributing fresh-cut flowers.

Slogan: "Satisfying Our Global Customers with Source, Supply and Service."

Statement: We have to earn our customers' respect and confidence on a daily basis. We have to earn their business every day.

299. Dixie Group Inc.
1100 S. Watkins St.
Chattanooga, TN 37404
Phone: (423) 698-2501

Dixie Group Inc. (NASDAQ; DXYN), formerly Dixie Yarns, manufactures floor-covering and textile products.

Dixie's Vision: Dixie's vision is to provide value-added products and services to consumers through retail channels of distribution or to consumer-driven manufactures, within distinctly defined floor-covering, textile, and related markets where we can be important. We shall perform these endeavors profitably, with integrity, adhering to our company's values and with a sense of urgency and responsiveness to our associates and customers.

300. DNA Plant Technology Corp.
6701 San Pablo Ave.
Oakland, CA 94608
Phone: (510) 547-2395

DNA Plant Technology Corp. (NASDAQ; DNAP) is a biotechnology company focused on the development and marketing of fruits and vegetables developed through advanced breeding, genetic engineering, and other biotechniques.

Statement: The company's business strategy is to use its technology to develop and market what it believes are superior, differentiated products.

301. Dominion Resources Inc.
901 E. Byrd St.
Richmond, VA 23219
Phone: (804) 775-5700
Web: http://www.domres.com

Dominion Resources Inc. (NYSE; D) is a holding company in the electric utility business and the financial services and real estate businesses.

Statement: Our strategy is to ensure that we remain a low-cost, high performance industry leader.

302. Donaldson Co. Inc.
1400 W. 94th St.
Minneapolis, MN 55431
Phone: (612) 887-3131

Donaldson Co. Inc. (NYSE; DCI) is a manufacturer of filtration products.

Slogan: "Filtration Solutions for a Cleaner World."

Statement: Our primary financial objective is to achieve consistent earnings growth as the driver of shareholder value over the long term — building value through price appreciation and dividend income. Internal performance goals, consistent with this objective, have been established throughout the organization.

Donaldson Creed: We believe all of the people of the Donaldson Company should strive to conduct themselves in such a manner that the company and those associated with it will stand for:

Integrity in our dealings with customers, employees, shareholders, government authorities, suppliers, neighbors and the public.

Quality in our products and services, in our manufacturing methods and general management.

Technology in our particular fields of research, product development, engineering and manufacturing.

Growth in sales, profits and strength within our areas of special interest and competence.

Progress toward an environment where our people have increasing opportunities for contribution, fulfillment and reward.

Donaldson Pledge: As an environmentally and socially responsible corporation, the Donaldson Company complies with all environmental laws and regulations and actively promotes:

A management commitment to the development of enlightened environmental principles and their implementation throughout the organization.

Pollution prevention at its source and the responsible management of any residual waste.

Recycling of raw materials, finished products and other resources.

Conservation of energy and natural resources through prudent use and reuse.

A product development process which considers environmental impacts throughout the product's life cycle.

A corporate commitment to minimize the environmental, health, and safety risks in the workplace and community.

303. (R. R.) Donnelley & Sons Co.
77 W. Wacker Dr.
Chicago, IL 60601
Phone: (312) 326-8000
Web: http://www.donnelley.com

R. R. Donnelley & Sons Co. (NYSE; DNY) is a provider of printing and related services.

Our Mission: It is the mission of R. R. Donnelley & Sons Company to be a preeminent worldwide provider of printing and related information and value added services and products for owners, publishers, and users of information.

Our Basic Commitments: To our customers: We will provide services of superior quality and value. Customer satisfaction will be the paramount consideration in the performance of every aspect of our work.

To each other: Each of us is entitled to and will be treated with dignity and respect. We will deal fairly and openly with each other as individuals and provide fair and equal employment opportunities to all. Each of us must act with integrity and adhere to the highest standards of business ethics.

To our shareholders: We will strive to provide our shareholders with a consistently superior financial performance measured against other medium-to-large publicly held companies of any kind. Lawful conduct will be present in every aspect of our business.

To quality and excellence: Quality must permeate everything about our company. Quality of our services and products must be preeminent. We will lead in the research, development and implementation of new technology as it applies to the growth and betterment of our business.

To profit and growth: We will consistently increase our earnings and maintain a superior return on shareholders' equity. We will grow profitably in order to meet our responsibilities to employees, shareholders, and others with whom we deal.

To others: We will deal fairly and honorably with our suppliers. We will be a responsible corporate citizen in the communities in which we have facilities and in society in general.

304. Dow Chemical Co. Michigan Division
2030 Dow Center
Midland, MI 48674
Web: http://www.dow.com

Dow Chemical Co., Michigan Division is a subsidiary of Dow Chemical Co. (NYSE; DOW), a worldwide manufacturer and supplier of chemicals, plastics, energy, agricultural products, consumer goods, and environmental services,

Mission: Our mission as a premier, world-competitive Division is to develop and manufacture specialty products and provide services for our customers' success.

The Michigan Division driven by quality performance, is the preferred supplier to our customers. As a team, we work incident-free and are a welcomed neighbor in our communities.

Statement: "If you can't do it better, why do it?" — Herbert H. Dow set forth the direction and purpose of the exploration that followed.

Today, as The Dow Chemical Company enters its second century, it embraces the passion and spirit of its founder with a renewed focus on chemistry and the value it can bring to employees, customers, shareholders, and society. Through purposeful and strategic navigation, Dow's exploration continues to result in greater discoveries as we expand our horizons and reach for new heights.

305. Dow Jones & Co. Inc.
200 Liberty St.
New York, NY 10281
Phone: (212) 416-2000
Web: http://www.dowjones.com

Dow Jones & Co. Inc. (NYSE; DJ) is in the business of gathering and distributing useful information to business, investment, consumer, and educational markets.

Statement: Our chief objective is to serve the public exceedingly well with quality publications and services. In this endeavor, our skilled and dedicated employees are the company's greatest strength. Their successful efforts enhance respect for Dow Jones, the foundation on which our century-old business is based.

Success in meeting our main objective helps us fulfill our responsibility of servicing well the company's stockholders. Profitability, in turn, provides the resources to better serve the public through improved products and services.

306. DQE Inc.
500 Cherrington Pkwy.
Suite 100
Corapolis, PA 15108
Phone: (412) 262-4700
Web: http://www.dqe.com

DQE Inc. (NYSE; DQE) is in the electric energy industry.

Mission Statement: Our primary focus is to efficiently and effectively satisfy the needs and requirements of our customers through the commitment and personal involvement of all Duquesne Light people.

We will be a low cost producer and profitable supplier of electricity and electric services, recognized for excellence and quality, dedicated to the protection of the environment, and responsible for the delivery of safe and reliable electric energy.

307. Dreyer's Grand Ice Cream Inc.
5929 College Ave.
Oakland, CA 94618
Phone: (510) 652-8187
Web: http://www.dreyers.com

Dreyer's Grand Ice Cream Inc. (NASDAQ; DRYR) is a manufacturer and marketer of premium ice cream.

Slogan: "Evidently, It's Not Your Normal Ice Cream."

Our New Mission: Become the preeminent ice cream company in the United States by achieving The Grand Plan.

308. DSC Communications Corp.
1000 Colt Rd.
Plano, TX 75075
Phone: (972) 519-3000
Web: http://www.dsccc.com

DSC Communications Corp. (NASDAQ; DIGI) is a company in the telecommunications industry.

Statement: The network vision of DSC Communications Corporation is global and comprehensive. It envisions the emergence of a multimedia, full-service distributed network, where end users control the information to their businesses and residences.

As DSC moves into the future, its goal is to provide cost-effective, evolvable product lines that allow different types of information to move across interconnected networks using the equipment of different suppliers — in a way that is profitable for DSC customers and transparent to their end users. DSC is weaving together technology and service in order to fulfill the corporate commitment ... to innovative solutions, global vision.

309. Duke Power Co.
422 S. Church St.
Charlotte, NC 28242
Phone: (704) 594-0887
Web: http://www.dukepower.com

Duke Power Co. (NYSE; DUK) produces and supplies electricity and related products and services.

Our Shared Vision: We will be the supplier of choice by our customers, the employer of choice by our co-workers, and our communities, the investment of choice by our owners and the model of integrity and excellence for business and industry.

Our Mission: We produce and supply electricity, provide related products and services and pursue opportunities that complement our business. We will continually improve our products and services to better meet our customers' needs and expectations, helping our customers, employees, owners and communities to prosper.

310. Dun & Bradstreet Corp.
One Diamond Hill Rd.
Murray Hill, NJ 07974
Phone: (908) 665-5000
Web: http://www.dnbcorp.com

Dun & Bradstreet Corp. (NYSE; DNB) provides information, software, and services.

Statement: D&B's strategy for the future revolves around one constant: change.

Statement of Values: As the men and women who are The Dun & Bradstreet Corporation, we are a team — one company united through shared values relating to our ethics, customers, ourselves, and our shareowners.

Ethics: We will practice the highest standards of personal ethics and integrity so that in all our relationships we can have pride in ourselves and our company.

Customers: We will strive relentlessly to exceed our customers' expectations so that they will want to continue to do business with us.

Ourselves: We will respect and treat each other as individuals who want the opportunity to contribute and succeed. Each of us will be accountable for quality and continuous improvement in all we do. We will work to be the best.

Shareowners: We will accept our responsibility to be effective stewards of our shareowners' resources so that through our performance shareowners are properly rewarded for their investment in Dun & Bradstreet.

By our living and working in accordance with these values, everyone who is affected by our behavior will say of us, "Customer focus is how they do business."

311. (E. I.) DuPont de Nemours and Co.
1007 Market St.
Wilmington, DE 19898
Phone: (302) 774-1000
Web: http://www.dupont.com

E. I. DuPont de Nemours and Co. (NYSE; DD) manufactures and markets chemicals, petroleum, and natural gas. Its subsidiary, Conoco, markets gasoline and other refined petroleum products.

Slogan: "Better Things for Better Living."

Values: Uniting all of DuPont's businesses are the values that shape the way we operate.

DuPont is a discovery company. Building on a long record of innovation. DuPont is committed to using science and technology to improve everyday life.

Excellence in science, technology, and engineering has also helped make the company a leader in environmental stewardship, with goals that in may cases go well beyond those required by law, wherever in the world DuPont does business.

One of DuPont's best-known values is our commitment to safety — protecting employees and neighboring communities. The company is widely recognized as the world leader in industrial safety.

Integrity in all aspects of business and everyday life, based on a strict code of ethics, is the foundation of DuPont's reputation as a premier company from the perspectives of customers, investors, employees, suppliers, and the communities in which we do business. DuPont is a good company to buy from, invest in, work for, sell to, and have as a neighbor.

312. Duracell Inc.
Berkshire Corporate Park
Bethel, CT 06801
Phone: (203) 796-4000
Web: http://www.duracell.com

Duracell Inc., a subsidiary of Gillette Co. (NYSE; G), manufactures and markets Duracell brand alkaline batteries. Duracell also markets nickel metal hydride rechargeable batteries and Durabeam, a line of lighting products.

Slogans: "You Can't Top the Copper Top." "No Battery Is More Advanced."

One World, One Brand: "One Brand" because Duracell's approach to marketing Duracell Brand batteries is the same whether the city is Shanghai or Stockholm. Consumers know and prefer Duracell batteries because the brand name stands for long life and good value. And whether it's the copper and black trade dress, the distinctive packaging, or the advertising message that consumers see on television, Duracell's strategy is the same the world over and fundamental qualities of the Duracell brand translate into every language.

313. Dynamics Corp. of America
475 Steamboat Rd.
Greenwich, CT 06830
Phone: (203) 869-3211

Dynamics Corporation of America (NYSE; DYA) is a diversified manufacturer of commercial and industrial products.

Statement: As we face the unknown opportunities and challenges of the future, we will remain vigilant to the economic uncertainties brought about by increasing interest rates, financial disorder related to losses in derivative investments, collapse of the peso and deterioration of the Mexican economy, rapid contraction of the defense industry, increasing trends of global competition, and signs that the U.S. economy is slowing.

We know the future will continue to bring a changing and challenging economy with opportunities for financially sound debt-free companies like DCA. While continuing to improve our operations and expand our markets, we will search for those opportunities which have best potential to bring about a still higher return on your investment in DCA.

314. Eagle Food Centers Inc.
Rte. 67 & Knoxville Rd.
Milan, IL 61264
Phone: (309) 787-7700

Eagle Food Centers Inc. (NASDAQ; EGLE) runs a regional supermarket chain.

Charter for Success: Our success and satisfaction are derived from meeting our commitment to our associates, our customers, and the communities we serve. Our commitment includes:

We will run an honest and fair business. We will seek to gain the trust of our associates and customers based on our actions. We will communicate, listen, and be willing to change. We will recognize those who help make Eagle a better place to work and shop.

We will run a successful business which meets its operating objectives and provides career opportunities for our associates. We will make decisions which will build our business for the long term based on a well-developed plan. We will seek support for

our plan by diligent, ongoing communications.

We will support our business with a well-developed marketing plan. We will apply discipline to ensure we have a focused, consistent marketing plan with a message that creatively supports our business plan.

We will develop a corporate culture that invites participation and results in satisfaction. We will seek to build a diversified, high-performance team. We will develop an environment which encourages teamwork, offers opportunities, and recognizes success.

We will provide shareholders with a good return on their investment by successful execution of the above-stated commitments.

315. Eagle Hardware & Garden Inc.
981 Powell Ave. SW
Renton, WA 98055
Phone: (206) 227-5740

Eagle Hardware & Garden Inc. (NASDAQ; EAGL) operates home improvement centers.

Slogan: "More of Everything."

The Eagle Advantage: Consumer surveys confirm that customers would rather shop in our stores than our competitors'. Why? Because our unique customer-friendly approach to store merchandising makes shopping at Eagle easier.

316. Eastern Enterprises
9 Riverside Rd.
Weston, MA 02193
Phone: (617) 647-2300
Web: http://www.efu.com

Eastern Enterprises (NYSE; EFU) is a holding company with two major subsidiaries. Boston Gas markets natural gas and Midland Enterprises is a water transportation carrier.

Mission Statement: Eastern's primary

objective is to maximize total return to its shareholders, by investing in companies which provide their customers with quality products and services, and managing those businesses in a manner that achieves, over time, sustainable earnings growth and an above average return on invested capital.

317. Eastman Kodak Co.
343 State St.
Rochester, NY 14650
Phone: (716) 724-4000
Web: http://www.kodak.com

Eastman Kodak Co. (NYSE; EK) is a large photography company.

Slogan: "Take Pictures Further."

Statement: Kodak is committed to greater growth, as the world leader in images and a key player in strategically important health care markets. We will reduce our debt, generate greater earnings and put customers first, through quality, excellence, and product and service leadership. We will be the world's best in these areas, and share the goal of achieving nothing less than total customer satisfaction.

318. Eaton Corp.
Eaton Crt.
Cleveland, OH 44114
Phone: (216) 523-5000
Web: http://www.eaton.com

Eaton Corp. (NYSE; ETN) manufactures a wide variety of electric and electronic products for the automotive, industrial, and defense industries.

Mission Statement: Producing the highest quality products at costs which make them economically practical in the most competitively priced markets.

To be achieved by our global commitment to:

Customer satisfaction.
Profitable growth.
Total quality leadership.
Continuous productivity improvement.

The Eaton philosophy of excellence through people.

Concern for our communities and environment.

And the highest standard of integrity.

319. Echlin Inc.
100 Double Beach Rd.
Branford, CT 06405
Phone: (203) 481-5751
Web: http://www.echlin.com

Echlin Inc. (NYSE; ECH) is, primarily, a manufacturer for the automobile aftermarket. The company produces brakes, engines, power transmissions, steering and suspension system products for a wide range of on- and off-road vehicles and equipment — most of the parts are replacement items, used to repair cars and trucks.

Statement: For three and a half decades, Echlin has reported the greatest sales of any aftermarket company.

To achieve this growth, we've followed three basic strategies. First, we focus our business in two of the steadiest, most important segments of our industry: Safety and efficiency related parts. Second, we continually broaden our product range, by incorporating new lines and expanding existing ones. Third, we deepen our market penetration, worldwide, by accessing every channel of distribution.

Shareholders entrust us to grow their investment as we grow the company.

Growth on the Horizon: Echlin continues to aggressively build its product and market base. Our objective is threefold: To present a full breadth of top quality parts, to deliver our products through every channel available, and to enlarge our customer group worldwide.

Philosophy: A basic philosophy has governed our growth. We've proposed, with our business lines, a policy of providing all the components needed for all the vehicles on the road. Whether it's a 1930 Ford or a 1996 Chrysler Caravan, we're bound to have replacement items for it.

320. Echo Bay Mines

Plaza Tower One
6400 S. Fiddlers Green Circle
Suite 1000
Englewood, CO 80111
Phone: (303) 714-8600
Web: http://www.echobay.com

Echo Bay Mines (AMEX; ECO) mines and processes gold.

Mission Statement: To be a premier gold mining company that operates in a safe, environmentally sound and profitable manner, and that provides a challenging and fulfilling atmosphere for the Echo Bay team.

Our Quality Policy: We will consistently achieve the highest quality of performance by:

Fully defining, understanding and conforming to all the requirements of our jobs.

Creating and maintaining the necessary work environment that will allow us to fully satisfy those requirements.

Continuously evaluating and improving our job requirements and work processes.

Achieving the highest quality of performance will enable us to fulfill Echo Bay's mission.

321. Ecogen Inc.

2005 Cabot Blvd. West
P.O. Box 3023
Langhome, PA 19047
Phone: (215) 757-1590

Ecogen Inc. (NASDAQ; EECN) is a biotechnology company, specializing in biopesticide products.

Mission Statement: Ecogen is committed to be the leader in the development of quality specialty biopesticide products for controlling insects and disease in agricultural and related markets.

322. Ecolab Inc.

Ecolab Ctr.
St. Paul, MN 55102
Phone: (612) 293-2233
Web: http://www.ecolab.com

Ecolab Inc. (NYSE; ECL) manufactures products for cleaning, sanitizing and maintenance needs.

Our Mission: Our business is to be a leading innovator, developer, and marketer of worldwide services, products, and systems, which provide superior value to our customers in meeting their cleaning, sanitizing, and maintenance needs, while conserving resources and preserving the quality of the environment and providing a fair profit for our shareholders.

323. (A. G.) Edwards & Sons Inc.

One North Jefferson
St. Louis, MO 63103
Phone: (314) 289-3000
Web: http://www.agedwards.com

A. G. Edwards & Sons Inc. (NYSE; AGE) provides investment and financial services.

Mission Statement: Our purpose is to furnish financial services of value to our clients. We should act as their agents, putting their interests before our own.

We are confident that if we do our jobs well and give value for what we charge, not only will mutual trust and respect develop, but satisfaction and a fair reward will result.

324. EG&G Inc.

45 William St.
Wellesley, MA 02181
Phone: (617) 237-5100
Web: http://www.egginc.com

EG&G Inc. (NYSE; EGG) manufactures scientific instruments and mechanical components.

Statement: EG&G is using its expertise and technology to respond to the needs of the nineties — and beyond. Our goals: To create a climate of technology transfer among businesses to produce new products for new markets, and to manage and support our customers with better, faster, and cheaper services.

325. El Paso Energy Corp.
1001 Louisiana
Houston, TX 77002
Phone: (713) 757-2131

El Paso Energy Corp. (NYSE; EPG), formerly El Paso Natural Gas Co., is one of the largest energy companies in the nation. The company has three business units with operations in natural gas transmission (El Paso Natural Gas Co. acquired Tenneco Energy); and Tennessee Gas Pipeline Co.), field and merchant services (El Paso Energy Resources), and international project development (El Paso Energy International).

Corporate Strategy: Produce 10-15% annual earnings growth by maximizing cash flow and earnings from regulated assets and reinvesting that cash flow to expand non-regulated businesses.

Statement: During 1997, we will focus on combining the talents and experience of the El Paso Energy and Tenneco Energy work forces into one cohesive unit. We have one of the most innovative and widely experienced management teams in the industry, leading a highly skilled and disciplined work force. As a newly merged organization, we look good on the map, and we look good on the balance sheet. Our management and our assets uniquely position us to realize opportunities arising from the convergence of the natural gas and electric utility industries resulting from evolving regulatory changes.

While we participate in this dynamic process, our corporate goal remains unchanged — to enhance shareholder value through annual earnings growth, growth that is fueled by deploying our considerable free cash flow into investment opportunities in our non-regulated and regulated businesses, by capitalizing on cost saving opportunities and by pursuing additional strategic acquisitions.

In short, El Paso Energy Corporation is now positioned to lead the energy as it changes to meet the future.

326. Elcor Corp.
Wellington Centre
Suite 1000
14643 Dallas Pkwy.
Dallas, TX 75240
Phone: (972) 851-0500
Web: http://www.elcor.com

Elcor Corp. (NYSE; ELK) produces roofing materials and industrial products.

Mission: Our mission is to achieve excellence in:

Meeting our present and evolving quality requirements for our customers, our employees, our shareholders, our suppliers and our community.

Continually improving everything we do to assure perpetuation of success and excellence in the future.

327. Electronic Arts Inc.
1450 Fashion Island Blvd.
San Mateo, CA 94404
Phone: (415) 571-7171
Web: http://www.ea.com

Electronic Arts Inc. (NASDAQ; ERTS) creates interactive entertainment systems, including cartridge systems, dedicated CD-ROM systems, and personal computers.

Slogan: "If It's in the Game, It's in the Game."

Mission: Electronic Arts' mission is to become the world's leading interactive entertainment software company.

328. Eli Lilly and Co.
Lilly Corporate Ctr.
Indianapolis, IN 46285
Phone: (317) 276-2000
Web: http://www.lilly.com

Eli Lilly and Co. (NYSE; LLY) develops, manufactures, and markets pharmaceuticals, medical instruments, and diagnostic products, and agricultural products.

Slogan: "Knowledge Is Powerful Medicine."

Mission: Eli Lilly and Company is a global research-based corporation that develops, manufactures, and markets pharmaceuticals, medical instruments and diagnostic products, and agricultural products.

To guide its affairs, the company follows certain fundamental principles. These principles, which we believe are in the best long-term interests of employees, customers, shareholders, and society as a whole, are the following:

The company is committed to the discovery and marketing of innovative products of the highest quality that offer benefits to customers in all markets.

The company is dedicated to the highest levels of ethics, integrity, and excellence in research, manufacturing, marketing, and all other phases of its operations.

The company recognizes a primary responsibility to its employees because of the key role employees play in the achievement of corporate goals. The company's objective is to attract and retain outstanding people at all levels and in all parts of the organization. It is committed to fair and equitable treatment of all employees, to the creation of an environment that recognizes the value of diversity, and to policies and programs that offer the opportunity for employees to develop meaningful and rewarding careers.

The company believes that it has an obligation to be a good corporate citizen wherever it operates and that it has a responsibility to conduct its operations in a manner that protects human health and the environment.

Vision: Eli Lilly and Company is committed to being a leader in the worldwide marketplace for products based on the life sciences.

The company's primary objective is to discover, through research, innovative products of the highest quality.

All company activities are to be conducted with a thirst for excellence, with the highest of ethical standards, and with a customer orientation.

In keeping with its tradition, the company continues to recognize its employees as its most important asset.

329. EMC Corp.
171 South St.
Hopkinton, MA 01748
Phone: 1-800-424-EMC2
Web: http://www.emc.com

EMC Corp. (NYSE; EMC) is a leader in information storage and retrieval technology. EMC is primarily known for its revolutionary Integrated Cached Disk Array design, which can be found in its Symmetrix products for mainframe computer systems, its Harmonix products for midrange (IBM AS/400) computer systems, and its Centriplex products for open systems computing environments.

Slogan: "The Storage Architects."

Statements: Our goal is to maintain our leadership in each segment of our market by continuing to be first to market with reliable and innovative storage solutions.

EMC is the only company in the world entirely focused on rapidly delivering strategic intelligent data storage solutions that allow corporations and organizations to leverage their growing volumes of information into profitability, growth, and competitive advantage.

330. Emery Worldwide
P.O. Box 10110
Palo Alto, CA 94303
Phone: (415) 855-9100

Emery Worldwide, a subsidiary of Consolidated Freightways Inc. (NYSE; CNF), is an international and domestic transporter of packages, parcels, and freight.

Our Mission: Our mission is to exceed our customers' expectations. We believe they deserve nothing less. Whether we meet in the customer's office, on the dock or over the telephone, we're honest and professional. Individually, we are proud of our work and our history of innovations. Together, we are a team of dedicated people working to satisfy our customers.

Emery Worldwide is an international and domestic transporter of packages, parcels, and freight. We also will handle envelopes for customers who require transportation of packages, parcels, and freight. No shipment is too large to be handled by Emery Worldwide. The company services business customers.

Emery Worldwide strives to provide total freight transportation to customers. Inbound packages, parcels, and freight are as important as our outbound.

We clearly understand each location's expense of performing service on behalf of each of our customers and govern our sales efforts and operational activities accordingly.

331. Empi Inc.
599 Cardigan
St. Paul, MN 55126
Phone: (612) 415-9000
Web: http://www.empi.com

Empi Inc. (NASDAQ); EMPI develops, manufactures, and markets therapeutic and rehabilitation products and services.

Slogan: "Passion for Patient Care."

Vision: To become the world technology leader in services and non-invasive products to improve the quality of life for people with functional disabilities.

Mission: Empi Inc. is a company that meets the needs of the rehabilitation, gynecology, urology, and neurology markets through the development, manufacture, and marketing of innovative, cost effective, electro-therapeutic and rehabilitation products and services to continuously improve the quality of life for the diseased and physically disabled.

Values: Passion for care of patients. Quality of life.

Integrity with all stakeholders. Rewarding and challenging workplace.

332. Empire District Electric Co.
602 Joplin St.
Joplin, MO 64801
Phone: (417) 626-5100
Web: http://www.empiredistrict.com

Empire District Electric Company (NYSE; EDE) provides electrical service to customers in Missouri, Oklahoma, Kansas, and Arkansas.

Slogan: "Team Empire."

Vision: Empire will be the provider of choice for electrical services.

Mission: Know our customers and exceed their expectations.

Provide increasing value to our shareholders.

Provide a safe, challenging and satisfying work environment.

Develop a corporate culture which will enable success in a competitive marketplace.

Provide financial strength to respond to an increasingly deregulated environment.

333. Energen Corp.
2101 Sixth Ave. North
Birmingham, AL 35203
Phone: (205) 326-2700
Web: http://www.energen.com

Energen Corp. (NYSE; EGN) is a diversified energy company. Its subsidiaries are Alagasco (natural gas utility) and Taurus Exploration (oil and gas exploration and production).

Statement: To enhance shareholder value, Energen blends the financial and operating strength of its natural gas utility with the growth potential of its oil and gas exploration and production company.

There is one specific reason Energen decided to diversify: To enhance shareholder value.

334. Energy West Inc.
One First Ave. South
Great Falls, MT
Phone: (406) 791-7500
Web: http://www.ewst.com

Energy West Inc. (NASDAQ; EWST) is an energy service holding company.

Mission Statement: The mission of Energy West is to maximize the company value by providing total quality energy services, empowering customer-oriented employees and growing through expansion, acquisition and new technology.

335. Engelhard Corp.
101 Wood Ave.
Iselin, NJ 08830
Phone: (908) 205-5000
Web: http://www.engelhard.com

Engelhard Corp. (NYSE; EC) is a provider of specialty chemical products, engineered materials, and precious metals management services.

Statement: By becoming an even more valuable partner to our customers, and by pursuing our other strategic thrusts, we expect steady sales growth to become the engine that drives profit growth. In this way, we will satisfy the expectations of our investors and provide opportunities for employees.

Agenda for the 90's: As our customers' preferred supplier, we will be the industry leader in performance, urgency, and integrity, and as a world-class competitor we will deliver superior value to our shareholders.

336. Ennis Business Forms Inc.
107 N. Sherman
Ennis, TX 75119
Phone: (972) 872-3100
Web: http://www.ennis.com

Ennis Business Forms Inc. (NYSE; EBF) makes and markets business forms and other business products for national distribution.

Statement: We are totally committed to long-term profitable growth for our company and the creation of value for our stockholders.

337. Enron Corp.
1400 Smith St.
Houston, TX 77002
Phone: (713) 853-6161
Web: http://www.enron.com

Enron Corp. (NYSE; ENE) markets natural gas and electricity.

Slogans: "Creating Energy Solutions Worldwide."

"Natural Gas. Electricity. And Endless Possibilities."

Vision: Become the world's leading energy company — creating innovative and efficient energy solutions for growing economies and a better environment worldwide.

338. ENSERCH Corp.
300 South St. Paul
Dallas, TX 75201
Phone: (214) 651-8700
Web: http://www.enserch.com

ENSERCH Corp. (NYSE; ENS) is an integrated natural gas company.

Statement: With the excellent people, properties, and potential of the company, combined with the financial resources to fund opportunities, we believe ENSERCH Explorations has a bright future.

We believe strongly in focusing our operations in areas in which we have a concentration of properties with the expertise to provide us the best profit opportunities.

339. Entergy Corp.
639 Loyola Ave.
New Orleans, LA 70161
Phone: (504) 529-5262
Web: http://www.entergy.com

Entergy Corp. (NYSE; ETR) is an energy company that extends it expertise and technology worldwide through the diversified energy and related services businesses it owns and operates. Entergy supplies electricity and related services to customers in Arkansas, Louisiana, Mississippi, and Texas, through regulated subsidiaries.

Slogan: "Entergy Has a Plan."

Vision: Winning through innovative and profitable actions — exceeding customers' expectations everywhere we serve.

Statement: Entergy is a major energy company in the midst of tremendous growth ... evidence of our determination to win in tomorrow's competitive marketplace. We have moved beyond the boundaries of our regulated utility business and are employing our core skills of power-plant operations, distribution-network management, and customer connections to expand globally, as well as compete more broadly in domestic markets. We've grown dramatically during this decade, extending our presence to five continents and practically tripling our retail customer base to about 4.8 million.

Tremendous opportunities lie ahead.

Playing to Win Strategy Update: Aggressively manage Entergy's core electricity business.

Broaden Entergy's global power-development business.

Expand domestically into energy-related services.

Manage an orderly transition to competition.

340. Enterprise Rent-A-Car
600 Corporate Park Dr.
St. Louis, MO 63105
Phone: (314) 512-5000
Web: http://www.pickenterprise.com

Enterprise Rent-A-Car, a private company, rents, leases, and sells automobiles, and other related services.

Slogan: "We'll Pick You Up."

The Enterprise Mission: Our mission is to fulfill the automobile rental, leasing, car sale, and related needs of our customers, and, in doing so, exceed their expectations for service, quality, and value. We will strive to earn our customers' long-term loyalty by working to deliver more than promised; being honest and fair; and "going the extra mile" to provide exceptional personalized service that creates a pleasing business experience. We must motivate our employees to provide exceptional service to our customers by supporting their development, providing opportunities for personal growth, and amply compensating them for their successes and achievements. We believe it is critical to our success to promote managers from within who will serve as examples of success for others to follow. Although our goal is to be the best and not necessarily the biggest or the most profitable, our success at satisfying customers and motivating employees will bring growth and long-term profitability.

341. Epitope Inc.
8505 SW Creekside Pl.
Beaverton, OR 97008
Phone: (503) 641-6115

Epitope Inc. (NASDAQ; EPTO) is in the biotechnology business.

Statement: We are excited about Epitope's future and dedicated to our vision of producing biotechnology used compassionately to better the health and well-being of people worldwide.

342. Equitable Companies Inc.
787 Seventh Ave.
New York, NY 10019
Phone: (212) 554-1234
Web: http://www.equitable.com

Equitable Companies Inc. (NYSE; EQ) provides insurance and asset management products.

Slogan: AXA — "Go Ahead. You Can Rely on Us."

Mission Statement: Equitable, together with its global partner AXA, seeks to be the world's premier provider of insurance and asset management products for financial security and retirement savings.

343. Estee Lauder Companies Inc.
767 Fifth Ave.
New York, NY 10153
Phone: (212) 572-4200

Estee Lauder Companies Inc. (NYSE; EL) manufactures and markets cosmetics and personal beauty products.

Vision: "Bringing the Best to Everyone We Touch."

Environmental Policy: The Estee Lauder Companies are committed to protect and preserve the environment and our natural resources through our continued responsible action in all aspects of business. Our commitment will be realized through the creation of safe and innovative ingredients, products, manufacturing processes, and packaging that meet consumer needs, while minimizing environmental impact.

344. Ethyl Corp.
330 South Fourth St.
P.O. Box 2189
Richmond, VA 23217
Phone: (804) 788-5000
Web: http://www.ethyl.com

Ethyl Corp. (NYSE; EY) is a company in the chemical specialty industry.

Our Vision: To be at the top of customers' lists of suppliers.

In the markets we serve, Ethyl's family of companies will be at the top of existing and potential customers' lists of companies from which they will choose to do business.

Environment: It is Ethyl's goal to provide workplaces for employees that are safe, healthy, and environmentally sound.

Likewise, our presence in communities will not adversely affect the safety, health, or environments of our neighbors.

345. Express Scripts Inc.
14000 Riverport Dr.
Maryland Heights, MO 63043
Phone: (314) 770-1666
Web: http://www.express-scripts.com

Express Scripts Inc. (NASDAQ; ESRX) is provider of mail order and retail pharmacy and health care management services.

Mission: Our mission at Express Scripts is to form a partnership with clients, employing innovative managed care principles and leading edge technology to provide a high-quality, cost-effective pharmacy benefit with superior customer service.

346. Exxon Corp.
5959 Las Colinas Blvd.
Irving, TX 75039
Phone: (972) 444-1000
Web: http://www.exxon.com

Exxon Corp. (NYSE; XON) explores, refines, and markets products in the oil, natural gas and chemical industries.

Slogans: "Rely on the Tiger." "The Best Way to Get There."

Statement: Exxon's continuing objective is to be the world's premier petroleum company and to provide shareholders a secure investment with a superior return. Attaining this goal requires excellent performance in the following areas:
Operational excellence.
Investment selectivity.
Asset management.
Technological leadership.
Sound financing.
Flexibility and objectivity.
Highly qualified people.

347. EZCORP Inc.
1901 Capital Pkwy.
Austin, TX 87846
Phone: (512) 314-3400

EZCORP Inc. (NASDAQ; EZPW) owns and operates a chain of pawn shops.

Statement: Our goal is to provide a range of superior financial services in a convenient format to segments of the population that do not have access or choose not to use conventional banking services. We believe that we can shape our goals into outstanding customer service, increased profitability, and attractive return to you — our stockholders.

348. Fab Industries Inc.
200 Madison Ave.
New York, NY 10016
Phone: (212) 592-2700

Fab Industries Inc. (AMEX; FIT) is a manufacturer of textile fabrics, laces, and knits. Additionally, the company produces comforters, sheets, blankets, and other bedding products.

Statement: Additional emphasis has been placed upon research efforts in the development of new fabrics for the consumer, and the recruitment, training and seasoning of a sound management team have been intensified. In this highly competitive environment, we shall continue to invest the funds necessary to maintain Fab at the forefront of the textile industry.

349. Family Dollar Stores Inc.
1401 Old Monroe Rd.
Matthews, NC 28105
Phone: (704) 847-6961
Web: http://www.familydollar.com

Family Dollar Stores Inc. (NYSE; FDO) is a growing discount store chain.

Statements: As our merchandising strategy moves away from promotional pricing and back towards everyday low prices, actions are being taken to minimize the impact on gross profit margins. Our merchants are working with vendors to bring costs down and additional em-

phasis is being given to higher margin categories of goods.

While gross profit margins have been lower as a result of the reduction of merchandise prices and the decrease in sales of higher margin apparel, our merchandising strategy is attracting new customers and positioning our company for future profitable growth.

350. Fedders Corp.
Westgate Corporate Center
505 Martinville Rd.
P.O. Box 821
Liberty Corner, NJ 07938
Phone: (908) 604-8686

Fedders Corp. (NYSE; FJC) manufactures and sells air conditioners and dehumidifiers.

Slogan: "Quality and Innovation."

Statement: The world and our company have changed dramatically over the century that Fedders has been in business. Yet, essential time-honored principles such as innovation and quality have remained cornerstones of our philosophy and continue to be instrumental in our success.

Fedders takes seriously its determination to be the low-cost producer of high-quality room air conditioners while maintaining its commitment to excellence.

351. Federal Express Corp.
2005 Corporate Ave.
Memphis, TN 38132
Phone: (901) 369-3600
Web: http://www.fedex.com

Federal Express Corp. (NYSE; FDX) is in the package and freight delivery service.

Slogans: "Our International Service Available in Small, Medium, and Large."

"All You Have to Do Is Point, Click, and Ship."

Corporate Mission and Strategy: Federal Express, based on a strong adherence to its People — Service — Profit philosophy, is dedicated to maximizing financial returns by providing totally reliable, competitively superior, global air-ground transportation of high priority goods and documents that require rapid, time-certain delivery.

352. Federal Home Loan Mortgage Corp.

8200 Jones Branch Dr.
McLean, VA 22102
Phone: (703) 903-2000
Web: http://www.freddiemac.com

The Federal Home Loan Mortgage Corp. (NYSE; FRE), Freddie Mac, is a shareholder owned corporation that provides financial products and services to homeowners and renters.

Mission: Freddie Mac is a shareholder-owned corporation whose people are dedicated to improving the quality of life by making the American dream of decent, accessible housing a reality. We accomplish this mission by linking Main Street to Wall Street by purchasing and securing home mortgages and ultimately providing homeowners and renters with lower housing costs and better access to home financing.

353. Federal National Mortgage Association

3900 Wisconsin Ave.
Washington, DC 20016
Phone: (202) 752-7000
Web: http://www.fanniemae.com

The Federal National Mortgage Association (NYSE; FNM), referred to as Fannie Mae, was created by Congress in 1938 to provide liquidity to the U.S. housing market. Fannie Mae has evolved into a shareholder-owned corporation that is a supplier of conventional home mortgage funds. Although, it does not make loans directly to consumers

Slogan: "Showing America a New Way Home."

Mission Statement: Since its creation by Congress in 1938 and its evolution into s shareholder-owned company in 1968, Fannie Mae's mission has been to provide financial products and services that increase the availability and the affordability of housing for low-, moderate-, and middle-income Americans.

354. Federal-Mogul Corp.

26555 Northwestern Hwy.
Southfield, MI 48034
Phone: 354-7700
Web: http://www.federal-mogul.com

Federal-Mogul Corp. (NYSE; FMO) is a distributor and manufacturer of a broad range of precision parts for automobiles, light and heavy-duty trucks, farm and construction vehicles and industrial products.

Statement: We are on track with implementation of our global strategy — to deliver the right part in the right place at the right time.

Maximizing shareholder value remains the top priority for the Board of Directors and management of Federal-Mogul.

355. Ferro Corp.

1000 Lakeside Ave.
Cleveland, Ohio 44114
Phone: (216) 641-8580

Ferro Corp. (NYSE; FOE) is a producer of specialty materials for industry, including coatings, colors, ceramics, chemicals, and plastics. The company is the world's largest supplier of ceramic glaze and porcelain enamel coatings. The company also holds leading positions in powder coatings, inorganic pigments and colorants, specialty plastic compounds and colorants, and polymer additives.

Slogan: "Ferro Touches Your Life ... Every Day."

Ferro's Corporate Mission: Ferro is organized and managed to achieve steady growth in operating profits, enhancement of shareholder value, and dividend payments commensurate with earnings growth.

Operations are directly to meeting the needs of customers for high-performance specialty materials, engineered products and services worldwide. These businesses will have sufficient size, technical scope and market position to provide opportunities for current and future growth.

Because a company's reputation is one of its most valued assets, Ferro conducts its business on sound ethical principles, based upon integrity and fairness to all constituencies.

While the company's ultimate responsibility is to its shareholders, Ferro also has a deep commitment to its employees, whose skills, attitudes and efforts are essential to the company's continued success.

Statement: A major focus of Ferro's marketing efforts, aimed at creating sustainable growth, is more closely assessing value of current and potential customers and directing resources toward those that are successfully growing and impacting their marketplace. Growth also will come from pursuing strategic alliances with other producers to meet a variety of customers' needs.

Outlook: Effective restructuring of our worldwide operations has strengthened our competitive stance, positioned us to exploit growth opportunities and reduced our vulnerability to business cycles. We will continue to restructure and organize to ensure we meet dynamic customer and market opportunities cost effectively. We will also capitalize on the core technologies that link our businesses and product lines to develop and sustain competitive advantages. We are dedicated to maintaining Ferro's momentum regardless of external circumstances.

356. FHP International Corp.
9900 Talbert Ave.
Fountain Valley, CA 92708
Phone: (714) 963-7233

FHP International Corp. (NASDAQ; FHPC) is a diversified health care company in three key lines of business. They are: A Health maintenance organization; a physician management company; and an insurance group.

Slogan: "Your Health Partner. For Life."

Statement: We are determined to improve profitability and are making fundamental changes to strengthen our competitive position.

357. Fieldcrest Cannon Inc.
One Lake Circle Dr.
Kannapolis, NC 28081
Phone: (704) 939-2000
Web: http://dama.tc2.com/fldcrest/
default.htm

Fieldcrest Cannon Inc. (NYSE; FLD) manufactures and markets bath and bedding products.

Statement: While competitively, Fieldcrest Cannon has the best brands in the industry, we are committed to improving business processes and implementing modernization programs that will increase our competitiveness and bring even greater value to our customers, shareholders and employees.

358. Fina Inc.
Fina Plaza
8350 N. Central Expwy.
Dallas, TX 75206
Phone: (214) 750-2400

Fina Inc. (AMEX; FI), through its subsidiaries, engages in crude oil and natural gas exploration and production and natural gas marketing; petroleum products refining, supply and transportation, and marketing; and chemicals manufacturing and marketing.

Statement: In the longer term, we will continue to focus on how we are, or can become, differentiated from our competitors, consistent with our vision to be among the best in our industry.

359. First Bank System Inc.

First Bank Plaza
601 Second Ave. South
Minneapolis, MN 55402
Phone: (612) 973-1111
Web: http://www.fbs.com/home.html

First Bank System Inc. (NYSE; FBS) is a regional bank holding company serving Midwestern and Rocky Mountain states.

Slogan: "We're Committed to Helping Our Communities Succeed."

Mission: We build high-performing banking franchises where we can create and sustain market leadership.

Goals: We will be one of the top-performing banks, measured in terms of market share and long-term profitability. We will achieve this goal through: Customer service commitment; cost control; credit quality; capital strength; core business concentration; cross-selling aggressively and effectively; community commitment; communicating clearly and honestly.

360. First Brands Corp.

83 Wooster Heights Rd.
Danbury, CT 06813
Phone: (203) 731-2300

First Brands Corp. (NYSE; FBR) is a leader in the branded consumer product markets. The company's products are sold under registered brand names, including Glad plastic wrap and bags, STP and Simoniz automotive products, and Scoop Away, Jonny Cat and Ever Clean pet products. First Brands' Himolene subsidiary is also a leader in the commercial trash bag market.

Slogans: Glad (food bags) — "Yellow and Blue Make Green." Glad (trash bags) — "Ties Are Out ... Flaps Are In!" STP — "The Racer's Edge." STP — "Drive a Better Car."

Statement: We will continue to look for growth opportunities through complementary acquisitions. First Brands has been especially adept at assimilating new businesses and quickly turning them into strong contributors.

361. First Chicago NBD Corp.

One First National Plaza
Chicago, IL 60670
Phone: (312) 732-4000
Web: http://www.fcnbd.com

First Chicago NBD Corp. is a regional commercial bank and a financial services company.

Slogan: "To Commit to Excellence in All We Do."

Mission: The mission of First Chicago NBD Corporation is to be a world-class financial services company distinguished by strong customer relationships, quality products, and excellent service.

362. First Data Corp.

401 Hackensack Ave.
Hackensack, NJ 07601
Phone: (201) 525-4700
Web: http://www.firstdata.com

First Data Corp. (NYSE; FDC) is a leading provider of information and transaction processing services. Services include transaction processing and back office support for card issuers; merchant and consumer payment services; debt collection and accounts receivable management; mutual fund processing; health care claims administration; data imaging and information management; and other related services.

Slogan: "The New First Data Corporation — The Leader in Payment Services."

Our Mission: To be the recognized leader in the markets we serve by providing high quality, value-added information processing services.

By achieving this we will satisfy an ever increasing number of clients and be integral to their success.

In turn, we will generate consistently high returns for our shareholders and provide meaningful challenges and rewards for our colleagues.

Our Values: All our activities and decisions must be based on, and guided by, these values: Embodying the highest ethical standards, satisfying clients by always exceeding their expectations, treating people with respect and dignity, and creating value for shareholders.

363. First Hawaiian Inc.
999 Bishop St.
Honolulu, HI 96813
Phone: (808) 525-7000
Web: http://www.fhb.com

First Hawaiian Inc. (NASDAQ; FHWN) is a bank holding company.

Mission: The primary mission of First Hawaiian Inc. is to be first in customer service and satisfaction. We of the First Hawaiian family are committed to the belief that Hawaiian is more than our middle name. The work expresses our corporate culture and commitment to our customers, owners, fellow employees, and community.

364. First Interstate Bancorporation
633 W. 5th St.
Los Angeles, CA 90071
Phone: (213) 614-3001
Web: http://www.wellsfargo.com

First Interstate Bancorporation, who merged with Wells Fargo Bank (NYSE; WFC), is in the commercial banking industry.

Mission Statement: At First Interstate Bank, our mission is to provide superior value and exceptional service to our customers.

We believe in being a preferred employer.

We believe in the importance of maintaining superior asset quality.

We believe in actively supporting the communities we serve.

We believe in maintaining the highest levels of professional integrity and personal ethics.

We believe in rewarding our shareholders with returns that consistently meet their expectations.

As a result, we will be recognized as a leader in the financial services industry.

365. First Union Corp.
One First Union Center
Charlotte, NC 28288
Phone: (704) 374-6565
Web: http://www.firstunion.com

First Union Corp. (NYSE; FTU) is a large bank holding company.

Slogan: "First Union Direct."

Strategic Priorities: Provide our customers unparalleled service, convenience, and responsiveness; balance earnings power through geographic and product diversity; provide the most innovative financing solutions and a broad array of products; increase the production of our specialty businesses; maximize operating efficiency; and emphasize capital strength and loan quality, with growth in loans, deposits, and fee income.

366. First Union Real Estate Investments
55 Public Sq.
Suite 1900
Cleveland, OH 44113
Phone: (216) 781-4030

First Union Real Estate Investments (NYSE; FUR) operates in the real estate industry.

Mission Statement: As owners and managers of real estate, we will maximize shareholder value, by providing quality service in a creative atmosphere of teamwork among our employees, customers, and communities.

Finance Mission Statement: To provide First Union with maximum financial flexibility by accessing the lowest cost capital available; to provide management, shareholders and investors with accurate, timely and insightful financial information; to protect the assets of the Trust through effective controls and risk management; to perform strategic planning, budgeting and financial analysis; and to maximize on our human resources by hiring, developing, retaining and supporting a dedicated, professional staff.

367. First Virginia Banks Inc.
One First Virginia Plaza
6400 Arlington Blvd.
Falls Church, VA 22042
Phone: (703) 241-4000
Web: http://www.firstvirginia.com

First Virginia Banks Inc. (NYSE; FVB) is a commercial bank which offers a variety of financial services.

The First Virginia Creed: Our goal is to provide friendly and professional service. We must continually strive to make our customers feel welcome. As an individual, you can accomplish this goal by greeting customers by name whenever possible, and by always thanking them for banking with us. And, when customers have questions, you should attempt to answer them as quickly and as accurately as possible. Collectively, we must carefully evaluate the needs of all customers and be sure to provide them with all the financial services they need.

Finally, we must realize that, individually and as a whole, we are responsible for creating the atmosphere that will make customers feel at home. Our fundamental responsibility is to consider how our attitudes and actions will affect customer opinion and satisfaction. Along with being fiscally responsible and earning an acceptable return for our stockholders, providing friendly, helpful service is a fundamental part of our business philosophy.

Iowa, Minnesota, Illinois, Arizona, and Florida.

Slogan: "To Get There, Start Here."

The Vision We Share: Firstar will create and retain mutually beneficial long-term relationships with our customers, employees, communities, and shareholders.

We will consistently provide outstanding customer satisfaction by conveniently delivering financial products and services that are valued for features, quality, and price. We will listen to our customers and use their insights to make continuous improvements.

The success of Firstar and its employees is interdependent. As an employer, Firstar will create a challenging environment that emphasizes professional growth, rewards performance, and affords equal opportunity to all of our people. As employees, we will work together in a spirit of teamwork and mutual respect. We will always adhere to the highest standards of ethics and integrity.

Firstar will be a good corporate citizen. We will actively support the economic, social and cultural well-being of our communities.

We will provide our shareholders a competitive return on their investment by consistently performing in the top quartile of our peer group.

We realize that the only way we can achieve this vision is to be a financially strong, consistently profitable, and growing organization. As we prioritize our activities, soundness is first, then profitability, and finally growth.

By fulfilling this vision, we will assure our future as one of the nation's most successful and respected financial institutions.

368. Firstar Corp.
777 East Wisconsin Ave.
Milwaukee, WI 53202
Phone: (414) 765-4321
Web: http://www.firstar.com

Firstar Corp. (NYSE; FSR) is a bank holding company operating in Wisconsin,

369. FIserv Inc.
255 FIserv Dr.
Brookfield, WI 53045
(414) 879-5000
Web: http://www.fiserv.com

FIserv Inc. (NASDAQ; FISV) provides ATM/POS services to more than 700 financial institutions and supports the operations of more than 2,500 ATMs.

Vision: Together, as FIserv, we will be known worldwide for our advanced service quality and held in the highest esteem by our clients, employees, shareholders, service partners, industry, and communities.

Mission: To be the leading provider of data processing and information management products and services to the financial industry. To deliver products and services that help our clients grow their businesses and enhance service to their customers. To enable our people to achieve outstanding job performance and personal growth. To produce a favorable level of earnings and consistent earnings growth for our company, and increased value for our shareholders.

370. Fisher-Price Inc.
636 Girard Ave.
East Aurora, NY 14052
Phone: (716) 687-3000

Fisher-Price Inc., a subsidiary of Mattel Inc. (NYSE; MAT), manufactures toys and other juvenile products.

Mission: Fisher-Price will design, engineer, produce and market the world's best children's products characterized by a tradition of uncompromised safety, quality, durability, innovation, and value.

We will continuously strive to improve our products and services to meet or exceed customer and consumer expectations to succeed as a profitable business.

371. Flagstar Companies Inc.
203 East Main St.
Spartanburg, SC 29319
Phone: (803) 597-8000

Flagstar Companies Inc. (NASDAQ; FLST), through its wholly-owned subsidiary, Flagstar Corporation, is one of the largest restaurant companies in the U.S., operating (directly and through fran-

chisees) Denny's, Hardee's, Quincy's and El Pollo Loco.

Slogan: Hardee's — "What Will They Think of Next."

Statement: Flagstar is working toward positioning itself for a lasting turnaround. With its many fine brands and the commitment and talent I see throughout the organization, I believe we can also become, once again, a growth company.

One common trait to great growth companies is an intense focus on doing the simple things that matter to their customers to near perfection. An acute understanding of what customers want drives their businesses. All of their energies go into fulfilling customer needs; they keep distractions to a minimum. They know their strengths — the things that keep their customer coming back — and they build upon those strengths.

Flagstar can be one of those companies. Each of our restaurant concepts enjoys a unique market position that is greatly enhanced by a particular strength that matters to our customers.

372. Fleet Financial Group Inc.
One Federal St.
Boston, MA 02110
Phone: (617) 346-4000
Web: http://www.fleet.com

Fleet Financial Group Inc. (NYSE; FLT) is a diversified financial services company.

Statement: The short-term challenge for us, of course, is to continue to offer competitive and profitable products and services whether or not we are the beneficiaries of new banking powers or regulatory relief. Toward that end, we are moving ahead with a far more aggressive target-marketing strategy which is heavily technology-driven. Should new business opportunities present themselves along the way, however, then we will be that much ahead of the game.

Longer-term challenges for Fleet's management team will be to continue to leverage internal growth with external acquisitions. Clearly the financial services industry will continue to consolidate through the balance of the decade to reduce overcapacity. We believe those that survive this process will exhibit such common traits as: Geographic breadth; product diversity; a low cost of service; a technological advantage; a renewed sales culture; a target-marketing approach; and depth of management.

373. Fleming Companies Inc.
6301 Waterford Blvd.
Oklahoma City, OK 73126
Phone: (405) 840-7200
Web: http://www.fleming. com

Fleming Companies Inc. (NYSE; FLM) is engaged primarily in the food wholesaling and distribution industry, with both wholesale and retail operations.

Our Mission: Become a world-class marketing and distribution company.

Position the customers we serve to win at retail.

Always remember that individuals make the difference.

Maintain a clear vision of our future direction.

374. Flowers Industries Inc.
U.S. Hwy. 19
P.O. Box 1338
Thomasville, GA 31799
Phone: (912) 226-9110
Web: http://www.flowersindustries.com

Flowers Industries Inc. (NYSE; FLO) operates in the packaged foods industry principally serving grocery, foodservice, restaurants, and fast-food markets. The company's products are marketed under a variety of registered trade names including: Flowers, Nature's Own, Stilwell, Cobblestone Mill, Dandee, Ideal, Holsum, Keebler, and others.

Statement: Redefined. Refocused. Reinvigorated. Flowers' strategies are paying

off. We're strong. We're profitable. We're pursuing new distribution channels, adding new plants, and boosting efficiencies. We're a leader in the fresh bakery business and a growing specialty frozen baked foods company. We've set ourselves apart. We're breaking away.

375. Fluke Corp.
6920 Seaway Blvd.
Everett, WA 98203
Phone: (206) 347-6100
Web: http://www.fluke.com

Fluke Corp. (NYSE; FLK) manufactures testing equipment.

Slogan: "Fluke Quality — A Continuing Tradition."

Mission Development: Three Considerations: Market dynamics and customer needs.

Fluke core competencies and strengths.

Competitive situation and opportunity to lead.

When we developed our mission, it was based on three fundamental considerations: The market opportunity must be sufficiently large and growing; we must build upon our strengths; and we must be able to realistically obtain and strengthen a position of leadership.

Vision for Our Future: The vision for our future contains seven key concepts. They describe what we will be like as an enterprise.

1. Creative understanding of user needs.

2. Creating new products and markets.

3. Delighting customers — with products and support.

4. Worldwide competitor.

5. Leadership in our chosen business area.

6. A great place to work.

7. Profitable growth.

Statement: We must never forget that our most fundamental focus is on the customer who buys and uses our products. We absolutely must build products that our customers will buy. Our products and their related services must not only be viewed as useful and needed, but their quality and value must meet or exceed customers' expectations and be superior to other choices they may have. Customer expectations and needs change; therefore, we must continuously improve our performance to meet this challenge. Every individual in the company has an impact on how well we meet these expectations and needs. We are the ones who translate words into results.

376. Fluor Corp.
3353 Michelson Dr.
Irvine, CA 92698
Phone: (714) 975-2000
Web: http://www.fluor.com

Fluor Corp. (NYSE; FLR) is an international engineering, construction, maintenance and diversified services company, with an important investment in low-sulfur coal. Fluor Daniel, the company's principal operating business, provides a broad range of technical services.

Mission: As Fluor Daniel employees, our mission is to assist clients in attaining a competitive advantage by delivering quality services of unmatched value.

Principles: To add value to our services, these principles are emphasized:

We are client focused.

We are innovative and flexible in meeting client needs.

We do our work better, faster, cheaper, and safer.

Philosophy: Our philosophy is based upon ethical conduct, mutual trust and teamwork. To ensure continuous improvement, we challenge, test, reevaluate and continually raise our standards of excellence.

As a service organization, our success depends upon the combined capabilities and contributions of all employees. Fluor Daniel is dedicated to fostering a work environment which challenges, enriches and rewards each individual.

377. FMC Corp.
200 East Randolph Dr.
Chicago, IL 60601
Phone: (312) 861-6000
Web: http://www.fmc.com

FMC Corp. (NYSE; FMC) is a producer of chemicals and machinery for industry, agriculture, and government. FMC participates in five broad markets: Performance chemicals, industrial chemicals, machinery and equipment, defense systems, and precious metals.

Statement: Increasing shareholder value through people, growth, and superb execution.

Priority: Our top priority is maximizing shareholder value.

378. Foamex International Inc.
1000 Columbia Ave.
Linwood, PA 19061
Phone: (610) 859-3000
Web: http://www.foamex.com

Foamex International Inc. (NASDAQ; FMXI) is a manufacturer of foam and related materials.

Mission: To be the premier supplier of foam and related products in markets in which we compete.

To maintain our dominant market position in North America, and by the year 2000 to be the premier global company supplying products that add comfort and value.

To maintain good employee relations.

Purpose: To develop, produce and market innovative products that provide comfort and value to our customers.

Good Community Citizenship: Our reputation is important. It will be determined by the standards and behaviors of all our people.

Contribute time and dollars to worthwhile community programs.

Take responsible care of the environment where we are located.

379. Food Lion Inc.
2110 Executive Dr.
Salisbury, NC 28144
Phone: (704) 633-8250
Web: http://www.foodlion.com

Food Lion Inc. (NASDAQ; FDLNB) operates a chain of supermarkets.

Statements: As one of America's leading supermarkets, Food Lion is strongly committed to assuring the quality and freshness of every item it sells.

Food Lion is committed to being the best supermarket in the neighborhood.

Gold Lion Guarantee: The Gold Lion Guarantee is our promise to customers to provide only the highest quality products in clean, efficient stores that are staffed with courteous and well-trained employees. Food Lion shoppers know we stand behind every item in every one of our stores. If it isn't right, we'll make it right. No questions asked.

380. Ford Motor Co.
The American Rd.
Dearborn, MI 48121
Phone: (313) 322-3000
Web: http://www.ford.com

Ford Motor Co. (NYSE; F) is the number two car manufacturer in the U.S. They manufacture and market Ford, Lincoln, Mercury, and Jaguar products.

Slogans: Ford — "Quality Is Job 1." Ford — "The Best Never Rest." Ford — "Winning the World Over." Mustang — "It Is What It Was and More." Ford — "Have You Driven a Ford Lately?" Ford — "Everything We Do Is Driven by You." Jaguar — "One Part Love, Two Parts Lust." Ford — "Not Just a New Ford ... A New Ford Attitude." Ford Trucks — "Build Ford Tough." Lincoln — "What a Luxury Car Should Be." Mercury — "Imagine Yourself in a Mercury." Jaguar — "Grace ... Pace ... Space." Mark VIII — "Drive Everything Else First." Escort and Taurus — "Ford Makes It Smart to Buy American."

Mission: Our mission is to improve continually our products and services to meet our customers' needs, allowing us to prosper as a business and to provide a reasonable return for our stockholders, the owners of the business.

Vision: How we accomplish our mission is as important as the mission itself. Fundamental to success for the company are these basic values:

People — Our people are the source of our strength. They provide corporate intelligence and determine our reputation and vitality. Involvement and teamwork are our core human values.

Products — Our products are the end result of our efforts, and they should be the best in serving customers worldwide. As our products are viewed, so are we viewed.

Profits — Profits are the ultimate measure of how efficiently we provide customers with the best products for their needs. Profits are required to survive and grow.

Growing Principles: Quality comes first.

Customers are the focus of everything we do.

Continuous improvement is essential to our success.

Employee involvement is our way of life.

Dealers and suppliers are our partners.

Integrity is never compromised.

381. FoxMeyer Corp.
1220 Senlac Dr.
Carrollton, TX 75006
Phone: (214) 446-4800

FoxMeyer Corp., a subsidiary of Fox-Meyer Health Corp. (NYSE; FOX), markets pharmaceutical products.

Mission: The mission of FoxMeyer Corporation is to enhance the effectiveness and efficiency of the health care delivery system while delivering superior value to our customers, suppliers, and shareholders.

382. FPL Group Inc.

700 Universe Blvd.
Juno Beach, FL 33408
Phone: (407) 694-4000
Web: http://www.fpl.com

FPL Group Inc. (NYSE; FPL) generates, transmits, distributes and markets
electric energy.

Statement: We will be the preferred
provider of safe, reliable, and cost-effective products and services that satisfy the
electricity-related needs of all customer
segments.

Goal: Our paramount goal is to provide superior total returns to our shareholders ... Today FPL Group is better prepared for success than at any time in the
past.

383. Franklin Quest Co.

2200 W. Parkway Blvd.
Salt Lake City, UT 84119
Phone: (801) 975-1776
Web: http://www.franklinquest.com

Franklin Quest Co. (NYSE; FNQ) is
a management consulting firm. The
company has been in the business of
teaching time management seminars and
selling day planners and related products.

Mission Statement: Franklin Quest is
in the business to help people gain control
over their lives and increase their productivity.

Company Governing Values: We
make a positive difference in people's
lives.

We search for, live by and teach correct
principles.

We produce quality.

We serve the customer.

We wisely manage corporate resources.

We value our employees.

We welcome innovation and adapt to
change.

We practice teamwork.

We value our shareholders.

384. Franklin Resources Inc.

777 Mariners Island Blvd.
San Mateo, CA 94404
Phone: (415) 312-2000

Franklin Resources Inc. (NYSE; BEN)
is a diversified financial services holding
company. Through its operating subsidiaries, the company provides a variety
of investment products and services to investors.

Mission: The companies within the
Franklin Resources, Inc. organization provide global investment management, advisory and distribution services to individual and institutional clients worldwide.
We are value investors, basing our decisions on original research and a flexible
policy of investing in equities and debt
obligations of companies and governments
throughout the world at what we believe
to be attractive prices.

The company's primary objective is to
provide superior investment results and
services to our clients.

385. Fremont General Corp.

2020 Santa Monica Blvd.
Suite 600
Santa Monica, CA 90404
Phone: (310) 315-5500

Fremont General Corp. (NYSE; FMT)
is a nationwide insurance and financial
services holding company.

Strategies: The primary operating
strategy of Fremont General is to build
upon its core business units through acquisition opportunities and new business
development. Fremont General's secondary strategy is to achieve income balance and geographic diversity among its
business units in order to limit the exposure of the company to industry, market,
and regional concentrations.

386. Fresh Choice Inc.

2901 Tasman Dr.
Suite 109
Santa Clara, CA 95034

Phone: (408) 986-8661

Fresh Choice Inc. (NASDAQ; SALD) operates casual, upscale restaurants.

Mission: The mission of Fresh Choice is to build and operate restaurants according to specifically defined performance standards. These standards or pillars of performance for restaurant operations include: Guest experience, physical environment, financial results, management and training, and employee experience.

387. (H. B.) Fuller Co.
2400 Energy Park Dr.
St. Paul, MN 55108
Phone: (612) 645-3401

H. B. Fuller Co. (NASDAQ; FULL) is a worldwide formulator, manufacturer and marketer of adhesives, sealants, coatings, paints, and other specialty chemical products.

Mission: The H. B. Fuller corporate mission is to be a leading and profitable worldwide formulator, manufacturer and marketer of quality specialty chemicals, emphasizing service to customers and managed in accordance with a strategic plan.

H. B. Fuller is committed to its responsibilities, in order of priority, to its customers, employees, shareholders, and communities. H. B. Fuller will conduct business legally and ethically, support the activities of its employees in their communities and be a responsible corporate citizen.

388. Funco Inc.
10120 W. 76th St.
Minneapolis, MN 55344
Phone: (612) 946-8883
Web: http://www.funcoland.com

Funco Inc. (NASDAQ; FNCO), through its FuncoLand stores, is a retailer of previously played interactive entertainment. The company's products include a wide selection of video games, related hardware, and accessories.

Company Strategy: The company's primary goal is to strengthen its position as a leading provider of previously played interactive entertainment.

389. Furon Co.
29982 Ivy Glenn Dr.
Laguna Niguel, CA 92677
Phone: (714) 831-5350

Furon Co. (NYSE; FCY) designs and manufactures highly specialized products for a wide range of applications. The company is a world leader in engineered polymer components.

Vision: Furon is committed to being the industry leader in satisfying its customers and providing them the highest quality goods and services. In doing so, employees share a sense of urgency in an environment of continuous learning and improvement.

390. Gannett Co. Inc.
1100 Wilson Blvd.
Arlington, VA 22234
Phone: (703) 284-6000
Web: http://www.gannett.com

Gannett Co. Inc. (NYSE; GCI) is a news and information company whose assets include USA Today, daily and weekly community newspapers, specialty publications, television and radio stations, alarm security services, and online news, information and advertising.

Slogan: "Dynamic by Definition."

Mission: To create and expand products through innovation and continue to make acquisitions in news, information, and communications and related fields that make strategic and economic sense.

Environment: It is Gannett's policy to operate its business as a corporate citizen committed to sound environment management and with concern for the well-being of our common environment. Our goal is to ensure that company facilities and operations are in compliance with federal, state, and local environmental standards. We believe that an appropriate balance can and should be achieved between environmental goals and economic health. We intend to be a leader in responsible environmental management.

Operating Principles: Provide effective leadership and efficient management.

Achieve a positive return on new and acquired products and properties in a reasonable period of time, while recognizing those with high growth potential may take more time.

Increase profitability and increase return on equity and investment over the long term.

Enhance the quality and editorial integrity of our products, recognizing that quality products ultimately lead to higher profits.

Guarantee respect for and fairness in dealing with employees.

Offer a diverse environment where opportunity is based on merit.

Show commitment and service to communities where we do business.

Deliver customer satisfaction.

Dispose of assets that have limited or no potential.

In all activities, we show respect for the First Amendment and our responsibility to it.

bility is a fact of company culture, in each of the communities in which it does business, the company has made it a priority to address the environment, work safety, and employment issues with which it comes in contact. The company encourages its employees as its headquarters, distribution centers, and in its stores to become involved actively in their communities. As a responsible member of the international business community, the company has made great efforts to ensure that the quality of its overseas vendors extends far beyond the goods and services they supply.

Statement: I have always wanted The Gap to be recognized as America's leading quality specialty store for casual clothing. Our Gap label products stand for quality and good taste, and today our brand sells the second most apparel units of any brand in the world, behind Levi.

We are unique in that we create, produce and sell our own products. We design, not copy, and our stores and our merchandise are distinctive and recognizable. This brand identity, plus our vertical integration at every stage of our business and our superb real estate locations, gives us major competitive advantages over any other specialty apparel retailer.

What this company has achieved in such a short time is almost impossible to imagine. It's like a fairy tale.

391. Gap Inc.
One Harrison
San Francisco, CA 94105
Phone: (415) 952-4400

The Gap Inc. (NYSE; GPS) is a specialty retailer which operates stores selling casual apparel for men, women, and children under five registered brand names: Gap, GapKids, babyGap, Banana Republic, and Old Navy Clothing Co.

Slogan: "Fall Into the Gap."

Teamwork: Teamwork has made us what we are today, and it will carry us for the next 25 years.

Social Responsibility: Social responsi-

392. Gateway 2000
610 Gateway Dr.
North Sioux City, SD 57049
Phone: (605) 232-2000
Web: http://www.gateway.com

Gateway 2000 is a direct marketer of personal computers.

Slogan: "You've Got a Friend in the Business."

Vision: To be the leading marketer of personal computer products in the world.

Values: Respect, caring, teamwork, common sense, aggressiveness, honesty, efficiency and fun.

Mission: To profitably grow our business faster than the competition by better understanding and serving the desires of our customers and aggressively marketing the highest value directly to our chosen markets.

393. Gaylord Entertainment Co.
One Gaylord Dr.
Nashville, TN 37214
Phone: (615) 316-6000

Gaylord Entertainment Co. (NYSE; GET) is a diversified entertainment and communications company operating principally in three industry divisions: Entertainment, cable networks, and broadcasting.

Mission: Gaylord Entertainment Company will be the internationally recognized source of country music, country lifestyle and family entertainment and provider of world-class convention and lodging facilities, thereby generating a 15% average annual increase in operating cash flow.

394. Genentech Inc.
460 Point San Bruno Blvd.
South San Francisco, CA 94080
Phone: (415) 225-1000
Web: http://www.gene.com

Genentech Inc. (NYSE; GNE), a public subsidiary (Hoffmann-La Roche, immediate parent), manufactures and markets pharmaceuticals produced by recombinant DNA technology.

Statement: The company's strategy is to utilize biotechnology to produce unique and useful pharmaceutical products to provide treatments for currently untreatable diseases, or to improve upon existing, but less adequate treatments. We are putting the necessary resources towards our goal of building the internal value of the company by maximizing sales of existing products, aggressively pursuing product development, increasing the pace

of forming strategic alliances and improving financial returns.

395. General Dynamics Corp.
3190 Fairview Dr.
Falls Church, VA 22042
Phone: (703) 876-3000
Web: http://www.gdeb.com

General Dynamics Corp. (NYSE; GD) is a supplier of sophisticated defense systems. The company has two main divisions: Electric Boat Division and the Land System Division. They design and build nuclear submarines and armored vehicles, respectively.

Statement: To give our customers more affordable products, our major businesses stepped up their efforts to lower costs. Scrubbing our costs for better efficiency is a never-ending process, central to the way we run the business. Our customers count on it, and our shareholders expect it. We believe that enhancing affordability for our customers and building value for our shareholders are sides of the same coin.

We believe consolidation of the defense industry will continue — and as it does, it may well present us with significant opportunities to build on our strengths. Accordingly, we remain open to business combinations, with several criteria firmly in place. Any opportunity must present real value for our shareholders; lead to more affordable products for our customers; enable us to improve margins in the backlog through increased efficiencies; and result in marketplace leadership and critical mass.

396. General Electric Co.
3135 Easton Tpk.
Fairfield, CT 06431
Phone: (203) 373-2211
Web: http://www.ge.com

General Electric Co. (NYSE; GE) is involved in the following businesses: Aircraft engines, broadcasting (through

NBC), industry (through Borg Warner, plastics, technical products and services, appliances, and financial services (through GE Capital).

Slogans: "Progress Is Our Most Important Product." "We Bring Good Things to Life." GE Capital — "Our Business Is Helping You."

G.E. Management Values: G. E. leaders, always with unyielding integrity:

Create a clear, simple, reality-based, customer-focused vision and are able to communicate it straightforwardly to all constituencies.

Set aggressive targets, understanding accountability and commitment, and are decisive.

Have a passion for excellence, hating bureaucracy and all the nonsense that comes with it.

Have the self-confidence to empower others and behave in a boundary-less fashion. They believe in and are committed to work-out as a means of empowerment and are open to ideas from anywhere.

Have, or have the capacity to develop, global brains and global sensitivity and are comfortable building diverse global teams.

Stimulate and relish change and are not frightened or paralyzed by it, seeing change as opportunity, not threat.

Have enormous energy and the ability to energize and invigorate others. They understand speed as a competitive advantage and see the total organizational benefits that can be derived from a focus on speed.

397. General Mills Inc.
1 General Mills Blvd.
Minneapolis, MN 55426
Phone: (612) 540-2311
Web: http://www.generalmills.com

General Mills Inc. (NYSE; GIS) produces cereals and other consumer foods. Registered trade names include Cheerios, Betty Crocker, Hamburger Helper, Gold Medal flour, Yoplait, and Bisquick.

Slogan: Cheerios — "The Only One."

Statement of Corporate Values: Consumers — Consumers choose General Mills because we offer competitively superior products and services.

Employees — Employees choose General Mills because we reward innovation and superior performance and release their power to lead.

Investors — Investors choose General Mills because we consistently deliver financial results in the top 10 percent of all major companies.

Commitment: Our commitment to our shareholders is to deliver financial results that place us in the top 10 percent of all major companies. This can only be accomplished with the personal commitment of each of us.

The persistency to bounce back from disappointments, the intensity to pursue the exceptionally difficult, and the reliability to deliver promised results are all part of our commitment to our shareholders, to each other, and to our pride in "The Company of Champions." This commitment is demonstrated by substantial and increasing levels of employee stock ownership.

398. General Motors Corp.
100 Renaissance Center
Detroit, MI 48243
Phone: (313) 556-5000
Web: http://www.gm.com

General Motors Corp. (NYSE; GM) is the world's largest auto maker, in addition to being the world's largest company.

Slogans: "People in Motion" GMC Trucks — "The Strength of Experience." Cadillac — "Creating a Higher Standard." Chevy — "Heartbeat of America." Oldsmobile — "New Generation of Olds." Oldsmobile — "Demand Better." Buick — "The New Symbol of Quality in America." Buick — "Now ... Wouldn't You Really Rather Have a Buick." Pontiac — "We Are Driving Excitement." Chevy — "Experience the Difference of Genuine Chevrolet." GMC Yukon —

"Comfortably in Command." Oldsmobile Bravada — "It Knows the Road." Chevy Venture — "Let's Go." Pontiac Bonneville — "Luxury with Attitude." Pontiac — "Wider Is Better."

Vision: Our vision is for GM to be the world leader in transportation products and services.

399. General Re Corp.
695 E. Main St.
Stanford, CT 06904
Phone: (203) 328-5000
Web: http://www.genre.com

General Re Corp. (NYSE; GRN) is a holding company providing, through its subsidiary General Reinsurance, reinsurance, insurance, and other related services.

Mission Statement: At General Re, we are committed to maintaining our status as the industry leader in evaluating, structuring, underwriting, and managing risk by providing reinsurance and other financial products and services that meet or exceed the needs and expectations of our clients worldwide. We will continue to improve existing products, services, and capabilities, as well as provide new and innovative services so that General Re and its staff, clients and shareholders grow and prosper, enabling us to continue to be the best reinsurance/financial services company in the world.

400. Genuine Parts Co.
2999 Circle 75 Pkwy.
Atlanta, GA 30339
Phone: (707) 953-1700
Web: http://www.genpt.com

Genuine Parts Co. (NYSE; GPC) is a major auto parts distributor.

Looking Ahead: We believe that it is our good fortune to operate in three sound business activities. The market for auto parts, industrial parts and supplies, and for office products will continue to experience modest but steady growth. Our strategy is directed toward growth at a rate

higher than industry rates and to be the best at what we do.

Each of our industries is experiencing rapid change which creates opportunities for us — we are pleased that our marketing plans seem to be working well and moving us ahead in a positive way.

401. Genzyme Corp.
One Kendall Sq.
Cambridge, MA 02139
Phone: (617) 252-7500
Web: http://www.genzyme.com/
welcome.shtml

Genzyme Corp. (NASDAQ; GENZ), a top biotechnology company, develops and markets therapeutic and diagnostic products and genetic diagnostic services. It also develops processes for manufacturing pharmaceuticals and novel chemicals.

Statement: The company focuses on developing innovative solutions to major unresolved human health care needs.

402. Geon Co.
One Geon Center
Avon Lake, OH 44012
Phone: (216) 930-1000
Web: http://www.geon.com

Geon Co. (NYSE; GON) is a producer of vinyl (PVC) resins and compounds.

Statement: We are continuing our program to position Geon at benchmark competitiveness in our industry.

Looking forward we see additional opportunities to create significant long-term shareholder value through growth.

403. Georgia-Pacific Corp.
133 Peachtree St. NE
41st Fl.
Atlanta, GA 30303
Phone: (404) 652-4000
Web: http://www.gp.com

Georgia-Pacific Corp. (NYSE; GP) manufactures and markets building and paper products.

Slogan: "You Take Care of the Things You Care About."

Vision: Being the best at everything we do.

To outperform our competitors and to generate the best investment returns, some of the right things are to:

Provide a safe working environment and rewarding careers for our employees.

Provide customers with products and services that meet or exceed expectations.

Promote environmental stewardship.

Improve operations and products continually.

Pursue aggressively being the best at everything we do and always uphold the highest standards of business conduct.

Environmental Policy: Georgia-Pacific's policy is to practice pollution prevention by minimizing environmental impacts of our products and operations, practicing sustainable development, and promoting continuous improvement through measurable goals.

404. Gerber Products Co.
444 State St.
Fremont, MI 49413
Phone: (616) 928-2000

Gerber Products Co., a subsidiary of Sandoz — Sandoz AG and Ciba-Geigy Ltd. merged to form Novartis AG (OTC; NVTSY) — makes and markets baby food.

Mission: The people and resources of the Gerber Products Company are dedicated to assuring that the company is the world leader in, and advocate for, infant nutrition, care, and development.

405. Gibson Greetings Inc.
2100 Section Rd.
Cincinnati, OH 45222
Phone: (513) 841-6600

Gibson Greetings Inc. (NASDAQ; GIBG) designs, manufactures, and markets greeting cards, gift wraps, and other specialty items.

Mission: Our mission is to provide the highest quality products that communicate personal expression; to support our retailers' business objectives through innovation, responsiveness and productivity; and to achieve the goals of our shareholders and our associates.

406. Giddings & Lewis Inc.
142 Doty St.
Fond du Lac, WI 54935
Phone: (414) 921-9400

Giddings & Lewis Inc. (NASDAQ; GIDL) manufactures machine tools and industrial products.

Quality Policy: Giddings & Lewis is committed to a policy of meeting our customers' requirements in all functions of our organization. We shall conform to those requirements without exception with a performance standard of "Do it right the first time."

Mission Statement: The mission of Giddings & Lewis, Inc. is to be a leading global company that provides our customers world-class manufacturing technology by developing, producing and marketing engineered products and services required for automated discrete manufacturing and to engage in the manufacturing of industrial products/components compatible with the expertise and capabilities of Giddings & Lewis, Inc.

407. Gillette Co.
Prudential Tower Bldg.
Boston, MA 02199
Phone: (617) 421-7000

Gillette Co. (NYSE; G) manufactures and markets consumer products, including razors, dental care products (Oral-B), pens (Parker; Paper Mate), and coffeemakers (Braun).

Slogans: Gillette — "The Best a Man Can Get." Braun — "Designed to Perform Better."

Statement: The strength of Gillette's

long-term business results and stock market performance is largely due to our continuing focus on carrying out the company's mission — to achieve or enhance clear leadership worldwide in the existing or new core consumer product categories in which we choose to compete. To achieve this, we emphasize geographic expansion and three primary "growth drivers" — research and development, capital spending and advertising.

408. Glaxo Wellcome PLC

Landsdowne House
Berkeley Sq.
London W1X 6BQ
United Kingdom
Phone: (44) 0171-493-4060
Web: http://www.glaxowellcome.co.uk

Glaxo Wellcome PLC (NYSE; GLX) is a major company competing in the pharmaceutical industry.

Mission Statement: Glaxo Wellcome is a research-based company whose people are committed to fighting disease by bringing innovative medicines and services to patients throughout the world and to the healthcare providers who serve them.

409. Golden Enterprises Inc.

2101 Magnolia Ave. South
Suite 212
Birmingham, AL 35205
Phone: (205) 326-6101

Golden Enterprises Inc. (NASDAQ; GLDC) is a holding company. Its only subsidiary is Golden Flake, a snack food company.

Slogan: "It's Where You Find the Flavor."

Statement: Golden Flake employees are committed to producing the best possible snack products, developing products that satisfy customer trends, meeting the service and snack sales needs of our valued customers and overall to be the "best in the industry." While we are committed to

the above, we are also working to deliver increasingly better financial results for our shareholders. As a group, Golden Flake employees are our company's second largest shareholder and therefore have a strong vested interest in the performance of our company.

410. (The) Good Guys Inc.

7000 Marina Blvd.
Brisbane, CA 94005
Phone: (415) 615-5000
Web: http://www.thegoodguys.com

Good Guys Inc. (NASDAQ; GGUY) is a retailer of electronic goods (audio/video specialists).

Slogan: "Our Name Is Our Way of Doing Business."

Statement of Mission: The Good Guys! is committed to giving every customer a superior consumer electronics shopping experience at competitive prices.

This will be achieved through:

An unrelenting commitment to interacting with our customers honestly; listening to their needs with sincere interest; providing them with superior product knowledge; and maintaining an attitude of overall customer respect; and our offering the broadest assortment of quality consumer electronics products from well-known manufacturers.

411. (B. F.) Goodrich Co.

4020 Kinross Lakes Pkwy.
Richfield, OH 44286
Phone: (216) 659-7600
Web: http://www.bfgoodrich.com

B. F. Goodrich Co. (NYSE; GR) is a manufacturer in the aircraft components industry. The company also manufactures plastics and specialty chemicals.

Mission: The basic purpose of The B. F. Goodrich Company is to provide customers with quality products, systems and services that represent the best use of our technological, financial and human resources. We achieve leadership positions in specialty markets by helping our customers improve the performance of their products and reducing their costs. By creating economic advantages for our customers, we generate wealth for our shareholders, provide rewarding careers for our employees and build our worldwide business in a profitable and responsible manner.

412. Goodyear Tire and Rubber Co.
1144 Market St.
Akron, OH 44316
Phone: (303) 796-2121
Web: http://www.goodyear.com

Goodyear Tire and Rubber Co. (NYSE; GT) is a diversified global manufacturer of tires and other rubber, plastic, and chemical products.

Slogans: "#1 in Tires." "The Best Tires in the World Have Goodyear Written All Over Them."

Mission: Our mission is constant improvement in products and services to meet our customers' needs. This is the only means to business success for Goodyear and prosperity for its investors and employees. Quality is the key to customer satisfaction.

Company Credo: "Protect Our Good Name."

Environment: As a diversified global manufacturer of tires and other rubber, plastic, and chemical products, Goodyear and its associates are committed to protecting the environment in the offices and in the production and sales facilities of its operation.

Fulfilling marketplace demands, while striving for the highest environmental standards, is a top corporate priority.

Goodyear associates are committed to a wide range of programs that protect the environment and conserve natural resources.

413. (W. R.) Grace & Co.
One Town Center Rd.
Boca Raton, FL 33486
Phone: (561) 362-2000
Web: http://www.gcp-grace.com

W. R. Grace & Co. (NYSE; GRA) is a global specialty chemicals and specialized health care company. Grace's focus is on its six core product lines: Packaging, catalysts and other silica-based products, construction products, water treatment and process chemicals, container sealants, and health care.

Slogan: "Commitment to Care."

The Company Tomorrow: Grace is now embarked on a far-reaching global strategy designed to maximize shareholder value by focusing, upgrading and integrating its core and specialty chemicals and specialized health care businesses. To propel the company's growth through the 1990s and beyond, Grace is focusing on aggressively growing its core product lines — packaging, catalysts and other silica-based products, construction products, water treatment and process chemicals, container products, and health care.

414. Graco Inc.
450 Olson Memorial Hwy.
Golden Valley, MN 56422
Phone: (612) 623-6000

Graco Inc. (NYSE; GGG) is a world leader in fluid handling systems and components.

Slogan: "First Choice When Quality Counts."

Corporate Mission: Graco's mission is to serve it customers, employees, shareholders, and communities by generating sustained profitable growth. Our goal is to be the world's leading supplier of fluid handling equipment and systems in the markets we serve.

Corporate Vision: Graco will be an independent, worldwide leader in fluid handling systems and components. Graco products move, measure, control dispense, and apply a wide range of fluids and viscous materials used in vehicle lubrication, commercial and industrial settings. The company's success is based on its unwavering commitment to technical excellence, world-class manufacturing and unparalleled customer service. Working closely with specialized distributors, Graco offers systems, products and technology which set the quality standards in a wide range of fluid handling applications, including spray finishing and paint circulation, lubrication, sealants, and adhesives, along with power application equipment for the contractor industry. Graco's ongoing investment in fluid management and control will continue to provide innovative solutions to a diverse global market.

415. (W. W.) Grainger Inc.

5500 W. Howard St.
Skokie, IL 60077
Phone: (847) 793-9030
Web: http://www.grainger.com

W. W. Grainger Inc. (NYSE; GWW) is a nationwide distributor of maintenance, repair, and operating supplies, and related information to commercial, industrial, contractor, and institutional customers.

Company Vision: The company has been successful since its founding in 1927. This success has been due in large part to a philosophy of management which will continue to guide us in the future. Our vision is:

To be the leader in the distribution of maintenance, repair, and operating suppliers and related information to commercial, industrial, contractor and institutional customers. To have the capabilities necessary to be a primary source through the breadth of our offering and a focus on the lowest total cost solution for each of our customers.

To operate with the highest moral, ethical, and legal standards.

To be committed to: Superior service and satisfaction for each of our customers; mutually fair, responsible, and beneficial arrangements with each of our suppliers; fairness, dignity, respect, and equal opportunity for all employees regardless of sex, age, race, or national origin; professionalism in all aspects of our business operations.

To operate for quality long-term growth while: Sustaining sound and conservative financial policies; achieving an attractive rate of return for our shareholders through continued improvements in economic earnings.

To foster a working environment that promotes: High integrity; high standards; initiative and creativity; respect and concern for other people as individuals; loyalty; continuous learning and business process improvement.

To be a good corporate citizen in the communities in which we operate.

Company Values: Agility — Challenge the status quo and be open to new ideas.

Empowerment and accountability — Give employees the authority to act and be responsible for their actions.

Ethics and integrity — Commit to fairness and honesty in all aspects of business.

Having fun — Celebrate achievements and encourage a healthy balance between work and personal life.

Learning — Seek and accept feedback and build upon both successes and failures.

Teamwork — Trust others and value differences.

416. GranCare Inc.

One Ravinia Dr.
Ste. 1500
Atlanta, GA 30346
Phone: (770) 393-0199

GranCare Inc. (NYSE; GC) is a health care organization that provides a comprehensive continuum of care for patients following their discharge from the acute hospital setting.

Slogan: "Commitment to Excellence."

The Vision: To be the innovator within the full spectrum of health care; to be a revolutionary force in shaping new cost-effective responses to the health needs of society well into the future; to achieve this vision through risk-taking; forming creative partnerships; attracting, involving, retaining and empowering talented staff; and progressively pushing the standards of quality to higher levels.

417. Grand Casinos Inc.

130 Cheshire Lane
Minnetonka, MN 55305
Phone: (612) 449-4002
Web: http://www.grandcasinos.com

Grand Casinos Inc. (NYSE; GND) is in the gaming business.

Our Mission: To operate premier casinos, balancing the needs of profitability, associates and guests.

To delight the guests — not just satisfy them.

To operate with a high level of excellence, innovation, integrity and ethics.

To attract, retain and develop a team of superior people.

To be focused, sensitive and responsive to the casinos' associates.

To be a welcome and positive corporate citizen of our resident communities.

Statement: Our goals ... are to fine-tune all properties and operate more efficiently, thereby improving margins and overall financial performance. We will continue to add amenities to further delight our guests by creating full-service destination resorts at each location. Additionally, we will continue our proactive search for exceptional opportunities to develop new gaming projects. With a superior management team already in place, we are positioned to grow. Finally, it is our goal and intention to continue to operate with a high level of integrity and ethics in all that we do.

418. Grand Metropolitan PLC

20 St. James's Sq.
London SW1Y 4RR
United Kingdom
Phone: (29) 0171-518-5200

Grand Metropolitan PLC (NYSE; GRM) is a food and liquor giant. Subsidiaries include Pillsbury, Burger King, Haagen-Dazs, Green Giant, Old El Paso, Progresso, and International Distillers & Vintners (Bailey's, J&B Rare, Smirnoff). Plans have been approved for the merger with Guinness.

Company Values: GrandMet is a market-driven company. We must continuously listen to what our customers and consumers tell us and genuinely respond to this. We will strive at all time to provide quality in our goods and services.

Through increased market orientation, we will grow our business by developing added-value food and drink brands. We will resist involvement in commodity and private label trading. The long-term health of our brands is the life blood of GrandMet's prosperity. All actions by the GrandMet board and all employees at all times should strengthen the position of our brands position in the marketplace. It is essential that we must all behave in accordance with the above principle to support our business mission, which is to maximize shareholder value over time by building brand equity.

419. GRC International Inc.

1900 Gallows Rd.
Vienna, VA 22182
Phone: (703) 506-5000
Web: http://www.grci.com

GRC International Inc. (NYSE; GRH) is a provider of professional and technical products and services to military, civil and commercial clients. The company has gained prominence for innovation in complex information systems, advanced technology development, interactive multimedia training, telecommunications, materials testing and other decision-support and productivity enhancement products and services.

Mission Statement: GRC International — Committed to our clients' success through the delivery of consistently superior decision-support and productivity-enhancement products and services.

420. Great Atlantic & Pacific Tea Co. Inc.
2 Paragon Dr.
Montvale, NJ 07645
Phone: (201) 573-9700
Web: http://www.aptea.com

Great Atlantic & Pacific Tea Co. Inc. (NYSE; GAP) operates a major supermarket chain.

Statement: Our desire to be the supermarket of choice in all our markets unifies our activities across all banners.

Quality and value are often subjective and difficult to define. At A&P we define quality and value by fine produce, choice deli and bakery goods, a pleasant shopping environment and exceptional store brands.

Our goal, now as always, is to consistently provide the highest quality at the lowest possible price.

A&P is dedicated to product improvement and product development.

421. Great Western Financial Corp.
9200 Oakdale Ave.
Chatsworth, CA 91313
Phone: (818) 775-3411
Web: http://www.gwf.com

Great Western Financial Corp. (NYSE; GWF) operates in the financial services industry. Divisions include mortgage banking, banking and investments, and consumer finance.

Strategic Objectives: Some six years ago, Great Western recognized that its core business, home mortgage origination, faced continuing competitive pressures, most notable, pricing pressures. To sustain and enhance profitability in an increasingly commodity-like marketplace,

the company concluded it was essential to lower its relative cost of funds and grow new sources of revenue.

These have been two components to the company's fundamental change in strategic direction. In 1989, Great Western began an effort to become more like a retail consumer bank with the twin goals of reducing its cost of funds and developing new sources of revenue. Concurrently, Great Western began to open real estate offices outside California to reduce its concentration of credit risk in California. The goal was to increase outside California originations to 50 percent annually, Using 1989 as a benchmark year, Great Western has made significant progress in achieving all of these strategic objectives during the past six years.

Statement: As the company looks to the future, its principal objectives are to:

Accelerate the drive to be more like a commercial bank.

Continue to lower its relative cost of funds.

Continue to exert strong control over expenses.

Create a substantially larger and broader book of retail consumer loan business.

Further develop distribution channels and cross-selling opportunities.

Become an even more efficient national mortgage lender.

422. Groundwater Technology Inc.
100 River Ridge Dr.
Norwood, MA 02062
Phone: (617) 769-7600

Groundwater Technology Inc. (NASDAQ; GWTI), an environmental consulting, engineering and remediation firm, is a leader in the development and application of cost-effective technologies for the restoration of environmentally impacted sites.

Slogan: "Excellence in Every Phase."

Vision: Our vision is to be the world leader in on-site remediation.

To achieve this, we will dedicate ourselves to total customer satisfaction, create opportunities for our fellow employees' development and success, encourage innovation and continuous improvement of our technology, aggressively pursue profitable growth ... while contributing to a better environment.

Our Mission: Groundwater Technology is committed to providing unsurpassed service to our customers in the restoration and protection of the environment. Our goal is to be recognized as the leader in the remediation of contaminated soil and groundwater.

We will seek to provide total customer satisfaction while applying proven and innovative technologies which reduce the risks associated with environmental contamination in the most cost-effective manner.

Our work will be driven by enthusiasm, discipline, and a commitment to continuous improvement in order to achieve steady growth and financial success while adhering to the highest professional, business, and ethical standards, We will pursue this mission with confidence and pride for the benefit of our customers, the public, our shareholders, and our employees.

423. GTE Corp.

One Stamford Forum
Stamford, CT 06904
Phone: (203) 965-2000
Web: http://www.gte.com

GTE Corp. (NYSE; GTE) is a very large telecommunications company. It is the largest U.S.-based local telephone company, with wireline and wireless operations in markets encompassing about a third of the U.S. population. GTE is also a leader in government and defense communications systems and equipment, directories, telecommunications-based information services and systems, and aircraft-passenger telecommunications.

Slogan: "It's Amazing What We Can Do Together."

Statement: Our talented and motivated employees remain committed to ensuring that our company is successful and that we take full advantage of the explosive opportunities available to us. Not only is our future bright, but our direction is clear as well. Our strategies are based on five major initiatives: Enhance wireless voice, accelerate wireless development, expand data services, pursue international opportunities, and enter video services.

Vision and Financial Performance: Three years ago we set forth a clear vision for GTE: Nothing less than market leadership in the telecommunications industry. We said that we'd achieve that vision by growing the business in five strategic areas: Wireline voice, wireless, data, video, and international.

We've made excellent progress in those areas. At the same time, we're delivering record financial results.

424. Guardian Life Insurance Co. of America

201 Park Ave. South
New York, NY 10003
Phone: (212) 598-8000
Web: http://www.theguardian.com

The Guardian Life Insurance Co. of America, a mutual company, is a provider of personal insurance and financial services.

Slogan: "The Intelligent Choice."

Corporate Mission Statement: The mission of The Guardian is to be the premier and primary provider of personal insurance and financial services to clearly identified individual and group markets based on satisfying consumer and corporate client needs.

We will follow a pattern of innovative management and prudent risk taking and will add value while safeguarding policyowner interests.

We will offer competitively priced, high quality products through a professional, personalized delivery system.

We will support our products and their

delivery systems with friendly, efficient services, utilizing modern technologies in a cost-effective manner.

Quality, financial strength and profitability will continue to be the hallmark of our corporate identity.

Our corporate culture has always been based on integrity and fair dealings with our clients, employees and agents. This will continue to be our guiding principle in the future for all our lines of business.

425. Guardsman Products Inc.

3033 Orchard Vista Dr. SE
Suite 200
Grand Rapids, MI 49501
Phone: (616) 957-2600

Guardsman Products Inc. (NYSE; GPI) is a leading producer of customized industrial coatings, resins and diversified consumer home-care products.

Mission: The mission of Guardsman Products Inc. is to manufacture and provide quality goods and services which enhance and maintain the value and appearance of products used in the home and the workplace. Guardsman is dedicated to excel in this mission for the benefit of its customers, employees and shareholders. We are dedicated to: Delivering goods and services of superior quality and value to our customer through innovative technology, unparalleled service and continuous improvement of our processes. Treating our employees in a fair and equitable manner and providing a stimulating, challenging and safe environment which promotes pride in the company, teamwork, personal growth, and respect for the individual. Acting as responsible corporate citizens and conducting our business with the highest levels of ethics and integrity. Being environmentally progressive. Providing our shareholders with increased value and favorable returns by achieving our financial goals.

426. Gymboree Corp.

700 Airport Blvd.
Suite 200
Burlingame, CA 94010
Phone: (415) 579-0600
Web: http://server1.service.com/
gymboree/home.html

Gymboree Corp. (NASDAQ; GYMB) is a specialty retailer of high quality apparel and accessories for children ages newborn to seven years old.

Business Strategy: The company's business strategy consists of the following principal elements: High quality apparel, brand name recognition, integrated operations (design, production and retailing), exclusive distribution channel, and merchandise focus.

427. Haemonetics Corp.

400 Wood Rd.
Braintree, MA 02184
Phone: (617) 848-7100
Web: http://www.haemonetics.com

Haemonetics Corp. (NYSE; HAE) is the world leader in automated blood processing.

Mission: To enhance the safety and quality of the world's blood supply and increase the availability of critical blood components.

428. Hallmark Cards Inc.

2501 McGee St.
Kansas City, MO 64108
Phone: (816) 274-5111
Web: http://www.hallmark.com

Hallmark Cards Inc., a private company, makes and markets greeting cards and other personal communications products.

Slogans: "When You Care Enough to Send the Very Best." "You'll Feel Better Inside."

Corporate Mission: Hallmark aspires to enrich people's lives and enhance their relationships.

429. Hamilton Beach/ Proctor-Silex Inc.

4421 Waterfront Dr.
Glen Allen, VA 23060
Phone: (804) 273-9777

Hamilton Beach/Proctor-Silex Inc., a subsidiary of NACCO Industries Inc. (NYSE; NC), manufactures household appliances.

Mission Statement: It is the mission of the Hamilton Beach/Proctor-Silex operations team to manufacture and deliver high quality products that meet or exceed customer expectations in the world market. All products and services will be delivered on time, with expected performance, and at competitive costs.

Leadership through world class manufacturing ... A commitment to excellence.

430. (M. A.) Hanna Co.

Suite 36-5000
200 Public Sq.
Cleveland, OH 44114
Phone: (216) 589-4000
Web: http://www.mahanna.com

M. A. Hanna Co. (NYSE; MAH) is a leading international specialty chemicals company.

Slogan: "The Power to Change."

Statement: M. A. Hanna's strategy is to be the single source where processors prefer to shop for any combination of compounds, color and additive concentrates and resins and where the major polymer companies prefer to take their materials to market.

431. Hannaford Bros. Co.

145 Pleasant Hill Rd.
Scarsborough, ME 04074
Phone: (207) 883-2911
Web: http://www.hannaford.com

Hannaford Bros. Co. (NYSE; HRD) is a multi-regional food retailer. The company is located throughout Maine, and in parts of New Hampshire, Vermont, Massachusetts, New York, North Carolina, South Carolina, and Virginia. The company operates under the names Stop 'n Shop, Hannaford, or Wilson's.

Mission Statement: We want to serve consumers so well that they will be our regular customers. We need to find out what they like and find the best ways to serve them. We can do this best if we work together enthusiastically. To be successful, we must satisfy our customers, our associates, our communities and our shareholders. To achieve this, we must practice the highest level of ethical, social, legal and professional behavior. We must constantly anticipate the changing needs and desires of our customers and respond quickly and effectively to those needs and desires. We are committed to distributing the goods and services consumers want with prices and quality that represent superior value. We are committed to the growth of all associates. To accomplish this, we need a growing business, a sharing of common goals and an atmosphere of mutual trust, openness and encouragement. We will support and participate in the efforts of local, state, and national organizations which best contribute to the quality of life. We will strive to earn, during any five-year period, an average return on equity in the upper quartile of companies in similar businesses. In the long run, we will best serve the interests of our shareholders by serving well our customers, associates, and communities.

Earth Matters: Hannaford Bros. Co. is committed to improving our environment. Through our Earth Matters programs, we are working in partnership with our customers, communities, associates, and suppliers. We are raising awareness of environmental issues and increasing community involvement in environmental programs. We are encouraging and practicing recycling, reuse of materials, and reduced use of natural resources. These efforts will benefit our communities, our business and our associates by maintaining an environment in which we can all thrive.

Our Vision: Our Vision: Grow the business. Seize opportunities. Keep learning. Take ownership. Win through excellent teamwork.

432. Harcourt General Inc.
27 Boylston St.
Chestnut Hills, MA 02167
Phone: (617) 232-8200

Harcourt General Inc. (NYSE; H) operates in publishing (Harcourt Brace), retailing (Neiman Marcus, NM Direct, Bergdorf Goodman and Contempo Casuals) and professional services (Drake Beam Morin).

Our Mission: Harcourt General is an international operating company founded upon and committed to a fundamental economic principle: Management is responsible for generating above-average returns to the company's shareholders on a consistent, long-term basis.

Our mission, therefore, is to aggressively, yet responsibly, manage our operating business to create steadily appreciating value for those who invest in our company. As we pursue this mission, we are guided by the following important values:

1. We will maintain an uncompromising commitment of quality and the highest levels of customer service in all our businesses and endeavors.

2. We will adhere to the highest levels of integrity and ethical standards in dealing with all constituencies, including customers, suppliers, and employees.

3. We will aspire to achieve a leadership position in every one of our operating businesses.

4. Our management decisions will emphasize long-term benefits to the value of our businesses, not short-term gains. We will employ capable, motivated people; follow sound management practices; utilize new technology efficiently; and reinvest earnings and new capital as required to grow our businesses and maintain the Corporation's financial health.

5. We will strive to maximize the potential of all employees and maintain a professionally challenging work environment.

6. We will be socially responsible and provide financial and human resources support for worthwhile causes, especially in those communities in which we operate.

433. Harley-Davidson Inc.
3700 W. Juneau
Milwaukee, WI 53201
Phone: (414) 342-4680
Web: http://www.harley-davidson.com

Harley-Davidson Inc. (NYSE; HDI) manufactures premium quality, heavyweight motorcycles.

Slogan: "It's Not the Destination, It's the Journey."

Statement: At Harley-Davidson, we don't run our business on a quarter-to-quarter basis. We also don't run our business for Wall Street, ourselves or even our customers. Our focus has been and will continue to be on the long term growth, which we believe is attainable only by balancing the interests of all of our stakeholders. This way, we all grow. Together.

Our Vision: Harley-Davidson Inc. is an action-oriented, international company — a leader in its commitment to continuously improve the quality of mutually beneficial relationships with stakeholders (customers, dealers, employees, suppliers, investors, governments, and society). Harley-Davidson believes the key to success is to balance stakeholders' interests through the empowerment of all employees to focus on value-added activities.

Base Philosophy: Organizations are people.

Business organizations only achieve success through the efforts of people.

Leadership adds unique value to the organization only to the extent to which leaders enhance the capability of people.

A leader's only success comes through the efforts of others.

Values:
Tell the truth.
Keep your promises.
Be fair.
Respect the individual.
Encourage intellectual curiosity.
Harley-Davidson Issues:
Quality.
Participation.
Productivity.
Flexibility.
Cash flow.

434. Harnischfeger Industries Inc.

P.O. Box 554
Milwaukee, WI 53201
Phone: (414) 797-6480

Harnischfeger Industries Inc. (NYSE; HPH) is a holding company with business segments involved in the manufacture, distribution, and service of equipment for papermaking, surface mining, underground mining, and material handling.
Slogan: "Focused Energy."
Statement: Our company continues to focus its energies on strengthening its core businesses globally. We are meeting customer needs by providing technologies, equipment and aftermarket support that deliver productivity and value.

435. Harrah's Entertainment Inc.

1023 Cherry Rd.
Memphis, TN 38117
Phone: (901) 762-8600
Web: http://www.harrahs.com

Harrah's Entertainment Inc. (NYSE; HET) is in the casino business. The company operates land-based casinos in Atlantic City, Lake Tahoe, Las Vegas, Laughlin (CO), Reno, and Auckland. They also operate riverboat and dockside casinoes in Joliet, North Kansas City, Shreveport, St. Louis, Tunica, and Vicksburg. Additionally Phoenix Ak-Chin and Skagit Valley are Indian casinos operated by Harrah's. The following are under development: Cherokee Smokey Mountains and Prairie Band-Topeka.
Slogan: "The Premier Name in Casino Entertainment."
Our Vision: Our vision at Harrah's Entertainment Inc. is to offer exciting environments and to be legendary at creating smiles, laughter and lasting memories with every guest we entertain.
Promise to Our Shareholders: To be industry leaders in financial performance, producing extraordinary results, not just extraordinary effort.
To create opportunities for our people who manage the corporation's assets to be significant shareholders, motivating them to create value for all shareholders.

436. Harris Corp.

1025 West NASA Blvd.
Melbourne, FL 32919
Phone: (407) 727-9100
Web: http://www.harris.com

Harris Corp. (NYSE; HRS) is a worldwide company with four major businesses — electronic systems, semiconductors, communications, and Lanier office systems.
Statement: The company uses advanced technologies to provide innovative and cost-effective solutions for our commercial and government customers and is committed to being a company of the highest quality in every aspect of its business activity.

437. Hasbro Inc.

1027 Newport Ave.
Pawtucket, RI 02862
Phone: (401) 431-8697
Web: http://www.hasbro.com

Hasbro Inc. (AMEX; HAS) is a worldwide leader in the design, manufacture and marketing of toys, games, puzzles, and infant care products.

Slogan: "Generation to Generation."

Statement: We are looking to the future — alert to the challenges and opportunities from a position of financial strength — and are making the changes and investments to provide for our long term growth and profitability.

438. HBO & Co.

301 Perimeter Center North
Atlanta, GA 30346
Phone: (707) 393-6000
Web: http://www.hboc.com

HBO & Co. (NASDAQ; HBOC) provides information systems to the healthcare industry.

Mission Statement: At HBO & Company, our people, products and services have a primary goal: To serve healthcare enterprises by putting the right information in the right hands at the right time. Every resource we employ and every task we undertake must deliver on that fundamental promise.

We will help every member of the caregiving team to improve the quality of patient care by providing them with software products, implementation and training services, and support to help them adapt to change and do their jobs better.

We will help every member of the healthcare delivery system to develop and manage effective healthcare enterprise networks by providing communications technologies that allow easy, immediate access to the exchange of information.

We will apply our experience and knowledge to help healthcare enterprises adapt to the fundamental, rapid changes occurring in the U.S. healthcare system by providing a foundation of innovative, flexible software solutions for future growth and success.

In the international marketplace, we will seek opportunities to apply our information technology solutions and expertise to the unique needs of healthcare delivery systems of other countries.

In all that we do, we are committed to a continuous pursuit of quality in fact and quality in perception, so that every product and service we offer is known as the best in the industry.

Vision: HBO & Company's vision is to be the acknowledged leader in healthcare informatics, such that the name "HBOC" will be synonymous with quality software products and related services, outstanding customer support, innovative thinking and successful information technology solutions.

439. HEALTHSOUTH Corp.

1 Healthsouth Pkwy.
Birmingham, AL 35243
Phone: (205) 967-7116
Web: http://www.healthsouth.com

HEALTHSOUTH Corp. (NYSE; HRC) provides rehabilitative health care services.

Statement: Our outpatient division has been streamlining its business processes to enable facilities to come on-line faster. We have been enhancing our clinical standards and protocols to increase the efficiency and efficacy of the delivery of care to our patients.

440. Heartland Express Inc.

2777 Heartland Dr.
Coralville, IA 52241
Phone: (319) 645-2728
Web: http://www.heartlandexpress.com

Heartland Express Inc. (NASDAQ; HTLD) provides short-haul trucking services.

Mission: "Delivering Quality First."

Statement of Mission: As an organization, Heartland Express is committed to providing our customers with the highest quality of service in the trucking industry. Excellence in service is our goal as a company. We measure ourselves by the high standards of our customers, and value their input. Mutual progress toward defined goals is our objective in working with our customers.

In order to provide this service to our external customers, Heartland is committed to internal quality processes. We are dedicated to achieving maximum efficiency and productivity in every area of operation. Every employee must understand how their job contributes to the overall operation and directly affects the customer, their ultimate employer.

Heartland Express is committed to continuous improvement and responsiveness to customer needs in all departments. We have made a long term commitment to developing programs that will enable our employees to function more efficiently. This will enable us to provide our customers with superior service and work with them to obtain mutual efficiencies. At Heartland, "Service for Success" enables ourselves and our customers to succeed in achieving overall quality that reflects organizational excellence.

441. (G.) Heileman Brewing Co. Inc.
100 Harborview Plaza
La Crosse, WI 54601
Phone: (608) 785-1000

G. Heileman Brewing Co. Inc., a private company acquired by Stroh Brewing Co., is in the business of brewing beer and other beverages.

Statement (prior to acquisition): G. Heileman is a team of highly motivated individuals focused on the production and sale of high quality beverages. Our strength is our commitment to our people, our industry, our investors, our wholesalers, our retailers, and our consumers.

442. (H. J.) Heinz Co.
600 Grant St.
Pittsburgh, PA 15219
Phone: (412) 456-5700
Web: http://www.hjheinz.com

H. J. Heinz Co. (NYSE; HNZ) is a major food processor.

Statement: Dissemination of pure products and nutritional services.

443. Hershey Foods Corp.
100 Crystal A Drive
Hershey, PA 17033
Web: http://www.hersheys.com

Hershey Foods Corp. (NYSE; HSY) is a leading manufacturer of chocolate and other confectionery products, and dry pasta products.

Slogan: "There's a Smile in Every Hershey's Bar."

Mission: Our mission is to be a focused food company in North America and selected international markets and a leader in every aspect of our business.

In North America, our goal is to enhance our number one position in confectionery and achieve number one positions in pasta and chocolate-related grocery products.

444. Hertz Corp.
225 Brae Blvd.
Park Ridge, NJ 07656
Phone: (201) 307-2000
Web: http://www.hertz.com

Hertz Corp. (NYSE: HRZ), a public subsidiary of Ford Motor Co. (NYSE; F), is in the car rental business.

Slogan: "There's Hertz, and There's Not Exactly." "Exactly."

Basic Beliefs/Values: We will conduct business ethically and honestly in dealing with our customers, suppliers and employees.

We will treat our employees in the same fashion as we expect them to treat our customers — with dignity and respect.

We will consistently provide the highest level of customer service and quality of vehicles, and differentiate ourselves from our principal competitors through innovation.

Profits are the ultimate measure of how efficiently we provide customers with the highest level of customer service and quality of vehicles. Profits are required to survive and grow.

The overall No. 1 position in airport revenue market share is a key measurement of industry leadership.

445. Hewlett-Packard Co.
3000 Hanover St.
Palo Alto, CA 94304
Phone: (415) 857-1501
Web: http://www.hp.com

Hewlett-Packard Co. (NYSE; HWP) is a leader in the manufacture of computers and related products.

Values: We have trust and respect for individuals.

We focus on a high level of achievement and contribution.

We conduct our business with uncompromising integrity.

We achieve our common objectives through teamwork.

We encourage flexibility and innovation.

Objectives: Profit: To achieve sufficient profit to finance our company growth and to provide the resources we need to achieve our other corporate objectives.

Customers: To provide products and services of the highest quality and the greatest possible value to our customers, thereby gaining and holding their respect and loyalty.

Fields of interest: To participate in those fields of interest that build upon our technology and customer base, that offer opportunities for continuing growth, and that enable us to make a needed and profitable contribution.

Growth: To let our growth be limited only by our profits and our ability to develop and produce innovative products that satisfy real customer needs.

Our people: To help HP people share in the company's success which they make possible; to provide employment security based on their performance; to ensure them a safe and pleasant work environment; to recognize their individual achievements;

and to help them gain a sense of satisfaction and accomplishment from their work.

Management: To foster initiative and creativity by allowing the individual great freedom of action in attaining well-defined objectives.

Citizenship: To honor our obligations to society by being an economic, intellectual, and social asset to each nation and each community in which we operate.

446. Hillenbrand Industries Inc.
700 State Route 46 East
Batesville, IN 47006
Phone: (812) 934-7000
Web: http://www.hillenbrand.com

Hillenbrand Industries Inc. (NYSE; HB) operates in the funeral services, health care, and high security lock markets.

The Hillenbrand Vision: Niche market leadership: We focus on and serve with excellence customers in only a few carefully chosen markets, rather than try to be all things to all customers.

Total customer satisfaction: We work to understand our customers' needs, exceed their expectations and build exceptional, long-term relationships with them. We know that the only way we create value is with satisfied customers.

Continuous improvement: We believe everything we do can be improved to the advantage of our customers.

Individual worth: We respect the value and worth of every individual by empowering each person to satisfy his or her customers. We do this with absolute honesty and integrity, and by living the spirit and letter of the law wherever we do business. This is the foundation of our relationship with our customers, our suppliers, our communities, and each other.

447. Hilton Hotels Corp.
9336 Civic Center Dr.
Beverly Hills, CA 90210
Phone: (310) 278-4321
Web: http://www.hilton.com

Hilton Hotels Corp. (NYSE; HLT) operates hotels and resorts, and is one of the preeminent companies in the hospitality, gaming and lodging businesses.

Mission: To be recognized as the world's best first-class hotel organization, to constantly strive to improve, allowing us to prosper as a business for the benefit of our guests, our employees, and our shareholders.

448. Hoechst Celanese Corp.
Route 202-206
Somerville, NJ 08876
Phone: (908) 231-2000
Web: http://www.hoechst.com

Hoechst Celanese, a subsidiary of the giant chemical and pharmaceutical producer Hoechst Group (OTC; HOEHY), manufactures and markets a diversified line of chemicals, fibers, advanced materials and technologies, and life sciences products, primarily to industrial customers.

Mission: We are a large, international company based in the United States. We operate a broad spectrum of chemistry-related businesses within the worldwide Hoechst organization.

We will be the recognized leader in our target markets.

We will be the preferred employer in our industry.

We recognize that people are our most valuable asset.

We will be the partner of choice for customers, suppliers, and other creators of innovative concepts.

We will be a major contributor to and take full advantage of the strong technological base of the Hoechst Group.

We will continually increase the long-term value of our company.

We operate in a decentralized manner, allowing each business to develop within our values.

Values: Performance: Preferred supplier, dedicated to understanding and meeting customer expectations; commitment to safety, employee health and protection of the environment; responsible corporate citizen; earnings to support long-term growth; consistently superior to competition; commitment to continual improvement.

People: Respect for individuals and appreciation for contributions each can make; diversity accepted and valued; concern and fair treatment for individuals in managing business change; equal opportunity for each employee to achieve his or her potential; employee pride and enthusiasm; informed employees through open communication.

Process: Openness and trust in all relationships; innovation, creativity and risk taking encouraged; teamwork throughout the organization; participative goal setting, measurement and feedback; decision making at the lowest practical level; actions consistent with clearly understood mission and long-term goals; recognition for quality achievements; resources committed to ongoing training and development.

Striving for "10 out of 10."

449. Hollywood Casino Corp.
2 Galleria Tower
Suite 2200
13455 Noel Rd. LB 48
Dallas, TX 75240
Phone: (972) 392-7777

Hollywood Casino Corp. (NASDAQ; HWCC) is in the gaming industry.

Statements: Total entertainment … that's where the gaming industry is going and Hollywood Casino Corporation is leading the way.

With its profitable casino operations, exciting Hollywood revues, award-winning restaurants, successful hotel operations, state-of-the-art technology and reputation as an involved corporate citizen, Hollywood Casino Corporation has built a solid foundation upon which the company plans to continue its growth.

We are committed to the continuous

excellence of our existing operations, and to strategic expansion into markets where our trademarked Hollywood theme will set a new standard in total entertainment.

450. Home Depot Inc.

2727 Faces Ferry Rd. NW
Atlanta, GA 30339
Phone: (770) 433-8211
Web: http://www.homedepot.com

Home Depot Inc. (NYSE; HD) is a home improvement retailer.

Slogan: "Low Prices Are Just the Beginning."

Statement: The heart and soul of The Home Depot are the people. We serve customers. We help our communities grow. We are never content, we always strive to improve.

We are driven by one common goal, to give the customer the best possible retail experience when they enter our stores. Building relationships with our customers happens because we are real people, because we believe in what we're doing, and we believe in doing it well.

In a lot of ways, our philosophies are the same as those of Olympic athletes. They are always striving to be number one — pushing, trying to do better than they have done before. These are the same values that we share at The Home Depot.

451. Honeywell Inc.

Honeywell Plz.
Minneapolis, MN 55408
Phone: (612) 951-1000
Web: http://www.honeywell.com

Honeywell Inc. (NYSE; HON) is a manufacturer of control systems for buildings, industry, and aerospace.

Statement: Honeywell's vision for the future is to achieve profitable growth by delighting our customers, and thus gaining undisputed global leadership in control.

By fulfilling the world's need for a cleaner environment, greater productivity, energy efficiency, enhanced comfort, increased safety, and national security, we will achieve this vision and realize the greatness we are capable of as a business, as an investment and as a place to work.

452. Household International Inc.

2700 Sanders Rd.
Prospect Hts., IL 60070
Phone: (847) 564-5000
Web: http://www.household.com

Household International Inc. (NYSE; HI) is a provider of financial services for consumers.

Building Shareholder Value: Our principle goal is to provide our shareholders with a superior return on their investment. By this we mean "total return," which is the appreciation in stock price that occurs over a period of time plus the value of dividends paid to shareholders and reinvested in Household common stock over the same period of time.

Vision ... and Commitment: Our vision for Household International is to be a premier financial services provider, recognized for leadership positions in our markets and superior returns for our shareholders.

We will realize this vision by fully leveraging our core strengths across all of our businesses, while adhering to a value system which is strongly held throughout the company.

We see our core strengths as these: A culture which encourages company-wide sharing of internal competencies; centralized financial oversight which ensures effective cost management and sound investment practice; economies of scale which give us competitive advantages; agility to adjust to changing business conditions to maximize opportunities, and the ability to develop financial products which appeal to a broadly-based customer audience and are marketed under a variety of brands and distribution channels.

The value system which is shared

throughout Household is based on commitments to our four principal constituencies: For our shareholders we will provide a superior return on investment, sustained long-term earnings growth, and timely and candid communication. For our customers, we will deliver need-based products and caring, respectful service. For our employees we will provide a work environment which embraces diversity and recognizes merit, encourages personal learning and growth, fosters open communication and demonstrates respect for family needs. In the communities in which we do business we will practice active good citizenship and absolute compliance to the letter and spirit of the law.

As we work to carry out these commitments, we will at all times adhere to the highest standards of ethical behavior.

Guided by our vision and our value system, we believe Household is and will be respected for the quality of our people, the reliability of our performance and the value of our word.

Building Value: Over the past two years we have built a leaner and more focused Household. Our purpose has been to concentrate on our strengths — and compete in businesses where we can win.

Today, Household is more efficient, responsive and profitable than ever before. We have achieved this by emphasizing four principles throughout the company:

1. Keep it simple — focus on high-return businesses.

2. Be efficient — drive down costs, be low-cost producers.

3. Serve the customer — use speed and agility to meet customers' changing needs.

4. Think like an owner — assume ownership of all we do.

453. Houston Industries Inc.
1111 Louisiana St.
Houston, TX 77210
Phone: (713) 207-3000

Houston Industries Inc. (NYSE; HOU) is a holding company involved in the electric utility industry. Its regulated subsidiary is Houston Lighting & Power Co. Shareholders of the company and NorAm Energy Corp. approved an agreement and plan of merger pursuant to which the company will merge into HL&P, and NorAm will merge into a subsidiary of the company.

Mission: The mission of Houston Industries Incorporated is to maximize shareholder value and satisfy customer needs, while providing employees a rewarding and productive work environment and conducting its affairs responsibly in the community.

Houston Industries will accomplish this mission by creating a corporate vision of successful growth, by carefully managing its assets, and by integrating its businesses through effective planning and allocation of resources.

Key Strategies: First, we are aggressively expanding our customer base domestically and internationally.

Second, we plan to become a major player in the wholesale gas and electricity trading markets.

Third, we plan to offer an array of new products and services to both existing and new markets.

454. Hudson Foods Inc.
1225 Hudson Rd.
Rogers, AR 72756
Phone: (501) 636-1100
Web: http://www.hudsonfoods.com

Hudson Foods Inc. (NYSE; HFI) is a producer of meat and poultry products.

Corporate Philosophy: We will strive to be a company whose worth in dollars is determined by its emphasis on human values, rather than a company whose human values is determined by its emphasis on dollars.

Corporate Objective: To grow and prosper — to do so we must:

Be efficient, lean, hungry, and eager.

Insist on fair play, both from our company to others, and from others to our company.

Recognize that a company is a group of

people; consequently we can be no better than our people.

Be a quality house with quality people and quality products for sound growth.

Create the kind of environment that encourages our people to enjoy their work and take pride in their company.

455. Hudson's Bay Co.
401 Bay St.
Suite 500
Toronto, Ontario
Canada M5H 2Y4
Phone: (416) 861-6112
Web: http://www.hbc.com

Hudson's Bay Co. (Toronto exchange) is Canada's largest department store retailer.

Mission: Our mission is to be Canada's best fashion department store by offering broad, dominant assortments, quality and value, fashion and trend leadership, a high level of customer service and an unremitting guarantee of performance.

456. Huffy Corp.
225 Byers Rd.
Miamisburg, OH 25342
Phone: (937) 866-6251
Web: http://www.huffy.com

Huffy Corp. (NYSE; HUF) operates in two distinct business segments — consumer products (Huffy Bicycles, True Temper Hardware, Huffy Sports, Gerry Baby Products Co.) and services for retail (Washington Inventory Service and Huffy Service First).

Vision: Huffy Corporation will be a leading supplier of name brand consumer products and retail services designed to improve consumer life-styles and enhance the business performance of its retail customers.

457. (GM) Hughes Electronics Corp.
7200 Hughes Terrace
Los Angeles, CA 90045

Phone: (310) 568-7200
Web: http://www.hughes.com

GM Hughes Electronics Corp. (NYSE; GMH), a public subsidiary of General Motors Corp. (NYSE; GM), is an electronics company serving the following segments: Automotive, space/telecommunications, defense, and commercial.

Vision: Electronics growth company driven by excellence, customer satisfaction and technology.

Goals: Leadership In: Return to our shareholders, growth in our markets and advancement of our employees.

Strategy: Cost competitive; technology leadership; continuous measurable improvement; alliances; invest/divest (as necessary to lead in our markets).

458. Hughes Supply Inc.
20 North Orange Ave.
Suite 200
Orlando, FL 32801
Phone: (407) 841-4755

Hughes Supply Inc. (NYSE; HUG) is a wholesale distributor that provides the construction and equipment industry with electrical, plumbing, utilities, building materials, pool & spa, tools, refrigeration, and water & sewer services and products.

Objectives:
1. To provide our customers quality service and products.

2. To develop employees in an environment of trust through a system of promotion from within.

3. To protect our stockholders' investment by generating sufficient profits to ensure continued growth and financial strength.

4. To maintain the highest level of integrity and promote fairness to all.

5. To support the communities in which we operate.

459. Humana Inc.
500 West Main St.
Louisville, KY 40201

Phone: (502) 580-1000
Web: http://www.humana.com/home.html

Humana Inc. (NYSE; HUM) is one of the nation's largest managed care companies.

Ours Is a Mission of Quality: We believe the ultimate purpose of us as a company, and of the entire health system, is remarkable in its simplicity: To help people of every age and physical condition live their lives to the fullest.

Toward achieving this goal, Humana has built strong, dynamic relationships with employers, plan members and health care providers through a single-minded commitment to quality of life and well-being. We believe the programs and systems born of this commitment place us years ahead of others in our industry.

460. Hunt Manufacturing Co.

One Commerce Sq.
2005 Market St.
Philadelphia, PA 19103
Phone: (215) 656-0300
Web: http://www.huntmfg.com

Hunt Manufacturing Co. (NYSE; HUN) is a producer of office and art/craft products.

Statement: Hunt has sustained its market penetration by remaining close to its various markets and introducing new products that complement existing product lines and satisfy customer needs.

The Hunt Way:

1. We are known by what we do, not what we say.

2. To take individual action is the highest value.

3. The customer is first.

4. People are to be respected and trusted.

5. Profit growth is a legitimate goal and a critical result.

6. Our company is a citizen of the communities in which it operates.

461. (J. B.) Hunt Transport Services Inc.

615 J. B. Hunt Corporate Dr.

Lowell, AR 72745
Phone: (501) 820-0000
Web: http://www.jbhunt.com

J. B. Hunt Transport Services Inc. (NASDAQ; JBHT) is in the trucking transport business.

Old Mission: To provide the best transportation services possible nationwide; to meet the varied and specialized needs of the shipping public, resulting in above average profits and growth.

New Mission: To dominate the full-load, containerizable transportation business in North America and to enter and compete in the worldwide distribution business.

462. Huntington Bancshares Inc.

One Huntington Ctr.
41 S. High St.
Columbus, OH 43287
Phone: (614) 480-8300
Web: http://www.huntington.com

Huntington Bancshares Inc. (NASDAQ; HBAN) is a regional bank holding company.

Slogan: "This Is Your Retirement Savings. This Is What You'll Need. And This Is How to Get It."

Mission: The mission of Huntington Bancshares Incorporated is to meet the financial service needs of individuals and businesses. We seek dominant position in the markets where we choose to compete by providing high quality, differentiated products and legendary customer service. Our thrust for business development is to penetrate existing markets, deliver products and services to new geographic markets, and strategically manage our business mix to achieve superior results.

463. Hyatt Corp.

Madison Plaza
200 W. Madison St.
Chicago, IL 60606
Phone: (312) 750-1234
Web: http://www.hyatt.com

Hyatt Corp., a private company, is in the hotel industry.

Social Consciousness: Operating quality hotels with innovative programs is not the only way Hyatt benefits consumers and local communities. Hyatt also plays a major role in social and environmental issues. Inherent within the company's philosophy is the goal to give back to the local community and environment wherever and whenever it can.

464. Hycor Biomedical Inc.
18800 Van Karman Ave.
Irvine, CA 92715
Phone: (714) 440-2000

Hycor Biomedical Inc. (NASDAQ; HYBD) specializes in the development, production and worldwide marketing of a broad range of diagnostic and medical products.

Statement: Hycor's focus is on allergy diagnostics and therapy, microscopic urinalysis, specialized immunodiagnostics and laboratory controls. Hycor's prospects for growth are enhanced by new product offerings, developing market opportunities, excellent financial condition, and an experienced management team.

465. IBP Inc.
P. O. Box 515
Dakota City, NE 68731
Phone: (402) 494-2061
Web: http://www.ibpinc.com

IBP Inc. (NYSE; IBP) processes meat—beef and pork. The company's principal products include boxed beef, pork, and variety meats, which are sold domestically and internationally to food retailers, distributors, wholesalers, restaurant and hotel chains and further processors. IBP also produces hides and other allied products used to make leather, animal feeds, and pharmaceuticals.

Statement: We believe our long-term focus on efficiency, value-added production, international growth, and the con-

tinued expansion of our core business will bring more success.

466. Idaho Power Co.
1221 W. Idaho St.
Boise, ID 83707
Phone: (208) 388-2200
Web: http://www.idahopower.com

Idaho Power Co. (NYSE; IDA) is a provider of electricity services.

Company Vision: In the old, tightly-regulated world, stockholder value was tied directly to and derived from our asset base, but in the new competitive world, the link is not as direct and value will derive from different sources:
Selective and efficient use of capital.
Customer orientation, and
Innovative, efficient operations.
This fundamental change in the basis for value creation is profound, and the future of Idaho Power Company rests on how well we adapt to the new world.

Environment: Idaho Power's business is to provide its customers the electricity they use in a safe, reliable and economical manner. In doing so, we incur a compelling obligation to a public which depends on us every single day for energy services that help safeguard human health, make prosperity possible and enhance individual opportunity for quality of life.

Fulfilling that obligation requires the construction, operation and maintenance of generating, transmission and distribution facilities that inevitably have an impact on the natural environment.

As part of our obligation to the public we serve, we incur a second compelling obligation to conduct our business in an environmentally conscientious manner. That obligation in part is a matter of law and in part the requirement of any business to meet the expectations of those it serves. But we readily accept our obligation to the environment in a broader context. We accept it as a fundamental corporate value.

We are convinced that sound environmental policy and sound business practice go hand in hand. We will pursue both for the benefit of our customers, shareholders, employees, and the communities we serve.

467. IDEX Corp.

630 Dundee Rd.
Northbrook, IL 60062
Phone: (847) 498-7070

IDEX Corp. (NYSE; IEX) manufactures an extensive array of proprietary, engineered industrial products sold to customers in a variety of industries.

Corporate Objectives Statement: Our objective is to earn a satisfactory return that will enable the company to grow and prosper, thereby creating opportunities for its employees in a desirable workplace. We aim to be the unquestioned leader in the markets served, and to be ethical in all of our relationships. To accomplish this, we must place our customers at the forefront, providing them with courteous and prompt service and quality products that are second to none.

468. IDEXX Laboratories Inc.

One IDEXX Dr.
Westbrook, ME 04092
Phone: (207) 856-0300
Web: http://www.idexx.com

IDEXX Laboratories Inc. (NASDAQ; IDXX) develops and commercializes advanced biotechnology-based and chemistry-based detection systems for veterinary, food and environmental testing applications.

Our Mission: To be viewed as a great company by our employees, customers and stockholders by creating exceptional long term value for their benefit through worldwide leadership in our business.

469. Illinois Tool Works Inc.

3600 West Lake Ave.

Glenview, IL 60025
Phone: (847) 724-7500

Illinois Tool Works Inc. (NYSE; ITW) is a manufacturer of fasteners, components, assemblies and systems.

Statement: ITW businesses are small and focused so they can work more effectively in a decentralized structure to add value to customers' products.

Teamwork is encouraged with each business unit, with customers, suppliers and other ITW units. By working together, ITW men and women create better working environments, better solutions and better products.

470. IMC Global Inc.

2100 Sanders Rd.
Northbrook, IL 60062
Phone: (847) 272-9200

IMC Global Inc. (NYSE; IGL) is one of the world's leading producers and marketers of phosphate and potash crop nutrients and animal feed ingredients. The company is also one of the nation's leading distributors of crop nutrients.

Statement: Looking to the future, IMC Global's long-term strategy remains focused on positioning the company's capital and human resources on worldwide agribusiness opportunities that provide the best returns for our shareholders. Our plan for continued profitable growth is a balanced approach that utilizes both internal and external opportunities. External opportunities include acquisitions, joint ventures, strategic alliances and other business combinations. As for internal growth, such opportunities as the increased use of precision agriculture techniques in farming also will contribute to your company's future success.

471. ImmuLogic Pharmaceutical Corp.

610 Lincoln St.
Waltham, MA 02154
Phone: (617) 466-6000

ImmuLogic Pharmaceutical Corp. (NASDAQ; IMUL) is a biotechnology company specializing in the development of peptide immunotherapeutics, with a primary focus on treating allergies and autoimmune diseases.

Statement: We believe that Immu-Logic's strength and ultimate success will come from a diligent pursuit of quality science, strong management, and sharp focus. We are confident in our ability to emerge as a successful biotechnology company.

472. Immune Response Corp.
5935 Darwin Ct.
Carlsbad, CA 92008
Phone: (760) 431-7080
Web: http://www.imnr.com

The Immune Response Corp. (NAS-DAQ; IMNR) develops, manufactures, and markets biopharmaceuticals.

We Believe: In maintaining a strong "people" orientation and demonstrating care for every employee.

In protecting and enhancing the corporation's high level of ethics and conduct.

In sustaining a strong results orientation coupled with a product approach to business.

Mission Statement: Develop, manufacture, and market biopharmaceuticals to treat life-threatening or crippling diseases.

473. In Focus Systems Inc.
27700B SW Parkway Ave.
Wilsonville, OR 97979
Phone: (503) 685-8888
Web: http://www.infocus.com

In Focus Systems Inc. (NASDAQ; INFS) produces LCD projection panels and related products.

Mission: To provide the highest value to our customers, employees and shareholders by being the market leader in projection products and services that revolutionize the effectiveness of group communications.

Values: We commit to fostering an innovative and creative environment which enables all employees, the company, and the customer to win. We individually and collectively value: Our customers; informed risk taking; results; quality; discipline and cooperation; a great place to work.

474. Inco Ltd.
145 King Street West
Suite 1500
Toronto, Ontario M5H 4B7
Canada
Phone: (416) 361-7511
Web: http://www.incoltd.com

Inco Ltd. (NYSE; N) is in the metal industry. The company is a major producer of nickel. They also produce copper and cobalt.

Slogan: "Stronger for Our Experience."

Statement: Inco is committed to the concept of sustainable development, which requires balancing the need for economic growth with good stewardship in the protection of human health and the natural environment.

475. Informix Corp.
4100 Bohannon Dr.
Menlo Park, CA 94025
Phone: (415) 926-6300
Web: http://www.informix.com

Informix Corp. (NASDAQ; IRMX) produces database systems for computer networks.

Strategy: Key to Informix's future growth and stability is the success of our core product technology. Informix is unique in its efforts to build database products based on an enduring, underlying architecture — a strategy designed to better enable our customers with scalable product technology, so they can successfully run their business today and in the future.

476. Ingersoll-Rand Co.
200 Chestnut Ridge Rd.
Woodcliff Lake, NJ 07675
Phone: (201) 573-0123
Web: http://www.ingersoll-rand.com

Ingersoll-Rand Co. (NYSE; IR) manufactures machinery, engineered equipment, bearings, locks, and tools.

Our Vision: Customers respond to our excellence in serving them by making Ingersoll-Rand Company their supplier and partner of choice.

Our Mission: Create an environment conducive for all of our people working productively together to make the changes needed to attain leadership in customer service, quality and financial returns. Focus on attaining leadership in all the businesses we commit to.

Our Passion: Ignite the desire within all of us to make the necessary changes to accomplish the mission. Develop an organization actively executing major change followed by continuous improvement. Reach out — make possible the impossible.

477. Insurance Auto Auctions Inc.
1270 Northwest Hwy.
Palatine, IL 60067
Phone: (847) 705-9550
Web: http://www.iaai.com

Insurance Auto Auctions Inc. (NASDAQ; IAAI) sells automobile salvage.

Our Corporate Mission: It is our mission to effectively leverage our nationwide industry leadership into the future by:

Utilizing the IAA purchase agreement method to provide low-cost salvage processing solutions to our vehicle supplier customers that yield maximum net returns while setting the highest standards of service with unparalleled integrity.

Effectively managing our company at every level to ensure continuous financial stability and steadily increasing shareholder value.

As a team, every employee in our national organization plays a vital role in achieving this mission.

478. Integrated Health Services Inc.
10065 Red Run Blvd.
Owings Mills, MD 21117
Phone: (410) 998-8714
Web: http://www.ihs-inc.com

Integrated Health Services Inc. (NYSE; IHS) offers an array of post-acute services: Subacute care, respiratory care, long term care, inpatient rehabilitation, outpatient rehabilitation, home care, diagnostic services, physician and outpatient clinics, hospice care, and skilled nursing care. The company, recently, bought RoTech Medical and assets from HEALTHSOUTH.

Slogan: "America's Leader in Post-Acute Care."

Statement: Our current strategy is to develop "at-risk" post-acute care networks which provide for the comprehensive management of the post-acute patient. Going forward, we will focus on (1) expanding these care networks, (2) increasing our home health business line as both a stand-alone business and as part of our network, and (3) increasing "at-risk" business through contracts with various payers including commercial managed care companies, Medicare HMOs, and states or Medicaid agencies.

479. Intel Corp.
220 Mission College Blvd.
Santa Clara, CA 95052
Phone: (408) 765-8080
Web: http://www.intel.com

Intel Corp. (NASDAQ; INTC) supplies the computing industry with chips, boards, systems, and software.

Slogan: "What Makes All Your Software Fall Into Place?"

Our Vision: PCs everywhere. We believe that the personal computer has the potential to become the universal general-purpose information appliance. The PC is the one tool that can incorporate inter-active entertainment, networked informa-tion services and real-time multimedia communications in one place.

480. Interface Inc.
2859 Paces Ferry Rd.
Suite 2000
Atlanta, GA 30339
Phone: (770) 437-6800
Web: http://www.ifsia.com

Interface Inc. (NASDAQ; IFSIA) mar-kets commercial floorcoverings, interior fabrics and specialty chemicals and sur-faces.

Statement: Immediate service, superior quality, zero waste, top styling, teamwork, and EcoSense. This is Interface today.

Pledge: We pledge to sustain and grow by:

Continuing our quality effort and strengthening our campaign to drive costs out of the business.

Growing our business through aggres-sive plans to win preemptive products specifications and capture market share.

Making substantial progress in the global imperative to sustain, conserve, and ultimately restore natural resources.

Fostering an environment of creative interchange and cooperation in the Inter-face, Inc. culture.

Creating the kind of corporation that other companies want to do business with.

Increasing the return on investment to our shareholders.

Becoming the preeminent name in commercial and institutional interiors, as we renew the world within work environ-ments today.

481. International Business Machines Corp.
1 Old Orchard Rd.
Armonk, NY 10504
Phone: (914) 765-1900
Web: http://www.ibm.com

International Business Machines Corp. (NYSE; IBM) is a leader in computer equipment, systems, software, and related services.

Data Processing Motto: "Think."

Slogans: "Solutions for a Small Planet." "Finding the Right Computer for All of You Is Easier Than You Think." "Operate at a Higher Level."

We Are IBM: We have two fundamen-tal missions. First, we strive to lead in the creation, development and manufacture of the industry's most advanced informa-tion technologies, including computer systems, software, networking systems, storage devices and microelectronics. Sec-ond, we translate these advanced tech-nologies into value for our customers worldwide — through our sales and pro-fessional services units in North America, Europe/Middle East/Africa, Asia Pacific and Latin America.

IBM Strategic Imperatives: Employ our technology.

Increasing our share of the client/server computing market.

Establishing leadership in the emerging network-centric computing world.

Realigning the way we deliver value to customers.

Rapidly expanding our position in key emerging geographic markets.

Leveraging our size and scale to achieve cost and market advantage.

Strategic Vision: A networked world that transforms the way people work, in-teract, learn, and do business.

482. International Dairy Queen Inc.
7505 Metro Blvd.
Minneapolis, MN 55439
Phone: (612) 830-0200
Web: http://www.dairyqueen.com

International Dairy Queen Inc. (NAS-DAQ; INDQA) franchises a system of stores (Dairy Queen; Orange Julius; Karmelkorn) featuring hamburgers, hot dogs, various dairy desserts and beverages.

Slogan: "Hot Eats, Cool Treats."

Statement: The company is continuously seeking to open new stores. The ability of the company to open new stores is most dependent upon recruiting qualified operators with suitable sites.

For more than 50 years, the Dairy Queen system's recipe for success has been simple. It's a combination of the hard-working people who own and operate the stores and great-tasting food and tempting treats served in the stores.

IDQ: We are in the business of managing diverse franchise systems, with current emphasis on those in the fast-food, treat and snack areas.

It is our intention to continue to grow in the franchising business, providing financial, management, marketing, operational, training, equipment, engineering, insurance, and supply systems to franchisees. We will continue to expand within the food franchise industry through the growth of existing systems and the acquisition of systems which complement the existing systems, and outside that industry through franchise systems in non-food categories.

We will maintain strong financial standards which will facilitate enhanced return to our stockholders, capital for our further business growth and market growth for our franchisees.

In each system we manage, we will be as professionally informed and skilled as the best operators within the category, so that the revenues we earn result from leadership, innovation and genuine service to our franchisees.

We will operate our business professionally and ethically, with appropriate concern for our franchisees, employees and the communities in which we conduct business.

483. International Flavors & Fragrances Inc.
521 West 57th St.
New York, NY 10019
Phone: (212) 765-5500

International Flavors & Fragrances Inc. (NYSE; IFF) creates and manufactures flavor and fragrance products used by other manufacturers to impart or improve flavor or fragrance in a wide variety of consumer products.

Statement: We believe that IFF's strong performance on a global basis during the past year confirms the basic human needs at all economic levels for the flavor and fragrance products we create. Our singular commitment is to pursue the fulfillment of that need and so enhance for all people the quality and enjoyment of everyday life.

484. International Game Technology
9295 Prototype Way
Reno, NV 89511
Phone: (702) 686-1200
Web: http://www.intgame.com

International Game Technology (NYSE; IGT) designs, manufactures, and markets gaming machines and proprietary software systems.

IGT Mission Statement: IGT is in business to provide for the needs of our customers, our employees and our shareholders, while recognizing our responsibility to the communities in which we operate.

IGT is committed to providing our customers with quality products at a competitive price which, together with excellent service and support, will assist them in maximizing their profitability.

IGT is committed to providing our employees with a stable and rewarding work environment, the opportunity to grow to the extent of their talents, and the opportunity to share in the success of the company which they make possible.

IGT is committed to providing our shareholders with an above average return on their investment, since our ability to serve the needs of our customers and employees is made possible only through their support.

IGT is committed to being a responsible corporate citizen in the communities in which we operate, and encourages our employees to individually be an asset to the community in which they live.

485. International Multifoods Corp.
33 South 6th St.
Minneapolis, MN 55402
Phone: (612) 340-3300
Web: http://www.multifoods.com

International Multifoods Corp. (NYSE; IMC) is a specialty foodservice distributor focusing on the service and product needs of pizza restaurants, and select limited-menu, multi-unit establishments.

Statement: At Multifoods, we define our success by the success of our customers.

We are driven by six trends that are having a major impact on customers: Away from home eating; freshness; nutrition; high-calorie rewards; brand identification; changing preferences.

486. International Paper Co.
Two Manhattanville Rd.
Purchase, NY 10577
Phone: (914) 397-1500
Web: http://www.ipaper.com

International Paper Co. (NYSE; IP) is a worldwide producer of paper, packaging, and forest products.

Slogan: "Roots As Deep As Your Own."

Environment: The environmental impact of papermaking and forestry operations is an important issue facing our industry, and International Paper has assumed a leadership role in addressing these concerns.

Looking Forward: We expect the business environment in our industry to improve further, assuming worldwide economic expansion continues for the next several years. Announced industry capacity additions are modest and we should continue to enjoy high operating rates for our major production lines. Given these conditions our earnings should increase dramatically from current levels.

Our strategies going forward are the same as those that underlie our current success: Expand higher value products in our core paper businesses; grow specialty products and distribution businesses; grow specialty products and distribution businesses; develop technologies to create innovative new products, improve our manufacturing processes and reduce costs; and continue to enter fast-growing markets worldwide.

Our objective continues to be the achievement of a 15 percent return on equity over a full economic cycle, and we believe that our current expansion and cost-improvement programs will enable us to reach that target. Our employees are critical to our success, and we are making excellent progress in obtaining their active participation and support of our goals. Their efforts are guided by the best management team in the industry, including senior managers who have a hands-on and entrepreneurial approach to their operations.

487. Inter-Regional Financial Group Inc.
60 South Sixth St.
Minneapolis, MN 55440
Phone: (612) 371-7750

Inter-Regional Financial Group Inc. (NYSE; IFG) is one of the nation's largest full-service regional brokerage and investment banking companies.

Vision: A holding company that is well capitalized and appropriately leveraged.

Strong regional firms that are independently managed and preeminent in their markets.

A strategically organized business with selected centralized services.

An organization that is passionate about quality client service.

Strong employee ownership that aligns employees' interests with the interests of shareholders.

A people-oriented company that earns the loyalty of its employees because it is a great place to work.

The end result — superior returns for shareholders.

488. Intuit Inc.

2535 Garcia Ave.
Mountain View, CA 94043
Phone: (415) 944-6000
Web: http://www.intuit.com

Intuit Inc. (NASDAQ; INTU) is a provider of financial services and software.

Our Mission: Revolutionize how individuals and small businesses manage their finances by delivering innovative, automated, financial solutions.

Our Vision of Intuit in the Year 2010: Intuit is the preeminent provider of automated financial solutions for individuals and small businesses. We are renowned as the company whose leadership and revolutionary innovations in financial services and software have delivered breakthrough value to our customers in every facet of their financial lives: Banking, borrowing, investing, planning, insurance, and beyond.

We are a large, growing multinational company. Both our competitors and our shareholders respect us for our ability to create and establish leadership in huge, new markets.

Intuit's customer focus is legendary. Our unwavering devotion to outstanding quality — in our customer care, as well as in our products and services — inspires our customers' confidence and enthusiasm.

Our products and services strike a careful balance between evolution-seeking out, understanding, and responding to our customers' needs and desires — and revolution — continually delighting our customers with valuable new ideas they haven't even thought of.

People around the world use our prod-ucts and access our services not only with computers, but with telephones, electronic wallets, and television. In short, we have become an integral part of their lives. Our customers rely on our solutions to help them simplify, organize, understand, and improve their finances; many confidently choose to put portions of their finances on autopilot.

Even though Intuit is known for the quality of its products and services, we know that the quality of our people is the foundation of our success.

489. Invacare Corp.

899 Cleveland St.
Elyria, OH 44036
Phone: (216) 329-6000
Web: http://www.invacare.com

Invacare Corp. (NASDAQ; IVCR) provides products and equipment for people with disabilities.

Worldwide Vision: To design, manufacture and distribute the best value in mobility products and medical equipment for people with disabilities and those requiring home health care.

490. Ionics Inc.

65 Grove St.
Watertown, MA 02172
Phone: (617) 926-2500
Web: http://www.ionics.com

Ionics Inc. (NYSE; ION) is a leading water purification company engaged worldwide in the supply of water and of water treatment. Ionics' products and services are used by the company or its customers to resalt brackish water and seawater, to purify and supply bottled water, to treat water in the home, to manufacture and supply water treatment chemicals and ultrapure water, to process food products, recycle and reclaim process water and wastewater, and to measure levels of water-borne contaminants and pollutants. The company's customers include industrial companies, consumers, municipalities, and utilities.

Statement: As people and industries continue to increase their requirements for cleaner water: As our society realizes, more and more, the importance of clean water to the health of our environment and life on this planet; and as we at Ionics continue to execute the achievement of our strategic vision, rebuilding upon nine consecutive years of record earnings and revenues with 30% annual growth in earnings per share and 16% annual growth in revenues over the nine-year period, it appears that the greatest opportunities for growth in the water business still lie ahead.

491. IPALCO Enterprises Inc.
One Monument Circle
Indianapolis, IN 46204
Phone: (317) 262-8261
Web: http://www.ipalco.com

IPALCO Enterprises Inc. (NYSE; IPL) is in the electric utility industry.

Mission: We discover and deliver energy solutions.

492. ITT Corp.
1330 Ave. of the Americas
New York, NY 10019
Phone: (212) 258-1000
Web: http://www.ittinfo.com

ITT Corp. (NYSE; ITT) is in the hospitality (Sheraton), entertainment/gaming (Caesars), and information services businesses. The "old" ITT has been separated into four separate, individual companies. The process began in 1994 with the Rayonier spin-off, and was completed in December 1995 with the creation of three additional companies: ITT Corporation, ITT Industries, and ITT Hartford Group.

Slogan: Sheraton Hotels — "Our World Revolves Around You."

ITT Sheraton Mission Statement: At ITT Sheraton, we are committed to becoming the number one hospitality company in the world by attracting and retaining the best employees, and by providing total customer satisfaction in order to increase long-term profits and value for our owners and ITT.

Focus: We are keeping to our long-range plan, but we are accelerating our short term actions in response to the marketplace. We are building what is the world's premier lodging and gaming company, focusing on the Sheraton and Caesars brands. We are moving rapidly to increase the value of our company, by monetizing or otherwise realizing the value of ITT's non-core assets.

It is your Board's conviction ... that ITT management is best equipped to accomplish the task of creating shareholder value — both short and long term.

493. ITT Educational Services Inc.
5975 Castle Creek Parkway, N. Drive
Indianapolis, IN 46250
Phone: (317) 594-9499

ITT Educational Services Inc. (NYSE; ESI) is a leading private college system focused on technology-oriented programs of study.

Mission: The mission of ITT Educational Services, Inc. and ITT Technical Institutes is to provide the highest quality of postsecondary education and required services to prepare a diverse student body for careers in education-related employment fields.

We will strive to establish an environment for our students and employees which promotes professional growth, encourages each person to achieve his or her highest potential and fosters ethical responsibility and individual creativity within a framework of equal opportunity and affirmative action.

494. ITT Hartford Group Inc.
Hartford Plaza
690 Asylum Ave.
Hartford, CT 06115

ITT Hartford Group Inc. (NYSE; HIG) is an international insurance and financial services organization offering personal, commercial, specialty and rein-surance property and casualty coverages and claim services as well as individual life and annuities, employee benefits, estate planning and retirement savings.

Slogan: "Bring It On."

Mission: Our mission is to be a world class financial services organization, not just an insurance company, and to target global high-growth markets where our skills and strengths create a competitive edge.

495. Jackpot Enterprises Inc.
1110 Palms Airport Dr.
Las Vegas, NV 89119
Phone: (702) 263-5555

Jackpot Enterprises Inc. (NYSE; J) is engaged in the gaming business, operating a gaming machine route, with video poker and other gaming machines.

Business Development Strategy: The company's business strategy is to enhance its position as a leader in the Nevada gam-ing route market and to apply its gaming management expertise, experience in mar-keting to middle market clientele, and ex-tensive regulatory and government expe-rience to pursue expansion opportunities in existing and emerging gaming markets for gaming route operations, strategic gaming activities and other nongaming areas. Specifically, the company's business strategy includes the following:

Enhance Nevada route operations.

Pursue gaming route operations in emerging jurisdictions.

Pursue other strategic gaming and nongaming opportunities.

Jackpot believes it is well positioned to expand its operations as additional states and local jurisdictions adopt legislation to allow the development of video gaming and casino entertainment. Although Jack-pot is actively pursuing potential gaming and nongaming opportunities, there can be no assurance that additional gaming or nongaming opportunities will be available on terms acceptable to Jackpot.

496. James River Corp. of Virginia
120 Tredagar St.
Richmond, VA 23219
Phone: (804) 644-5411
Web: http://www.jamesrivercorp.com

James River Corp. of Virginia (NYSE; JR) is a manufacturer and marketer of consumer products, food and consumer packaging and communications paper. Product lines include such registered brand names as Quilted Northern bath-room tissue; Brawny paper towels; Vanity Fair and Dixie premium foodservice prod-ucts; Eureka! recycled and Word Pro busi-ness printing papers; and Delta Brite pub-lishing papers.

Statement: James River employees worldwide are bound together by a uni-versal commitment to finding new and better ways to provide superior value to customers and consumers at the lowest possible cost. This fundamental belief in a strategy we call finding A Better Way will guide James River now and in the fu-ture as the company continues to trans-form itself to serve evolving market needs.

497. Jefferson-Pilot Corp.
100 N. Greene St.
Greensboro, NC 27401
Phone: (910) 691-3000
Web: http://www.jpc.com

Jefferson-Pilot Corp. (NYSE; JP) oper-ates primarily in the insurance business. The company also provides information and entertainment services through three network television and thirteen radio sta-tions.

Slogan: "The Vision to Power Your Dreams."

Our Vision: Jefferson-Pilot will be a market leader ...

We will provide competitive products and superior service which meet or exceed the needs of our existing and prospective clients.

We will grow faster than our competitors and strive to be one of the largest providers in each of our target product and geographic segments.

... in selected insurance, financial services, and communications businesses ...

We will focus on selected products and markets.

We will not attempt to be all things to all people.

... by building on our financial quality ...

We will remain one of the most soundly capitalized companies in the life insurance industry, retaining our AAA rating.

We will invest prudently in acquisitions and internal growth.

... our reputation ...

We will build on and capitalize on our strong reputation in the Southeast.

We will continue to epitomize integrity and quality in our relationship with clients and communities.

... and the skills of our people ...

We will provide challenging and rewarding career opportunities through training, career planning, and other aspects of human resource management.

... while achieving superior long-term results for shareholders.

We will strive to increase earnings per share by ten percent per year.

We will require superior returns on capital from each of our businesses.

498. JLG Industries Inc.
1 JLG Dr.
McConnellsburg, PA 17233
Phone: (717) 485-5161

JLG Industries Inc. (NYSE; JLG) manufactures material handling equipment.

Our Mission: JLG Industries Inc. is committed to being the provider of choice worldwide for access and material handling equipment.

Our Vision: Through leadership, teamwork and dedication, we will provide world-class excellence in quality, service and delivery to our distributors and customers; opportunity and enrichment for our employees; and superior performance for our shareholders.

Our Values: Customer focus; highest quality standards; world class products; uncompromising integrity; constant pursuit of excellence; teamwork.

499. John Hancock Mutual Life Insurance Co.
John Hancock Place
P.O. Box 111
Boston, MA 02117
Phone: (617) 572-6000
Web: http://www.jhancock.com

John Hancock Mutual Life Insurance Co., a mutual company, offers insurance products and financial products and services nationally and internationally.

Mission Statement: The mission of John Hancock financial services is to be the highest quality financial services company.

Core Values: Customers are the reason we are in business. In order to establish lasting relationships, we provide the best customer service in the financial services industry.

We care about the dignity of each person in this organization. In order to be successful, we treat others with the same respect we seek for ourselves.

500. Johnson & Johnson
One Johnson & Johnson Plaza
New Brunswick, NJ 08933
Phone: (908) 524-0400
Web: http://www.jnj.com

Johnson & Johnson (NYSE; JNJ) produces and markets a wide range of consumer health care products, toiletries, medical supplies and equipment, pharmaceuticals, hygienic and dental products.

Slogan: Mylanta — "My Doctor Said Mylanta."

Our Credo: We believe our first responsibility is to the doctors, nurses and patients, to mothers and fathers and all others who use our products and services. In meeting their needs everything we do must be of high quality. We must constantly strive to reduce our costs in order to maintain reasonable prices. Customers' orders must be serviced promptly and accurately. Our suppliers and distributors must have an opportunity to make a fair profit.

We are responsible to our employees, the men and women who work with us throughout the world. Everyone must be considered as an individual. We must respect their dignity and recognize their merit. They must have a sense of security in their jobs. Compensation must be fair and adequate, and working conditions clean, orderly, and safe. We must be mindful of ways to help our employees fulfill their family responsibilities. Employees must feel free to make suggestions and complaints. There must be equal opportunity for employment, development and advancement for those qualified. We must provide competent management, and their actions must be just and ethical.

We are responsible to the communities in which we live and work and to the world community as well. We must be good citizens — support good works and charities and bear our fair share of taxes. We must encourage civic improvements and better health and education. We must maintain in good order the property we are privileged to use, protecting the environment and natural resources.

Our final responsibility is to our stockholders. Business must make a sound profit. We must experiment with new ideas. Research must be carried on, innovative programs developed and mistakes paid for. New equipment must be purchased, new facilities provided and new products launched. Reserves must be created to provide for adverse times. When we operate according to these principles, the stockholders should realize a fair return.

501. Johnson Controls Inc.
5757 N. Green Bay Ave.
Milwaukee, WI 53201
Phone: (414) 228-1200
Web: http://www.gci.com

Johnson Controls Inc. (NYSE; JCI) participates in fours businesses: Automotive seating, building controls, plastics, and batteries.

Our Creed: We believe in the free enterprise system. We shall consistently treat our customers, employees, shareholders, suppliers, and the community with honesty, dignity, fairness, and respect. We will conduct our business with the highest ethical standards.

Our Mission: Continually exceed our customers' increasing expectations.

502. Johnson Worldwide Associates Inc.
1326 Willow Rd.
Sturtevant, WI 53177
Phone: (414) 884-1500
Web: http://www.jwa.com

Johnson Worldwide Associates Inc. (NASDAQ; JWAIA) manufactures fishing, camping, and diving equipment.

Statement: We are dedicated to earn the goodwill of the users of our products, and we commit ourselves to:

Provide products and services which differentiate us in the minds of our consumers by working closely with consumers; developing, monitoring and maintaining high standards of quality; developing and marketing superior products; maintaining a strong commitment to product innovation; maintaining high advertising standards of integrity and good taste; packaging and labeling our products so that consumers can make informed value judgements.

Ensure that all products developed and marketed by JWA ensure the health and safety of consumers when used as directed by meeting or exceeding all relevant regulations; providing clear and adequate directions for use; designing products which minimize potential misuse; researching new technologies that enhance product safety.

Provide an effective consumer interface with key JWA personnel by handling all inquiries, complaints and service needs in a prompt and efficient manner; regularly disseminating information to consumers.

503. Jostens Inc.
5501 Norman Center Dr.
Minneapolis, MN 55497
Phone: (612) 830-3300
Web: http://www.jostens.com

Jostens Inc. (NYSE; JOS) provides yearbooks, class rings, gifts for graduation, and other customized products and services for students, alumni, and others.

Mission Statement: Jostens' mission is to enhance the development and motivation of individuals and organizations. Through a strong customer focus Jostens will be the foremost marketer of programs and services which address instructional, recognition, identity, tradition, training and achievement needs.

Jostens will adhere to certain basic principles in fulfilling this mission. These are:

Enhancing stakeholders' interests through superior sales and earnings growth and responsible financial management.

Adhering to the highest level of ethical standards and corporate citizenship.

Creating and maintaining a challenging and rewarding work environment.

Participating in businesses in which we either have or expect to attain a market leadership position.

504. Kansas City Power & Light Co.
1201 Walnut St.
Kansas City, MO 64106
Phone: (816) 556-2200
Web: http://www.kcpl.com

Kansas City Power & Light Co. (NYSE; KLT) is an electric power producer.

Slogan: "Ask Us About Energy."

Mission Statement: To be the regional energy supplier of choice.

Environment: The environment. It's our right to inhabit it. It's our privilege to appreciate it. It's our responsibility to preserve it. It's our obligation to perpetuate it. It's not just an issue, it's a way of thinking. It's an EnvironMentality.

505. Katy Industries Inc.
6300 South Syracuse Way
Englewood, CO 80111
Phone: (303) 290-9300
Web: http://www.Katyindustries.com

Katy Industries Inc. (NYSE; KT) carries on business through three principal operating groups: Industrial machinery, industrial components, and consumer products.

Statement: The challenge we now face is to develop Katy into an economic vehicle that investors can better understand and evaluate. We intend to do this primarily through an acquisitions program focused on our higher margin, growth companies, and to foster internal growth in our other operations.

Mission: Katy's mission is to exceed our customers' expectations and create value for our shareholders.

506. Kellwood Co.
600 Kellwood Pkwy.
Chesterfield, MO 63107
Phone: (314) 576-3100

Kellwood Co. (NYSE; KWD) is an international marketer, merchandiser, and manufacturer of apparel and recreational camping soft goods.

Slogan: "Creating a World of Value…."

Our Mission: To strengthen our ability to be a leading international marketer, merchandiser and manufacturer of value-oriented products in each of our portfolios of soft goods companies.

To maintain a strong customer focus by building partnerships with retailers in world markets, providing them with a distinctive merchandising mix of branded and private label programs that add value and improve profitability.

To encourage and support our employees, for it is through their high standards, creativity and commitment, that our company will prosper.

To achieve long-term growth of profits and return on shareowner investment through sound financial management practices and operating disciplines.

507. Kelly Services Inc.
999 W. Big Beaver Rd.
Troy, MI 48084
Phone: (810) 362-4444
Web: http://www.kellyservices.com

Kelly Services Inc. (NASDAQ; KELYA) is a leading international staffing services company, providing office, marketing, professional, technical, and light industrial staffing and related human resources services.

Slogan: "The Quality Solution."

Mission: To serve our customers, employees, shareholders and society by providing a broad range of staffing services and products.

To achieve our mission:

We will develop innovative staffing services which meet the needs of our customers and contribute to their success.

We will foster an environment which stimulates professional excellence and encourages contribution by all employees.

We will provide our shareholders a fair return on their investment.

We will demonstrate good corporate citizenship through the ethical conduct of our business.

Vision: To be the world's best staffing services company and to be recognized as the best.

508. Kendall-Jackson Winery Ltd.
421 Aviation Blvd.
Santa Rosa, CA 95403

Phone: (707) 544-4000
Web: http://kj.com

Kendall-Jackson Winery Ltd., a private company, makes and markets distinctive wines from the following: Chardonnay, pinot noir, cabernet sauvignon, merlot, sauvignon blanc, and zinfandel.

Slogan: "When You're Passionate About Winemaking, It Shows."

Statement: Flavor first is the driving philosophy behind all Kendall-Jackson wines. The belief that behind every award winning wine lies a rich layering of distinctive varietal flavors. Flavors that are intense. Complex. A delight to enjoy. It begins in our estate vineyards. Each estate is carefully selected for the ideal harmony of soil and micro-climate creating the perfect expression of a single varietal.

509. Kennametal Inc.
Route 981
at Westmoreland County Airport
Latrobe, PA 15650
Phone: (412) 539-5000
Web: http://www.kennametal.com

Kennametal Inc. (NYSE; KMT) markets, manufactures, and distributes a broad range of tools for the metalworking, mining and highway construction industries. Kennametal is one of the world's leading producers of cutting tools and wear resistant parts made of cemented carbides and other hard materials.

Mission: Kennametal's mission is to be our customers' first choice worldwide for cutting tools, tooling systems, supplies and technical services in the metalworking, mining and highway construction industries. We will market and manufacture, as appropriate, these products and services while increasing shareholder value through long-term financial performance.

510. Kent Electronics Corp.
7433 Harwin Dr.
Houston, TX 77036
Phone: (713) 780-7770

Kent Electronics Corp. (NYSE; KNT) manufactures and distributes electronics.

Slogans: "Working as a Team, KENT Associates Exceed Customer Expectations." "Making the Right Connections."

Corporate Objective: To become the best national specialty electronics distribution company with sales offices and distribution centers in the major U.S. markets and to establish K*TEC as one of the largest multi-plant specialty electronic custom contract manufacturers.

Environment: KENT is concerned about global environmental deterioration. The world's future quality of life is being threatened by the serious consequences of environmental problems such as acid rain, hazardous and toxic waste, and depletion of the ozone layer. These problems cannot be brought under control without the positive efforts of those in the corporate community. KENT, as a member of the corporate community, agrees to share in the responsibility to attempt to find ways to solve the environmental problems confronting our society.

511. Kerr-McGee Corp.

123 Robert S. Kerr Ave.
Oklahoma City, OK 73125
Phone: (405) 270-1313

Kerr-McGee Corp. (NYSE; KMG) is in the chemical and energy businesses.

Our Mission: Create value for shareholders through energy and selected chemical businesses.

Our Vision: To be an innovative, respected global energy and chemical company, recognized as outstanding by employees, investors, customers, and the public; and to be the standard by which other businesses are measured.

Our Beliefs: Respect for the individual.

Ethical business dealings.

Safe working practices.

Responsible corporate citizenship.

Responsible care for the environment.

Continuous improvement.

512. KeyCorp Management Co.

127 Public Sq.
Cleveland, OH 44114
Phone: (216) 689-3000
Web: http://www.keybank.com

KeyCorp Management Co. (NYSE; KEY) is a bank holding company with full-service commercial banks and specialized financial services affiliates.

Our Mission: We maintain a leadership role within the financial services industry by providing our customers with innovative products, services, and delivery methods; by providing shareholders with ongoing enhancement of their investment; by concerning ourselves with our employees' quality of life through career development and professional advancement opportunities; and by sharing our talents and resources to improve the communities we serve.

Our Vision: To be the first choice of those seeking world-class financial products and services.

513. Keystone Consolidated Industries Inc.

Three Lincoln Centre
5430 LBJ Freeway
Suite 1740
Dallas, TX 75240
Phone: (972) 458-0028
Web: http://www.redbrand.com

Keystone Consolidated Industries Inc. (NYSE; KES) is a leading manufacturer of fabricated wire products, industrial wire and carbon steel rod for the agricultural, industrial, construction, original equipment manufacturer and retail consumer markets.

Strategy for the Future: The company's operating strategy is to enhance profitability by:

Internal growth and expanding its downstream wire products business through selective acquisitions of additional wire products manufacturing or distribution facilities.

Shifting its product mix towards higher margin, value-added products.

Achieving manufacturing cost savings and production efficiencies through capital improvements and investment in new and upgraded wire and steel production equipment. Establishing a leading position as a supplier of choice among its fabricated wire products and industrial wire customers by satisfying customer quality and service requirements through a broad product line offering.

Keystone is committed to increasing its profitability and level of competitiveness and believes this operating strategy, combined with its strong customer focus, high degree of vertical integration and strategic manufacturing locations, will enable the company to achieve these goals. The successful implementation of this operating strategy will aid in insuring the long-term viability of Keystone, as well as maximize shareholder values.

514. Keystone Investments Inc.

200 Berkeley St.
Boston, MA 02116
Phone: (617) 338-3200

Keystone Investments Inc. provides investment management and support services for investors and others.

Mission Statement: Our goal is to provide excellence in investment management and support services for investors and their advisers that exceed their expectations. We are committed to maintaining the highest ethical and professional standards and providing an energized, supportive work environment. In all that we do, we must earn trust and confidence. We must strive to create value for our customers, employees, owners and the community.

Corporate Goal: To be the investment company of choice.

515. KFC: Kentucky Fried Chicken Corp.

1441 Gardiner Lane
Louisville, KY 40213
Phone: (502) 456-8300

Kentucky Fried Chicken Corp., a leading chicken restaurant chain, together with Taco Bell and Pizza Hut, has spun off from PepsiCo to become TRICON Global Restaurants (NYSE; YUM).

Slogans: "Everybody Needs a Little KFC." "Finger Lickin' Good."

Our Mission: To be the leading restaurant chain in the world by satisfying customers' demands for quality quick service eating occasions with a chicken-dominant menu.

516. Kimball International Inc.

1600 Royal St.
Jasper, IN 47549
Phone: (812) 482-1600
Web: http://www.kimball.com

Kimball International Inc. (NASDAQ, KBALB) is a diversified company, providing a wide range of products and services for customers.

Our Mission: Kimball International is a diversified company whose purpose is to create high value products and services that consistently exceed our customers' expectations, thereby providing excellent return to share owners and a high quality of life for employees and communities in which we operate.

517. Kimberly-Clark Corp.

351 Phelps Dr.
Irving, TX 75038
Phone: (972) 281-1200
Web: http://www.kimberly-clark.com

Kimberly-Clark Corp. (NYSE; KMB) makes and markets personal care and other consumer products. The company's registered trade names include Huggies, Kleenex, and Scott Paper, to name a few.

Slogan: Huggies Supreme — "The Ultimate in Care."

Statement: At Kimberly-Clark everyone is focused on the mission of making and selling the finest products and maintaining the confidence and loyalty of our customers. We do our best to work harder and smarter than our competitors — and to have fun doing it.

518. KLM Royal Dutch Airlines USA

565 Taxter Rd.
Elmsford, NY 10523
Phone: (914) 784-2000
Web: http://www.klm.nl

KLM Royal Dutch Airlines USA, a subsidiary of KLM Royal Dutch Airlines (NYSE; KLM), is one of the largest international passenger airlines.

Mission: KLM is positioned as an airline operating world-wide from a European base, providing professional service for passengers and shippers demanding high-quality products at competitive prices with a reliable and punctual product and caring and friendly service.

519. Kroger Co.

1014 Vine St.
Cincinnati, OH 45202
Phone: (513) 762-4000
Web: http://www.krogerusa.com

Kroger Co. (NYSE; KR) is a leader in the grocery store industry.

Slogan: "Your Total Value Leader."

Mission: Our mission is to be a leader in the distribution and merchandising of food, health, personal care, and related consumable products and services. In achieving this objective, we will satisfy our responsibilities to shareholders, employees, customers, suppliers, and the communities we serve.

We will conduct our business to produce financial returns that reward investment by shareowners and allow the company to grow. Investments in retailing, distribution and food processing will be continually evaluated for their contribution to our corporate return objectives.

We will consistently strive to satisfy consumer needs better than the best of our competitors. Operating procedures will reflect our belief that the organizational levels closest to the consumer are best positioned to respond to changing consumer needs.

We will treat our employees fairly and with respect, openness and honesty. We will solicit and respond to their ideas and reward meaningful contributions to our success.

We value America's diversity and will strive to reflect that diversity in our work force, the companies with whom we do business, and the customers we serve. As a company, we will convey respect and dignity to each individual.

We will encourage our employees to be active, responsible citizens and will allocate resources for activities that enhance the quality of life for our customers, our employees and the communities we serve.

520. Laclede Steel Co.

One Metropolitan Sq.
St. Louis, MO 63102
Phone: (314) 425-1400

Laclede Steel Co. (NASDAQ; LCLD) produces steel and steel products.

Statement: As we look at the steel market in the future, we see an ever-growing number of single product mini-mills producing high quality steel, using scrap fed electric arc furnaces. These mills produce bar, rods and hot rolled coil. As this production supply increases, in periods of slack demand downward pressure is exerted on steel prices. At the same time new electric furnace capacity creates more demand for ferrous scrap. We have felt the negative effects of the added demand for scrap in the form of higher costs over the last three years. However in the case of our future rod purchases, the surplus capacity in North America, as well as worldwide, will help us buy at very attractive prices, thus lowering our costs.

Unfortunately the increase in new sheet capacity helps our competitors, who buy hot rolled coil to produce tubular products. We will face severe competitive pressure in our tubular business for some years ahead. This makes our move to the more efficient continuous cast process even more important.

521. Lafarge Corp.

11130 Sunrise Valley Dr.
Suite 300
Reston, VA 22091
Phone: (703) 264-3600

Lafarge Corp. (NYSE; LAF) is engaged in the cement construction materials and waste conversion businesses.

Our Mission: To be the best North American company in the cement construction materials and waste conversion businesses.

Our Guiding Principles: Lafarge Corporation is involved in many businesses of varying size throughout North America. Although there are inherent differences in some of our operations, all are guided by four broad principles of management:

1. Responsiveness to our shareholders, customers, employees, and communities.

2. Orientation to our customers' needs.

3. Respect for common human resource beliefs.

4. Implementation of a cohesive operating philosophy.

Communities: The prosperity of Lafarge Corporation is closely linked to the prosperity of the communities in which we operate; our resources and the talents of our employees can therefore play an active role in improving those communities. As a responsible community member, Lafarge Corporation will conduct all of its business in an environmentally sound manner.

522. Lance Inc.

8600 South Blvd.
Charlotte, NC 28273
Phone: (704) 554-1421

Lance Inc. (NASDAQ; LNCE) produces food and related products for consumers.

Mission Statement: To be a consumer driven company providing quality food and related products in an ever-changing, international market for the benefit of those who participate in our success.

Our Philosophy: We believe we should help develop the people in our organization to the maximum potential in a climate that creates a high degree of employee morale.

We believe in being good citizens ... in encouraging our employees to practice thrift ... take an active interest in the church of their choice ... and in community projects and government.

We believe that the products and services we offer should be of the highest quality that we may merit the respect, confidence and loyalty of our customers and consumers.

We believe we should be a source of strength to our suppliers and that all of our transactions with them should be based on honesty and truth.

We believe all of our activities should be planned and executed so the company can expand its leadership and be regarded as a model in industry.

We believe we should earn a reasonable profit so the company will remain financially strong and may perpetuate this philosophy.

523. Land O'Lakes Inc.

4001 Lexington Ave. North
Arden Hills, MN 55126
Phone: (612) 481-2222
Web: http://www.landolakes.com

Land O'Lakes Inc., a cooperative, is a leader in the food and agricultural businesses.

Mission: We are a market- and customer-driven cooperative committed to optimizing the value of our members' dairy, crop and livestock production.

Vision: To be one of the best food and agricultural companies in the world.

524. Lands' End Inc.

1 Lands' End Lane
Dodgeville, WI 53595
Phone: (608) 935-9341
Web: http://www.landsend.com

Lands' End Inc. (NYSE; LE) is a leading direct marketer of traditionally styled apparel, domestics, soft luggage and other products. The company's products are offered through regular mailings of its monthly primary catalog and its specialty catalogs.

Growth Strategy: The company's growth strategy has four key elements. First, the company seeks to increase sales from its regular catalogs in the United States both by expanding its customer base and by increasing sales to its existing customers. Second, the company endeavors to generate additional sales by making targeted mailings of its specialty catalogs to existing and prospective customers. Third, the company is actively pursuing opportunities to apply its merchandising, marketing and order fulfillment skills abroad by increasing its efforts in the United Kingdom and Japan, as well as entering other countries. Finally, the company continues to explore the development of new brands and product lines, marketed primarily through additional specialty catalogs to targeted customers, and the acquisition of new businesses.

Principles of Doing Business:

1. We do everything we can to make our products better. We improve material, and add back features and construction details that others have taken out over the years. We never reduce the quality of a product to make it cheaper.

2. We price our products fairly and honestly. We do not, have not and will not participate in the common retailing practice of inflating markups to set up a future phony "sale."

3. We accept any return for any reason, at any time. Our products are guaranteed. No fine print. No arguments. We mean exactly what we say: GUARANTEED. PERIOD.

4. We ship faster than anyone we know of. We ship items in stock the day after we receive the order.

5. We believe that what is best for our customer is best for all of us. Everyone here understands that concept. Our sales and service people are trained to know our products and to be friendly and helpful. They are urged to take all the time necessary to take care of you. We even pay for your call, for whatever reason you call.

6. We are able to sell at lower prices because we have eliminated middlemen; because we don't buy branded merchandise with high protected markups; and because we have placed our contracts with manufacturers who have proved that they are cost conscious and efficient.

7. We are able to sell at lower prices because we operate efficiently. Our people are hard working and intelligent, and share in the success of the company.

8. We are able to sell at lower prices because we support no fancy emporiums with their high overhead. Our main location is in the middle of a 40-acre cornfield in rural Wisconsin.

525. Lawson Products Inc.

1666 E. Touhy Ave.
Des Plaines, IL 60018
Phone: (847) 827-9666

Lawson Products Inc. (NASDAQ; LAWS) is a distributor of parts and specialty items.

Credo: Lawson Products Inc., as an independent distributor of parts and specialty items, serving many industries across the nation, maintains a unique and distinguished position in its field.

Its growth, now and in the future is and shall be, the result of public recognition of the quality of its organization, services, products, personnel, policies and integrity.

The welfare of its own employees and of the customers they serve is, and shall be, its primary objective.

Its responsibilities to industry, to the community and to the nation as a whole are discharged with a full sense of the importance of preserving free enterprise and the American democratic way of life.

A strong and healthy corporate pattern, the result of dealing fairly with its suppliers, vigorously and openly with its competition, alertly and progressively in its services to customers, considerately with its employees, realistically in its pricing policies and profitably for the benefit of all, characterizes this — the Lawson Organization.

Environmental Position: As a leader in the field of maintenance products, Lawson Products recognizes that we must conduct our business in a manner that demonstrates the highest concerns for the safety and health of our employees, our customers, the public and the environment. To ensure compatibility between our products, actions and services to that of the environment, we have adopted the following positions:

We will strive at all times to be in compliance with the requirements of all federal and state environmental laws and regulations.

Through the creation of proactive programs we will operate with the objective of protecting and enhancing the environment.

Through interaction with our customers and suppliers we will continuously review and improve the performance of our products and services with consideration given to their environmental impact.

We will educate and promote responsibly the real advantages of our products. We will avoid confusing or misleading statements of environmental benefits.

We will encourage environmental quality improvements and the use of recycled materials for our cartons, packages, and paper needs.

Because we understand the importance of interacting responsibly with our surroundings, our corporate resources are committed to supporting Lawson's environmental position.

526. La-Z-Boy Inc.
1284 N. Telegraph Rd.
Monroe, MI 48161
Phone: (313) 242-1444

La-Z-Boy Inc. (NYSE; LZB) manufactures and markets chairs, recliners, and other furniture products.

Slogan: "We Make the Rooms That Make a Home."

Commitment: To listen with care, and let our customers inspire and shape our thinking. . .

To lead, be inventive and bold, and perform beyond expectations. . .

To continue to develop quality business solutions which reflect the integrity of our name and rich heritage. . .

And to always embrace a passion for excellence in our relationships with our employees, suppliers, representatives, dealers and ultimately our customers, who make this commitment possible.

527. Legg Mason Inc.
Legg Mason Tower
111 South Calvert St.
P.O. Box 1476
Baltimore, MD 21203
Phone: (410) 539-0000
Web: http://www.leggmason.com

Legg Mason Inc. (NYSE; LM) is engaged as a securities brokerage with investment advisory services, corporate and public finance, and real estate services.

Statement: Our primary approach to investing is sill the "Value Approach," focusing on investments that are fundamentally sound and have attractive growth prospects, but appear to be undervalued by the marketplace. But now we offer not only domestic equities and high quality municipal bonds, but also international and even emerging market equities, overlooked or specially created corporate bonds, global bonds and high yield debt. Although we avoid product fads and fancies, we use increasingly advanced technology to improve client service, to help clients evaluate their investments, and to diversify clients' investments so as to maximize their returns without exceeding their individual tolerance for risk.

528. Lehman Brothers Holding Inc.

3 World Financial Center
New York, NY 10285
Phone: (212) 526-7000
Web: http://www.lehman.com

Lehman Brothers Holding Inc. (NYSE; LEH) is a global investment bank serving the financial needs of corporations, institutions, governments, and high-net-worth investors worldwide.

Statement: Lehman Brothers engages in a "client/customer" driven strategy which uniquely positions the firm in the global investment banking business. Our complete focus on serving the needs of a targeted group of issuing and advisory clients and investing customers has been the hallmark of our organization. The premise of this strategy is to develop lead relationships in the coverage of our clients and customers worldwide to capture the majority of their flow business. This positions the firm as a dynamic global facilitator between institutions looking to raise capital and those requiring investment products and services. Lehman Brothers' management has operated successfully under this framework, and newer members have chosen to join the firm because of this unabated emphasis on clients and customers through a seamless integration of our investment banking, institutional and private client sales, product trading and research efforts on a global basis.

529. Levi Strauss Associates Inc.

1155 Battery St.
San Francisco, CA 94111
Phone: (415) 544-6000
Web: http://www.levi.com

Levi Strauss Associates Inc., a private company, is a leading apparel manufacturer. Registered trade names include Levi jeans and jeans-related products, as well as Dockers and Brittania branded products and other casual sportswear.

Code of Ethics: Levi Strauss & Co. has a long and distinguished history of ethical conduct and community involvement. Essentially, these are a reflection of the mutually-shared values of the founding families and of our employees.

Our ethical values are based on the following elements:

A commitment to commercial success in terms broader than merely financial measures.

A respect for our employees, suppliers, customers, consumers and stockholders.

A commitment to conduct which is not only legal but fair and morally correct in a fundamental sense.

Avoidance of not only real, but the appearance of conflict of interest.

530. LIDAK Pharmaceuticals

11077 North Torrey Pines Rd.
La Jolla, CA 92037
Phone: (619) 558-0364

LIDAK Pharmaceuticals (NASDAQ; LDAKA) is a development-stage biopharmaceutical company engaged in the research and development of innovative therapeutic products targeting viral diseases, inflammatory disorders, and cancer.

Statement: The company's ultimate mission continues to be developing and marketing proprietary therapeutic products worldwide, beginning with the commercialization of LIDAKOL, in collaboration with strategic development and marketing partners. Strategic objectives established in support of that mission include (1) generating near-term cash flow through the out-licensing of LIDAKOL in the United States and other territories where it is not yet licensed, additional contract sales of existing assay products and/or the acquisition of currently available and marketable products, (2) expanding the company's product pipeline through internal development and/or the acquisition of new products and technologies and (3) preparing LIDAK to be in a position to raise additional capital when it is needed.

531. Life Technologies Inc.
9800 Medical Center Dr.
Rockville, MD 20850
Phone: (301) 840-8000
Web: http://www.lifetech.com

Life Technologies Inc. (NASDAQ; LTEK), a public subsidiary of Dexter Corp. (NYSE; DEX) produces cell culture and molecular biology research products.

Customers: Customer satisfaction is our highest priority. We will ensure the success of our customers by anticipating their needs and responding with the right products and services. We strive to be their first choice.

Employees: We appreciate and will use the skills and abilities of all of us. We will foster teamwork and cooperation by recognizing and rewarding individual and team performance. We take responsibility for our individual actions, learning, and growth. In return, we expect to be treated with candor, dignity, and respect. And have fun in the process.

Shareholders: Sustained growth, market leadership and technical innovation define our success and assure credibility with our shareholders. We will seize opportunities to grow our business around the world. We will take prudent, calculated risks to ensure that success. We will challenge ourselves and each other to meet or exceed our business objectives.

Community: We behave as responsible stewards of the environment. We will be responsive to the health and safety needs of our employees, our customers, and our communities in the daily conduct of our business.

532. Lilly Industries Inc.
733 S. West St.
Indianapolis, IN 46225
Phone: (317) 687-6700

Lilly Industries Inc. (NYSE; LI) is a manufacturer of industrial coatings and specialty chemical products.

Mission Statement: To effect a worldwide leadership position in industrial coatings and other differentiated high value added specialty coatings through internal and external development, and to be the leader in the quality and value of the products and services we provide to customers.

533. Limited Inc.
Three Limited Pkwy.
Box 16000
Columbus, OH 43216
Phone: (614) 479-7000

The Limited Inc. (NYSE; LTD) is a leading specialty retailer of fashion clothing and personal care products.

Our Commitment: Our commitment is to offer the best customer shopping experience, the best merchandise, the best merchandise presentation, the best customer service, the best value, the best everything that a customer sees and experiences, and to treat all the women, men, and children who enter our stores with the same respect and dignity we accord to our family and friends.

To achieve this goal:

We must maintain a restless, bold, and daring business spirit noted for innovation and cutting-edge style.

We must be tough-minded, disciplined, demanding, self-critical and yet supportive of each other, our team, and our suppliers.

We must seek and retain Associates with an unquestioned reputation for integrity and respect for all people: Customers, suppliers, shareholders, and fellow Associates.

We must continue to make risk acceptable by rewarding the risk-taker who succeeds — that goes without saying — and not penalizing the one who fails.

We must utilize our capacity to set qualitative and quantitative standards for our industry.

We are determined to surpass all standards for excellence in retailing by thinking — and thinking small. By staying close to our customers and remaining agile, we will continue as a major force in retailing.

534. Lincoln Electric Co.
22801 St. Clair Ave.
Cleveland, OH 44117
Phone: (216) 481-8100
Web: http://www.lincolnelectric.com

Lincoln Electric Co. (NASDAQ; LECOA) designs, manufactures, and markets arc welding and thermal cutting products and electric motors.

Slogan: "Lincoln Is Moving to Broaden Its World Leadership."

Statements: We firmly believe that the corporate culture resulting from the incentive management system has increased productivity, led to enhanced operating flexibility and contributed to the company's industry leadership position.

Manufacturing efficiencies, flexibility, and quality are enhanced by the company's high degree of vertical integration.

Focused growth in new markets: The Lincoln Electric Company believes that international markets will provide expanded opportunities for increased sales of both basic and advanced technology products. Part of the company's growth strategy is focused on marketing its existing products into Central Europe, Asia, Latin America, and other developing countries to take advantage of the significant number of infrastructure projects planned in these economies in the next decade.

Outlook: Looking toward the future, the company expects to build on its position as a leader in the domestic U.S. arc welding industry with continued market penetration facilitated by new product offerings and further capacity additions. This domestic plan is coupled with an aggressive campaign to strengthen international market share and capture developing infrastructure businesses. Also, the company has expanded its integral horsepower industrial electric motor facility and anticipates continued development of this business.

535. Lincoln National Corp.
200 East Berry St.
P.O. Box 7832
Fort Wayne, IN 46801
Phone: (219) 455-2000
Web: http://www.lnc.com

Lincoln National Corp. (NYSE; LNC) is an insurance holding company.

Vision: Lincoln National Corporation will be a high performance financial services company achieving benchmark service, growth and profit.

Mission: Lincoln National Corporation exists to satisfy the financial security needs of individuals and businesses. In so doing, LNC must create superior value for shareholders, offer quality products and services to customers, provide satisfying jobs for employees and be a responsible citizen in the communities in which it operates.

Goals: LNC will maximize long-term shareholder value through superior operating performance and returns, as measured by:

15% annual return on equity; and 9% annual growth in book value.

Shared Values: Lincoln National Corporation seeks to live up to the reputation of Abraham Lincoln, and with this statement of values, LNC reaffirms that "Our name indicates our character."

Integrity: Integrity implies trustworthiness and incorruptibility to a degree that one is incapable of being false to a trust or responsibility. It requires firm adherence to both applicable laws and relevant moral standards. This uprightness of character is essential in men and women who conduct business that is affected with a public interest.

Commitment to Excellence: We have a long history of doing some things in a first-class manner and are committed to achieve that level of performance in all aspects of our business. In particular, we seek to excel in continuous learning and improvement, creativity and innovation both individually and through teamwork, and above all else, the quality of the products and services we provide to our customers. We also seek balanced personal and professional lives and happily confess a desire to have fun in all our endeavors!

Responsibility: We are each personally accountable for what we say and do. If we are responsible for any part of a project, we are responsible for all of it. We are responsible to our customers for fair dealing in providing quality products and services. We are responsible to each other to act in accordance with our shared values. We are responsible to our shareholders and regulators to conduct business in a safe, prudent, and lawful manner. Finally, we are responsible as citizens for responding to the needs, values, and traditions of the communities in which we work and live.

536. Litton Industries Inc.
21240 Burbank Blvd.
Woodland Hills, CA 91367
Phone: (818) 598-5000
Web: http://www.littoncorp.com

Litton Industries Inc. (NYSE; LIT) is in the aerospace/defense industry. The company is a primary builder of large multimission surface combatant ships and manufacturer of electronics for the U.S. Navy and a major provider of overhaul, repair, modernization, ship design and engineering services. The company has acquired Racal Marine Group (marine electronic equipment producer) and SAI Technology (mobile computing equipment and systems supplier).

Statement: Our goal is to build value for you, the investor, while also serving

our customers, our employees, and our country. The company is focused on a strategy of long-term growth. We have talented employees, an experienced and capable board of directors, and a strong management team committed to meeting the challenges ahead. From this foundation we are building a new and exciting Litton.

537. Lockheed Martin Corp.
6801 Rockledge Dr.
Bethesda, MD 20817
Phone: (301) 897-6000
Web: http://www.lockheed.com

Lockheed Martin Corp. (NYSE; LMT), the result of a merger of Lockheed Corp. and Martin Marietta Corp., is a diversified technology company. The company is involved in space, aeronautics, electronics, missile systems, information and other services. Lockheed Martin and Northrop Gruman have made an agreement to merge, at the time of this writing.

Our Vision: Our vision is for Lockheed Martin to be recognized as the world's premier systems engineering and technology enterprise.

Our mission is to build on our aerospace heritage to meet the needs of our customers with high-quality products and services.

And in so doing, produce superior returns for our shareholders and foster growth and achievement for our employees.

Overarching Principles: In realizing our vision, we will adhere to the highest standards of ethical conduct in everything we do. We will achieve mission success for our customers, create opportunity for our employees, provide strong returns for our shareholders, and serve the communities where we live and work. Our actions are guided by certain unifying principles:

Ethical conduct in dealing with our colleagues, customers, shareholders, suppliers and the public, providing the basis for earned trust.

Mission success as we carry out our responsibility to achieve superior performance and to provide our customers the quality products and services they have a right to expect.

Technological leadership in all disciplines that contribute to fulfilling our vision.

Financial strength and profitability to meet the expectations of our shareholders and enable us to aggressively pursue new business opportunities.

Competitiveness through attention to cost, efficiency and continuous improvement.

Fair treatment and candid communication with the diverse work force from whom our enterprise derives its strength.

Decisiveness and responsiveness in addressing our internal and external challenges.

Active, responsible citizenship to the nation and the communities in which we live and work.

538. Lomak Petroleum Inc.
500 Throckmorton St.
Suite 2104
Fort Worth, TX 76102
Phone: (817) 870-2601

Lomak Petroleum Inc. (NYSE; LON) explores for oil and gas reserves.

Lomak Purpose: The purpose of Lomak Petroleum Inc. is to maximize the net wealth position of its shareholders by profitably building value through the acquisition, development, exploration, and efficient management of oil and gas reserves.

Lomak Principles: Conduct business in an honest and fair manner.

Believes growth is necessary for the company to be successful.

Embraces change which represents new ideas and opportunities for growth.

Encourages each employee to contribute to company goals and rewards employees for results achieved.

Seizes opportunity, makes fact-based

decisions, and establishes clear expectations and accountability.

Achieves maximum success through a shared vision of the company purpose and goals.

539. Long John Silver's Restaurants Inc.
300 W. Vine St.
Kincaid Towers
Lexington, KY 40507
Phone: (606) 388-6000
Web: http://www.ljsilvers.com

Long John Silver's Restaurants Inc., a private company, operates a quick-service seafood restaurant chain.

Slogan: "The Meal You've Been Missing."

Promise: Long John's promise, triple quality inspection.

Our Mission: Long John Silver's is positioned for dramatic growth. Since 1990, Long John's has crafted a corporate mission statement which effectively guides decision making at every level. This clearly focused corporate mission, along with a restructured, committed culture and an acute awareness of the marketplace will enable the company to achieve its guest-driven goal: We want to be America's best quick-service restaurant chain.

Our Promise: We will provide each guest great tasting, healthful, reasonably priced fish, seafood and chicken in a fast, friendly manner on every visit.

Our Culture: We will maintain a work environment that encourages team members to put forth their best efforts to serve our guests. We will respect each team member as we work together to achieve excellence.

The participation of team members in our success is an essential part of our culture. Highly regarded training programs for all team members are based on a simple philosophy: Hire innovative people and train them using proven methods.

540. Louisiana Land and Exploration Co.
909 Poydras St.
New Orleans, LA 70112
Phone: (504) 566-6500

Louisiana Land and Exploration Co. (NYSE; LLX) is an explorer and producer of crude oil and gas.

Statement: The ultimate goal of LL&E's business strategy is creation of shareholder value. To achieve this we are building on our core strengths: A well-focused asset base; financial capacity; technical capability; organizational flexibility; global perspective; and a shared commitment to excellence.

541. Lowe's Companies Inc.
State Highway 268 East (Elkin Hwy.)
North Wilkesboro, NC 28659
Phone: (336) 651-4000
Web: http://www.lowes.com

Lowe's Companies Inc. (NYSE; LOW) is a retailer, serving the do-it-yourself home improvement, home decor, home electronics, and home construction markets.

Slogan: "Lowe's Knows."

Lowe's Vision: Lowe's is in the business of providing the products to help our customers build, improve, and enjoy their homes. Our goal is to outservice the competition and be our customers' 1st choice store for these products.

542. Luby's Cafeterias Inc.
2211 Northeast Loop 410
P.O. Box 33069
San Antonio, TX 78265
Phone: (210) 654-9000
Web: http://www.lubys.com

Luby's Cafeterias Inc. (NYSE; LUB) operates a chain of cafeterias.

Motto: "Good Food from Good People."

Statements: Each day is a new day in the cafeteria business. We're no better than the last meal you ate with us.

We can serve wonderful food yesterday; but if we don't serve good food today, people aren't going to come back.

Our founders were visionary pioneers who had that perfect blending of idealism and practicality. First, they had a dream; then they set about to make this dream come true.

As one goal was accomplished another was instituted; thus, movement has always been upward. From this emanates an optimism that touches every employee of the company.

543. Lukens Inc.
50 S. First Ave.
Coatesville, PA 19320
Phone: (610) 383-2000

Lukens Inc. (NYSE; LUC), a holding company, manufactures stainless steel, carbon, alloy and steel plate.

Vision: Lukens' vision for the next decade is to grow as an innovative, world-class industrial organization providing products and services which exceed customer expectations for quality and value, thereby benefiting all stakeholders.

Mission: Lukens will exceed customer expectations for quality, innovation and value while providing carbon and specialty steels, industrial products and services to a diverse global market. Growth, an essential element of Lukens' long-range strategies, will be accomplished through internal and external programs that are closely aligned with our strengths. Success will be measured by how effectively we achieve excellence in customer satisfaction, develop our employees, create a climate conducive to continuous improvement and provide value to our shareholders.

544. Lyondell Petrochemical Co.
One Houston Center
Suite 1600
1221 McKinney St.
Houston, TX 77253

Phone: (713) 652-7200
Web: http://www.lyondell.com

Lyondell Petrochemical Co. (NYSE; LYO) is a petrochemical producer. The company manufactures ethylene, propylene, butadiene, methanol, methyl tertiary butyl ether (MTBE), special chemicals, and aromatics.

Lyondell's Strategy: Building on the basics of low cost, flexibility and high productivity. By building on its strengths in the businesses Lyondell knows best, the company expects to meet its goals of customer satisfaction, employee productivity, corporate responsibility, and financial success.

545. MagneTek Inc.
26 Century Blvd.
Nashville, TN 37229
Phone: (615) 316-5100
Web: http://www.magnetek.com

MagneTek Inc. (NYSE; MAG) core businesses consist of electric lighting products, motors, generators, drives, power supplies, and transformers. These products are purchased by original equipment manufacturers and systems integrators.

Motto: "T.E.A.M. — Total Excellence at MagneTek"

Statement: To win, we need more than a vision of what we want MagneTek to become. We must have winning technical, manufacturing and marketing strategies for each of our product lines. And underpinning those strategies, we must have a company-wide strategy that gives us a leg up on competitors whoever and wherever they may be. That "master strategy" consists of 10 points:

1. Competence and compensation. We will employ "the best and the brightest" and compensate them at above-average levels for above-average performance.

2. Personal growth. We will foster a system of personal development, assessment and training that will provide the best possible opportunities for the growth of each deserving associate.

3. Customer service. We will know our customers and their markets well, our efforts will be driven by their needs, and we will serve them in an outstanding manner consistent with our profit goal.

4. Technology. We will perform advanced and applied R&D, alone and with others, to assure that our processes and products represent the latest in technology.

5. Productivity. We will continuously assess, invest in and utilize the latest and most efficient tools and processes available.

6. Cost-consciousness. We will constantly compare all costs of operation against those of our peers and others to be certain we are the lowest total-cost producer in the electro-industry.

7. Accountability. We shall be personally accountable for solving problems and pursuing opportunities, and will take no order that will create known losses without the explicit authorization — and justification — of senior management.

8. Profit-consciousness. We will grow both internally and through acquisitions, but never at the expense of profitability.

9. Financial stability. We shall maintain the financial stability of the company and the reserves necessary to achieve our operating objectives.

10. Integrity. At all times, we shall conduct business and our individual tasks with the highest levels of corporate and personal integrity.

546. Mallinckrodt Inc.
7733 Forsyth Blvd.
St. Louis, MO 63105
Phone: (314) 854-5200
Web: http://www.mallinckrodt.com

Mallinckrodt Inc. (NYSE; MKG), formerly Mallinckrodt Group Inc., is an international growth company serving specialty markets in human healthcare, chemicals and animal health. The company is a major producer of pain relief pharmaceuticals, diagnostic imaging agents, medical devices, animal pharmaceuticals and vaccines, catalysts, and laboratory and microelectric chemicals.

Slogan: "Improving Healthcare and Chemistry."

Statement: We value integrity, service, and achievement.

Our Vision: To create extraordinary value for our shareholders through exceptional growth in sales and profitability driven by innovation and productivity in our specialty human and animal health and chemicals businesses.

Objective: Mallinckrodt Group's objective is to be an exceptional growth company, with long-range plans for average annual growth in sales of at least 10 percent and 12 to 15 percent in earnings.

Our Goals for Leadership: To fully satisfy our customers.

To provide our employees with opportunities for growth and development.

To fulfill our social responsibilities.

To build extraordinary value for our shareholders.

To be widely recognized and respected by all of our constituencies.

To leave a legacy for great success in the 21st century.

Growth Strategies: These initiatives are adding value to our core business while enhancing performance and shareholder value:

Enhancing management systems and processes.

Managing our base business for growth.

Discovering and marketing new technologies.

Enhancing our business portfolio.

547. Manitowoc Co. Inc.
500 South 16th St.
Manitowoc, WI 54221
Phone: (414) 684-4410
Web: http://www.manitowoc.com

Manitowoc Co. Inc. (NYSE; MTW) is a diversified capital goods manufacturer. The company manufactures, distributes and provides customer support services to a broad range of capital goods markets, including ice machines and commercial refrigeration equipment for foodservice, lodging, healthcare and convenience-store applications; lattice-boom cranes and boom trucks for heavy-construction, duty-cycle, dockside, and crane-rental operations; plus ship-repair and conversion service for freshwater and saltwater vessels operating on the Great Lakes.

Mission Statement: Manitowoc's mission is to continuously add value for its customers, employees, suppliers, and shareholders by efficiently providing market-leading engineered capital goods and services to selected niche markets.

Toward the New Millennium: While it is unlikely Manitowoc will make another large acquisition in the next year or two, we will continue to fine-tune and prune present operations to reposition Manitowoc and gain greater control of our destiny by dampening the impact of the normal economic cycles in which we operate.

548. MAPCO Inc.
1800 South Baltimore Ave.
Tulsa, OK 74101
Phone: (918) 581-1800

MAPCO Inc. (NYSE; MDA) is involved in the production and transportation of natural gas and the refining and marketing of petroleum.

Vision: MAPCO's vision is to be the best and most successful provider of quality energy and energy-related products and services to our customers.

Statement: To achieve business growth we will:

Make strategic acquisitions and internal investments.

Develop niche markets that provide a competitive advantage.

Establish strategic business alliances.

Encourage responsible risk taking.

549. Mark IV Industries Inc.
One Towne Centre
501 John James Audubon Pkwy.

Amherst, NY 14226
Phone: (716) 689-4972

Mark IV Industries Inc. (NYSE; IV) is a worldwide manufacturer of proprietary and other products, primarily for power and fluid transfer applications. In addition, the company also provides audio products to the professional audio market.

Statement: Mark IV became a more focused company through the expansion of its power and fluid transfer business — a strategy that has positioned our company to meet the challenges of the coming years.

550. Marriott International Inc.
10400 Fernwood Rd.
Bethesda, MD 20817
Phone: (301) 380-3000
Web: http://www.marriott.com

Marriott International Inc. (NYSE; MAR) is in the hospitality/hotel business under the following registered trade names: Marriott, Ritz-Carlton, Courtyard, Residence Inn, TownePlace Suites, and Fairfield Inn.

Mission Statement: We are committed to being the best lodging and management services company in the world by treating employees in ways that create extraordinary customer service and shareholder value.

551. Mary Kay Cosmetics Inc.
16251 Dallas Pkwy.
Dallas, TX 75248
Phone: (972) 687-6300
Web: http://www.marykay.com

Mary Kay Cosmetics Inc., a private company, is in the cosmetics/personal care products industry.

Vision: To be preeminent in the manufacturing, distribution, and marketing of personal care products through our independent sales force.

To provide our sales force an unparalleled opportunity for financial independence, career achievement and personal fulfillment.

To achieve total customer satisfaction worldwide by focusing on quality, value, convenience, innovation, and personal service.

Product Safety Testing: Mary Kay Cosmetics, Inc. does not use animals in the testing of its products, and has no testing involving the use of animals done by anyone else on its behalf.

552. Masco Corp.
21001 Van Born Rd.
Taylor, MI 48180
Phone: (313) 274-7400
Web: http://www.masco.com

Masco Corp. (NYSE; MAS) is a leading manufacturer of home improvement, building, and home furnishings products.

Mission Statement: Masco's corporate mission is to continue to build a leadership brand-name consumer products company with above-average growth and profitability.

Business Objectives: We expect to achieve our planned profit growth by continued focus on several key objectives:

Focus on our core businesses — providing products for the home and family — and continue to strengthen our well-defined product and brand franchises.

Offer a wide range of products at varying price points and through a variety of distribution channels that provide a choice of style, value and convenience to the customer, and be a profitable resource to our trade customers.

Maintain or enhance our profit margins and growth through a balance of new product introductions, product improvements, cost-reduction initiatives, market share gains and the strategic acquisition of complementary companies and product lines.

Strategies: Our strategies to achieve these objectives involve:

Fostering a culture that reflects a commitment to excellence and an ethic of continuous improvement.

Being primarily driven by the needs and desires of consumers while being responsive to the requirements of our dealers, distributors and other trade customers.

Leveraging the myriad strengths contained in our collection of companies and taking advantage of the natural synergies that exist among them.

Retaining the entrepreneurial spirit of our individual operating companies while cooperatively manufacturing and marketing our products.

Continuing to invest in our companies to ensure that our core competencies remain or become world class.

553. Massachusetts Mutual Life Insurance Co.

1295 State St.
Springfield, MA 01111
Phone: (413) 788-8411
Web: http://www.massmutual.com

Massachusetts Mutual Life Insurance Co. (MassMutual) is a premier mutual life insurance company. The company offers a complete portfolio of life and health insurance, asset accumulation products, health and pension employee benefits, and investment management services.

Slogans: "We Help You Keep Your Promises." "A Promise to Teach You the Value of Standing Up for What You Believe In. A Promise I'll Remember. It's Never Too Early in the Day to Eat Ice Cream. A Promise to Watch Over You Now and Always."

Vision Statement: MassMutual is a life insurance company of impeccable integrity, indisputable financial strength, and operational excellence. The company is composed of business organizations that provide value-added insurance and asset accumulation products and services to individuals, businesses, and their employees. Our products and services protect against the adverse financial consequences of one or more of the basic human risks — death, illness, disability or outliving one's

financial resources — and meet other money management needs.

554. Material Sciences Corp.

2300 E. Pratt Blvd.
Elk Grove Village, IL 60007
Phone: (847) 439-8270

Material Sciences Corp. (NYSE; MSC) manufactures a variety of coating materials, composites, and laminates.

Corporate Beliefs: Our customers: Material Sciences Corporation's principal responsibility is to our customers. We see ourselves as partners in serving our customers' markets. Only with this attitude can we be truly knowledgeable and foresightful about our customers' needs and motivations.

In performing for those who have entrusted their business to us, we raise to the highest level of importance — our obligation to deliver consistent, superior quality. We are also committed to provide expert, personal service to our customers so that we will remain a sought after partner. Finally, we will constantly strive to reduce costs, so that such relationships will be practical in a highly competitive environment.

Achieving the above we believe will create for Material Sciences Corporation a sustainable competitive advantage based upon delivering superior value to our customers.

Our employees: We are no less responsible to the men and women of Material Sciences Corporation than to our customers and investors. Their dignity as individuals must be honored by management at all levels, their ideas actively encouraged, their employment opportunities equalized. Working conditions must be safe, healthful and well ordered. Most importantly each person must be provided encouragement and the opportunity to develop to his or her maximum potential.

In the communities where our companies operate we are dedicated to standards of citizenship and environmental quality which make our people proud of their association.

Our investors: To our shareowners, whose confidence in the company is essential to our growth and success, Material Sciences Corporation is committed to achieving optimum investment returns and value. This is often a delicate balance of short-term and long-term gains, but it is approached in the knowledge that long-term success is the goal of most investors.

Adequately funding the future while rewarding the present can be one of management's most challenging tasks. We must take into account the fact that future growth will be supported only if ongoing financial targets are achieved at a level which encourages investment.

Return on ethics: We pledge that the honesty and integrity we demand of ourselves must involve every aspect of our business, including relations with our customers, employees, suppliers, the government and our competitors.

We operate on the premise that one of management's primary tasks is to demonstrate how company values and personal values can be consonant, and how ethical behavior is consistent with profit-building long term goals. We believe there is a "return on ethics."

555. Mattel Inc.
333 Continental Blvd.
El Segundo, CA 90245
Phone: (310) 252-2000
Web: http://www.hotwheels.com

Mattel Inc. (NYSE; MAT) is a toy manufacturer focused on four principal core registered brands: Barbie, Fisher-Price, Disney, and Hot Wheels.

Statement: A commitment to in-house manufacturing of core brand products assures the lowest cost, as well as maximum flexibility in meeting "just-in-time" inventory requirements.

Core brand products are in greatest demand and change the least from year to year. By concentrating its in-house manufacturing on these time-tested staple products, the company is assured of being the low cost manufacturer in its core categories.

556. Maxus Energy Corp.
717 N. Harwood St.
Dallas, TX 75201
Phone: (214) 953-2000

Maxus Energy Corp. (NYSE; MXS) is active in the exploration and production of oil and gas.

Maxus Vision: Our aim is to be a financially successful exploration and production company capable of competing worldwide.

Strategic Direction: We intend to generate and pursue profitable and repeatable investment opportunities with primary emphasis on the areas where we now produce.

Strategy: Retrench when oil prices are low.

Reduce program spending.

Reorganize company.

Reduce operating costs.

Develop proven reserves and economic prospects.

557. MAXXIM Medical Inc.
104 Industrial Blvd.
Sugar Land, TX 77478
Phone: (713) 240-5588

MAXXIM Medical Inc. (NYSE; MAM) develops, manufactures, and markets a diversified group of specialty medical products and is a leading supplier of disposable sterile procedure trays to hospitals, clinics and outpatient surgery centers. The company has four distinct operating divisions. They are: Argon, Boundary, Henley and Sterile Design.

Strategy:

1. To continue to pursue acquisitions with an emphasis on those that increase MAXXIM's vertical integration or include products that complement or expand its existing product lines.

2. To accelerate the development of new products that complement existing product lines.

3. To emphasize cross-selling to large buying groups and health care provider networks.

4. To expand international operations.

5. To increase productivity by maximizing the utilization of existing facilities.

558. May Department Stores Co.
611 Olive St.
St. Louis, MO 63101
Phone: (314) 342-6300
Web: http://www.maycompany.com/index.html

May Department Stores Co. (NYSE; MAY) operates regional department store companies.

Statement of Corporate Responsibility: The May Department Stores Company has a long-standing commitment to being a responsible corporate citizen. May's commitment applies to its role as an employer, as a buyer of goods and services from other businesses, and as a resident of the cities it serves.

As the communities in which May operates become increasingly diverse. May seeks a business environment that reflects the cultural diversity of those communities. May believes that this makes business sense for the company and for its future operations.

May is working to build diversity and a sensitivity to diversity into the basic fabric and culture of the company.

559. Maybelline Inc.
3030 Jackson Ave.
Memphis, TN 38112
Phone: (901) 324-0310
Parent's Web:
http://www.lorealcosmetics.com

Maybelline Inc., a subsidiary of L'Oreal S.A. (OTC; LORLY), is a leader in the domestic mass-market cosmetics business,

manufacturing eye, face, lip and nail cosmetics and personal care products.

Slogan: "Maybe She's Born with It. Maybe It's Maybelline."

Statement: Maybelline Inc. remains focused on three strategic objectives: (1) To increase core business sales and market share; (2) to strengthen financial performance and operational efficiency; and (3) to develop sources of incremental growth.

560. Maytag Corp.
403 W. 4th St. N.
Newton, IA 50208
Phone: (515) 792-8000
Web: http://www.maytagcorp.com

Maytag Corp. (NYSE; MYG) manufactures and markets home appliances under the registered brand names Maytag, Jenn-Air, Admiral, Magic Chef, and Hoover.

Slogan: Maytag — "The Dependability People."

Mission: To improve the quality of home life by designing, building, marketing and servicing the best appliances in the world.

Our Values: Values provide a common "language" for everyone to speak. In addition, they can foster a sense of pride and culture and imply a way of life for Maytag as a means of achieving our mission:

Customer first.
World quality.
Business innovation.
Total teamwork.
Profitable achievement.
Constant evolution.

Our Guiding Principles: We believe in the inherent worth of all people.

We believe in focusing on individual strengths.

We believe in being stewards for the future.

We believe in leadership training.

561. MBNA Corp.
1100 King St.
Wilmington, DE 19801

Phone: (302) 453-9930
Web: http://www.mbnainternational.com

MBNA Corp. (NYSE; KRB) is in the banking and financial services industry. The company, additionally, is a major issuer of credit cards.

Statement: Getting the right customers is not enough — to be successful, we have to keep them. We keep customers by exceeding their expectations every single time they come in contact with us.

MBNA is a company of people committed to:

Providing the customer with the finest products backed by consistently top-quality service.

Delivering these products and services efficiently, thus ensuring fair prices to the customer and a sound investment for the stockholder.

Treating the customer as we expect to be treated — putting the customer first every day — and meaning it.

Being leaders in innovation, quality, efficiency, and customer satisfaction. Being known for doing the little things of MBNA, makes the unassailable difference.

562. McCormick & Co. Inc.
18 Loveton Circle
Sparks, MD 21152
Phone: (410) 771-7301
Web: http://www.mccormick.com

McCormick & Co. Inc. (NASDAQ; MCCRK) is the largest spice company in the world. The company is the leader in the manufacture, marketing, and distribution of spices, seasonings, flavors, and other food products to the food industry — retail, foodservice, and food processors.

Slogan: "Flavor Up!"

Mission: The primary mission of McCormick & Company, Incorporated is to profitably expand its worldwide leadership position in the spice, seasoning, and flavoring markets.

Our Core Values: We believe in adding value for our shareholders.

We believe customers are the reason we exist.

We believe in successful achievement through teamwork and participation.

We believe in doing business ethically and honesty.

We believe in respect and concern for one another.

563. McDermott International Inc.
1450 Poydras St.
New Orleans, LA 70160
Phone: (504) 587-5400
Web: http://www.mcdermott.com

McDermott International Inc. (NYSE; MDR) is a leading supplier of energy-related products and services.

Mission Statement: McDermott International, Inc. is a leading supplier of products and services that help the world's industries and government produce energy. Our mission is to provide these products and services to the highest standards of quality, always meeting the needs of our customers, providing consistent and satisfactory returns to our shareholders, and creating safe and rewarding environments for our employees.

In order to accomplish our mission, we will:

Consistently provide high quality products and services to effectively and promptly meet the needs of our customers.

Develop or acquire new technologies which will make our products and services the best the market can offer.

Hold ourselves to the highest standards of quality and ethical conduct.

Provide for the professional and technical development of our employees, empower them through Total Quality Management, and foster in them the spirit of innovation and teamwork.

Support and protect the well-being of the natural environment and the communities in which we work.

Compete in new markets where our core competencies, both new and traditional, benefit the customer and provide opportunities for our growth.

Our dedication to this mission provides the foundation for the continued growth and success of McDermott International, Inc.

564. McDonald's Corp.

McDonald's Plaza
Oak Brook, IL 60521
Phone: (630) 623-3000
Web: http://www.mcdonalds.com

The McDonald's Corporation (NYSE; MCD) is the largest foodservice organization in the world. The company has pioneered food quality specifications, equipment technology, marketing and training programs, and operational and supply systems, all of which are considered the standards of the industry throughout the world. Products include, in part, the Big Mac, Quarter Pounder with Cheese, the Happy Meal, McChicken sandwich, Filet-o-Fish, Egg McMuffin, Big Breakfast, Chicken McNuggets, salads, sundaes, cheeseburgers, and hamburgers.

Mottoes: "Billions Served." "Whatever It Takes." "QSC; Quality, Service, and Cleanliness."

Slogans: "My McDonald's." "Look for the Golden Arches." "You Deserve a Break Today — So Get Up and Get Away to McDonald's." "Good Time, Great Taste." "Twoallbeefpattiesspecialsaucelettucecheesepicklesonionsonaseasameseedbun." "It's a Great Time for the Great Taste of McDonald's." "You Know the One, McDonald's, for Food, Folks, and Fun." "What You Want Is What You Get at McDonald's." "You Get More for Your Money at McDonald's Today." "Have You Had Your Break Today?" "Take a Break at McDonald's." "We Do It All for You." "You, You're the One." "Go for Goodness at McDonald's." "Nobody Can Do It Like McDonald's Can."

Our Vision: To become the world's eas-

iest quick-service restaurant choice for customers.

Global Strategies & Competencies: McDonald's vision to become the easiest choice for customers throughout the global foodservice industry is driven by six strategies. Our goal, through the implementation of these strategies, is to generate attractive returns to shareholders, thereby becoming the easiest choice for investors as well.

Value. We will consistently deliver the kind of low prices, special offers and quality experiences that motivate customers to think of McDonald's as a better value than our competitors.

Service. We will continue to provide fast, accurate, friendly and hassle-free service.

Site. We will serve our products wherever customers live, work, shop or gather while enhancing profits through long-term investments.

Food. We will continue to offer good, hot, easy-to-eat foods to attract more customer visits.

Experience. We will ensure that our customers' relationships and experiences with McDonald's exceed their expectations.

Focus. We will create and implement the leadership and management processes necessary to improve performance.

Commitment to the Environment: McDonald's Policy Statement — McDonald's believes it has a special responsibility to protect our environment for future generations. This responsibility is derived from our unique relationship with millions of consumers worldwide whose quality of life will be affected by our stewardship of the environment. We share their beliefs that the right to exist in an environment of clear air, clean earth, and clean water is fundamental and unwavering. We realize that in today's world, a business leader must be an environmental leader as well. Hence, our determination to analyze every aspect of our business in terms of its impact on the environment, and to take actions beyond what is expected if they hold the prospect of leaving future generations an environmentally sound world. We will lead, both in word and in deed. Our environmental commitment and behavior are guided by the following principles:

Effectively manage solid waste — We are committed to taking a "total lifecycle" approach to solid waste, examining ways of reducing materials used in production and packaging, and diverting as much waste as possible from the solid waste stream. We will follow three main courses of action: Reduce, reuse, and recycle.

565. MCI Communications Corp.
1801 Pennsylvania Ave.
Washington, DC 20006
Phone: (202) 872-1600
Web: http://www.mci.com

MCI Communications Corp. (NAS-DAQ; MCIC) provides a full range of integrated communication services. MCI was originally positioning itself for the closure of the merger with British Telecommunications to form Concert PLC. However, the BT/MCI merger has been cancelled. Due in large part to a better offer, MCI has agreed to be bought by WorldCom Inc. (NASDAQ;WCOM) to form MCI WorldCom.

Slogan: "Is This a Good Time, or What?"

Statement: The alliances with Telefonica and PT reinforce two strategies that are central to the success of Concert: One, the aggressive pursuit of explosive opportunities worldwide, and two, the solidifying of powerful partnerships with major communications providers. As the global communications market rapidly deregulates, control of a critical mass of international traffic flow becomes essential to global leadership and success. Strong partnerships worldwide provide this control.

Mission Statement: Our key mission through networkMCI, our strategic

vision, is to continue to grow domestic market share profitably, expand our global capabilities, and take full advantage of the emerging technologies to meet our customers' needs and become a leader in the coming world of multimedia.

MCI's strengths in the marketplace are its people, its responsiveness to customers' needs, the development of innovative products based on MCI's flexible, intelligent network platform — integrating the most advanced technologies from the world's leading suppliers.

566. McKesson Corp.
McKesson Plaza
1 Post St.
San Francisco, CA 94104
Phone: (415) 983-8300
Web: http://www.mckesson.com

McKesson Corp. (NYSE: MCK) distributes pharmaceutical and healthcare products, primarily to stores and the company, also, markets and distributes pure drinking water.

Corporate Vision: Over the past decade, McKesson has transformed from a broadly diversified conglomerate into a company actively focused on distribution and on providing related support services to its customers and suppliers. McKesson was founded early in the 19th century, and as we approach the 21st century we are firm in the believe that our future prospects are enhanced by a sharper focus on our two core businesses:

Distributing and marketing pharmaceutical and health and beauty care products and providing related retail, hospital, and managed prescription care services.

Bottling, marketing and distributing pure drinking water.

In addition to these businesses, McKesson also owns a prized asset: an 83% stake in Armor All Products Corporation. McKesson will continue to provide Armor All with a foundation and framework to develop its own independent identity and to reach its full business potential.

We are committed to an aggressive program to build Armor All's long-term future as the premier worldwide distributor of automotive appearance products.

By pursing this course, we can build value for the shareholders of both McKesson and Armor All.

Principles: Pharmaceutical distribution and pure drinking water, each serving essential human needs and each offering opportunity for steady growth, form the stable, balanced core of McKesson. We believe we will perform best by focusing on those two core businesses. In so doing, we will create superior products and services for our customers and suppliers and a rewarding and challenging work environment to our employees.

We firmly subscribe to conducting all of our business activities in accordance with the highest ethical standards and in full compliance with both the letter and spirit of the law. Recognizing the critical need to maintain the highest possible quality in our products and services, we will accept no compromise in our operations that endangers human health and safety. Working in conjunction with the McKesson Foundation, we are committed to playing a constructive role in those communities where we operate and to encouraging the participation of our employees in civic and non-profit activities.

In measuring progress toward realizing our vision, we will focus not only on financial success but also on the ability to attract, develop and retain talented people. As a distributor, we appreciate the central role played by employees in providing superior customer service. We will continue to rely on these employees to exercise their distinctive creativity, initiative and dedication.

As we achieve our vision, McKesson should produce superior returns for shareholders. By the second half of this decade, we expect to be positioned in the top quartile of U.S. companies, measured in terms of return on equity and growth and become established as one of the country's most admired service corporations.

567. Mead Corp.

Court House Plaza N.E.
Dayton, OH 45463
Phone: (937) 495-6323
Web: http://www.mead.com

Mead Corp. (NYSE; MEA) manufactures and markets paper, lumber, and other wood products and byproducts.

Mead's Vision: To become recognized by the results we achieve for customers, shareowners, and employees.

To act in ways consistent with a set of shared values:

Honesty, integrity and candor.
Customer focus.
Individual participation.
Results driven.
Learning organization.

To use a common set of tools to achieve results:

Total customer satisfaction.
Productivity improvement.
High performance management.

Mead's Mission: To become number one in customer satisfaction in the markets we choose to serve.

568. Media General Inc.

333 E. Grace St.
Richmond, VA 23219
Phone: (804) 649-6000
Web: http://www.media-general.com

Media General Inc. (AMEX; MEG/A) is an independent, publicly owned communications company with interests in metropolitan newspapers, broadcast television, cable television, newsprint production and diversified information services.

Mission: Our corporate mission is to be the leading provider of high quality news, information, and entertainment services in the Southeast by continually building our position of strength in strategically located markets.

569. Mellon Bank Corp.

One Mellon Bank Ctr.

Pittsburgh, PA 15258
Phone: (412) 234-5000
Web: http://www.melon.com

Mellon Bank Corp. (NYSE; MEL) through its subsidiaries is in the banking (Mellon Bank), financial services (Boston Co. and Mellon Financial Services), and mutual fund (Dreyfus Corp.) industries.

Vision: Mellon Bank Corporation will be well known for its commitment to total quality and consistent excellence in performance, and broadly recognized for successfully meeting customers' needs.

570. Merchants Bancshares Inc.
164 Church St.
Burlington, VT 05401
Phone: (802) 658-3400
Web: http://www.merchantsbankvt.com

Merchants Bancshares Inc. (NASDAQ; MBVT) is in the banking and financial services industry.

Mission Statement: The mission of The Merchants Bank is to be a customer-centric, high performance community bank committed to delivering value to our customers, our shareholders, and the communities we serve.

Corporate Vision: The financial services industry will continue to undergo radical change including continued consolidation, a proliferation of new competitors as a result of deregulation and technological advances, and a shift in focus and resources for most banks toward concentration on a few key strategic businesses. Many of these key businesses are today dominated by non-bank providers who have developed significant competitive advantages through advanced information technology and delivery. As Merchants continues to move through the transition to a community-based financial services company, we will focus on building four key characteristics of success.

A fortress balance sheet that generates a sound, stable, and consistent earnings

stream balanced between intermediation and fee income.

A leading edge, technologically based delivery system that allows our customers to bank "anytime, anywhere, and anyplace."

A unique style of business that differentiates Merchants in the marketplace and adds value to all customer relationships.

A proper balance between central direction (organizational control/risk containment) and entrepreneurial benefits at the customer level.

571. Merck & Co. Inc.
One Merck Dr.
Whitehouse Station, NY 08889
Phone: (908) 423-1000
Web: http://www.merck.com

Merck & Co. Inc. (NYSE; MRK) is a leading research-driven pharmaceutical products and services company. Merck discovers, develops, manufactures and markets a broad range of innovative products to improve human and animal health.

Slogan: "Committed to Bringing Out the Best in Medicine."

Statement: Merck works to improve quality of life and lower overall health-care costs. In addition to delivering these benefits to society, Merck is committed to providing superior returns for shareholders and a stimulating work environment for employees.

Major Goals: First, we established an overriding goal that Merck will remain a top-tier growth company. Specifically, it is our goal that Merck will perform in the top 25% of leading health-care companies.

Second, to achieve this financial objective, we are strengthening our focus on Merck's core business as a research-based ethical pharmaceutical company in human and animal health. For Merck, therefore, "diversification" will mean having innovative products in many therapeutic categories, not being in different businesses.

572. Meredith Corp.
1716 Locust St.
Des Moines, IA 50309
Phone: (515) 284-3000
Web: http://www.home-and-family.com

Meredith Corp. (NYSE; MDP) is a diversified media company.

Our Mission: We are Meredith Corporation, a publicly held media company founded upon service to our customers. Our cornerstone is knowledge and understanding of the home and family market. From that, we have built businesses which serve well-defined readers and viewers, deliver the messages of advertisers, and extend our franchises and related expertise to other special markets. Our products and services distinguish themselves on the basis of quality, customer service, and value that can be trusted.

Our Principles: Our actions are guided by these principles:

Our primary focus is success over the long term.

Our loyal customers are the company's lifeblood. We are dedicated to building enduring relationships with them and to understanding and meeting their needs with high-quality, high-value products, and with service beyond their expectations.

We believe good citizenship requires concern for the communities in which we operate. We encourage corporate and employee participation.

We treasure the good reputation of our company, its products, its services, and its people. Our reputation matters to us in everything we do.

Our shareholders, who have demonstrated faith in our company, deserve a superior return on their investments through market appreciation and dividends.

Our Objectives: Improve the effectiveness of customer service. Maintain better connections between each employee and the needs of the customer.

Strengthen succession planning and employee development.

Improve the linkage between corporate objectives and employee standards, incentive systems, rewards and recognition.

Increase core business profitability.

Grow the earnings base through product development and acquisitions.

573. Meridian Diagnostics Inc.
3471 River Hills Dr.
Cincinnati, OH 45244
Phone: (513) 272-3700

Meridian Diagnostics Inc. (NASDAQ; KITS) develops, manufactures, and markets a diverse line of immunodiagnostic test kits, purified reagents, and related diagnostic products. The company is a leader in the area of rapid diagnosis of infectious human diseases.

A Plan for Growth: At Meridian, our core growth continues through our strong commitment to research and development.

The growth strategies of Meridian Diagnostics are the foundations that guide us to immuno-diagnostic leadership and help us compete successfully in the rapidly changing health care industry. Fundamental to the attainment of our long-term growth objectives is the internal development of innovative new products through research and development. We continually improve our core products and apply proven technologies in an effort to increase accuracy, simplicity and speed.

574. Merrill Lynch & Co. Inc.
North Tower
250 Vesey St.
New York, NY 10281
Phone: (212) 449-1000
Web: http://www.ml.com

Merrill Lynch & Co. Inc. (NYSE; MER) is one of the largest brokerage firms. Additionally, the company supplies financing, insurance, and other related services.

Slogans: "The Difference Is Merrill Lynch." "A Tradition of Trust." "A Breed Apart."

Statement: Our corporate culture at Merrill Lynch is the sum total of what we believe and think, how we work together as colleagues and how we conduct ourselves as individuals.

It is the way we treat our clients, our shareholders, our fellow employees, our neighbors and the public in general.

It is who we are.

And while our corporate culture is by nature indefinable, it begins and ends with certain principles that underlie our success as a business and as individuals.

Our future growth and prosperity depend on our continued commitment to these principles and our ability to instill them in others:

Client focus.

Respect for the individual.

Teamwork.

Responsible citizenship.

Integrity.

575. Metropolitan Life Insurance Co.

One Madison Ave.
New York, NY 10010
Phone: (212) 578-2211
Web: http://www.metlife.com

Metropolitan Life Insurance Co. offers mutual life insurance and other financial products and services.

Slogans: "Get Met. It Pays." "MetLife Gives You Great Protection." "MetLife Whole Life ... Because You've Got Your Whole Life Ahead of You."

Mission: The mission of Metropolitan Life and its family of companies is to provide our customers with high-quality, innovative, and cost-effective insurance and other financial products and related services. The objective of each Met Life business is to grow and to be the best in its field, while balancing the interests of customers, employees, and the community.

Our Goals: To be one of the leading insurance and financial institutions in the world as measured by assets, market share and return on assets.

To increase our financial strength by profitable growth, prudent risk management, and sound and progressive investments.

To provide insurance to our mutual policyholders as close to cost as feasible.

To build on our traditions of integrity, reliability and financial strength.

To obtain feedback from our customers on an on-going basis, since meeting or exceeding their expectations is the foundation of our corporate commitment.

576. Micron Technology Inc.

8000 S. Federal Way
Boise, ID 83707
Phone: (208) 368-4000
Web: http://www.micron.com

Micron Technology Inc. (NYSE; MU) and its subsidiaries design, manufacture, and market DRAMs, very fast SRAMs, other semiconductor components, board-level and system-level products, and personal computers.

Mission: Our mission is to be a world-class team developing advantages for our customers.

577. Microsoft Corp.

One Microsoft Way
Redmond, WA 98052
Phone: (206) 882-8080
Web: http://www.microsoft.com

Microsoft Corp. (NASDAQ; MSFT) develops and markets systems and applications software.

Slogan: "Where Do You Want to Go Today?"

Vision: At Microsoft, one vision drives everything we do: A computer on every desk and in every home.

Commitment to the Environment: While many corporations utilize some form of recycling, Microsoft has a wide-ranging environmental program that includes conservation, reuse, and recycling.

We conserve everything from paper, electricity and water.

We reuse a variety of products including toner cartridges and trees and shrubs displaced by construction. The company also donates floppy disks and videotapes to local schools for reuse.

We recycle paper products, plastics, glass and metals to reduce waste and cut costs.

In addition, Microsoft is committed to completing this cycle by regularly purchasing products with recycled content, including paper for product packaging and manuals as well as office supplies.

578. Mikohn Gaming Corp.
1045 Palms Airport Dr.
Las Vegas, NV 89119
Phone: (702) 896-3890

Mikohn Gaming Corp. (NASDAQ; MIKN) manufactures, markets, and distributes high-technology systems, products, and services for the casino industry.
Strategic Growth Plan:
1. Acquiring high quality companies with complementary products.
2. Obtaining the manufacturing and/or distribution rights on existing top-of-the-line products.
3. Broadening our own product mix through research, development, and enhancement of new systems.
4. Expanding our network of sales, service, and manufacturing facilities to better serve active new jurisdictions.
5. Attracting and retaining talented, experienced people in order to further strengthen our management depth and capabilities.

579. Miller Brewing Co.
3939 W. Highland Rd.
Milwaukee, WI 53208
Phone: (414) 931-2000

Miller Brewing Co., a wholly-owned subsidiary of Philip Morris Inc. (NYSE; MO), is the second largest brewer in the U.S., behind Anheuser-Busch. Miller produces and distributes a full range of beer products. Their light beer category includes Miller Lite and Lite Ice. In the premium category they offer Miller Genuine Draft, MGD Lite, Icehouse, and Red Dog. In the near premium category they offer Miller High Life, Miller High Life Lite, and Miller High Life Ice. In the below premium category they offer Meister Brau, Milwaukee's Best, and Magnum Malt Liquor. In the specialty category they offer Miller Reserve Amber Ale and Miller Reserve Velvet. They also produce Sharp's, a non-alcohol beverage. Miller owns and operates Molson Breweries USA. They have a license agreement with Lowenbrau.
Slogans: "Miller Time." "Life Is Good." "Making the World a Very Cool Place." Red Dog — "You Are Your Own Dog." "Reach for What's Out There." "It's Time for a Good Old Macro Brew."

Vision: Miller Brewing Company will be the most successful brewer in the world through an unwavering commitment to our customers, the profitable growth of our business and the effectiveness of our people.

Miller Values: Quality; customer focus; acting with urgency; results orientation; innovation/creativity; open/honest communication; legal, moral, and ethical behavior; diversity; teamwork.

580. Millipore Corp.
80 Ashby Rd.
Bedford, MA 01730
Phone: (617) 275-9200
Web: http://www.millipore.com

Millipore Corp. (NYSE; MIL) manufactures and markets filtration and water analysis products.
Millipore's Mission: To be the worldwide leader in the eyes of our customers, employees, shareholders and suppliers in

the high-value-added separations industry.

To achieve leadership through a global focus on customer satisfaction, employee participation and technological excellence.

To improve the quality of life through products which advance achievement in science and technology.

581. Minnesota Mining and Manufacturing Co.

3M Ctr.
St. Paul, MN 55144
Phone: (612) 733-1110
Web: http://www.mmm.com

Minnesota Mining and Manufacturing Co. (NYSE; MMM) manufactures a variety of products, many using bonding and coating technology, such as pressure-sensitive tape.

Slogan: "3M Innovation."

Statement: At 3M, we are committed to satisfying our customers with superior quality and value; providing investors with an attractive return through sustained, high-quality growth; respecting our social and physical environment; and being a company of which employees are proud.

Corporate Goals and Objectives: 3M is an organization of employees and stockholders who have combined their resources to pursue common goals in providing useful products and services, creating rewarding employment, assuring an adequate return to investors and contributing toward a better social and economic environment for the public generally.

Fundamental Principles: The first principle is the promotion of entrepreneurship and insistence upon freedom in the work place to pursue innovative ideas. Policies, practices and organizational structure have been flexible and characterized by mutual trust and cooperation.

The second is the adherence to uncompromising honesty and integrity. This is manifested in the commitment of the highest standards of ethics throughout the organization and in all aspects of 3M's operations.

Third is the preservation of individual identity in an organization structure which embraces widely diverse businesses and operates in different political and economic systems throughout the world. From this endeavor there have developed an identifiable 3M spirit and a sense of belonging to the 3M family.

582. Minnesota Power & Light Co.

30 West Superior St.
Duluth, MN 55802
Phone: (218) 722-2641

Minnesota Power & Light Co. (NYSE; MPL) is in the electric utility industry.

Mission Statement: Our purpose is to manage our diversified company to significantly enhance total shareholder return from 1996 through the year 2000 and beyond. Our goal is to provide by the year 2000 a total return to our shareholders in the upper quartile of our peer group of diversified electric companies.

Core Values: Minnesota Power is a diverse set of businesses benefiting from specific industry knowledge and corporate staff expertise.

Our customers are the key to our success. We must respect them; we must walk in their shoes. Understanding their needs and serving them properly must be the driving passion of us all. We have to see our products and services from their viewpoint. Solving their problems and bringing them value is our job. We will look at our organization from the outside in, as our customers view us.

We are entrusted with the capital of our shareholders. Our obligation is to be responsible stewards of their funds and to provide a healthy return on their investment. Our mindset is one of uncompromising performance, and our incentive systems will be driven by the results we achieve for shareholders.

Minnesota Power respects all its employees and will reward them based on their performance and contribution. We will treat our people fairly and ethically. We will provide a stimulating workplace environment where participation and cooperation are expected and success is appreciated and rewarded. We expect our people to operate with a bias for action and to accept responsibility.

Minnesota Power operates in many communities. We will continue to be responsible corporate citizens both as individuals and operating companies. We will operate in the communities we serve in a way that distinguishes us from others, because it is the right thing to do.

Minnesota Power has a core philosophy that strongly supports environmental stewardship and safety. We will focus on preventing environmental problems before they become environmental mistakes. Environmental stewardship and safety are good business and set an example for others to emulate.

We expect our work environment to be fun and enjoyable. We share our workdays and we need to enjoy each other's company. We will enthusiastically celebrate victories, laugh at absurdity, enjoy our camaraderie and not take ourselves too seriously.

We will value our differences and diversity, yet support one another. We can agree to disagree and still be friends.

583. Mirage Resorts Inc.
3400 Las Vegas Blvd.
Las Vegas, NV 89109
Phone: (702) 791-7111
Web: http://www.mirageresorts.com

Mirage Resorts Inc. (NYSE; MIR) is a leading operator of casino-based resorts.

Statement: Once upon a time, there were three little pigs. One built his house of straw. Another used wood. But the smartest and most astute pig built his house of bricks.

Every child knows this wonderful fairy tale. The big, bad wolf arrives, of course, and blows down the houses of straw and wood, but cannot harm the house of bricks.

We have always thought that this simple fairy tale is the most absolute and fundamental lesson for success in our industry. Resorts that are built with a long-term viewpoint, those that provide for excellent customer service and maximum employee satisfaction, will prosper in any market, at all times. Clearly, the house of bricks will always prevail over those of straw or wood.

Each of our resorts, our houses of brick, were constructed with this long-term view in mind. No matter how exciting and prosperous their initial years may be, their best years will always be ahead of them.

As an organization, we are dedicated to the belief that excellence breeds success. I've always thought that the third pig understood this very well and that his experiences demonstrated the premise.

584. Molson Companies Ltd.
Scotia Plaza
40 King St. West
Suite 3600
Toronto, Canada M5H 3 Z5
Phone: (416) 360-1786
Web: http://www.molson.com

The Molson Companies Ltd. (Montreal, Toronto, Vancouver exchanges; MOL.A and MOL.B) is a diversified corporation in the following principal businesses: Molson Breweries (Canada's leading brewer), Diversey Corp. (chemical specialties), Beaver Lumber (retailing), and the Montreal Canadians (NHL hockey team/sports and entertainment).

Statement: Our plan is to exit from non-core businesses in an orderly manner. Over the next few years we will divest our retailing interests and other non-core assets.

In the longer term, the Corporation is expected to consist of two businesses at the top of their industries, as well as our highly valued sports and entertainment assets.

Brewing: Molson Breweries' aim, as expressed in its mission statement, is "to be Canada's number one brewer, a major competitor in North America and a respected player in select international markets."

585. Monarch Machine Tool Co.
615 N. Oak St.
Sidney, OH 45365
Phone: (937) 492-4111

Monarch Machine Tool Co. (NYSE; MMO) designs and manufactures machinery and related products.

Mission Statement: Profitable growth through the design and manufacture of machinery and allied products, and as a provider of manufacturing processes.

Priorities:
1. Quality: Reliability; accuracy; aesthetics.
2. On time delivery.
3. Profitability.

Quality Policy: We will design, produce and deliver products and services that meet or exceed our customers' expectations of quality.

These expectations are met by the commitment of all of our employees, distributors and subcontractors to continuous improvement of procedures and processes in all aspects of our operations.

586. Money Store Inc.
2840 Morris Ave.
Union, NJ 07083
Phone: (908) 686-2000
Web: http://www.themoneystore.com

The Money Store Inc. (NASDAQ; MONE) is a financial services company engaged primarily in the business of originating, purchasing, and servicing consumer and commercial loans.

Strategy: The Money Store's strategy has four elements:

Focus on growth niche markets.
Control credit and financial risk.
Invest heavily in advertising and technology.
Develop multiple growth drivers.

587. Monsanto Co.
800 N. Lindbergh Blvd.
St. Louis, MO 63167
Phone: (314) 694-1000
Web: http://www.monsanto.com

Monsanto Co. (NYSE; MTC) and its subsidiaries manufacture and sell a diversified line of agricultural products, chemical products and food products, including low-calorie sweeteners. Currently, Monsanto reports its business under four industry segments: The agricultural group, the chemical group, Searle, and NutraSweet.

Statement: We will continue to drive for shareowner value.

We will concentrate on net income gains and cash flow results in order to reach and sustain our financial return on equity target.

We will continue to use excess cash not needed for reinvestment to repurchase shares.

We will drive our research investments relentlessly to commercial success.

We will continue to find innovative ways to add value for our customers.

Strategic Goals: Achieve the full profit potential of key products.

Aggressively control costs and improve the productivity of our capital base.

Establish the products of the future.

Environmental Statement: "We pledge to be part of the solution."

It is our pledge to:

Reduce all toxic and hazardous releases and emissions, working toward an ultimate goal of zero effect;

Ensure no Monsanto operation poses any undue risk to our employees and our communities;

Work to achieve sustainable agriculture through new technology and practices;

Ensure groundwater safety;

Keep our plants open to our communities and involve the community in plant operations;

Manage all corporate real estate, including plant sites, to benefit nature; and

Search worldwide for technology to reduce and eliminate waste from our operations, with the top priority being not making it in the first place.

588. (J. P.) Morgan & Co.
60 Wall St.
New York, NY 10260
Phone: (212) 483-2323
Web: http://www.jpmorgan.com

J. P. Morgan & Co. (NYSE; JPM) is a holding company in the banking and finance industries.

Statement: Drawing on commercial, investment, and merchant banking traditions, we strive to be an international leader in capability and character, to channel capital to productive uses, and to earn superior returns over time for our stockholders.

Our Business Principles at Work: We strive to build relationships of trust and discretion over the long term. We put our clients' interests first, and we are resolute in defending those interests.

Our research is driven by analytical rigor and a commitment to objectivity. These elements work to ensure that our recommendations reflect the best information available and adhere to our clients' best interests.

Our perspective is global. Our international network of financial specialists provides expertise in, and access to, all major financial markets — not only in industrially developed regions but also in emerging economies around the world.

Our solid capital base and high credit rating often translate into added financial stability and flexibility for our clients. Our financial position and institutional reputation enable us to execute unusually large and complex transactions.

589. Morton International
100 North Riverside Plaza
Chicago, IL 60606
Phone: (312) 807-2000
Web:
http://www.mortonintl.com/home.htm

Morton International (NYSE; MII) is a manufacturer and marketer of specialty chemicals, automotive inflatable restraint systems, and salt.

Goal: Morton's goal is to be the market leader in the industries it serves by providing products which meet or exceed customers' expectations.

590. Mosinee Paper Corp.
1244 Kronewetter Dr.
Mosinee, WI 54455
Phone: (715) 693-4470

Mosinee Paper Corp. (NASDAQ; MOSI) produces specialty papers and towel and tissue papers. The company's specialty papers, including wax laminates, are used in an array of industrial and consumer products.

Mission: Mosinee Paper Corporation's mission is to increase shareholder value through capital appreciation and dividends. The continued development of strong and dependable cash flow from operations provides the means to expand the value-producing capabilities of the company.

591. Motorola Inc.
1303 E. Algonquin Rd.
Schaumburg, IL 60196
Phone: (847) 576-5000
Web: http://www.mot.com

Motorola Inc. (NYSE; MOTO) is one of the world's leading providers of wireless communications, semiconductors, and advanced electronic systems, components, and services. Major equipment businesses include cellular telephone, two-way radio, paging and data communications, personal communications, automotive, defense and space electronics and computers.

Slogans: "Leading the Way in Wireless Communications." "Quality Means the World to Us." "Know Now." "What You Never Thought Possible."

Statement: As stockholders, you have invested in a company with a distinctive culture that incorporates an obsession with quality, uncompromising ethics and respect for people. These values create the foundation for our success. They have helped us to create new technology platforms and to open new markets throughout the world.

592. M.S. Carriers
3171 Directors Row
Memphis, TN 38116
Phone: (901) 332-2500

M.S. Carriers (NASDAQ; MSCA) is in the trucking business.

Slogan: "Delivering Your Future."

Vision Statement: Excellence through: People — Top athletes in every position. Processes — Best service in industry through the application and continuous improvement of our processes.

Results — Superior shareholder value.

593. Murphy Oil Co.
200 Peach St.
El Dorado, AR 71731
Phone: (870) 862-6411
Web: http://www.murphyoilcorp.com

Murphy Oil Co. (NYSE; MUR) is a worldwide oil and gas exploration and production company.

Statement: The company completed the spin-off of its timer, farm, and real estate subsidiary and sold high-cost U.S. on-shore producing properties. These strategic initiatives will allow the company's management to focus more fully on the exploration for and production of high-margin oil and gas properties to deliver on its commitment to enhance shareholder value.

594. Mycogen Corp.
5451 Oberlin Dr.
San Diego, CA 92121
Phone: (619) 453-1053
Web: http://www.mycogen.com

Mycogen Corp. (NASDAQ; MYCO) provides a variety of technology-based products and services to control agriculture pests and improve food and fiber production.

Strategy: Mycogen's strategy is to use its proprietary *Bacillus thuringiensis* bio-toxin gene technology to expand its portfolio of biopesticide products and develop planting seeds with built-in insect resistance. It is also using plant transformation and other advanced plant science techniques to develop corn, cotton and other crop plants with improved nutritional, chemical and fiber characteristics.

Mission: Mycogen's mission is to be a fully integrated company involved in the invention, manufacturing and marketing of products to control pests and increase food production. Our products will be compatible with the environmental and social needs of a changing world.

We will build our reputation on the quality of our products and the excellence of our research; we will build our legacy on the quality of our people and our contributions to society and the environment.

595. NAC Re Corp.
One Greenwich Plaza
P.O. Box 2568
Greenwich, CT 06836
Phone: (203) 622-5200

NAC Re Corp. (NYSE; NRC) is the holding company for NAC Reinsurance Corporation and its wholly-owned insurance and reinsurance domestic and foreign subsidiaries.

Vision: NAC Re's vision is to be the best professional reinsurer as measured by our shareholders, clients, and employees. We will strive to become one of the top 5 domestic reinsurers — top 25 globally — in terms of profitability, premiums and surplus. To accomplish this we will distinguish ourselves in the following ways:

Client value — We seek to be rated first, by our clients, in service and innovation, in every market we enter.

Financial security — We will remain committed to maintaining a balance sheet of unquestioned strength.

Shareholder value — We will seek to be an industry leader in long-term returns to shareholders.

Organizational excellence — We intend to be the employer of choice in our industry by fostering an environment that encourages and rewards teamwork, involvement, trust, honesty, and continuous improvement.

596. Nalco Chemical Co.

1 Nalco Ctr.
Naperville, IL 60563
Phone: (630) 305-1000
Web: http://www.nalco.com

Nalco Chemical Co. (NYSE; NLC) produces specialty chemicals used in water and in waste treatment and other processes.

Statement: Nalco seeks to find customer needs and fill them through the application of specialty chemicals and technology. We enhance the profitability of our customers' business by providing products and services that add value to their operations and provide them in acceptable return on their investment.

597. National Beverage Corp.

One North University Dr.
Fort Lauderdale, FL 33324
Phone: (954) 581-0922
Web: http://www.natbev.com

National Beverage Corp. (AMEX; FIZ) serves as a holding company for various operating subsidiaries that develop, produce, market, and distribute its registered brand name soft drinks: Shasta, Faygo,

Big Shot, and Spree. The company also produces soft drinks for retail grocery chains, warehouse clubs, wholesalers, and other soft drink companies.

Slogan: "Taste That Stands the Test of Time."

Corporate Mission: The achievement ... the ultimate respect of its most adept competition in which 'they' profusely recognize National Beverage as the King of Flavors ... the admiration that the beverage industry will place on the speed and innovation of National Beverage's techniques relative to the taste and packaging creativity of its products. And finally, the most revered of our mission ... the first class status dignifying our management and its performance.

The foregoing will be the result of the sustained growth, profitability and innovation of the company.

This goal is paramount in our every decision. The people awareness and growth atmosphere within our company today gives self-fulfilling prophecy to this mission.

Statement: We all view the world a little differently. Seeing ... is achieving. As we look to the future, together we will create a company that will exceed all our expectations. Our vision will be realized because our focus is clear ... the fantasy of flavor is becoming a reality.

598. National Semiconductor Corp.

2900 Semiconductor Dr.
Santa Clara, CA 95051
Phone: (408) 721-5000
Web: http://www.nsc.com

National Semiconductor Corp. (NYSE; NSM) manufactures linear and digital integrated circuits.

Our Mission and Beliefs: Our mission is to excel in serving chosen markets by delivering semiconductor-intensive products and services of the highest quality and value, thereby providing a competitive advantage to our customers worldwide.

599. Nationwide Insurance Enterprise

One Nationwide Plaza
Columbus, OH 43216
Phone: (614) 249-7111
Web: http://www.nationwide.com

Nationwide Insurance Enterprise is a family of companies primarily engaged in providing mutual insurance and other financial security products and services for individuals, families, businesses, and organizations.

Slogan: "Nationwide Is on Your Side."

Our Vision: We are the Nationwide Insurance Enterprise. We exist to serve our customers. We will be the best in our core businesses, building on our leading positions in insurance and financial services. We value ethical behavior, diversity, and our mutual heritage. We will manage as a financially strong enterprise, rewarding results, teamwork, and creativity.

600. Natural Wonders

4209 Technology Dr.
Fremont, CA 94538
Phone: (510) 252-9600

Natural Wonders (NASDAQ; NATW) is a retailer of nature and science products.

Our Mission: To be an excellent national specialty retailer of nature and science products achieving high profitability and growth.

601. Navistar International Corp.

455 N. Cityfront Plz.
Chicago, IL 60611
Phone: (312) 836-2000
Web: http://www.navistar.com

Navistar International Corp. (NYSE; NAV) manufactures trucks and school bus chassis and diesel engines.

Corporate Mission: Our primary enterprise objective is to increase the value of shareowners' investment by managing our resources and serving our customers better than and more efficiently than our competitors.

We will grow in markets where we can create enough advantage to earn a good return for our shareowners. We will redeploy resources from markets where we cannot.

By achieving our objectives, we expect to reward our shareowners, whose continuing investment in the company is vital, and to reward our employees, whose creativity and commitment to winning through teamwork is the key to our competitiveness.

602. Neiman Marcus Group Inc.

27 Boylston St.
Chestnut Hill, MA 02167
Phone: (617) 232-0760
Web: http://www.neimanmarcus.com

Neiman Marcus Group Inc. (NYSE; NMG), a subsidiary of Harcourt General Inc. (NYSE; H), is a retailer of fine merchandise.

Slogan: "How to Look."

Our Mission: Our mission is to be the leading specialty retailer of fine merchandise to discerning, fashion-conscious customers from around the world. We will strive to exceed customer expectations for service, quality and value as we build upon our long-standing tradition of excellence.

603. NeoRx Corp.

410 West Harrison
Seattle, WA 98119
Phone: (206) 281-7001

NeoRx Corp. (NASDAQ; NERX) is dedicated to finding treatments for cancer and cardiovascular disease through biotechnology.

Mission: NeoRx Corporation develops targeted biopharmaceuticals to treat cancer and cardiovascular disease.

604. Nestle USA Inc.
800 North Brand Blvd.
Glendale, CA 91203
Phone: (818) 549-6000
Web: http://www.nestle.com

Nestle USA Inc., a subsidiary of Nestle Ltd. (OTC; NSRGY) is among the largest food and beverage companies in the nation. Registered brand names include, in part, Nestle, Baby Ruth, Butterfinger, Hills Bros., Coffee-mate, Stouffer's, Taster's Choice, Nescafe, Nestea, Contadina, Libby's, Friskies, Mighty Dog, and Berringer.

Our Vision: To be the premier diversified food company in the United States.

Strategies to Achieve Nestle USA's Vision: Develop a strong Nestle organization and culture.

Provide superior value to consumers and customers through continuous quality improvement.

Invest to strengthen brand equity and build loyalty to our brands.

Achieve leadership positions in our core businesses.

Achieve financial performance in the top quartile of diversified food companies.

605. NetFRAME Systems Inc.
11545 Barber Lane
Milpitas, CA 95035
Phone: (408) 474-1000
Web: http://www.netframe.com

NetFRAME Systems Inc. (NASDAQ; NETF) is a leading supplier of continuous availability network servers.

Mission: NetFRAME's mission is to provide customers with computing systems that solve real, business critical problems. In a time of growing competition, NetFRAME's family of ClusterServers enables corporations to utilize their networks to gain a strategic advantage. By deploying the client/server approach on an enterprise-wide scale, NetFRAME users are able to provide information to workers and managers quickly, enabling them to make better informed decisions, work more productively, and respond more efficiently to changing business conditions. It is through this commitment to providing state-of-the-art information solutions that NetFRAME intends to maintain its leadership position in the enterprise network server market, as well as gain a competitive edge in the midrange computing system market.

606. Neurogen Corp.
35 Northeast Industrial Rd.
Branford, CT 06405
Phone: (203) 488-8201

Neurogen Corp. (NASDAQ; NRGN) is a neuropharmaceutical company using molecular biology, medicinal chemistry and neurobiology to develop the next generation of psychotherapeutics, drugs to treat central nervous system disorders like anxiety, depression, dementia, epilepsy, psychosis, and eating, sleep and stress related disorders.

Statement: Ratcheted growth through successive collaborations — We are firmly committed to a very deliberate growth strategy based on ratcheting up our capabilities through successive successful corporate partnerships.

Strategy: Neurogen's strategy is to discover and develop highly specific drugs without the negative side effects typically associated with many currently prescribed psychotherapeutic medications.

607. New England Electric System
25 Research Dr.
Westborough, MA 01582
Phone: (508) 389-2000
Web: http://www.nees.com

New England Electric System (NYSE; NES) is a provider of electric services.

Commitment: We pledge to provide our customers the highest possible value by continuously improving electric service, managing costs, and reducing adverse environmental impacts.

608. New York Life Insurance Co.

51 Madison Ave.
New York, NY 10010
Phone: (212) 576-7000
Web: http://www.newyorklife.com

New York Life Insurance Co. family of companies provides traditional mutual life, group, annuity, disability products, managed health care, institutional asset management and investment products such as mutual funds.

Slogan: "The Company You Keep."

Vision: New York Life and its affiliates are in the business of providing financial security. We are committed to being the soundest, strongest, and easiest company to do business with. Every decision we make, every action we take has one overriding purpose: To be here when our customers need us.

609. New York State Electric & Gas Corp.

4500 Vestal Pkwy. East
Binghamton, NY 13903
Phone: (607) 729-2551
Web: http://www.nyseg.com

New York State Electric & Gas Corp. (NYSE; NGE) produces and distributes electric and gas service, chiefly to parts of New York state.

Vision: We put energy into action, providing ever better quality and value to those we serve. We seek to set the standard for excellence, leadership, and integrity in the utility industry.

Mission: NYSEG's diversified business units are committed to:

Providing quality services and products at competitive prices.

Pursuing opportunities in emerging and existing markets.

Offering our employees opportunities for personal and professional growth.

Earning an attractive return for our shareholder.

Protecting our environment.

Supporting the needs and visions of our communities.

610. New York Stock Exchange Inc.

11 Wall St.
New York, NY 10005
Phone: (212) 656-3000
Web: http://www.nyse.com

New York Stock Exchange Inc., a not-for-profit company, is a renowned securities marketplace.

Mission Statement: Add value to the capital-raising and asset-management process by providing the highest-quality and most cost-effective self-regulated marketplace for the trading of financial instruments, promote confidence in and understanding of that process, and serve as a forum for discussion of relevant national and international policy issues.

611. Newell Co.

29 E. Stephenson St.
Freeport, ID 61032
Phone: (815) 235-4171
Web: http://www.newellco.com

Newell Co. (NYSE; NWL) is a consumer products company. Registered brand names include Mirro cookware, Anchor Hocking glassware, Levelor blinds, and Rolodex card files, to name some.

Statement: Newell's basic strategy is to merchandise a multi-product offering of brand-name staple products, with an emphasis on excellent customer service, in order to achieve maximum results for our stockholders.

612. NeXstar Pharmaceuticals Inc.

2860 Wilderness Place

Boulder, CO 80301
Phone: (303) 444-5893

NeXstar Pharmaceuticals Inc. (NAS-DAQ; NXTR) is an integrated pharmaceutical company engaged in the discovery, development, manufacture, and sale of pharmaceutical products.

Statement: Prior to the merger (Neptune — a wholly owned subsidiary of the company — and Vestar), NeXstar was primarily engaged in the discovery and development of novel oligonucleotide-based pharmaceuticals. As a result of the merger, the company combined its drug discovery program and financial resources with Vestar's proprietary drug delivery technology, existing products and product pipeline, and Vestar's manufacturing, marketing and regulatory capabilities.

To Our Shareholders: It is not our intention, though, to ever rest on past or present accomplishments, which is why we continue to develop our proprietary drug discovery and delivery technologies. It is our strong belief that we must use those technologies to continually fill our product pipeline. Our ultimate goal, in fact, is to file at least one investigational new drug application each year. Although this will at times be a difficult goal to achieve, we believe that such an approach minimizes risk by letting us pick among the best possible clinical candidates in our chosen areas of focus: Oncology, inflammation/immunology, and infectious diseases. To improve our chances of meeting this goal, we have prioritized our research programs and terminated several internal and external programs that either were not within our core focus or which we believe were not competitive.

613. Nextel Communications Inc.

201 Route 17 North
Rutherford, NJ 07070
Phone: (201) 438-1400
Web: http://www.nextel.com

Nextel Communications Inc. (NAS-DAQ; NXTL) is in the telecommunication business.

Our Vision: To be the leading provider of wireless communications for the mobile work force.

614. Niagara Mohawk Power Corp.

300 Erie Blvd. W.
Syracuse, NY 13202
Phone: (315) 474-1511
Web: http://www.nimo.com

Niagara Mohawk Power Corp. (NYSE; NMK) is primarily an electric and gas utility company.

Vision: We will become the most responsive and efficient energy services company in the Northeast to achieve maximum value for customers, shareholders and employees.

Mission: Niagara Mohawk is an energy services company committed to maximizing value to its customers, shareholders and employees.

The company seeks to satisfy customers' energy needs with high quality, competitively priced electric and gas energy products and services; increase shareholder value through above average growth in earnings; and provide an atmosphere for employees which promotes empowerment and rewards excellence.

Niagara Mohawk promotes safe and efficient practices in the supply, delivery and use of energy. The company is committed to a cleaner, healthier environment through an active, positive approach to its environmental responsibilities. The company supports improvement in the social and economic well-being of the communities it serves and seeks cooperative and constructive relationships with all of its regulators.

Niagara Mohawk's business emphasis focuses on results, aggressive and responsible leadership, responsiveness to customer needs and continuous improvement in operations.

615. NIKE Inc.

One Bowerman Dr.
Beaverton, OR 97005

Phone: (503) 671-6453
Web: http://www.nike.com

NIKE Inc. (NYSE; NKE) designs, develops, and markets high quality footwear, apparel, and accessory products.
Slogans: "Just Do It."
"P.L.A.Y.— Participate in the Lives of America's Youth."
Mission Statement: To maximize profits to the shareholders through products and services that enrich people's lives.

616. Noble Drilling Corp.
10370 Richmond Ave.
Suite 400
Houston, TX 77042
Phone: (713) 974-3131

Noble Drilling Corp. (NYSE; NE) is a provider of diversified services for the oil and gas industry worldwide.
Strategy: The company's business strategy has been to expand its international and deepwater offshore capabilities through acquisitions, redeployments, and rig modifications, and to position itself in geologically promising areas.

617. NorAm Energy Corp.
1600 Smith
32nd Fl.
Houston, TX 77002
Phone: (713) 654-5699
Web: http://www.noram.com

NorAm Energy Corp. (NYSE; NAE) provides electric and gas services.
Vision: NorAm will be recognized as the leader in the customer-driven energy services business. We will be the 'provider of choice' of natural gas, electric power, and related value-added services to energy users in the national and international markets we serve.

618. Nordstrom Inc.
1501 5th Ave.
Seattle, WA 98101
Phone: (206) 628-2111

Nordstrom Inc. (NASDAQ; NOBE) is a specialty retailer.
Our Goal: To become America's store of choice through the commitment of each employee to provide our customers the very best in quality, value, selection and service.

619. Norfolk Southern Corp.
3 Commercial Pl.
Norfolk, VA 23510
Phone: (757) 629-2680
Web: http://www.nscorp.com

Norfolk Southern Corp. (NYSE; NSC) provides rail service.
Vision: Be the safest, most customer-focused and successful transportation company in the world.
Mission: Norfolk Southern's mission is to enhance the value of our stockholders' investment over time by providing quality freight transportation services and undertaking any other related businesses in which our resources, particularly our people, give the company an advantage.

620. Norsk Hydro USA Inc.
800 Third Ave.
New York, NY 10022
Phone: (212) 688-6606
Web: http://www.hydro.com

Norsk Hydro USA Inc. (NYSE; NHY) is a subsidiary of Norsk Hydro A. S., Norway's largest publicly owned industrial concern, with its major activities concentrated in agriculture, oil and gas, light metals, and petrochemicals.
Business Philosophy: Norsk Hydro is an industrial group, based on the processing of natural resources to meet needs for food, energy and materials.
Hydro's aim is to initiate development and growth in areas where, by being highly competitive, the company can achieve good profitability.
Hydro intends to satisfy customer requirements by focusing on market orientation, competence and creativity.

In all its activities Hydro will emphasize quality, efficient use of resources and care for the environment.

Hydro's Environmental Mission: We will make care for the environment and for the wellbeing of future generations the basis of our company policy and decision making.

We will conduct our business activities in accordance with the demands of the environment. Our task is to satisfy the world's need for the goods we provide, in ways which do not diminish the ability of future generations to meet their own needs.

To succeed in our mission we must define and promote specific environmental objectives and plans in all areas of our business.

621. North American Coal Corp.
14785 Preston
Dallas, TX 75240
Phone: (972) 239-2625

North American Coal Corp., a subsidiary of NACCO Industries (NYSE; NC), is a leading producer of lignite.

Mission: We, the North American Coal Corporation Companies, will provide exceptional service to our customers and maximum value to our shareholders. We will conduct our business in an ethical, professional, safe, environmentally sound manner.

Vision: By the year 2000, the North American Coal Corporation will be the largest lignite producer in North America, and will produce an additional ten million tons of monlignite Western coal annually. The company will be a major contribution to enhancing the image of the industry.

622. North Indiana Public Service Co.
5265 Hohman Ave.
Hammond, IN 46320

Phone: (219) 853-5200
Web: http://www.nipsco.com

North Indiana Public Service Co., a subsidiary of NIPSCO Industries Inc. (NYSE; NI) (a holding company for regulated utility and non-utility companies), is engaged in supplying natural gas and electric energy to the public.

Vision Statement: NIPSCO Industries will achieve superior earnings growth by being the premier supplier of energy products and services in the industrial heartland of America.

623. Northern States Power Co.
414 Nicollet Mall
Minneapolis, MN 55401
Phone: (612) 330-5500
Web: http://www.nspco.com/index.htm

Northern States Power Co. (NYSE; NSP) provides electric, gas, and other energy-related services to customers in parts of Minnesota, Wisconsin, South Dakota, North Dakota, and Michigan.

Slogan: "Creating Your Energy Future."

NSP Vision: NSP will be the quality provider of electric, gas, and energy-related services in the region. We will continuously improve the value of our products and services for our customers. We will enhance our opportunities for success and growth by balancing the needs of customers and shareholders, valuing our employees, supporting our communities and protecting the environment.

Future: In creating your energy future, NSP is shaping an environment in which the company can prosper as the electric industry becomes increasingly competitive. Our strategy for success includes taking significant steps to prepare for competition and change.

624. Northrop Grumman Corp.
1840 Century Park E.
Los Angeles, CA 90067
Phone: (310) 553-6262
Web: http://www.northgrum.com

Northrop Grumman Corp. (NYSE; NOC) is a government defense contractor. The company has agree to merge with Lockheed Martin.

Our Mission: Northrop provides products and services which contribute in the defense and technological strength of our nation. Our goal is to be one of the top two firms in our chosen segments of the military/commercial aircraft and defense electronics markets. Our aim is to satisfy customer needs with innovative, high quality products and services at a competitive price. We are committed to sustained excellence in all dimensions of our business and to providing a fair return for our shareholders. Outstanding performance will provide the resources necessary for Northrop to grow as a world-class aerospace company.

625. Northwest Airlines
2700 Lone Oak Pkwy.
Eagan, MN 55111
Phone (612) 727-2111
Web: http://www.nwa.com

Northwest Airlines, a subsidiary of Northwest Airlines Corp. (NASDAQ; NWAC), is a major company in the airline passenger industry.

Slogan: "Some People Just Know How to Fly."

Our Mission: To build together the world's most preferred airline with the best people, each committed to exceeding our customer's expectations.

626. Northwestern Mutual Life
720 East Wisconsin Ave.
Milwaukee, WI 53202
Phone: (414) 271-1444

Northwestern Mutual Life is a mutual company in the insurance industry. The company's current product portfolio includes a complete range of permanent and term life insurance, disability income, and annuity plans for the personal, business, estate planning and pension markets.

Slogan: "The Quiet Company."

Mutual Way: The ambition of the Northwestern has been less to be large than to be safe; its aim is to rank first in benefits to policyowners rather than first in size. Valuing quality above quantity, it has preferred to secure its business under certain salutary restrictions and limitations rather than to write a much larger business at the possible sacrifice of those valuable points which have made Northwestern pre-eminently the policyowners' company.

627. Norwest Corp.
Norwest Center
Sixth and Marquette
Minneapolis, MN 55479
Phone: (612) 667-1234
Web: http://www.norwest.com

Norwest Corp. (NYSE; NOB) operates in the financial services industry.

Slogan: "To the Nth Degree."

Goal: Our goal is continued great performance year after year.

Nth Degree: Our success will not be determined primarily by our products, services, or technology. The difference will be our talented employees and their ability to provide outstanding customer service time after time after time and to earn 100 percent of every creditworthy customer's business. That's the spirit of our new "To the Nth Degree" marketing initiative—finding better ways to serve our customers. It shows how much we care about our customers, our colleagues, our company and our communities.

628. NovaCare Inc.
1016 West Ninth Ave.
King of Prussia, PA 19406
Phone: (610) 992-7200
Web: http://www.novacare.com

NovaCare Inc. (NYSE; NOV) serves

patients with rehabilitation services.

Credo: "Helping Make Life a Little Better."

Purpose: To effectively meet the rehabilitation needs of our patients through clinical leadership.

Beliefs: Respect for the individual; service to the customer; pursuit of excellence; commitment to personal integrity.

629. Novartis AG
Lichtstrasse 35
CH-4002
Basel, Switzerland
Phone: (011) 41-61-324-111
Web: http://www.novartis.com

Novartis AG (OTC; NVTSY), a new company formed after the merger of Ciba-Geigy Ltd. and Sandoz Ltd., core businesses are pharmaceuticals, agribusiness, and nutrition.

Strategic Vision and Merger Objectives: Launch of an innovation-led world leader first in life sciences.

Critical competitive mass to shape our business environment.

Accelerated growth potential.

Fast, focused, flexible and modern, lean management.

Leadership for the 21st century.

630. Nucor Corp.
2100 Rexford Rd.
Charlotte, NC 28211
Phone: (704) 366-7000
Web: http://www.newc.com/nbs/

Nucor Corp. (NYSE; NUE) manufactures steel products.

Statement: Nucor has been able to remain a growing profitable steel and steel products producer because Nucor's work force is strongly committed to Nucor's basic philosophy — to build steel manufacturing facilities economically and to operate them productively.

631. NYNEX Corp.
1095 Avenue of the Americas
New York, NY 10036
Phone: (212) 395-2121
Web: http://www.nynex.com

NYNEX Corp., who merged with Bell Atlantic, is grouped into five segments: Telecommunications, cellular, publishing, financial services, and other diversified operations.

Our Corporate Mission: NYNEX Corporation's mission is to be a world-class leader in helping people communicate using information networks and services. NYNEX provides wireline and wire-free telecommunications services, directory publishing, and information delivery services.

632. Oakwood Homes Corp.
7800 McCloud Rd.
Greensboro, NC 27409
Phone: (910) 664-2400

Oakwood Homes Corp. (NYSE; OH) markets manufactured housing products and related services.

Mission: The mission of Oakwood Homes Corporation is to satisfy consumers' needs for superior quality, affordable manufactured housing products and related services through a fully integrated organization. In carrying our this mission, we will serve in a fair and balanced manner the interests of our shareholders, customers and employees through adherence of high standards of profitability and financial soundness, professionalism, business ethics and corporate citizenship.

633. Occidental Petroleum Corp.
10889 Wilshire Blvd.
Los Angeles, CA 90024
Phone: (310) 208-8800
Web: http://www.oxychem.com

Occidental Petroleum Corp. (NYSE; OXY) explores for, develops, produces, and markets crude oil and natural gas.

Priority: To achieve even more substantial efficiencies in all of our businesses on a unit-of-production basis — and hence to strengthen profit margins on an ongoing basis. All of our operations will be judged as much on how effectively they further reduce costs as on how much profit they produce in a given year. The latter is, in part, a reflection of prices — and if prices go up, they also can go down. The former, however, is a reflection of efficiency, and its benefits will continue year after year. It is efficiency that we are focusing on.

Meantime, Occidental continues to pursue strategies designed to build long-term strength into its core businesses.

634. Octel Communications Corp.
1001 Murphy Ranch Rd.
Milpitas, CA 95035
Phone: (408) 321-2000
Web: http://www.octel.com

Octel Communications Corp. (NASDAQ; OCTL) provides consumers and businesses communications products and services.

Mission: Our corporate mission is to provide products and services that improve communications using a phone as a terminal.

635. Office Depot Inc.
2200 Old Germantown Rd.
Delray Beach, FL 33445
Phone: (561) 278-4800

Office Depot Inc. (NYSE; ODP) is an office products retailer.

Slogan: "Taking Care of Business."

Mission Statement: Office Depot's mission is to be the most successful office products company in the world. We will achieve success by an uncompromising commitment to:

Superior customer satisfaction.

Associate-oriented environment.

Industry leading value/selection/service.

Ethical business conduct.

Shareholder value.

636. Ogden Corp.
Two Pennsylvania Plz.
New York, NY 10121
Phone: (212) 868-6100
Web: http://www.ogdencorp.com

Ogden Corp. (NYSE; OG) provides support services, such as housekeeping, maintenance, security, and food services.

Strategy: Our strategy is to increase the Corporation's intrinsic value and ensure premier market positions in the areas of aviation, entertainment, environmental, and energy services, and waste to energy. We will achieve that through long-term investments, strategic acquisitions, and the development of new business opportunities in these key areas.

All over the world, the Ogden service network is expanding to address and solve business and management problems.

In effect, Ogden is creating a leading global service organization that is expected to achieve steady growth despite economic uncertainties or market volatility in any one area.

637. Ohio Casualty Corp.
136 North Third St.
Hamilton, OH 45025
Phone: (513) 867-3000
Web: http://www.ocas.com

Ohio Casualty Corp. (NASDAQ; OCAS) is a holding company and is principally engaged, through its direct and indirect subsidiaries, in the business of property and casualty insurance and insurance premium finance.

Vision: To provide security for policyholders.

Mission: To respond to our policyholders' needs and expectations for products and services that assure their security, so long as our business choices create value for the company's shareholders.

Values: Customer-driven quality; innovation; stewardship; teamwork; integrity.

638. Ohio Edison Co.
76 S. Main St.
Akron, OH 44308
Phone: (330) 384-5100
Web: http://www.ohioedison.com

Ohio Edison Co. (NYSE; OEC), through Ohio Edison and Penn Power, provides electric utility service to parts of Ohio and Pennsylvania.

Slogan: "The Energy Maker."

Vision: We will become the best performing energy service company in our region and remain our customers' supplier of choice.

Vision for Success: Focus on core business. Become an industry leader. Take action now.

639. OHM Remediation Services Corp.
16406 U.S. Route 224 East
Findlay, OH 45839
Phone: (419) 423-3529

OHM Remediation Services Corp. is a subsidiary of OHM Corp., a company that provides a broad range of environmental, hazardous nuclear waste remediation services to clients located primarily in the United States.

Statement: The new OHM is committed to being the most customer-driven, service-competitive company in the remediation business.

640. Olsten Corp.
175 Broad Hollow Rd.
Melville, NY 11747
Phone: (516) 844-7800
Web: http://www.olsten.com

Olsten Corp. (NYSE; OLS) is a provider of home health care services and staffing services.

Slogan: "America Is Coming Home with Us."

Statement: Olsten Kimberly Quality Care is dedicated to providing the highest quality, most cost-effective home care services in North America.

We deliver the care you need, right where you need it — at home.

641. Omnicare Inc.
2800 Chemed Center
255 East Fifth St.
Cincinnati, OH 45202
Phone: (513) 762-6666

Omnicare Inc. (NYSE; OCR) is a leading provider of professional pharmacy and related consulting services for long-term care institutions such as nursing homes, retirement centers and other institutional health care facilities.

Strategy: Omnicare's strategy is to acquire high quality regional pharmacy providers. We then seek to achieve strong internal growth in the companies we acquire through increased market penetration, the expansion of services and improved operating efficiencies.

642. Oncogene Science Inc.
106 Charles Lindberg Blvd.
Uniondale, NY 11553
Phone: (516) 222-0023
Web: http://www.oncogene.com

Oncogene Science Inc. (NASDAQ; ONCS) is a biopharmaceutical company which is researching and developing innovative products for the diagnosis and treatment of cancer, cardiovascular disease, and other diseases associated with abnormalities of cell growth and control.

Goal: Our goal is to put at least one new compound into clinical development every year.

Statement: The company's principal approach to the development of therapeutics is the identification of compounds which act at the level of gene transcription. Gene transcription is the process by which genes signal cells either to produce or stop producing particular cellular proteins such as enzymes. The company believes that its proprietary gene transcription technology will lead to the development of a new class or orally active small molecular weight pharmaceuticals.

643. Oracle Corp.
500 Oracle Pkwy.
Redwood City, CA 94065
Phone: (415) 506-7000
Web: http://www.oracle.com

Oracle Corp. (NASDAQ; ORCL) creates database management systems software.

Statement: At Oracle, we believe the principal legacy of every endeavor is information. Our company is dedicated to enabling the information age by placing information within everyone's reach to conduct business, to educate, to advance technology — in short, to promote understanding and enrich the lives of people everywhere.

To succeed in fulfilling our vision, we have devoted our efforts toward providing the industry's premier technology, striving always to solve the most challenging information management and automation problems.

Oracle's quality strategy is designed to ensure ongoing leadership through quality. Our mission is to create a work environment in which every Oracle employee is committed to the belief that … Quality is our guarantee to our customers and ourselves that each task we perform, each product we build, and each service we give represents the highest standard of excellence to which we can aspire.

644. Orange and Rockland Utilities Inc.
One Blue Hill Plaza
Pearl River, NY 10965
Phone: (914) 352-6000

Orange and Rockland Utilities Inc. (NYSE; ORU) is an investor-owned utility serving electric and natural gas customers in southeastern New York state and sections of northern New Jersey and northeastern Pennsylvania.

Vision: Consistent growth of shareholder return through the creation and delivery of energy services of greater value than any competitor.

645. Oregon Steel Mills Inc.
1000 SW Broadway
Suite 2200
Portland, OR 97205
Phone (503) 223-9228
Web: http://www.osm.com

Oregon Steel Mills Inc. manufactures and sells steel and steel products.

Mission Statement: The environmentally committed, low cost steel manufacturer that customers prefer — where employees make the difference.

646. Organogenesis Inc.
150 Dan Rd.
Canton, MA 02021
Phone: (617) 575-0775
Web: http://www.organogenesis.com

Organogenesis Inc. (AMEX; ORG) designs, develops, and manufactures innovative medical therapeutics using living human cells and natural connective tissue components.

Mission Statement: Organogenesis' mission is to develop and manufacture technologically innovative medical products based upon the use of living cells and natural connective tissue components. These products are intended to interact with the body to enhance the normal healing process in order to promote the establishment of new tissues that maintain, restore or improve biological function.

647. Oryx Energy Co.
13155 Noel Rd.
Dallas, TX 75240
Phone: (972) 715-4000
Web: http://www.oryx.com

Oryx Energy Co. (NYSE; ORX) explores for and produces oil and natural gas.

Mission: Its mission is to create value for shareholders by finding, developing, producing, and marketing oil and natural gas.

648. OshKosh B'Gosh Inc.
112 Otter Ave.
Oshkosh, WI 54901
Phone: (414) 231-8800

OshKosh B'Gosh (NASDAQ; GOSHA) manufactures and markets casual apparel and related products.

Mission: Our mission at OshKosh B'Gosh is to enhance shareholder value. This will be accomplished by becoming a leading resource for quality casual apparel and related products for all members of the American family and their counterparts in all markets of the world. The mission will be accomplished by maintaining a corporate structure that provides directional and financial support to operating units whose goals are:

To attain continual growth by creating strategic advantage through superior customer service, quality, value and innovation.

To profitably grow the OshKosh B'Gosh branded business worldwide, utilizing wholesale and direct channels of distribution.

To develop or acquire appropriate apparel brands, sub-brands, companies, or service entities that support our primary mission, growth opportunities, and financial objectives.

We will fulfill this mission in a manner consistent with the heritage and ethical values of OshKosh B'Gosh, Inc. and in partnership with our employees, customers, and all those with whom we do business.

649. Outback Steakhouse Inc.
550 N. Reo St.
Suite 200
Tampa, FL 33609
Phone: (813) 282-1225

Outback Steakhouse Inc. (NASDAQ; OSSI) operates and franchises full-service restaurants featuring a limited menu of steaks, prime rib, chops, ribs, chicken, fish, pasta, and appetizers — including the "Bloomin' Onion."

Slogan: "No Rules. Just Right."

Statement: The company's strategy is to differentiate its restaurants by emphasizing consistently high quality food and service, generous portions at moderate prices, and a casual atmosphere suggestive of the Australian outback.

650. Outboard Marine Corp.
100 Sea-Horse Dr.
Waukegan, IL 60085
Phone: (847) 689-6200
Web: http://www.omc-online.com

Outboard Marine Corp. (NYSE; OM) is a manufacturer and marketer of marine engines, boats and accessories, primarily for recreational use.

Statements: We believe it's not enough to simply ride the cyclical tides of the marine industry. We must find ways to overcome the cyclicality of our business and consistently build shareholder value.

In any new venture we undertake, our approach will be strategically driven, based on a clear understanding of marketplace dynamics, and capable of establishing a strong market position for OMC.

651. Owens & Minor Inc.
4800 Cox Rd.
Glen Allen, VA 23069
Phone: (804) 747-9794

Owens & Minor Inc. (NYSE; OMI) is a wholesale distributor of national branded medical/surgical and nontraditional supplies.

Mission: To provide our customers and suppliers with the most responsive, efficient and cost-effective distribution system for the delivery of healthcare products and services in the markets we serve, to earn a return on our invested capital consistent with being and industry leader, and to manage our business with the highest ethical standards in a socially responsible manner, with particular emphasis on the welfare of our employees and the communities we serve.

Vision: Owens & Minor is committed to accomplishing, without question, the following three objectives by the year 2000 or before:

To be recognized by our customers, suppliers and competitors for having the lowest cost and best service in the industry.

To deliver sustained, superlative returns to our shareholders.

To remain a great company for which to work.

652. Owens Corning
One Owens Corning Pkwy.
Toledo, OH 43659
Phone: (419) 248-8000
Web: http://www.owens-corning.com

Owens Corning (NYSE; OWC) is a manufacturer of building insulation and roofing materials.

Slogan: "We Make the Difference."

Statement: Owens-Corning is dedicated to expanding its global leadership.

We strive for excellence through our commitment to three guiding principles:

Customer satisfaction.

Individual dignity.

Shareholder value.

By focusing on these ideals and the values they represent, we will build on our proud heritage of innovation and achievement, develop new technologies, launch new products, and grow our businesses around the world.

653. Owens-Illinois Inc.
One SeaGate
Toledo, OH 43666
Phone: (419) 247-5000

Owens-Illinois Inc. (NYSE; OI) is a diversified manufacturer of packaging products.

Strength: Our strength is built on technical leadership — and the ability to translate that know-how into continuous improvement in manufacturing performance and product innovation.

A Rich Legacy: Our strategy is built on the fundamental strengths of our company, the most important of which is leadership in technology.

By focusing on the strengths and special opportunities offered by each of our core businesses in glass and plastic packaging, we have developed a strategy that is realistic, straightforward, and achievable. It consists of the following elements:

Improve domestic glass operating margins.

Expand international glass container operations.

Grow in plastic packaging.

654. Packard Bell Inc.
One Packard Bell Way
Sacramento, CA 95828
Phone: (916) 388-0101
Web: http://www.packardbell.com

Packard Bell Inc., a private company, markets IBM clones.

Statement: Packard Bell's quality policy is to make an impact in the daily lives of people by providing a positive computing experience through quality, innovation, and efficiency in an ever-changing world. This will be accomplished with an empowered, cost-efficient work force through continuous process improvement.

We are proud of our products and strive daily to fulfill our quality policy.

655. Pall Corp.
2200 Northern Blvd.
East Hills, NY 11548

Phone: (516) 484-5400
Web: http://www.pall.com

Pall Corp. (NYSE; PLL) is in the business of purifying liquids and gases. It has a broad-based line of filtration and separation products.

Slogan: "Filtration. Separation. Solution."

Statement: Pall Corporation is committed to being the preeminent supplier of filtration products within each geographic area and industry it serves. We enter only those markets where we can provide superior products which are recognized by our customers as delivering clear and compelling benefits. Pall products and support services must provide users with the most economical and reliable solution to their filtration and separation requirements. We call this standard "Absolute Performance."

656. Parker Drilling Co.

Eight East Third St.
Tulsa, OK 74103
Phone: (918) 585-1058
Web: http://www.parkerdrilling.com

Parker Drilling Co. (NYSE; PKD) is one of the industry leaders in international and U.S. land drilling services. Customers include major oil companies, independent oil and gas producers and governments.

Mission: The mission of Parker Drilling is to provide total and unsurpassed service to all who have a shared interest in the success of our company.

Our Shareholders: Strive for long-term profitability of every contract.

Make decisions guided by economics without compromising our integrity.

Build economic value to the highest level possible.

657. Parker-Hannifin Corp.

17325 Euclid Ave.
Cleveland, OH 44112
Phone: (216) 531-3000

Parker-Hannifin Corp. (NYSE; PH) manufactures hydraulic and pneumatic components for fluid power systems.

Parker's Charter: To be a leading worldwide manufacturer of components and systems for the builders and users of durable goods. More specifically, we will design, market and manufacture products controlling motion, flow, and pressure. We will achieve profitable growth through premier service.

658. Paychex Inc.

911 Panorama Trail South
Rochester, NY 14625
Phone: (716) 385-6666
Web: http://www.paychex.com

Paychex Inc. (NASDAQ; PAYX) provides computerized payroll accounting services.

Statement: Successful businesses embody the best of entrepreneurial values — a focus on creating a needed product at a fair price.

Our company culture empowers each employee to deliver quality service. Individual motivation and a focus on excellence are what set us apart from other choices.

659. PECO Energy Co.

2301 Market St.
Philadelphia, PA 19103
Phone: (215) 841-5555
Web: http://www.peco.com

PECO Energy Co. (NYSE; PE) is an electric and gas utility company.

Mission: Our core business is to provide safe and reliable electric and gas services in southeastern Pennsylvania and northeastern Maryland.

Vision: We will become a premier regional energy services company by achieving superior customer satisfaction and shareholder value through the involvement of committed employees. We will work as a quality focused team to achieve our vision.

PECO Energy's New Vision: By the year 2000, we will transform PECO Energy into a competitive energy supplier with high customer loyalty.

By becoming the best we can be, we will excel in supplying products and services which enable our customers to be successful and improve their quality of life.

We will seek out emerging opportunities for growth which capitalize on our skills and assets.

660. (J. C.) Penney Inc.
6501 Legacy Dr.
Plano, TX 75024
Phone: (972) 431-1000
Web: http://www.jcpenney.com

J. C. Penney Inc. (NYSE; JCP) is a major department store retailer.

Slogan: "I Love Your Style."

Company Mission: Our mission at J. C. Penney has changed little since Mr. Penney founded the company in 1902: It was, and is, to sell merchandise and services to consumers at a profit, primarily but not exclusively in the United States, in a manner that is consistent with our company ethics and responsibilities.

661. Pennzoil Co.
700 Milam
Houston, TX 77002
Phone: (713) 546-4000
Web: http://www.pzl.com

Pennzoil Co.'s (NYSE; PZL) primary business is oil and gas exploration and production and refining and marketing of premium motor oil.

Slogans: "Performance. Protection. Quality."

"Stop. Go. Pennzoil."

Goal: Our goal is to increase the profitability of the core businesses in order to provide superior returns to our shareholders.

We will achieve this goal by:

Capitalizing on our medium size, which

enables us to act quickly and innovatively to meet the needs of our business partners and customers.

Maintaining the exceptional quality and customer service that differentiates our products from those of our competitors.

Expanding our international operations, building on Pennzoil motor oil's worldwide brand recognition and emphasizing in our oil and gas operations the intelligent use of technology and personal, long-term relationships with our partners and customers.

662. Peoples Energy Corp.
130 East Randolph Dr.
Chicago, IL 60601
Phone: (312) 240-4000
Web: http://www.pecorp.com

Peoples Energy Corp. (NYSE; PGL) is in the natural gas distribution utility business in Illinois.

Statement: Certainly, our good equity position and strong bond ratings will help us thrive in a more competitive environment. So too will our numerous strengths: Our residential customer base; our diverse portfolio of supplies; and our location at the convergence of several pipeline systems.

663. PepsiCo Inc.
700 Anderson Hill Rd.
Purchase, NY 10570
Phone: (914) 253-2000
Web: http://www.pepsico.com

PepsiCo Inc. (NYSE; PEP) manufactures, distributes and markets soft drinks and soft drink concentrates under the registered trade names Pepsi-Cola, Diet Pepsi, Mountain Dew, Slice, Mug, and within Canada, 7-Up. The company spun off its restaurant chains (Taco Bell, Pizza Hut, and KFC) into TRICON Global Restaurants Inc. (NYSE; YUM).

Slogans: "You've Got the Right One, Baby, Uh-Huh." "Generation X." "Nothing Else Is a Pepsi." "Pepsi Generation." "Drink Pepsi. Get Stuff."

Pepsi-Cola Co. Statement: We dedicate ourselves to creating a truly outstanding Pepsi-Cola Company, broadly recognized as a great company to do business with, as a great place to work and as a driving force in making PepsiCo one of the best long-term investments.

PepsiCo Mission Statement: PepsiCo's overall mission is to increase the value of our shareholders' investment. We do this through sales growth, cost controls, and wise investment of resources. We believe our commercial success depends upon offering quality and value to our consumers and customers; providing products that are safe, wholesome, economically efficient and environmentally sound; and providing a fair return to our investors while adhering to the highest standards of integrity.

664. Perrigo Co.
117 Water St.
Allegan, MI 49010
Phone: (616) 673-8451
Web: http://www.perrigo.com

Perrigo Co. (NASDAQ; PRGO) is a manufacturer of over-the-counter pharmaceuticals, personal care and vitamin products for the store brand market.

Slogan: "Building the Business of Store Brands."

Mission Statement: To achieve profitable growth and maintain our leadership position by providing our customers with high quality products and excellent service at competitive prices. We will accomplish this by developing, marketing, and manufacturing over-the-counter drugs, vitamins, health and beauty aids, toiletries, and related products sold as store brand, value brand or contract manufacturing through established distribution channels.

665. Petrolite Corp.
369 Marshall Ave.
St. Louis, MO 63119
Phone: (314) 961-3500

Petrolite Corp. (NASDAQ; PLIT) is in the chemical industry.

Mission Statement: To provide recognized and superior customer value in each segment in which we choose to compete. To be the acknowledged industry leader in providing innovative performance based solutions through differentiated products and requisite services managed by systematic account management. Achieve overall real productivity through relentless pursuit of continuous improvement.

666. PETsMART Inc.
10000 N. 31st Ave.
Suite C
Phoenix, AZ 85051
Phone: (602) 944-7070
Web: http://www.petsmart.com

PETsMART Inc. (NASDAQ; PETM) provides pet food, supplies and services.

Slogan: "Where Pets Are Family."

Vision: To be the premier organization in nurturing and enriching the bond between people and animals.

Mission: To be the dominant provider of pet food, supplies and services in each of the markets that we serve.

667. Pfizer Inc.
235 E. 42nd St.
New York, NY 10017
Phone: (212) 573-2323
Web: http://www.pfizer.com

Pfizer Inc. (NYSE; PFE) is a health care company serving pharmaceutical and medical needs.

Slogan: Ben Gay — "Medicine for Your Moving Parts."

Mission: Our mission is to discover and develop innovative, value-added products that improve the quality of life of people around the world and help them enjoy longer, healthier and more productive lives.

668. Pharmacia & Upjohn Inc.

7000 Portage Rd.
Kalamazoo, MI 49001
Phone: (616) 323-4000
Web: http://www.pharmacia.se

Pharmacia & Upjohn Inc., created by a merger between Upjohn Inc. and Pharmacia AB (NYSE; PNU) is a very large pharmaceutical company.

Upjohn Mission Statement: The Upjohn Company remains dedicated to bringing high quality, innovative health and nutritional products to our customers worldwide through the meaningful commercial application of science and medicine, while consistently returning value to our shareholders.

Upjohn is committed to total quality improvement — in service to our customers, our products, and our performance in the work place — and to conducting our business in an environmentally and socially responsible manner.

New Pharmacia & Upjohn Mission Statement: Our mission is to help people live longer and fuller lives by meeting medical needs through innovative research and development.

669. Phelps Dodge Corp.

2600 N. Central Ave.
Phoenix, AZ 85004
Phone: (602) 234-8100

Phelps Dodge Corp. (NYSE; PD) is a major producer of copper and copper products.

Mission Statement: We are an international mineral resource and industrial manufacturing company. We are committed to providing superior quality products, produced at internationally competitive costs, to customers around the globe. We seek to prosper by forging partnerships with our customers and suppliers.

Our mission in conducting business is to create and enhance long-term value for our shareholders and our employees, and

to do so in an environmentally responsible manner as good citizens of the communities in which we live and work.

670. Philip Morris Companies Inc.

120 Park Ave.
New York, NY 10017
Phone: (212) 880-5000

Philip Morris Companies Inc. (NYSE; MO) is a major consumer packaged goods company. The company's registered brands include Kraft, Oscar Mayer, Maxwell House, Tang, Miller beer, Marlboro, and Post cereals.

Slogans: Oscar Mayer Lunchables — "Lunch Will Never Be the Same." Maxwell House Coffee — "Good to the Last Drop." Kraft — "Everybody's Got a Taste for Kraft." Post — "Breakfast Made Right for Everyone." Miller Beer — "Life Is Good."

Mission: Our mission is to be the most successful consumer packaged goods company in the world, as demonstrated by our:

Outstanding overall quality of people, products, and business plans and execution.

Superior understanding and service of customer and consumer wants and needs.

Excellent, growth-driven financial performance.

Honesty, integrity, and responsibility in all aspects of operations.

The pursuit of this mission is intended to benefit our shareholders, our customers, and consumers, our employees, and the communities in which we operate.

671. Philips Electronics North America Corp.

100 E. 42nd St.
New York, NY 10017
Phone: (212) 850-5000
Web: http://www.philips.com

Philips Electronics North America Corp., a subsidiary of Philips Electronics

N.V. (NYSE; PHG), is the third largest electronics company behind Sony and Matsushita.

The Philips Way: Delight customers.

Value people as our greatest resource.

Deliver quality and excellence in all actions.

Achieve premium return on equity.

Encourage entrepreneurial behavior at all times.

672. Phillips Petroleum Co.
411 S. Keeler Ave.
Bartlesville, OK 74004
Phone: (918) 661-6600
Web: http://www.phillips66.com

Phillips Petroleum Co. (NYSE; P) operates in the petroleum and chemical industries.

Slogans: "The Performance Company."

"Because We Recycle Over 100 Million Plastic Bottles a Year, Landfills Can Be Filled with Other Things.

Like Land, for Instance."

Our Mission: Our mission is to achieve superior financial returns for our shareholders.

Our Vision: Our vision is to be the top performer in everything we do.

Long-Term Strategy: Expand production volumes in upstream businesses.

Achieve greater profitability in refining, marketing, and transportation.

Maintain market presence with selective, long-term growth in NGL (natural gas liquids), chemicals, and plastics.

Reduce operating break-even costs and improve asset management in all areas.

673. Phillips-Van Heusen Corp.
1290 Avenue of the Americas
New York, NY 10104
Phone: (212) 541-5200

Phillips-Van Heusen Corp. (NYSE; PVH) manufactures and markets men's and women's clothing and shoes.

Mission Statement: We, the associates of Phillips-Van Heusen are entrepreneurial, consumer responsive marketers, committed to delivering value, while consistently exceeding our customers' expectations.

We pledge to be honest, open, ethical and fair.

We pledge to treat people of all ages, genders, races, religions, and nationalities equally.

We are empowered to maximize our individual and collective potential, while developing and achieving a financial responsible strategic growth plan.

We desire to impact positively the community and the environment. This obligates us to incorporate social responsibility in all our decisions.

674. Pier 1 Imports Inc.
301 Commerce St.
Suite 600
Fort Worth, TX
Phone: (817) 878-8000
Web: http://www.pier1.com

Pier 1 Imports Inc. (NYSE; PIR) is a specialty retailer of unique home furnishings and gifts.

Slogan: "Pier 1 Imports — For a Change."

Statement: A major element of the company's strategy was to upgrade and broaden the merchandise assortment and more clearly define category emphasis.

675. Pilgrim's Pride Corp.
110 S. Texas St.
Pittsburg, TX 75686
Phone: (903) 855-1000

Pilgrim's Pride Corp. (NYSE CHX) produces a variety of chicken and related products.

Vision: To be a world class chicken company.

Statement: From the beginning vertical integration at Pilgrim's Pride has added quality to our products, and profits to our company. We started by selling grain, then mixing our own blend of feed. Soon we were selling chickens that ate our feed. Today, our concept of vertical integration extends all the way to the dining table.

676. Pillsbury Bakeries and Foodservice
200 South Sixth St.
Minneapolis, MN 55402
Phone: (612) 330-4966

Pillsbury Bakeries and Foodservice, a subsidiary of Grand Metropolitan PLC (NYSE; GRM), is a giant in the food industry. Pillsbury has leadership position in baking and specialty products, prepared dough products, vegetables, pizza, ice cream, frozen yogurt, Mexican foods, and foodservice. The company has two of the most recognized symbols in the food industry — The Pillsbury Doughboy and the Jolly Green Giant.

Mission: The mission of Pillsbury is to be the best food company in the world.

677. Pioneer-Standard Electronics Inc.
4800 East 131st St.
Cleveland, OH 44105
Phone: (216) 587-3600
Web: http://www.pios.com

Pioneer-Standard Electronics Inc. (NASDAQ; PIOS) is in the electronics industry.

Mission Statement: We will be the preferred strategic link between our suppliers and customers.

We will service today's needs for electronic components, systems, and services ... and tomorrow's needs for technology.

We will be among the top independent distributors.

We will provide our investors with attractive financial growth and our employees with an equal opportunity for personal and professional growth.

We take pride in our culture, dedicated to: Integrity, fairness, flexibility, growth, quality, success in all regards.

We are committed to doing what we say we will do.

678. Pizza Hut Inc.
1441 Gardiner Lane
Louisville, KY 40213
Phone: (502) 456-8300
Web: http://www.pizzahut.com

Pizza Hut Inc., a pizza restaurant fomerly a subsidiary of PepsiCo (NYSE; PEP), has spun off (together with KFC and Taco Bell) into TRICON Global Restaurants Inc. (NYSE; YUM).

Slogans: "There's a New Spirit at Pizza Hut." "You'll Love the Stuff We're Made Of." "A Good Time in No Time." "Making It Great, Again and Again."

Mission: To be the 1st choice for every pizza occasion by always providing 100% customer satisfaction.

Makin' It Great ... Always!

For our customers, team members, and shareholders.

679. Placer Dome U.S. Inc.
1 California St.
San Francisco, CA 94111
Phone: (415) 986-0740
Web: http://www.placerdome.com

Placer Dome U.S. Inc., a global mining company, is a subsidiary of Placer Dome Inc. (NYSE; PDG).

Mission Statement: Placer Dome is a global mining company whose primary emphasis is gold. We are committed to long-term profitable growth. The added value to our company will be achieved by investing in our strategy and in people whose combined skills will lead to successful exploration, property acquisition, mine development and mine operations.

We believe in integrating the efficient extraction of mineral resources with responsible environmental stewardship and providing a safe and healthy work place for our employees.

680. Plum Creek Timber Co. LP

999 Third Ave.
Suite 2300
Seattle, WA 98104
Phone: (206) 467-3600

Plum Creek Timber Co. LP (NYSE; PCL) produces wood products.

Slogan: "Leaders in Environmental Forestry."

Statement: A clear, compelling strategy has the power to direct and energize a company's actions toward its worthiest goals. At Plum Creek, our entire company is united in carrying out the key strategies that are central to our future growth: Expanding our asset base with high-quality acquisitions. Managing our lands to maximize their value. Continually improving upon our market-driven, value-added product focus. And leading the industry in environmentally responsible resource management.

Environment: Plum Creek practices stewardship that protects and enhances the environment values of the forest while providing economical timber growth and harvest. Plum Creek will be responsible to public expectations for water and air quality, wildlife and ecological diversity. Plum Creek practices forestry based on sound scientific and economic principles, and is dedicated to the future growth, productivity, diversity and health of its forests.

681. PNC Bank Corp.

One PNC Plaza
249 Fifth Ave.
Pittsburgh, PA 15222
Phone: (412) 762-1553
Web: http://www.pncbank.com

PNC Bank Corp. (NYSE; PNC) is a major company in the banking industry.

Statement: We're a hard-working, high-energy, no-nonsense bank, committed to operating at the highest levels of service and profitability. We're tough competitors who have streamlined systems and organized management to provide customers with unmatched products and services. We care about and respond to the needs of our customers, employees, and communities. And that's where performance counts.

To continue our record of profitable growth, we must become an exceptional marketing company. Everything we do must be with a clear focus on identifying and satisfying our customers' needs and desires in a profitable way. We must grow the business by investing in and maintaining a strong and enabling infrastructure, providing products and services of exceptional quality and delivering them efficiently.

682. Polaroid Corp.

549 Technology Sq.
Cambridge, MA 02139
Phone: (617) 386-2000
Web: http://www.polaroid.com

Polaroid Corp. (NYSE; PRD) manufactures and markets cameras, film, and related products.

Slogan: "What We Capture, We Capture Instantly."

Vision: The imaging industry in the 1990s is the fastest growing industry outside of pharmaceuticals and biotechnology — and it is much broader than instant or 35mm photography. Our goal is to double the company's net sales in seven years by participating in high-growth areas of the imaging field that are good "fits" for Polaroid, given our skills and technology.

Environment: Polaroid's goal is to carry on our industrial activity in harmony with natural ecosystems so as to achieve the minimum adverse effect on land, air, and water quality.

We will make a continuing effort to identify and assess the environmental consequences of each part of our operations. We will strive to develop and maintain standards of performance that not only comply with laws and regulations but also are consistent with our own environmental values.

683. Polo Ralph Lauren Corp.
650 Madison Ave.
New York, NY 10022
Phone: (212) 318-7000

Polo Ralph Lauren Corp. (NYSE; RL) is a specialty retail clothing company, featuring fashion apparel.

Ralph Lauren's Philosophy: His ability to stay true to his point-of-view despite the seasonal vagaries of fashion has helped make Ralph Lauren the leading American designer in the classic tradition. Mr. Lauren has always believed that fashion is a function of lifestyle. He believes that clothes should be natural, comfortable, and elegant, for the way people live today. His clothes have a timeless grace and become more personal with age. For Mr. Lauren, the starting point is always his overriding concern for quality and attention to detail, but the creative drama comes from his own romantic sense of authenticity and elegance. Always true to his own American vision of fashion, his products are nearly as diverse as the country that inspires them.

"I believe in clothes that last, that are not dated in a season," states Mr. Lauren. "They should look beautiful years after they are bought. People who wear my clothes don't think of them as 'fashion.' They like good clothes, and they like to feel comfortable in them." Arising from this philosophy is the perfection of a classic look that offers new excitement each season.

684. Portland General Corp.
One World Trade Center
121 SW Salmon St.
Portland, OR 97204
Phone: (503) 464-8820
Web: http://www.pge-online.com

Portland General Corp. (NYSE; PGN) is an electric service company.

Slogan: "Building Our Energy Future Together."

Guiding Behaviors: Be accountable. Earn trust. Dignify people. Team behavior. Positive winning attitude. Make it happen.

685. Potlatch Corp.
One Maritime Plaza
San Francisco, CA 94111
Phone: (415) 576-8800

Potlatch Corp. (NYSE; PCH) is a forest products company.

Business Philosophy: Potlatch is a forest products company committed to increased earnings and a superior rate of return; achieved by talented, well-trained and highly motivated people; properly supported by a sound financial structure; and with a keen sense of responsibility for the environment and to all the publics with whom the company has contact.

Company Objectives: Within the framework of this business philosophy, the company will strive to:

Achieve increased earnings and a superior rate of return, giving proper recognition to the inherent cycles in the economic climate.

Establish a balance between a disciplined drive for current earnings and a broad gauged program for long-term growth.

Manage a decentralized group of forest products businesses fully competitive within their own operating environments. Each business will be managed to capitalize upon its own strength as well as utilize the overall capabilities of the company, while operating within the parameters established by total company objectives and policies for planning, coordination, and control.

Be sensitive to the needs and desires of employees.

Utilize efficiently all human, financial, physical, and natural resources.

Maintain a sound financial structure, flexible enough to finance unique opportunities or unforeseen difficulties.

Provide quality products and services to our customers.

Fulfill our total commitment of environmental responsibility.

Maintain high ethical standards and open, forthright relationships with all publics.

Enhance and protect the natural life cycle of our renewable forests.

686. PPG Industries Inc.
One PPG Place
Pittsburgh, PA 15272
Phone: (412) 434-3131
Web: http://www.ppg.com

PPG Industries Inc. (NYSE; PPG) is a manufacturer and leading supplier of products for manufacturing, building, automotive, processing and numerous other world industries.

Slogan: "World Leaders in Car Finishes."

Mission: PPG Industries' mission is to serve customers through effective use of our resources, to provide a fulfilling workplace for our employees, to be recognized as an outstanding corporate citizen, and to generate superior returns to our shareholders. In achieving this mission, our enterprise will be publicly owned, diversified and global in operation.

687. Praxair Inc.
39 Old Ridgebury Rd.
Danbury, CT 06810
Phone: (203) 837-2000
Web: http://www.praxair.com

Praxair Inc. (NYSE; PX) provides industrial gases.

Statement: Performance incentives, tied to earnings per share, will motivate Praxair people to continue to maximize value for shareholders.

688. Premark International Inc.
1717 Deerfield Rd.
Deerfield, IL 60015
Phone: (847) 405-6000
Web: http://www.premarkintl.com

Premark International Inc. (NYSE; PMI) manufactures and markets consumer and other products, such as West Bend, Harto, and Wilsonart.

Mission: Premark's mission is to be an outstanding, diversified, consumer-driven international company. It will achieve its mission by leading its industries in developing and marketing products that meet customers' needs. It will do so through a universal commitment to excellence in customer satisfaction, and in partnerships with the various groups in which the company comes in contact, including employees, customers, suppliers, and communities.

689. Price Costco
999 Lake Dr.
Issaquah, WA 98027
Phone: (206) 313-8100
Web: http://www.pricecostco.com

Price Costco (NASDAQ; COST) operates a network of wholesale clubs.

What We Believe: Our Mission Statement — Obey the law; take care of our customers, take care of our employees, respect our vendors. If we do these four things throughout our organization, we will realize our ultimate goal: Reward our shareholders.

690. Primark Corp.
1000 Winter St.
Suite 4300
Waltham, MA 02154
Phone: (617) 466-6611
Web: http://www.primark.com

Primark Corp. (NYSE; PMK) is a global information services company whose businesses are strategically focused in the financial information, applied information technology and weather markets.

Mission: To help its customers become more effective and efficient in their own pursuits by providing them with advanced information technology applications and timely, reliable data.

Business Strategy: Primark's business strategy is to capitalize on its competitive advantages and to pursue growth opportunities such as rapid expansion of global investing by U.S. institutions; global access to financial investors for integrated product offerings; commercial applications of technology developed through government contracts; expanded access to new customers through electronic distribution; and increased United States government demand for information technology.

691. Principal Financial Group
711 High St.
Des Moines, IA 50392
Phone: (515) 247-5111
Web: http://www.principal.com

The Principal Financial Group, a subsidiary of Principal Mutual Life Insurance Company (The Principal), operates in the mutual insurance and financial services industry.

Slogans: "Our One by One Approach to Securing Your Financial Future Gives You an Edge." "The Financial Company That Gives You an Edge." "The Principal Edge." "Your Edge on the Future." "We Give You an Edge."

Mission: What we do. To help individuals, groups and businesses meet their financial goals by providing high quality insurance and financial services.

Vision: Where we want to be. To become the financial services company of choice for individuals, groups, businesses and their employees, and communities around the world.

692. Procter & Gamble Co.
One Procter & Gamble Plaza
Cincinnati, OH 45202
Phone: (513) 983-1100
Web: http://ww.pg.com

Procter & Gamble Co. (NYSE; PG) manufactures and markets a wide range of consumer products — Cheer, Tide, Crest, Ivory, Charmin, Folger's, to name a few.

Slogan: Tide — "Tide's in ... Dirt's Out."

Statement of Purpose: We will provide products of superior quality and value that best fill the needs of the world's consumers.

We will achieve that purpose through an organization and a working environment which attracts the finest people; fully develops and challenges our individual talents; encourages our free and spirited collaboration to drive the business ahead; and maintains the company's historic principles of integrity and doing the right thing.

Through the successful pursuit of our commitment, we expect our brands to achieve leadership share and profit positions and that, as a result, our business, our people, our shareholders, and the communities in which we live and work, will prosper.

693. Production Operators Corp.
11302 Tanner Rd.
Houston, TX 77041
Phone: (713) 466-0980

Production Operators Corp., a subsidiary of CAMCO International (NYSE; CAM), provides energy services for clients engaged in gas gathering, injection, treating and processing applications.

Company Mission: Production Operators, Inc. (POI) consistently develops and delivers optimal, cost-effective solutions for gas compression and other energy related challenges in close consultation with our clients.

POI is a growth company. We plan for growth. We grow by improving the profitability of our clients and shareholders.

POI is a learning organization with a

challenging and fun work environment. We use a teamwork approach to making decisions as near to the client as possible. Each of us commits to continual personal growth.

694. Progressive Corp.
6300 Wilson Mills Rd.
Mayfield Village, OH 44143
Phone: (216) 461-5000
Web: http://www.auto-insurance.com

Progressive Corp. (NYSE; PGR) is a holding company operating in the insurance business.

Vision: We seek to be an excellent, innovative, growing and enduring business by reducing the human trauma and economic costs of auto accidents in cost-effective and profitable ways that delight customers. We seek to earn a superior return on equity and to provide a positive environment to attract quality people and achieve ambitious growth plans.

695. Promus Hotel Corp.
1023 Cherry Rd.
Memphis, TN 38117
755 Crossover Lane
Memphis, TN 38117
Phone: (901) 374-5000
Web: http://www.promus.com

Promus Hotel Corp. (NYSE; PRH) is a hotel company operating under the names Hampton Inn, Embassy Suites, and Homewood Suites.

Our Vision: Our vision is to provide the best experience to our hotel customers by having the best people trained empowered and pledged to excellence, delivering the best service, quality and value to every customer, every time ... guaranteed.

696. Prudential Insurance Company of America
710 Broad St.
Newark, NJ 07102

Phone: (973) 802-6000
Web: http://www.prudential.com

Prudential Insurance Company of America, a mutual company, provides a wide range of insurance products.

Slogans: "The Rock." "Own a Piece of the Rock." "Peace of Mind. It Comes with Every Piece of the Rock."

Vision: We are The Prudential. We strive to be the best at helping each of our customers achieve financial security and peace of mind. Our values and our heritage as a mutual company provide a rock-solid foundation of strength and a tradition of trust.

We will build lasting relationships with our customers by providing superior advice, products, and services in three areas:

Insurance, investments and home ownership for individuals and families.

Health-care management and other benefit programs for employees of companies and members of groups.

Asset management for institutional clients and their associates.

Our commitment is to live our values, keep our promises, deliver for our customers, and achieve outstanding performance.

697. PSI Energy Inc.
1000 E. Main St.
Plainfield, IN 46168
Phone: (317) 839-9611

PSI Energy Inc., a subsidiary of PSI Resources Inc. (NYSE; PIN), provides electric services.

Vision Statement: We will be a leader in the emerging energy services industry by challenging conventional wisdom and creating superior value in a safe and environmentally responsible manner.

698. Public Service Company of Colorado
P.O. Box 840
Denver, CO 80201

Phone: (303) 571-7511
Web: http://www.psco.com

Public Service Company of Colorado (NYSE; PSR) is a public electric and natural gas utility company.
Corporate Strategy: Increase shareholder and customer value by:
Minimizing loss of existing market share.
Expanding the market through value-added services within and outside of PSCo's service territory.
Expanding market share/value through alliances, acquisitions, and divestitures.

699. Puget Sound Energy Inc.
10608 NE Fourth St.
Bellevue, WA 98004
Phone: (206) 454-6363

Puget Sound Energy Inc. (NYSE; PSD) is an electric utility company — the result of a merger between Puget South Power & Light Co. and Washington Energy Co.
Vision: The Northwest's leading provider of energy and related services to homes and businesses.

700. Pulte Corp.
33 Bloomfield Hills
Bloomfield Hills, MI 48304
Phone: (810) 647-2750
Web: http://www.pulte.com

Pulte Corp. (NYSE; PHM) operates in the homebuilding industry.
Mission Statement: Our strategy is to provide innovative, value-oriented, for-sale housing and related products and services within well-located communities across geographically-diverse markets.
Our housing products and service will be designed to meet the evolving needs, e.g. lifestyles and income levels, of a broad range of home buyers. We will be a leader in the markets and niches we choose to enter.
Our efforts will be concentrated where our financial strength and decentralized

management, operating under broad operating and financial guidelines, offer a clear, competitive advantage.

701. Quaker State Corp.
225 E. John Carpenter Fwy.
Irving, TX 75062
Phone: (972) 868-0400

Quaker State Corp. (NYSE; KSF) manufactures and markets motor oil, lubricants, and related products.
Slogans: "For a Clean Running Engine." "The Quality Your Car Deserves."
Mission Statement: Quaker State Corporation shall be a world-class leader in providing complete "cradle-to-cradle" lubricants and lubricant services for industrial, commercial, and individual business segments. In addition to growing our lubricant businesses, we plan to actively pursue selective business opportunities that capitalize on our technology, distribution, and customer service competencies.

702. Quanex Corp.
1900 West Loop South
Suite 1500
Houston, TX 77027
Phone: (713) 961-4600

Quanex Corp. (NYSE; NX) is a manufacturer of specialized metal products made from carbon and alloy steel and aluminum.
Mission: We will provide shareholders with an above-average return on their investment through a combination of growth in dividends and share price.

703. Questar Corp.
180 East 100 South
P.O. Box 45433
Salt Lake City, UT 84145
Phone: (801) 324-5000
Web: http://www.questarcorp.com
Questar Corp. (NYSE; STR) finds, produces, and markets oil and gas.

Vision: Questar's vision is to be a leading provider of energy-related products and services in regional and, eventually, national markets.

704. RailTex Inc.
4040 Broadway
Suite 200
San Antonio, TX 78209
Phone: (210) 841-7600

RailTex Inc. (NASDAQ; RTEX) is a company operating in the railroad industry.

Vision Statement: We are a growing, international, rail-oriented, logistics company that is customer focused, locally managed and centrally supported. We value quality of life, character, personal initiative, creativity, teamwork, and perseverance.

We are highly motivated, innovative, and multi-skilled. We are trained to understand and empowered to rapidly respond to our customers' needs in a safe, effective, and efficient manner.

Our success in converting opportunities into realities benefits our co-workers, customers, shareholders, and the communities we serve.

705. Rauscher Pierce Refsnes Inc.
2711 N. Haskell
Suite 2400
Dallas, TX 75205
Phone: (214) 989-1102

Rauscher Pierce Refsnes, a subsidiary of Inter-Regional Financial Group Inc. (NYSE; IFG), is a full-service brokerage and investment banking firm.

Mission: The mission of Rauscher Pierce Refsnes is to provide information and advice which is timely, accurate, and adds value; and to provide high quality service which leads to the highest levels of satisfaction for individual, institutional, corporate, and municipal clients.

706. Raychem Corp.
300 Constitution Dr.
Menlo Park, CA 94025
Phone: (415) 361-3333
Web: http://www.raychem.com

Raychem Corp. (NYSE; RYC) is a materials science company.

Statement: Raychem is a global corporation dedicated to creating and manufacturing unique products based on leadership in materials science.

We aim: To delight our customers with excellent service and products; to be proud of our performance, our people, our practices, and our products; to generate superior returns for our shareholders.

707. Raymond Corp.
S. Canal St.
Greene, NY 13778
Phone: (607) 656-2311

Raymond Corp. (NASDAQ; RAYM) operates in the narrow aisle segment of the materials handling market. The company is a recognized leader in lift truck technology.

Mission: Raymond's mission is to provide customers with increasingly productive solutions to their warehousing and distribution needs, while maintaining a commitment to building shareholder value.

708. Raymond James Financial Inc.
880 Carillon Parkway
P.O. Box 12749
St. Petersburg, FL 33733
Phone: (813) 573-3800
Web: http://www.rjf.com

Raymond James Financial Inc. (NYSE; RJF) is a diversified financial services holding company.

Mission: Our primary mission is to protect our clients' principal and its buying power from inflation and taxation, and then to enhance it through income generation and/or capital appreciation.

709. Rayonier Inc.

1177 Summer St.
Stamford, CT 06905
Phone: (203) 348-7000
Web: http://www.rayonier.com

Rayonier Inc. (NYSE; RYN) is a leading international forest products company producing and marketing specialty pulp, timber, and wood products.

Commitment: Our commitment is to provide long-term value to shareholders. We won't be satisfied with anything less than financial performance consistently within the top quartile of our industry. We will achieve these business objectives while maintaining high ethical standards and meet our responsibilities to our communities, the environment, and our employees.

710. Rayovac Corp.

601 Rayovac Dr.
Madison, WI 53711
Phone: (608) 275-3340
Web: http://www.rayovac.com

Rayovac Corp., a private company, manufactures and markets batteries, lights, and related products.

Mission Statement: To be an innovative and responsive worldwide developer, manufacturer, and marketer of a broad line of branded high quality and environmentally safe batteries, lights, and related products that provide steady profitable growth through corporate commitment to continuous improvement.

711. Raytheon Co.

141 Spring St.
Lexington, MA 01273
Phone: (617) 862-6600
Web: http://www.raytheon.com

Raytheon Co. (NYSE; RTN) is a diversified, multi-industry, technology-based company organized into four business segments: Electronics, aircraft products, energy and environmental, and major appliances.

What Raytheon Stands For: Respect for stockholders — working our hardest to provide stockholders with full value.

Integrity — honesty in everything we do with our co-workers, domestic and international customers, suppliers, stockholders, and competitors. We play to win, but we play fair.

Respect for the environment — embedding environmental thinking in everything we do. Raytheon's goal is to put respect for the environment in the hands and hearts of our people — through an environmental ethics training program, an environmental, health, and safety audit program, principles of environmental quality, and most importantly, through the focused commitment of employees worldwide.

712. Read-Rite Corp.

345 Los Coches St.
Milpitas, CA 95035
Phone: (408) 262-6700
Web: http://www.readrite.com

Read-Rite Corp. (NASDAQ; RDRT) is a leading supplier of magnetic recording heads for rigid disk drives.

Statement: We plan to continue our focus on customer satisfaction, technology, innovation, and cost reduction through Total Quality Management. We are very proud of the worldwide team we have assembled and are committed to continuing to create value for our shareholders.

713. Rehabilicare Inc.

1811 Old Highway 8
New Brighton, MN 55112
Phone: (612) 631-0590

Rehabilicare Inc. (NASDAQ; REHB) manufactures and markets products and support services for the care of the acutely ill and occupational medicine markets.

Mission Statement: We will be a worldwide customer-driven organization, focusing on the design, manufacture and distribution of quality products and support services to the rehabilitative, acute care, and occupational medicine markets in a cost effective manner.

We will build on our expertise in electrotherapy products to achieve a dominant presence in the home therapy application of clinical treatments.

Every employee of Rehabilicare Inc. will be empowered to achieve continued improvement and will participate in setting, managing and achieving goals, resulting in growth of revenue, profit, and shareholder world.

714. Revco D.S. Inc.
1925 Enterprise Pkwy.
Twinsburg, OH 44087
Phone: (216) 425-9811

Revco D.S. Inc. (NYSE; RXR) operates a chain of drugstores.

Slogan: "A Friend for Life."

Statement: Revco must invest in technology to improve productivity, and leverage costs against pressured prescription margins, to respond effectively in a consolidating industry.

715. Reynolds Metals Co.
6601 W. Broad St.
Richmond, VA 23261
Phone: (804) 281-2000
Web: http://www.rmc.com

Reynolds Metals Co. (NYSE; RLM) is a producer of aluminum and aluminum-related products.

Slogans: "Working Together Our Quality Shines Through." "Reynolds Has It All Wrapped Up."

Our Vision: We, the men and women of Reynolds Metals Company, are dedicated to being the premier supplier of aluminum and other products in the global markets we serve.

Our Mission: Working together, our mission is to provide our customers with uncompromising quality, innovation and continuous improvement, which will result in the profitable growth and financial strength of our company.

716. Rhone-Poulenc Rorer Inc.
500 Arcola Rd.
Collegeville, PA 19426
Phone: (610) 454-8000
Web: http://www.rpr.rpna.com
Parent Web: http://www.rhone-poulenc.com

Rhone-Poulenc Rorer Inc., a public subsidiary of Rhone-Poulenc S.A. (NYSE; RPR), is a discoverer, developer, manufacturer, and marketer of pharmaceutical products.

Mission: Rhone-Poulenc's corporate mission is to use its innovations in the areas of life science, and chemistry to create products and services that make people's lives better.

Core Competencies: Chemical; fibers and polymers; health; agro.

717. Rio Hotel & Casino Inc.
3700 West Flamingo Rd.
Las Vegas, NV 89103
Phone: (702) 252-7733

Rio Hotel & Casino Inc. (NASDAQ; RIOH) operates in the gaming/hotel industry. The Rio utilizes a colorful Brazilian carnival and rain forest theme to enhance its customers' gaming and resort experience.

Statement: Our goal for growing the company extends beyond the Rio, although its success is the yardstick we use to measure the viability of other investments.

718. Rite Aid Corp.
30 Hunter Lane
Camp Hill, PA 17011
Phone: (717) 761-2633
Web: http://www.riteaid.com

Rite Aid Corp. (NYSE; RAD) operates a chain of discount drugstores.

Statement: Rite Aid is positioned for growth in the years ahead — as our country adjusts to changes in health care and general marketplace conditions. We have refocused our resources on our drugstore business and have undertaken extensive efforts to generate rapid growth in prescription revenues.

719. RJR Nabisco Holding Corp.
1301 Avenue of the Americas
New York, NY 10019
Phone: (212) 258-5600
Web: http://www.rjrnabisco.com

RJR Nabisco Holding Corp. (NYSE; RN) is a holding company engaged in the production and sale of cigarettes and consumer packaged goods, such as Camel, Salem, Oreo, Planters, Grey Poupon, Life Savers, Cream of Wheat, Egg Beaters.

Slogan: Grey Poupon — "One of Life's Finer Pleasures." Salem — "Move to Smooth." Life Savers — "Life Savers ... Yummm."

Mission: RJR Nabisco's mission is to increase the wealth of all its shareholders through stock price appreciation, dividend payments or a combination of the two. This can only be accomplished by producing strong growth over time in earnings.

Strong earnings growth is driven by an unabashed, company-wide pursuit of profit and revenue growth. We must produce uniform-quality products at the lowest possible cost that provide better value to consumers than our competitors.

720. Roadway Express Inc.
1077 Gorge Blvd.
Akron, OH 44310
Phone: (330) 384-8184
Web: http://www.roadway.com

Roadway Express Inc. (NASDAQ; ROAD) is a motor carrier operating in the trucking/transportation industry. Road-

way Express has been spun off from Roadway Services. Roadway Services has changed its name to Caliber System Inc.

Mission: Roadway Services Inc., through its operating companies, is in the business of satisfying customers by meeting their requirements for value added transportation and logistic services, thereby creating value for our shareholders.

We will be quality driven and customer focused in pursuit of this mission. We will be the best there is at the art and science of satisfying the customer.

We will be efficient in the use of human and other resources.

We will provide our people with a challenging and satisfying work experience.

We will conduct our affairs with integrity as a responsible corporate citizen.

721. Rochester Gas and Electric Corp.
89 East Ave.
Rochester, NY 14649
Phone: (716) 546-2700

Rochester Gas and Electric Corp. (NYSE; RGS) is in the gas and electric utility industry.

Vision: We will be the market leader in bringing people a higher quality of life through the use of energy.

Mission: We market and provide energy and energy-related services to people, in their homes and businesses, with 100% customer satisfaction 100% of the time.

722. Rockwell International Corp.
2201 Seal Beach Blvd.
Seal Beach, CA 90740
Phone: (562) 797-3311
Web: http://www.rockwell.com

Rockwell International Corp. (NYSE; ROK), the result of a merger between Rockwell Standard and North American

Aviation, is an aerospace/defense company.

Credo: We believe maximizing the satisfaction of our customers is our most important concern as a means of warranting their continued loyalty.

We believe in providing superior value to customers through high-quality, technologically-advanced, fairly-priced products and customer services, designed to meet the needs better than all alternatives.

We believe Rockwell people are our most important assets, making the critical difference in how well Rockwell performs; and, through their work and effort, separating Rockwell from all competitors.

We believe we have an obligation for the well-being of the communities in which we live and work.

We believe excellence is the standard for all we do, achieved by encouraging and nourishing:

Respect for the individual.

Honest, open communication.

Individual development and satisfaction.

A sense of ownership and responsibility for Rockwell's success.

Participation, cooperation and teamwork.

Creativity, innovation and initiative.

Prudent risk-taking.

Recognition and rewards for achievement.

723. Rohm and Haas Co.
100 Independence Mall West
Philadelphia, PA 19106
Phone: (215) 592-3000
Web: http://www.rohmhaas.com

Rohm and Haas Co. (NYSE; ROH) is a manufacturer of specialty chemicals and plastics.

Vision Statement: Rohm and Haas is a highly innovative, growing global specialty polymer and chemical company building on an ever-broadening technical base.

Our customers regard us as indispensable to their success. We are their best and most consistent supplier of products and services. The general public views the company as a valued corporate citizen and a good neighbor.

Our employees behave as owners and feel accountable for their performance and the success of the company.

Ethical behavior, teamwork, fast action, and a passion for constant improvement are the hallmarks of our culture.

724. Rollins Environmental Services Inc.
One Rollins Plaza
Wilmington, DE 19899
Phone: (302) 426-2700

Rollins Environmental Services Inc. (NYSE: REN) treats and disposes of chemical waste for industry.

Mission Statement: Provide the highest quality, customer centered, safe and environmentally sound hazardous waste management services at the lowest possible cost through an organization of skilled people dedicated to the highest standards of service.

725. Ross Stores Inc.
8333 Central Ave.
Newark, CA 94560
Phone: (510) 505-4400
Web: http://www.rossstores.com

Ross Stores Inc. (NASDAQ; ROST) operates specialty retail stores featuring name-brand apparel, accessories, and footwear for the family.

Slogan: "Dress for Less."

Mission: Ross Stores' mission is to offer competitive values to customers by focusing on the following key strategic objectives:

Achieve an appropriate level of brands and labels at strong discounts throughout the store.

Meet customer needs on a regional basis.

Deliver an in-store shopping experience that reflects the expectations of the off-price customer.

Manage real estate growth to maintain dominance or achieve parity with the competition in key markets.

726. Roto-Rooter Inc.
2600 Chemed Center
255 E. 5th St.
Cincinnati, OH 45202
Phone: (513) 762-6900

Roto-Rooter Inc. (NASDAQ; ROTO), a public subsidiary of Chemed Corp. (NYSE; CHE), is a leading provider of sewer and drain cleaning services.

Vision: We have expressed our vision simply:

Be a great place to work.

Provide world-class service.

Grow our business.

727. Royal Caribbean Cruises Ltd.
1050 Caribbean Way
Miami, FL 33132
Phone: (305) 539-6000
Web: http://www.royalcaribbean.com

Royal Caribbean Cruises Ltd. (NYSE; RCL) operates a fleet of vacation cruise vessels.

Slogan: "Like No Vacation on Earth."

Statement: Our focus at Royal Caribbean is much broader than the worldwide deployment of our ships; it involves a dedicated effort to cultivate the global marketplace for cruise vacations.

728. Royal Crown Co. Inc.
1000 Corporate Dr.
Ft. Lauderdale, FL 33334
Phone: (954) 351-5600

Royal Crown Co. Inc., a major subsidiary of Triarc Companies Inc. (NYSE; TRY), is the 3rd largest producer of cola, behind Coca-Cola and Pepsi.

Slogans: "RC Cola: It's the Taste." "My RC." "Shake Things Up." "The Cola That Never Left." "Gettin' Back to the Taste."

Mission: Securing a stronger market position is the immediate mission of Royal Crown Company. Royal Crown believes that a small, quick, innovative organization — properly using the brand equity that is part of its heritage — can compete successfully against big companies with large infrastructures.

729. Rubbermaid Inc.
1147 Akron Rd.
Wooster, OH 44691
Phone: (330) 264-6464
Web: http://www.rubbermaid.com

Rubbermaid Inc. (NYSE; RBD) manufactures and markets rubber and plastic products for consumers, commercial, and industrial markets.

Slogan: "Ideas That Last."

Vision and Mission: Rubbermaid's vision is to grow as a leading global business by creating the best value solutions as defined by our customers and consumers.

Our mission is to be the leading marketer under our global umbrella brands of products and services which are responsive to consumer needs and trends and make life more productive and enjoyable. We will achieve this mission by creating the best value for the consumer, commercial, and industrial markets.

730. Ruby Tuesday Inc.
4721 Morrison Dr.
Mobile, AL 36609
Phone: (334) 344-3000

Ruby Tuesday Inc. (NYSE; RI), formerly Morrison Restaurants Inc., operates a chain of restaurants under a variety of names, including Ruby Tuesday, Tia's Tex-Mex, and Mozzarella's cafes.

Mission: Our mission is to be a great restaurant company that provides the highest quality and greatest value to every guest, every team member, and every share owner we serve.

731. Ruddick Corp.
2000 Two First Union Center
Charlotte, NC 28282
Phone: (704) 372-5404

Ruddick Corp. (NYSE; RDK) is a diversified holding company which, through its subsidiaries, is engaged in four primary businesses: Harris Teeter Inc. operates a chain of supermarkets; American & Efird Inc. manufactures and distributes industrial and consumer sewing thread and sales yarn; Jorday Graphics Inc. produces and distributes business forms; and R.S. Dickson & Co. operates an investment management, real estate development and venture capital company.

Mission: Ruddick Corporation's goal is to provide long-term financial value to its shareholders. The company's strategies are based on meeting or exceeding the quality, service and value needs of its customers.

732. Russell Corp.
755 Lee St.
Alexander City, AL 35010
Phone: (205) 329-4000

Russell Corp. (NYSE; RML) designs, manufactures, and markets leisure and sports apparel.

Vision: To provide the highest quality branded and private label apparel and textiles with superior customer value and unparalleled service, globally to consumers of all ages, through selected channels of distribution. We will conduct this endeavor in a manner responsible to our employees, business partners and our environment.

Credo: To have the most satisfied customers and consumers in every business in which we compete.

Mission: Russell Corporation will conduct business in a directed and disciplined manner fostering an open and communicative environment which empowers each employee to contribute their full potential to the Corporation. We recognize the importance of consumer brand awareness and, directed by clearly defined and focused marketing strategies, we will build the consumer franchises appropriate for our brands.

Our decisions will be toward building consumer brand awareness, providing unparalleled customer service to both our internal and external customers and all decisions will be tempered by an awareness of efficiency and cost effectiveness. We are committed to product leadership through market directed product innovation and quality and through leveraging our vertical manufacturing strengths.

733. Ryan's Family Steak Houses Inc.
405 Lancaster Ave.
Greer, SC 29652
Phone: (864) 879-1000

Ryan's Family Steak Houses Inc. (NASDAQ; RYAN) operates a chain of restaurants.

Mission Statement: To be an innovative, profitable, growth company, committed to customer satisfaction by always providing high quality food at affordable prices with friendly service in clean and pleasant surroundings.

734. Ryder System Inc.
3600 NW 82 Ave.
Miami, FL 33166
Phone: (305) 500-3726
Web: http://www.ryder.com

Ryder System Inc. (NYSE; R) operates in two segments: vehicle leasing and highway transportation of cars and trucks. The company sold its consumer truck rental business.

Vision: Ryder will serve its customers with the best value in logistics and transportation solutions around the world or around the corner.

735. Sacramento Bee

2100 Q Street
Sacramento, CA 95816
Phone: (916) 321-1000
Parent Web: http://www.nando.net/
mcclatchy

The *Sacramento Bee* is one of the city newspapers owned by McClatchy Newspapers Inc. (NYSE; MNI). McClatchy owns 12 daily and 15 community newspapers.

Mission: To serve our public as its leading, most trusted and most respected provider of news and information necessary to the informed practice of citizenship and enhancement of the quality of life.

Such functions can be sustained only by an organization capable of competing successfully in the modern marketplace of ideas, services, and products.

Values: Continually improve the quality of the newspaper; exceed customer expectations; operate ethically and safely; protect our financial health; promote and maintain diversity in the workplace and in our work; encourage innovation and celebrate creativity; respect individual rights and opinions; offer opportunities for growth to our employees; be an active partner in our communities.

736. Safeguard Scientifics Inc.

800 The Safeguard Building
435 Devon Park Dr.
Wayne, PA 19087
Phone: (610) 293-0600
Web: http://www.safeguard.com

Safeguard Scientifics Inc. (NYSE; SFE) is in the information services industry.

Mission: Safeguard Scientifics Inc. develops advanced technology-oriented, entrepreneurially-driven companies, with an emphasis on information systems markets.

Safeguard's goal is to achieve maximum returns for its shareholders by:

Providing to its companies and associated venture funds active strategic management, operating guidance and innovative financing, and transferring that value directly to shareholders via rights offerings.

737. Safety-Kleen Corp.

1000 N. Randall Rd.
Elgin, IL 60123
Phone: (847) 697-8460
Web: http://www.safety-kleen.com

Safety-Kleen Corp. (NYSE; SK) is a business-to-business marketing and service company focusing on the environmental needs of business through recycling and reuse of fluid waste.

Corporate Mission: To maximize the value of the company's unique marketing, distribution, and recycling capabilities by becoming the world's leading specialty reclaimer of hazardous and quasi-hazardous automotive and industrial fluids, with primary emphasis placed on serving the needs of the small quantity generator of these fluids.

738. Safeway Inc.

5918 Stoneridge Mall Rd.
Pleasanton, CA 94588
Phone: (510) 467-3000
Web: http://www.safeway.com

Safeway Inc. (NYSE; SWY) is one of the world's largest food retailers.

Marketing Strategy: Safeway's marketing strategy is to offer superior quality perishables, selection and service at competitive prices in first class facilities.

Priorities: The first is to reduce the cost of doing business in our stores and support facilities.

Our second priority is to reinvest cost savings to increase sales. The savings are funding improved store standards, enhanced service, and more competitive pricing.

Our third priority is to manage capital effectively — specifically, to maximize returns on capital investments, reduce working capital and strengthen our capital structure.

739. St. Jude Medical Inc.

1 Lillehei Plaza
St. Paul, MN 55117
Phone: (612) 483-2000
Web: http://www.sjm.com

St. Jude Medical Inc. (NYSE; STJ) designs, manufactures, and markets cardiovascular medical devices and provides related services.

Mission: St. Jude Medical Inc. is committed to helping our customers worldwide save lives, restore health, and improve the quality of life in their patients through the design, manufacture, and marketing of the highest quality cardiovascular medical devices and services.

We will accomplish our mission by:

Providing the most innovative and highest value-added products which create a clinical benefit.

Emphasizing quality and innovation in the design, manufacture, and distribution of our products.

Developing and maintaining superior relationships with our customers and the community.

Providing a challenging and rewarding work environment which enables our employees to reach their fullest potential.

By achieving our mission we will create additional value in the company and greater rewards for our shareholders.

740. St. Paul Bancorp Inc.

6700 West North Ave.
Chicago, IL 60635
Phone: (312) 622-5000
Web: http://www.stpaulbank.com

St. Paul Bancorp Inc. (NASDAQ; SPBC) provides banking and financial services.

Mission Statement: At St. Paul Bancorp Inc. our mission is to provide quality, innovative and competitive consumer financial products and services to our customers and the communities we serve. We believe our success is rooted in sound business practices — coupled with respect for and responsiveness to our customers, stockholders, employees, and communities.

741. St. Paul Companies Inc.

385 Washington St.
St. Paul, MN 55102
Phone: (612) 310-7911
Web: http://www.stpaul.com

St. Paul Companies Inc. (NYSE; SPC) operates in the insurance industry.

Statement: At the St. Paul, we're committed to being the preferred insurer or insurance broker in the markets we choose to serve. We'll achieve that through products and services that are clearly superior and competitively priced.

For the St. Paul, the priority is finding opportunities in the myriad changes that confront every business and individual.

742. Santa Fe Energy Resources Inc.

1616 South Voss
Suite 1000
Houston, TX 77057
Phone: (713) 507-5000

Santa Fe Energy Resources Inc. (NYSE; SFR) is engaged in the exploration, development and production of crude oil and natural gas.

Statement: We have an aggressive plan for further international exploratory drilling.

743. Sara Lee Corp.

3 1st National Plaza
Chicago, IL 60602
Phone: (312) 726-2600
Web: http://www.saralee.com

Sara Lee Corp. (NYSE; SLE) is a very large food and consumer products company. Registered brand names include, in part, Sara Lee, Ball Park, Jimmy Dean, Hillshire Farm, Mr. Turkey, Kahn's, Bryan, Superior coffee and foods, Hanes, Playtex, L'eggs. Champion, Isotoner, Bali, Aris, Kiwi, and Maison du Cafe.

Slogans: L'eggs — "Nothing Beats a Great Pair of L'eggs." Hanes — "Just Wait 'Til We Get Our Hanes on You." Sara Lee — "Nobody Doesn't Like Sara Lee."

Mission: Sara Lee Corporation's mission is to be a premier, global branded consumer packaged goods company. We shall aspire to have the leading position in each product category and in each world marketplace in which we choose to participate.

744. Saturn Corp.
1420 Stephenson Hwy.
Troy, MI 48007
Phone: (313) 524-5000
Web: http://www.saturn.com

Saturn Corp., a division of General Motors (NYSE; GM), manufactures and markets automobiles.

Slogan: "A Different Kind of Company. A Different Kind of Car."

Mission: Market vehicles developed and manufactured in the United States that are world leaders in quality, cost and customer satisfaction through the integration of people, technology, and business systems and to transfer knowledge, technology, and experience throughout General Motors.

745. (R. P.) Scherer Corp.
2075 W. Big Beaver Rd.
Troy, MI 48007
Phone: (810) 649-0900
Web: http://www.rpscherer.com

R. P. Scherer Corp. (NYSE; SHP) is a leading international developer and manufacturer of drug delivery systems.

Mission: Enhance shareholder value by consistently earning economic returns in excess of the company's cost of capital. Increase earnings by accelerating the growth of Scherer's softgel business through new, high value-added applications, while reinvesting cash flows in facilities for expansion into new geographic markets and for investments necessary to become a leader in advanced drug delivery systems.

746. Schering-Plough Corp.
1 Giralda Farms
Madison, NJ 07940
Phone: (201) 822-7000
Web: http://www.sch-plough.com

Schering-Plough Corp. (NYSE; SGP) discovers, manufactures, and markets pharmaceutical and consumer products.

Statement: Schering-Plough has staked its future on research, targeting therapeutic projects capable of bringing immense value to humankind. No novice to dramatic changes involving policy making and competition, the company is investing with confidence, enhancing its ability to introduce value-added products and reward its shareholders.

747. Scientific-Atlanta Inc.
One Technology Pkwy. South
Norcross, GA 30092
Phone: (707) 903-5000
Web: http://www.sciatl.com

Scientific-Atlanta Inc. (NYSE; SFA) provides products and services needed to develop the advanced terrestrial and satellite networks. The company's products connect information generators with information users via broadband terrestrial and satellite networks, and include applications for the converging cable, telephone, and data networks.

Strategy: Our strategy for the future includes: Investing in our markets; investing in our customers' strategies; investing in technology; investing in our processes.

748. Scios Nova Inc.
2450 Bayshore Pkwy.
Mountain View, CA 94043
Phone: (415) 966-1550

Scios Nova Inc. (NASDAQ; SCIO) is focused on the development of products to treat acute illness, primarily in the areas of cardio-renal disease and inflammation.

Strategy: Our strategy for building a major biopharmaceutical business is to target our R&D investment towards acute-care products, while supporting these efforts with cash flow from commercial operations and corporate partner-funded projects focused on chronic-care products.

749. Scotsman Industries Inc.
775 Corporate Woods Pkwy.
Vernon Hills, IL 60061
Phone: (847) 215-4500

Scotsman Industries Inc. (NYSE; SCT) is a manufacturer of refrigeration products, food preparation workstations, and related products.

Slogan: "The One the World Relies On."

Mission: It is our mission to: achieve total customer satisfaction and be recognized as the best at what we do; maximize shareholder value by maximizing cash flow and achieving superior financial results; increase our international presence and global market share; and provide employees with work that challenges, rewards and affords opportunity for personal growth.

750. (E. W.) Scripps Co.
312 Walnut St.
28th Fl.
Cincinnati, OH 45201
Phone: (513) 977-3000
Web: http://www.scripps.com

E. W. Scripps Co. (NYSE; SSP) is involved in the publication of newspapers, broadcast television, cable television, and entertainment.

Mission: The company aims at excellence in the products and services it produces and responsible service to the communities in which it operates. Its purpose is to engage in successful, growing enterprises in the field of information and entertainment. The company intends to expand, to develop and acquire new products and services, and to pursue new market opportunities. Its focus shall be long-term growth for the benefit of its stockholders and employees.

751. Seagate Technology Inc.
920 Disc Dr.
Scotts Valley, CA 95066
Phone: (408) 438-6550
Web: http://www.seagate.com/home.shtml

Seagate Technology Inc. (NYSE; SEG) designs, manufactures, and markets data storage products and components for the computer systems and data technology industries.

Statement: Seagate is committed to those core technologies which will enable the innovation of systems and products that will extend advanced capabilities to ever broadening markets and applications. The vision of companies playing in this arena must expand to embrace not only the challenges of their current business, but the challenges that will arise in the next three to five years as technology continues to advance and new opportunities are created. Only the fittest will survive. For in this dynamic environment, only those companies with strong balance sheets, an adept management team and a visionary approach to this new digital world will be in a position to capitalize on the opportunities ahead.

752. Seagram Co. Ltd.
1430 Peel St.
Montreal, Quebec
H3A 1S9
Canada
Phone: (514) 849-5271

Seagram Co. Ltd. (NYSE; VO) is in the alcoholic beverage (Seagram), fruit juice (Dole), and entertainment (Universal Studios, formerly MCA) industries.

Mission Statement: The mission of the Seagram Company Ltd. is to be the best-managed beverage company in the world. To accomplish this goal, we will improve our financial performance and competitive position, build an organization that encourages individuals to contribute to our success, and create an environment in which all employees are valued and motivated.

We will achieve a long-term pattern of earnings growth and enhanced returns on our assets and sales in order to continue to provide superior returns to our shareholders.

We will strengthen our portfolio of premium brands and focus on improving their profitability and competitive position. We will build on our other sources of strength: Our worldwide beverage distribution network; our family tradition; and the knowledge, skill and dedication of our employees.

We will place authority and accountability as close to the customer as possible. We will encourage innovation and prudent risk taking. We will ensure that recognition and rewards are based on performance.

Integrity and the highest ethical standards will guide all our actions. We will foster a spirit of teamwork throughout the organization, and we remain committed to equality of opportunity and to the development of the full potential of all our employees.

753. Sealed Air Corp.
Park 80 East
Saddle Brook, New Jersey 07663
Phone: (201) 791-7600
Web: http://www.sealedaircorp.com

Sealed Air Corp. (NYSE; SEE) is engaged primarily in the manufacture and sale of a wide variety of protective and specialty packaging materials and systems.

Mission: Our corporate mission is to provide worldwide leadership in protective and specialty packaging. While there are a wide range of products in the vast market for packaging materials, protective packaging materials differ from these other types of packaging in that the benefits they provide are measurable.

754. Sears, Roebuck and Co.
3333 Beverly Rd.
Hoffman Estates, IL 60179

Phone: (847) 286-2500
Web: http://www.sears.com

Sears, Roebuck and Co. (NYSE; S) is a major department store retailer.

Slogans: "Come See the Many Sides of Sears." "Come See the Softer Side of Sears."

Our Mission: To provide total satisfaction for our customers by delivering the best combination of merchandise and related services, customer service, and competitive prices.

755. Sensormatic Electronics Corp.
951 Yamato Rd.
Boca Raton, FL 33431
Phone: (561) 989-7000
Web: http://www.sensormatic.com

Sensormatic Electronics Corp. (NYSE; SRM) is a manufacturer and provider of electronic security products and systems.

Slogan: "World Leader in Electronic Security."

Mission: Our mission is to provide innovative, cost-effective solutions that address the problems of loss prevention and security for business and industry. These solutions provide organizations with powerful tools that reduce costs through security automation as well as help to promote safety, security, and peace-of-mind.

756. Service Merchandise Co. Inc.
7100 Service Merchandise Dr.
Brentwood, TN 37027
Phone: (615) 660-6000
Web: http://www.servicemerchandise.com

Service Merchandise Co. Inc. (NYSE: SME) is a retailer of jewelry and a wide selection of brand-name hardgoods.

Slogans: "America's Leading Jeweler." "A Better Way to Shop, a Better Way to Save."

Statement: Our objective is to break down any operational barriers to achieving complete customer satisfaction.

Our plan relies on our company's greatest strength ... our people.

757. ServiceMaster Co.
One ServiceMaster Way
Downers Grove, IL 60515
Phone: (708) 964-1300
Web: http://www.svm.com

ServiceMaster Co. (NYSE; SVM) provides services to customers through several companies: TruGreen-ChemLawn, for lawn, tree, shrub, and interior plant care; Terminix for termite and pest control; American Home Shield for home warranties; ServiceMaster Residential/Commercial Services for heavy cleaning and disaster restoration; Merry Maids for residential maid service; Furniture Medic for on-site furniture repair; and AmeriSpec for home inspections.

The ServiceMaster Objectives:
To honor God in all we do.
To help people develop.
To pursue excellence.
To grow profitably.

758. Shared Medical Systems Corp.
51 Valley Stream Pkwy.
Malvern, PA 19355
Phone: (610) 219-6300
Web: http://www.smed.com

Shared Medical Systems Corp. (NASDAQ; SMED) is a provider of healthcare information system and service solutions to hospitals, multi-entity healthcare corporations, integrated health networks, physician groups, and other healthcare providers.

Mission: Through long-term partnerships in the healthcare industry, SMS helps our customers improve their quality of care, financial performance, and strategic position by providing superior, cost-effective information system and service solutions.

759. Shoney's Inc.
1727 Elm Hill Pike
Nashville, TN 37202
Phone: (615) 391-5201

Shoney's Inc. (NYSE; SHN) operates and franchises a chain of family-style restaurants.

Statement: Shoney's seeks to differentiate itself from competing restaurants by offering excellent service, warm hospitality, and attractive prices to afford a high-quality overall dining experience.

760. Showboat Inc.
2800 Fremont St.
Las Vegas, NV 89104
Phone: (702) 385-9141

Showboat Inc. (NYSE; SBO) is in the gaming industry.

Statement: We are committed to structuring transactions so that all parties leave the transaction better off than when they entered it.

761. Shuffle Master Inc.
10921 Valley View Rd.
Eden Prairie, MN 55344
Phone: (612) 943-1951

Shuffle Master Inc. (NASDAQ; SHFL) is a manufacturer of card shuffling systems.

Mission Statement: Shuffle Master Gaming will, through product innovation and superior quality and service, be a leading contributor to the continued growth, professionalism, and prosperity of the gaming industry.

762. Silicon Graphics Inc.
2011 N. Shoreline Blvd.
Mountain View, CA 94043
Phone: (415) 960-1980
Web: http://www.sgi.com

Silicon Graphics Inc. (NYSE: SGI) is a supplier of visual computing solutions.

Mission: Our mission is to inspire dramatic change in what users expect from their computers, allowing people to create, capture, and communicate their ideas as never before.

763. SkyWest Airlines
444 So. River Rd.
St. George, UT 84770
Phone: (801) 634-3000
Web: http://www.skywest-air.com

SkyWest Airlines (NASDAQ; SKYW) operates in the airline industry.

Our Commitment: We pledge to provide airline service that exceeds our customers' expectations. Each of us at SkyWest is dedicated to excellence in service as part of the Delta Air Lines transportation system.

We will provide each customer with a quality of service that will clearly demonstrate our commitment to excellence. We will be well trained, honest, courteous and professional in our responsibilities and will not forget that we are here solely to serve our customers.

Our flights will operate on time, in clean, well-maintained aircraft. Our commitment to safety, in all that we do, will not be compromised under any circumstance. We will anticipate and resolve service failures to the complete satisfaction of our customers.

We clearly recognize that the success of our organization in fulfilling our responsibilities to our employees, to our stockholders and to each of the communities we serve, depends entirely upon our ability to provide service that exceeds our customers' expectations.

764. (A. O.) Smith Corp.
One Park Plaza
11270 W. Park Place
Milwaukee, WI 53224
Phone: (414) 359-4000
Web: http://www.aosmith.com

A. O. Smith Corp. (NYSE; AOS) is engaged in four business segments: Original equipment manufacturer, water products, fiberglass products, and agricultural products.

Statement: While we intend to aggressively pursue growth opportunities, that does not mean we plan to neglect our core businesses. We must strike a balance between growth and continuously improving the returns of our existing business. Over the next three years, our capital plans continue to include aggressive spending for cost reduction projects in an on-going effort to maintain the competitive advantages we worked so hard to attain.

765. Smith International Inc.
16740 Hardy St.
Houston, TX 77032
Phone: (281) 443-3370

Smith International Inc. (NYSE; SII) provides drilling tools and services.

Mission: Our people and technology make us a world leader in drilling tools and services. We work together to constantly improve customer satisfaction, employee opportunity, and shareholder value.

766. Smithfield Foods Inc.
900 Dominion Tower
999 Waterside Dr.
Norfolk, VA 23510
Phone: (757) 365-3000

Smithfield Foods Inc. (NASDAQ; SFDS) is a leading pork processor and marketer.

Statement: Quality. Consistency. Value. The overarching strategy of Smithfield Foods Inc. is vertical integration along the entire hog-production and pork-marketing chain. The company is committed to lean genetics. Three principles guide the company's growth: Quality in fresh pork and processed meats comes from a base of the best raw materials and the modern facilities needed to bring that meat to market in perfect condition. Smithfield's products are lean, perfectly trimmed and expertly packaged. Consistency has become an absolute requirement in the marketplace. Every cut must be the same as the one that came before and the one that follows, case after case, truckload after truckload. In every respect Smithfield strives for consistency. Value flows naturally from quality and consistency. Smithfield's customers offer consumers America's finest pork products. And Smithfield, in turn, has begun to benefit from the value of its highly differentiated product line.

767. SmithKline Beecham
One Franklin Plaza
Philadelphia, PA 17101
Phone: (215) 751-4000
Web: http://www.sb.com

SmithKline Beecham, a subsidiary of SmithKline Beecham PLC, (NYSE; SBH) develops, manufactures, and markets human pharmaceuticals, over-the-counter medicines, consumer healthcare products and clinical laboratory testing services.

Slogan: "Striving to Make People's Lives Better."

The "Promise": At SmithKline Beecham, healthcare — prevention, diagnosis, treatment and cure — is our purpose. Through scientific excellence and commercial expertise we provide products and services throughout the world that promote health and well-being.

The source of our competitive advantage is the energy and ideas of our people; our strength lies in what we value: Customers, innovation, integrity, people, and performance.

At SmithKline Beecham, we are people with a purpose, working together to make the lives of people everywhere better, striving in everything we do to become the 'Simply Better' healthcare company as judged by all those we serve: Customers, shareholders, employees, and the global community.

768. Snap-on Inc.
2801 80th St.
Kenosha, WI 53141
Phone: (414) 656-5200
Web: http://www.snaponcto.com

Snap-on Inc. (NYSE; SNA) is a leading developer, manufacturer and distributor of tools and equipment.

Statement: It is vital to the future success of Snap-on Tools that all stakeholders understand and share the vision of the company. That future success is contingent upon planning for and implementing actions necessary to provide increasing value for our shareholders and to ensure continued prosperity for Snap-on's dealers, distributors, customers, employees, and suppliers.

Our Vision: Snap-on will be the global leader in professional tool and equipment markets by retaining, developing or acquiring a meaningful market share in selected regions of the world.

Our major customers are those who service transportation equipment, maintain industrial plants, or manufacture products.

Our products will consist of those tools and equipment required by our customers.

We will utilize any distribution channel to serve our customers.

We will be the highest quality and most cost-efficient manufacturer utilizing the best technologies, methods, and systems.

We will achieve a superior return on investment for Snap-on's shareholders.

We will always adhere to the highest ethical standards.

Mission: Snap-on's mission is to create value by providing innovative solutions to the transportation service and industrial markets worldwide.

769. Sofamor Danek Group Inc.
1800 Pyramid Place
Memphis, TN 38132
Phone: (901) 396-2695
Web: http://www.sofamordanek.com

Sofamor Danek Group Inc. (NYSE; SDG) manufactures and markets spinal implant devices.

Slogan: "The Spine Specialist"

Mission Statement: We, Sofamor Danek, are dedicated to: Providing our customers with innovative services and products of the highest quality; exceeding the expectations of the spinal medical community; and continuous profit and growth for our employees and shareholders.

770. Software Spectrum
2140 Merritt Dr.
Garland, TX 75041
Phone: (972) 840-6600
Web: http://www.swspectrum.com

Software Spectrum (NASDAQ; SSPE) is a reseller of microcomputer software and a supplier of software and related services.

Mission Statement: Software Spectrum is committed to providing superior customer service and value through the timely delivery of products and quality technical information and services.

771. Solectron Corp.
777 Gibraltar Dr.
Milpitas, CA 95035
Phone: (408) 957-8500
Web: http://www.solectron.com

Solectron Corp. (NYSE; SLR) is a provider of customized, integrated manufacturing services to original equipment manufactures in the electronics industry.

Strategy: Solectron's strategy is to establish manufacturing partnerships with its customers by providing a full spectrum of services. This process begins with an evaluation of the manufacturability and testability of the product design, continues with materials procurement and management, and follows with printed circuit board-level assembly, computer-aided test, system assembly, and final test before shipment to the end user.

772. Sonic Corp.
101 Park Ave.
Suite 1400
Oklahoma City, OK 73102
Phone: (405) 280-7654
Web: http://www.sonicdrivein.com

Sonic Corp. (NASDAQ; SONC) franchises and operates drive-in restaurants.

Slogan: "America's Drive In."

Strategy: The company's business strategy involves the continued enhancement of the profitability of the existing Sonic restaurants, the development of new franchised restaurants, and the growth in the number of company-owned restaurants through the opening of new company-owned restaurants and the acquisition of restaurants from existing franchisees. The company has considered in the past and may consider in the future the acquisition of other restaurant chains.

773. Sonoco Products Co.
One N. Second St.
Hartsville, SC 29550
Phone: (803) 383-7000
Web: http://www.sonoco.com

Sonoco Products Co. (NYSE; SON) is a global packaging company.

Mission Statement: Sonoco will be a customer-focused, global packaging leader, recognized for superior quality and high-performance results, integrity and a commitment to excellence will be the hallmark of our culture.

Strategy Statement: We will achieve this mission by satisfying customers, creating value through the consistent delivery of products and services which clearly meet the present and future needs of our customers worldwide.

774. Southern Co.
270 Peachtree St.
Atlanta, GA 30303
Phone: (770) 393-0650
Web: http://www.southernco.com

Southern Co. (NYSE; SO) is a producer of electricity. It is the parent firm of five electric utilities: Alabama Power, Georgia Power, Gulf Power, Mississippi Power, and Savannah Electric. Other subsidiaries include Southern Communications Services, Southern Development and Investment Group, Southern Nuclear, and the Southern Company Services.

Slogan: "Energy to Serve Your World."

Core Values: The Southern Company is committed to the highest ethical standards. We pledge integrity, trust, and candor in our business relationships. Through our actions, we will be worthy of public confidence — both as individuals and as a company.

775. Southland Corp.
2711 N. Haskell Ave.
Dallas, TX 75204
Phone: (214) 828-7011
Web: http://www.7-11.com

Southland Corp. (NASDAQ; SLCM) is in the convenience retailing industry.

Statement: 7-Eleven is continually changing to satisfy convenience customers through a reliable selection of quality products and services.

776. Southwest Airlines Co.
2702 Love Field Dr.
Dallas, TX 75235
Phone: (214) 792-4000
Web: http://www.iflyswa.com

Southwest Airlines Co. (NYSE; LUV) is in the domestic passenger airline industry.

Slogans: "The Low Fare Airline." "The All-Time On-Time Airline."

Mission: The mission of Southwest Airlines is dedication to the highest quality of customer service delivered with a sense of warmth, friendliness, individual pride, and company spirit.

777. Spartan Motors Inc.
1000 Reynolds Rd.
Charlotte, MI 48813
Phone: (517) 543-6400

Spartan Motors Inc. (NASDAQ; SPAR) is a leader in the engineering and manufacturing of custom chassis for fire trucks, recreational vehicles, transit buses, and other specialty vehicles.

Slogan: "Growing Into the 21st Century by Continuing to Take One Right Step at a Time."

Statement: The company will continue to grow by: Serving the customer; building a product of the highest quality and value, as determined by the customer; moving quickly and continuously to be an industry leader and innovator; being dramatically different and unique in how we operate ... the Spartan way.

778. Spiegel Inc.
3500 Lacey Rd.
Downers Grove, IL 60515
Phone: (630) 986-8800
Web: http://www.spiegal.com/spiegal

Spiegel Inc. (NASDAQ; SPGLA) is one of the largest catalog companies in the United States, serving as a fashion resource for women.

Mission: Spiegel Inc.'s mission is to provide the best collection of special shopping experiences for our customers. In our catalogs, stores, and electronic media, we strive to maximize customer value through an optimum combination of quality, style, price, convenience and service. We follow a long-term growth strategy that calls for increasing market share by staying close to our customers, capitalizing on synergies among our businesses to be a low-cost operator, and targeting market niches that have growth potential. As a company, we are committed to nurturing the professional and personal growth of our associates, supplying the tools they need to build long-term customer relationships, and assisting the community as a responsible corporate citizen.

779. Sprint Corp.
2330 Shawnee Mission Pkwy.
Westwood, KS 66205

Phone: (913) 624-3000
Web: http://www.sprint.com

Sprint Corp. (NYSE; FON) is a diversified telecommunications company providing global voice, data, and video-conferencing services and related products.

Slogans: "Be There Now." "We'll Help Your Business Do More Business." "Real Business. Real Problems. Real Solutions. Real Results." "It All Makes Sense."

Vision Statement: To be a world-class telecommunications company — the standard by which others are measured.

780. SPX Corp.
700 Terrace Point Dr.
Muskegon, MI 49443
Phone: (616) 724-5000
Web: http://www.spx.com

SPX Corp. (NYSE; SPW) makes and manufactures specialty service tools and original equipment components for the motor vehicle industry.

Mission: SPX Corporation's mission is to build long-term stakeholder value through global market leadership in specialty service tools and original equipment components for the motor vehicle industry.

In the global specialty service tool and equipment market, SPX is the world leader. The driving force behind this worldwide market leadership is the company's close partnership with its original equipment and aftermarket customers, and its unique ability to anticipate and meet customer needs.

SPX is also a leader in the global market for proprietary original equipment components. The driving force behind the company's leadership in this market is its design, production and technology capabilities, market position, and its differentiated quality products and services.

SPX intends to be the leader in each of the product/market sectors it services and will provide its business units with the resources required for building value when:

There is an acceptable contribution to building long-term value.

The unit has a high probability of sustained growth in earnings and cash flow.

There is a clear synergy or match between the investment and the company's strategic domestic and international markets.

The unit has a strategic commitment to total quality, people empowerment, teamwork and continuous improvement.

Moving forward, SPX will consider value building opportunities that complement existing businesses and build on their strengths. SPX will also provide guidance and resources to assist its business units to identify their future strategies, providing human, material, and information resources as appropriate.

781. Standard Federal Bank
2600 W. Big Beaver Rd.
Troy, MI 48007
Phone: (810) 643-9600
Parent Web: http://www.abnamro.nl

Standard Federal Bank, a subsidiary of ABN Amro Holding N.V. (Amsterdam; public), is in the savings and financial services industry.

Slogan: "Creating Value in a Changing Financial World."

Statement: Standard Federal Bancorporation Inc. provides its customers with superior financial products and services, and its investors with an outstanding return.

782. Standard Microsystems Corp.
80 Arkay Dr.
Hauppauge, NY 11788
Phone: (516) 435-6000
Web: http://www.smc.com

Standard Microsystems Corp. (NASDAQ; SMSC) products enable a personal computer to be connected to a network and permit LANs to be connected to each other.

Vision: SMC component products division's vision is to achieve and maintain our status as a world class supplier of semiconductor products and associated technology products while continuing to grow and remain profitable.

Statement: The young, spirited and innovative thinking that has driven networking to its current level of achievement is mirrored by Standard Microsystems' commitment to deliver products that enhance networking capabilities and performance worldwide. It is this new breed of networking that will benefit the global community for generations to come.

783. Standard Products Co.

2401 South Gulley Rd.
Dearborn, MI 48124
Phone: (313) 561-1100

Standard Products Co. (NYSE; SPD) manufactures parts for the automotive industry.

Vision: Our vision is to be a growth-oriented industry leader driven by delighted customers, inspired employees, and committed suppliers, all of whom significantly contribute to shareholder value.

Mission: We are committed to enhance our position as a preferred supplier to the North American automotive industry. We will focus our efforts and continuously improve our core competencies to provide value and state-of-the-art solutions which exceed our customers' expectations.

784. Standard Register Co.

600 Albany St.
Dayton, OH 45401
Phone: (937) 443-1000
Web: http://www.stdreg.com

Standard Register Co. (NYSE; SR) is a leader in document products and services.

Slogan: "Paperwork Simplification."

The Vision: Standard Register's vision is to be a customer-driven organization whose primary direction is to serve the information and transactional needs of business, focused on key market segments.

It is our purpose to increase revenues and profits by providing high quality, value-desired products and services through innovation and technological development.

Key to the achievement of the company's growth plans and strategies is the Standard Register employee, who through his or her daily commitment to quality work and customer service, makes our vision a reality.

The Mission: A commitment to excellence.

We are a people-oriented, customer-focused organization:

Committed to providing exceptional service to our customers.

Committed to sustaining growth over the long term.

Committed to showing appreciation to our dedicated employees.

Committed to encouraging a free flow of information and an open style of management with emphasis on the team concept.

Committed to contributing to the communities in which we operate.

Committed to supporting and expanding on environmentally acceptable programs.

Committed to providing an acceptable return for our corporate shareholders.

785. Stanley Works

1000 Stanley Dr.
New Britain, CT 06053
Phone: (860) 225-5111
Web: http://stanleyworks.com

Stanley Works (NYSE; SWK) is a manufacturer and marketer of tools, hardware, and specialty hardware products for home improvement, consumer, industrial, and professional use.

Vision: To please our customers so well that our products are their first choice.

Mission: To be the world's most effective producer and marketer of tools, hardware and specialty hardware for home improvement, consumer, professional, and industrial use.

786. Starbucks Corp.
2203 Airport Way South
Seattle, WA 98124
Phone: (206) 447-1575
Web: http://www.ooc.com/starbucks

Starbucks Corp. (NASDAQ; SBUX) is a retailer, roaster, and brand of specialty coffee.
Mission Statement: Establish Starbucks as the premier purveyor of the finest coffee in the world while maintaining our uncompromising principles as we grow.

787. State Farm Mutual Automobile Insurance Co.
One State Farm Plaza
Bloomington, IL 61710
Phone: (309) 766-2311
Web: http://www.statefarm.com

State Farm Mutual Automobile Insurance Co., a mutual company, is a provider of a variety of insurance policies.
Slogans: "Like a Good Neighbor, State Farm Is There."
"Being in Good Hands Is the Only Place to Be."
Statement: State Farm is determined to stay efficient, flexible, and responsive into the next century.

788. Stone Container Corp.
150 North Michigan Ave.
Chicago, IL 60601
Phone: (312) 346-6600

Stone Container Corp. (NYSE; STO) is a global paper and packaging company.
Our Commitments: Our goal is to fully understand our customers'—and their customers'—requirements and to continually work to meet these needs better than any competitor.

Statement: Debt reduction and strengthening our balance sheet remain top priorities. While we successfully used leverage in the past to expand our business, the volatility of recent industry cycles has made substantial leverage too costly. We have implemented a program to reduce leverage to more appropriate levels, with the goal of reaching investment grade on our indebtedness no later than the end of this decade.
Environmental Principles: Treat environmental, health, and safety considerations as top priorities.
Recognize the environmental, health, and safety effects of our manufacturing processes and our products.
Monitor the environmental, health, and safety performance of our facilities.
Give employees the information they need to understand their environmental, health, and safety responsibilities.
Support research and development that will improve environmental, health, and safety performance.
Talk honestly, openly and accurately about environmental, health, and safety issues.
Participate in the development of public policies on environmental, health, and safety matters.
Conserve energy to the greatest possible extent.

789. Stop & Shop Companies Inc.
1385 Hancock St.
Quincy, MA 02169
Phone: (617) 380-8000
Parent Web: http://www.ahold.nl

Stop & Shop Companies Inc., a subsidiary of Royal Ahold N.V. (NYSE; AHO), is a leading supermarket retailer in New England.
Statement: Stop & Shop is dedicated to serving the families of the nineties with superstores that offer quality, value, variety, and convenience.

790. Stride Rite Corp.
191 Spring St.
Lexington, MA 02173
Phone: (617) 824-6000
Web: http://www.striderite.com

Stride Rite Corp. (NYSE; SRR) is a leading marketer of children's footwear, and is a major marketer of athletic and casual footwear for children and adults.

Statement: The Stride Rite we will create builds on the foundation we have inherited, affirms the best of our company's traditions, and makes our policies and practices consistent with our principles.

Our goal is to sustain responsible financial success by achieving superior profitability. To accomplish this, we will build a company where associates are proud and committed, and where all have an opportunity to contribute, learn, grow, and advance based on merit. Associates will be respected, treated fairly, heard, involved, and challenged. Above all, we want satisfaction from accomplishments, balanced personal and professional lives, to support the community, and to have fun in our endeavors.

791. Stroh Brewery Co.
100 River Place
Detroit, MI 48207
Phone: (313) 446-2000

The Stroh Brewery Co., a private company, is the 4th largest U.S. brewery (behind Anheuser-Busch, Miller, and Coors).

Slogans: "Brewing Today's Great Beers." "Perfecting the Art of Brewing."

Vision: Our vision of The Stroh Brewery Company is one of a growing and prospering company with a dynamic and motivated organization providing our shareholders with a reasonable return on their investment.

Mission: To achieve this vision, our mission is to produce, distribute, and market a variety of high-quality beers in a manner that meets or exceed the expectations of our customers.

Values: Our company values provide a constant point of reference of all of our efforts and confirm our commitment to Stroh employees and to all of our customers. The core values of Quality, Integrity, and Teamwork will serve as the foundation upon which we will build success.

792. Stryker Corp.
2725 Fairfield Rd.
Kalamazoo, MI 49002
Phone: (616) 385-2600

Stryker Corp. (NASDAQ; STRY) develops, manufactures, and markets specialty surgical and medical products, including orthopaedic implants, powered surgical instruments, endoscopic systems, and patient care and handling equipment.

Statement: Stryker's growth reflects the depth of our commitment to building shareholder value. We grow, in part, because we constantly remind ourselves — and each other — that we need to grow.

793. Student Loan Marketing Association
1050 Thomas Jefferson St. N.W.
Washington, DC 20007
Phone: (202) 333-8000
Web: http://www.slma.com

Student Loan Marketing Association (NYSE; SLM) — Sallie Mae — provides loans that make it possible for students to meet the costs of going to college.

Mission: Our mission is to help make higher education possible. The need and the opportunity have never been greater.

Objectives: To create value for shareholders.

To help make higher education possible.

To provide college and universities innovative solutions that simplify the lending process and lower their costs.

To provide student and parent borrowers superior customer service and benefits that lower their financing costs.

To offer our lending partners superior

back-office processing to improve their student loan business.

To help institutions of higher learning make education more affordable.

794. Summa Industries
21250 Hawthorne Blvd.
Suite 500
Torrance, CA 90503
Phone: (310) 792-7024

Summa Industries (NASDAQ; SUMX) manufactures hydraulic apparatus and other engineered components.

Mission: Become a very profitable enterprise with $100,000,000 in revenue in the year 2000, the smallest business unit of which will be $10,000,000 in revenue and $1,000,000 in operating income.

795. Summit Bancorp
301 Carnegie Center
Princeton, NJ 08543
Phone: (609) 987-3200

Summit Bancorp (NYSE; SUB)—formerly UJB Financial Corp.—provides banking and financial services. The company has an extensive banking network in New Jersey, and eastern Pennsylvania, as well as lending offices in New York and Connecticut.

Mission Statement: Summit Bancorp will be the most consistent regional provider of profitable, quality financial services. We seek a preeminent position in the marketplace.

Summit will lead by delivering:

Superior products and excellent customer service.

An environment in which employees share mutual respect and operate as a team. Employees will be trained, empowered and rewarded for excellence.

The commitment and support to enhance the quality of life in our communities.

Long-term shareholder value.

796. SUPERVALU Inc.
11840 Valley View Rd.
Eden Prairie, MN 55344
Phone: (612) 828-4000
Web: http://www.supervalu.com

SUPERVALU Inc. (NYSE; SVU) is the largest food wholesaler in the United States.

Creed of SUPERVALU: We shall so effectively serve our retailers with both merchandise and services that they experience continuing success and satisfactory growth under all competitive conditions. The future successful growth of SUPERVALU must always result from our achievement of this meaningful goal.

Since the future success of both SUPERVALU and our retailers is relative to, limited by, and dependent upon the future success of each other, there must always exist between us a strong personal bond with mutual responsibilities to each other.

797. Sybase Inc.
6475 Christie Ave.
Emeryville, CA 94608
Phone: (510) 922-3500

Sybase Inc. (NASDAQ; SYBS) is a database provider.

Vision: Our vision: A world without barriers. No barriers separating people from the information they need.

Mission: Provide customers with the world's greatest architecture, development technology, and solutions for creating, collecting, distributing and using information.

798. Synovus Financial Corp.
One Arsenal Place.
901 Front Ave.
Columbus, GA 31901
Phone: (706) 647-2387
Web: http://www.snv.com

Synovus Financial Corp. (NYSE; SNV) is a financial services company.

Mission Statement: Goal: To exceed the expectations of our customers by delivering the finest quality customer service.

Empowerment: Through well-trained and highly motivated employees who provide continuous quality improvements.

Results: That produce the highest levels of corporate performance and enhanced value for our shareholders.

799. T. Rowe Price Associates Inc.
100 E. Pratt St.
Baltimore, MD 21202
Phone: (410) 547-2000
Web: http://www.troweprice.com

T. Rowe Price Associates Inc. (NASDAQ; TROW) is a financial services company.

Slogan: "Invest with Confidence."

Mission: T. Rowe Price seeks to enhance its position as a premier financial services company by providing the highest quality investment products and services.

In pursuit of this goal, we will strive continually to:

Provide superior investment returns.

Provide a competitive line of value-added products.

Maintain a professional and challenging environment which recognizes and rewards outstanding performance.

Build a profitable, diversified, and financially stable company which gives high return to its stockholders.

800. Tandy Corp.
1800 One Tandy Center
Fort Worth, TX 76102
Phone: (817) 390-3700
Web: http://www.tandy.com

Tandy Corp. (NYSE; TAN) is an electronics retailer.

Slogans: "Gift Express." "You've Got Questions. We've Got Answers."

Mission Statement: Tandy — the new retail electronics company is dedicated to extraordinary value for the customer through knowledgeable personnel, unparalleled product selection and availability and commitment to satisfaction.

The management of our retail operations are charged with the responsibility to set the standards for customer value. We believe this strategy will accelerate growth and enhance value for our shareholders.

801. Tech Data Corp.
5350 Tech Data Dr.
Clearwater, FL 34620
Phone: (813) 539-7429
Web: http://www.techdata.com

Tech Data Corp. (NASDAQ; TECD) markets data processing supplies such as tape, disk packs, and custom and stock tab forms for mini and mainframe computers directly to end users.

Business Strategy: Operating efficiencies and economies of scale. The company's operations are structured to realize operating efficiencies both for itself and its customers, to benefit from economies of scale in product purchasing, financing, and working capital management, and to provide an efficient distribution system focusing on ease of order placement, speed of delivery, facilitation of product returns and reduction of freight costs.

802. Tektronix Inc.
26600 S.W. Pkwy.
Wilsonville, OR 97970
Phone: (503) 627-7111
Web: http://www.tek.com

Tektronix Inc. (NYSE; TEK) manufactures electronic equipment.

Vision: As convergence takes place, adapting to its changes forces markets to solve today's problems even as they evolve in anticipation of future changes. Tektronix is in the enviable position to win on all fronts.

803. Teleflex Inc.

630 Germantown Pike
Plymouth Meeting, PA 19462
Phone: (610) 834-6301
Web: http://www.teleflex.com

Teleflex Inc. (NYSE; TFX) is a manufacturer of products and services for the automotive, marine, industrial, aerospace and medical markets worldwide.

Strategic Objectives:
Seek leadership in technical market niches.
Maintain balance and diversification among our markets.
Emphasize our international activities.
Search for new technology in current markets.

804. Telephone and Data Systems Inc.

30 North LaSalle St.
Suite 4000
Chicago, IL 60602
Phone: (312) 630-1900
Web: http://www.teldta.com

Telephone and Data Systems Inc. (AMEX; TDS) is a diversified telecommunications company with established cellular telephone, local telephone and radio paging operations and developing personal communications services.

Mission: To rapidly grow customers and revenues by exceeding each customer's expectations for excellent quality and value communications services.

805. Tenet Healthcare Corp.

3820 State St.
Santa Barbara, CA 93105
Phone: (805) 563-7000
Web: http://www.tenethealth.com

Tenet Healthcare Corp. (NYSE; THC) is in the healthcare business, operating hospitals, specialty care facilities, outpatient centers, home health agencies, and related businesses.

Slogan: "Tenet Is Redefining Healthcare."

Vision: Tenet will distinguish itself as a leader in redefining healthcare delivery and will be recognized for the passion of its people and partners in providing quality, innovative care to the patients it serves in each community.

Tenet: Meet the needs of each and every patient whose care is our primary purpose and mission.

806. Tennant Co.

701 North Lilac Dr.
Minneapolis, MN 55440
Phone: (612) 540-1208

Tennant Co. (NASDAQ; TANT) makes and markets floor cleaning products.

Vision: To work for a cleaner and safer world.

Mission: To be the preeminent company in nonresidential floor maintenance equipment, floor coatings, and related product offerings.

807. Tenneco Inc.

1010 Milam
Houston, TX 77252
Phone: (713) 757-2131

Tenneco Inc. (NYSE; TGT) manufactures packaging (Hefty, Baggies, One-Zip) and automotive parts.

Slogan: Hefty — "There's the Hard Way or the Hefty Way."

Statement: Shareholder value comes first. Tenneco will continue to build value by hitting the demanding targets our shareholders expect. We will continue to build on the momentum we have created in producing results and meeting our operating cost leadership commitments with the confidence of knowing what we are doing already is working ... only knowing we need to do it better, faster, and smarter.

Our goal is to build increased value in each of our businesses so that we create additional opportunities to capture future value for our owners. In that regard,

Tenneco will continue the action-oriented response to opportunity that has come to characterize this company ... the willingness to identify practical and necessary goals and to take prompt action to meet them.

Our ultimate goal is to emerge from the pack as a standard setter of world-class performance in every essential area in which we operate.

808. Terra Industries Inc.
600 Fourth St.
Sioux City, IA 51102
Phone: (712) 277-1340
Web: http://www.terraindustries.com

Terra Industries Inc. (NYSE; TRA) produces and markets nitrogen fertilizer, crop protection products, seed and services for farmers, dealers, and professional growers.

Mission: Our mission is to be the supplier of choice.

809. Texas Industries Inc.
1341 W. Mockingbird Lane
Dallas, TX 75247
Phone: (972) 647-6700

Texas Industries Inc. (NYSE; TXI) is a leading producer of steel and construction materials, including cement, aggregates, and concrete.

Mission: We will be the most efficient, high value supplier of cement and aggregate products and will provide superior service in the markets we serve. We will continue to grow in our industry through innovation and geographic diversification.

810. Texas Instruments Inc.
13500 N. Central Expwy.
Dallas, TX 75265
Phone: (972) 995-2011
Web: http://www.ti.com

Texas Instruments Inc. (NYSE; TXN) manufactures and markets electronics and electrical equipment.

Mission: Texas Instruments exists to create, make, and market useful products and services that satisfy the needs of customers throughout the world.

811. Texas Utilities Co.
1601 Bryan St.
Dallas, TX 75201
Phone: (214) 812-4600
Web: http://www.tu.com

Texas Utilities Co. (NYSE; TXU) is in the electric utility business.

Vision for the Future: Texas Utilities will be recognized as the best supplier of electric energy services and will pursue other energy related opportunities that enhance shareholder value.

812. Thomas Industries Inc.
4360 Brownsboro Rd.
Suite 300
Louisville, KY 40232
Phone: (502) 893-4600
Web: http://www.thomasind.com

Thomas Industries Inc. (NYSE TII) has two main businesses: lighting and pumps.

Mission: Thomas Industries Inc. is dedicated to the long-term enhancement of shareholder value through growth and improved profitability. In our two core businesses, lighting and compressors and vacuum pumps, our goal is to provide high quality products that represent innovative solutions to each customer's application.

The people of Thomas Industries are dedicated to maintaining ethical business practices with customers, suppliers, employees and the communities in which we live and work.

813. Thomas Nelson Inc.
501 Nelson Place
Nashville, TN 37214
Phone: (615) 889-9000

Thomas Nelson Inc. (NYSE; TNM) is a publisher of bibles and inspirational books, and a publisher and distributor of Christian music.

Philosophy: To grow through fairness and integrity in distinctive service to all.

Purpose: Nelson's purpose is to publish, produce and market products that honor God and serve humanity, and enhance shareholders' value.

814. 3Com Corp.
5400 Bayfront Plaza
Santa Clara, CA 95052
Phone: (408) 764-5000
Web: http://www.3com.com

3Com Corp. (NASDAQ; CMS) is a supplier of networking systems.

Statement: A data networking company asserts industry leadership by anticipating change, perceiving needs, and creating solutions. But sustained leadership means applying this combination of foresight and insight to both the company's technology and its business infrastructure.

815. Three-Five Systems Inc.
1600 N. Desert Dr.
Tempe, AZ 85281
Phone: (602) 389-8600

Three-Five Systems Inc. (NYSE; TFS) designs, develops, and manufactures custom display modules and user-interface systems for original equipment manufacturers.

Statement: We want to be known as the leading U.S.-based supplier of all displays, small or large, segmented or pixel.

816. Tiffany & Co.
727 Fifth Ave.
New York, NY 10022
Phone: (212) 755-8000

Tiffany & Co. (NYSE; TIF) in a retailer of jewelry, watches, clocks, crystal, silverware, stationery and writing instruments, fragrances and accessories.

Statement: Building upon its heritage that began in 1837, it is the company's intention to exceed even the highest customer expectations.

It is the mission of Tiffany & Co. to be the world's most respected jewelry retailer.

817. Timberland Co.
200 Domain Dr.
Stratham, NH 03885
Phone: (603) 772-9500

Timberland Co. (NYSE; TBL) designs, manufactures and markets footwear, apparel and accessories.

Mission: Human history is the experience of individuals confronting the world around them. Timberland participates in this process, not just through our products or through our brand, but through our belief that each individual can and must, make a difference in the way we experience life on this planet. As a team of diverse people motivated and strengthened by this belief, we can and will deliver world-class products and services to our customers and create value for shareholders around the world.

The Timberland boot stands for much more than the finest waterproof leather. It represents a call to action. Pull on your boots and make a difference. With your boots and your beliefs, you will be able to interact responsibly and comfortably within the natural and social environments that all human beings share.

When confronting the world around you, nothing can stop you.

818. Time Warner Companies Inc.
75 Rockefeller Plaza
New York, NY 10019
Phone: (212) 484-8000
Web: http://pathfinder.com/Corp

Time Warner Companies Inc. (NYSE; TWX) is engaged in entertainment, news, information, and telecommunications.

Statement: From the beginning, this

has been a company with a profound sense of the importance of controlling distribution in generating more business, keeping a larger share of the profits and creating products that increase consumers' understanding and enjoyment. Distribution is an essential part of who we are and what we do.

Together, content and distribution are at the center of our strategic mission: Time Warner is home to the world's premier journalists and creative artists. We distribute the products of their minds and imaginations to the broadest audience across the globe.

819. Times Mirror Co.

Times Mirror Sq.
220 W. First St.
Los Angeles, CA 90053
Phone: (213) 237-3700
Web: http://www.latimes.com

Times Mirror Co. (NYSE; TMC) is a media and information company. The company publishes the *Los Angeles Times* and *Newsday*.

Mission: Our mission is to be the information partner of choice in each market we serve — helping people gain the knowledge they need to work, live, and govern themselves.

820. Timken Co.

1835 Dueber Ave. SW
Canton, OH 44706
Phone: (330) 438-3000
Web: http://www.timken. com

Timken Co. (NYSE; TKR) manufactures bearings and alloy steel products.

Our Mission: We are an independent organization with a leadership position in high-quality antifriction bearing and alloy steel products. To maximize shareholder value and sustain our competitive position, we will capitalize on the relationships between our businesses, emphasize the application of technology of products and processes, and combine these with un-

matched customer service. Through the strength of our people, we will strive to become the best manufacturing company in the world.

821. Tootsie Roll Industries Inc.

7401 South Cicero Ave.
Chicago, IL 60629
Phone: (312) 838-3400

Tootsie Roll Industries Inc. (NYSE; TR) is engaged in the manufacture and sale of candy under familiar registered brand names, such as Tootsie Roll, Sugar Daddy, Sugar Babies, Bow Pop, and Cella's.

Corporate Principles: We believe that the differences among companies are attributable to the caliber of their people, and therefore we strive to attract and retain superior people for each job.

We believe that an open, family atmosphere at work combined with professional management fosters cooperation and enables each individual to maximize his or her contribution to the company and realize the corresponding rewards.

We do not jeopardize long-term growth for immediate, short-term results.

We view our well known brands as prized assets to be aggressively advertised and promoted to each new generation of consumers in the United States and selected foreign markets.

We run a trim operation an continually strive to eliminate waste, minimize cost and implement performance improvements.

We invest in the latest and most productive equipment to deliver the best quality product to our customers at the lowest cost.

We seek to vertically integrate operations to the greatest practical extent.

We maintain a conservative financial posture in the employment and management of our assets.

822. Toro Co.

8111 Lyndale Ave. South
Bloomington, MN 55420

Phone: (612) 888-8801
Web: http://www.toro.com

Toro Co. (NYSE; TTC) is in the business of selling products for lawn and turf care maintenance and beautification.

Purpose Statement: Toro exists to help our customers beautify and preserve the outdoor environment ... to make the landscapes "green," healthy and safe ... with superior quality, innovative and environmentally-sound products, services, and systems.

Mission Statement: Our mission is to be the preeminent marketer of outdoor beautification and maintenance products and services worldwide.

823. Toyota Motor Co.

1, Toyota-cho
Toyota City, Aichi Prefecture 471
Japan
Phone: (81) 565-28-2121
Web: http://www.toyota.co.jp

Toyota Motor Co. (NASDAQ; TOYOY) manufactures and markets cars and trucks.

Slogan: "I Love What You Do for Me."

Statement: Basically, we intend for Toyota to keep growing and to grow in ways that fulfill the highest social expectations of our products and operations. We are taking concrete steps to make Toyota a better company in terms of those goals.

Our measures center on five priorities.

In product planning, we can and will do a better job of anticipating demand and responding quickly with competitive products.

In technology, we are refocusing our whole R&D organization on the subjects of biggest concern for people everywhere: Safety, the environment, and energy conservation.

Globally, the time has come to localize our far-flung activities further by integrating operations by region.

In Japan, we are mobilizing all our marketing resources, including our 5,000 new-car sales outlets, to bolster our market share.

And we are making an unprecedented commitment to developing new and expanded business in nonautomotive products and services.

Sharing our growth with our shareholders also is a high priority.

824. Toys "R" Us Inc.

461 From Rd.
Paramus, NJ 07652
Phone: (201) 262-7800
Web: http://www.tru.com

Toys "R" Us Inc. (NYSE; TOY) is a children's specialty retail chain.

Statement: We intend to aggressively pursue all of our strategic initiates and are committed to building market share and profitability in the years to come. We will work hard to continue being the most trusted store in town.

825. Transamerica Corp.

The Transamerica Pyramid
600 Montgomery St.
San Francisco, CA 94111
Phone: (415) 983-4000
Web: http://www.transamerica.com

Transamerica Corp. (NYSE; TA) provides specialized financial and life insurance products and services.

Goal: Our goal is to maximize shareholder value.

826. TransTexas Gas Corp.

1300 East North Belt
Suite 310
Houston, TX 77032
Phone: (281) 987-8600

TransTexas Gas Corp. is a producer and marketer of natural gas.

Future: The essence of TransTexas' strategy is focus — on our reserve base, achieving substantial improvements in annual production and expanding our operations while keeping our costs low.

In the year ahead, our primary goal is to build long-term value for our shareholders.

827. Travelers Group Inc.
388 Greenwich St.
New York, NY 10013
Phone: (212) 816-8000
Web: http://www.travelers.com/index.htm

Travelers Group Inc. (NYSE; TRV) offers life insurance, investment, consumer finance, corporate investments, and property and casualty insurance services.
Slogans: "The Symbol of Financial Leadership." "America's Umbrella."
Statement: We at Travelers Group remain focused on an immutable obligation: To reward our shareholders with superior returns, over time, on their investment.
Guiding Principles: As we move ahead, the "new" Travelers will be governed by the same business philosophy that drove Primerica's steady advance over the past years. That philosophy is unique and seemingly paradoxical — combining fiscal prudence and conservatism with willingness to take risk, and strict managerial discipline with entrepreneurial flexibility.

828. Tribune Co.
435 N. Michigan Ave.
Chicago, IL 60611
Phone: (312) 222-9100
Web: http://www.tribune.com

Tribune Co. (NYSE: TRB) is a leading information and entertainment company. The company publishes daily newspapers, books and information in print and digital formats. The company, also, operates a broadcasting and entertainment business.
Mission: Tribune's mission is to develop leading sources of information and entertainment. We will continue to grow in major metropolitan markets, as well as through related businesses of national and international scope.

829. TRINOVA Corp.
3000 Strayer Rd.
Maumee, OH 43537
Phone: (419) 867-2200

TRINOVA Corp. (NYSE; TNV) is a manufacturer and distributor of engineered components and systems for industry.
Our Mission: Our mission is to create economic value for our shareholders through superior growth and profitability.

To accomplish our mission, we will develop strategies that create sustainable competitive advantage, and we will build an organization fully capable of implementing these strategies.

Our success will not be a matter of change, but of commitment to the core values that distinguish us:

We listen to our customers and respond to their needs.

We provide quality in everything we do.

We invest in technology to enhance our productivity and effectiveness.

We take personal initiative for constructive change.

We conduct ourselves ethically, respect the dignity of the individual and are responsible community citizens.

We work as a team across functions, businesses, and cultures.

We are the force for fulfilling TRINOVA's mission and achieving its goals. By personalizing these core values and by working hard, we will win and we will all share in our success.

830. TRW Inc.
1900 Richmond Rd.
Cleveland, OH 44124
Phone: (216) 291-7000
Web: http://www.trw.com

TRW Inc. (NYSE; TRW) is a provider of high-tech products to customers in space, defense, auto, and information system markets.
Mission: TRW is a global company focused on providing superior products and

services to customers in the space and defense, automotive, and information systems markets. Our mission is to achieve leadership positions in these markets by serving the needs of our customers in innovative ways — by being the best in everything we do. We will create value for our shareholders by balancing short-term performance and long-term financial strength.

831. Tultex Corp.
101 Commonwealth Blvd.
Marinville, VA 24113
Phone: (504) 632-2961

Tultex Corp. (NYSE; TTX) makes and markets sportswear apparel.

Vision: To be the world's best apparel company.

Mission: Our mission is to provide superior returns to our shareholders.

Values: Trust; integrity; respect.

832. Tyson Foods Inc.
2210 W. Oaklawn Dr.
Springdale, AR 72762
Phone: (501) 290-4000
Web: http://www.tyson.com

Tyson Foods Inc. (NASDAQ; TYSNA) produces and distributes poultry products.

Slogans: "Feeding You Like Family." "We're Chicken."

Mission Statement: We are dedicated to producing and marketing quality food products that fit today's changing lifestyles.

833. UniFirst Corp.
68 Jonspin Rd.
Wilmington, MA 01887
Phone: (508) 658-8888
Web: http://www.unifirst.com

UniFirst Corp. (NYSE; UNF) is in the garment service industry, providing occupational garments, career apparel, and imagewear programs to a wide variety of businesses.

Mission Statement: UniFirst Corporation's mission is to be recognized as the leading provider of quality uniform products and services. We guarantee total customer satisfaction.

Our continuous customer focus enables us to grow, to provide and equitable return on investment, and to create development opportunities for our employees.

We are committed to conducting our business in a fair, honest and responsible manner in accordance with all environmental and governmental regulations.

Guiding Principles: Customers are the focus of everything we do. We will consistently meet our customers' requirements. Our reputation is built on total customer satisfaction and "doing it right the first time."

People are the driving force behind our level of service. They determine our company's reputation and vitality. We will invest in our people's development, growth, and job satisfaction and encourage employee participation at every level of the organization.

Profits measure how well we satisfy our customer's needs. Profits ensure a return to our investors and fuel future growth and success for the company and our employees.

834. Unilever United States Inc.
390 Park Ave.
New York, NY 10022
Phone: (212) 888-1260
Web: http://www.unilever.com

Unilever United States Inc., a subsidiary of Unilever PLC (NYSE; UN), is a major packaged consumer goods company with the following product lines: Lever Brothers Co. (Lever 2000, Caress, Dove, Surf, Wisk, All, Snuggle, Sunlight); Thomas J. Lipton Co. (Breyers, Klondike, Good Humor, Lipton, Lawry's); Van den Bergh Food Co. (Ragu, Five Brothers, I Can't Believe It's Not Butter, Country Crock, Brummel & Brown); Chesebrough-

Pond's USA Co. (Ponds, Vaseline, Mentadent, Q-tips, Brut Actif Blue, Rave, Aqua Net); Elizabeth Arden Co. (True Love, Elizabeth Taylor brands, Ceramide); Calvin Klein Cosmetics Co. (Obsession, Eternity, Escape, cK one); and National Starch and Chemical Co. (specialty chemicals).

Slogans: Breyers — "The All-Natural Ice Cream." Breyers — "So Real You Can Taste It." Lipton — "The Newest Way to Be a Lipton Tea Lover." Lipton — "Lipton: A Better Tea Bag. A Perfect Cup of Tea." Dove — "Dove Creams Your Skin While You Wash." Dove — "Dove Contains 1/4 Moisturizing Cream. It Won't Dry Your Face Like Soap." Q-tips — "Just the Thing." Q-tips — "The Safe Swab." Pond's — "New Face of Pond's." Lever 2000 — "It's Best for Your Skin."

Unilever Worldwide: One of the reasons for our success around the world is the leadership position of our brands. Maintaining the No. 1 or No. 2 market position is especially important in the highly competitive categories in which we operate.

Another important element of Unilever's 65-year success in managing a global business rests on a philosophy of decentralizing business decisions in order to meet local consumer needs. A key element of success is the ability to "think globally" but "act locally." At the same time, the company centralizes such functions as finance and research in order to gain economies of scale.

Unilever Research U.S.: The laboratory mission statement is: "To efficiently and consistently deliver to our business partners innovative technology that provides consumer-desired benefits, in order to achieve sustained and profitable global market growth."

835. Union Camp Corp.
1600 Valley Rd.
Wayne, NJ 07470
Phone: (201) 628-2000
Web: http://www.unioncamp.com

Union Camp Corp. (NYSE; UCC) is a manufacturer of paper, packaging, chemicals, and wood products. Its core business is paper and packaging. Its core product lines include linerboard and packaging, uncoated free sheet, chemicals, and forest resources. The company owns a controlling interest in Bush Boake Allen (NYSE; BOA), a leading manufacturer of flavors, fragrances, and aroma chemicals.

Slogan: Great White Shark Paper — "One Less Thing to Worry About."

Investment Philosophy & Strengths: Union Camp Corporation has followed a consistent philosophy of creating wealth by investing to enhance the company's competitive edge in its highly capital intensive and cyclical businesses. The company has continually reinvested capital in a few select businesses that are ideally suited to the company's manufacturing assets, resource base, expertise, and market presence. This continually reinvestment has enabled Union Camp to create a manufacturing system that is at the forefront of product quality and efficiency. It has also enabled Union Camp to remain a strong generator of cash, which funds dividends and the investment program.

The investment philosophy led to five key strengths:

1. Market position — Union Camp is a market leader in uncoated free sheet and linerboard.

2. Operating leverage — Capital investment has increased production capacity and quality while strengthening the company's superior cost position to capture global growth.

3. Financial strength — Continual reinvestment to improve productivity and quality, coupled with disciplined asset management, provides strong cast generating capabilities to maximize investment option.

4. Strong cyclical performer — The company's cost position, product mix and strong balance sheet enable the company to be a strong performer through the cycle by achieving superior results during the

up-turns and by maintaining profitability through the most severe down-turns.

5. Shareholder oriented strategy — While building its global business, the company remains committed to using its wealth to fund a strong dividend and build new shareholder value.

836. Union Carbide Corp.
39 Old Ridgebury Rd.
Section C2
Danbury, CT 06817
Phone: (203) 794-2000
Web: http://www.unioncarbide.com

Union Carbide Corp. (NYSE; UK) operates in two general segments of the chemicals and plastics industry: (1) Specialties and Intermediates (produces a diverse group of chemicals and polymers serving industrial customers. This segment also provides technology services to the oil and gas and petrochemicals industries); (2) Basic Chemicals and Polymers (produces polyethylene, polypropylene, and ethylene oxide/glycol for sale to third-party customers, as well as propylene, ethylene oxide for consumption by the Specialties and Intermediate segment).

Corporate Mission: To grow the value of the Corporation by successfully pursing strategies that capitalize on our business strengths in chemicals polymers.

To successfully execute wealth creation strategies that consistently deliver value to all stakeholders over the course of the business cycle.

Corporate Vision: Union Carbide is a leading global chemical company, focused on being the low cost and preferred supplier of chemicals and polymers in the industry segments in which we participate.

A Commitment for the '90s: We know where we are going: Our leadership is committed to getting us there.

We have a strategy to make us winners; we can prosper and grow.

Carbide's competitive advantage is significant and sustainable.

Employees, shareholders, and customers will benefit from our success.

837. Union Electric Co.
1901 Chouteau Ave.
P.O. Box 149
St. Louis, MO 63166
Phone: (314) 621-3222
Web: http://www.ue.com

Union Electric Co. (NYSE; UEP) supplies energy (electric and gas) to an area that covers most of eastern Missouri and a small part of Illinois.

Slogan: "Smart. Moving Ahead."

Statement: We are a business enterprise — dependent for success on the high quality and fair price of our service; on the skill, courtesy, and loyalty of our employees; on the confidence of our investors; and on the ability of our management to forecast and provide for the energy requirements of our area.

In the conduct of our business, we will render service of the highest quality to our customers — promptly, courteously and efficiently — at the lowest prices consistent with paying fair wages and affording job satisfaction and security to our employees; providing modern facilities for our customers' expanding needs for energy service; and paying a fair return to our investors who have provided the funds to make such service possible.

As a private enterprise entrusted with an essential public service, we recognize our civic responsibility in the communities we serve. We shall strive to advance the growth and welfare of these communities and shall participate in civic activities which fulfill that goal ... for we believe this is both good citizenship and good business.

Focus: Our focus is to continue doing what we have done so well for so long: Grow by expanding the business we know; hold down customer prices; control costs; improve service continually; reward stockholders fairly. We've proven it works.

838. Union Pacific Corp.
8th & Eaton Aves.
Bethlehem, PA 18018

Phone: (610) 861-3200
Web: http://www.up.com:80/

Union Pacific Corp. (NYSE; UNP) operates through its subsidiaries in the rail transportation business (Union Pacific Railroad Co. and Missouri Pacific Railroad Co.) and in the trucking business (Overnite Transportation Co.). The Corporation has acquired Southern Pacific.

Statement: Union Pacific Corporation is dedicated to being an industry leader in quality customer service, the most advanced technology, and the highest degree of employee involvement.

839. United Airlines

1200 E. Algonquin Rd.
Elk Grove Township, IL 60007
Phone: (847) 952-4000
Web: http://www.ual.com

United Airlines, a major air carrier of passengers and cargo, is the primary subsidiary of the holding company UAL Corp. (NYSE; UAL). It also operates a low-fare, short-haul service: Shuttle by United. The majority of UAL stock in owned by its employees.

Slogans: "Rising." "Come Fly Our Friendly Skies." "The Friendly Skyline."

Mission: To be recognized worldwide as the airline of choice.

As a company committed to safety.

As a company committed to service.

As a company of owners.

Dedicated employees: Reliable, and responsive to every customer we serve. Taking pride in a tradition of teamwork and trust. Leading in industry, integrity, innovation and opportunity.

United in values, United in vision.

840. United Asset Management Corp.

One International Place
Boston, MA 02110
Phone: (617) 330-8900
Web: http://www.uam.com

United Asset Management Corp. (NYSE; UAM), a holding company, acquires and owns firms that provide investment advisory services chiefly to institutional investment clients. Some firms manage assets for mutual funds and individuals.

Slogan: "A Tradition of Growth Through Serving Institutional Investors."

Mission: UAM's mission is to manage:

All classes of assets.

In all parts of the world.

Primarily for institutional clients.

841. United Dominion Industries Inc.

2300 One First Union Center
301 South College St.
Charlotte, NC 28202
Phone: (704) 347-6800

United Dominion Industries Inc. (NYSE; UDI) is a leading manufacturer of engineered products for industrial and building customers worldwide. The company's Industrial Products Segment serves selected markets with engineered equipment for heating, air drying and purification, fluid handling, heat exchange, compacting, food processing and aerospace applications. The Building Products Segment manufactures a variety of complementary products ranging from steel doors, to leading dock equipment, to wall and roof systems, to complete pre-engineered metal building systems, primarily for the non-residential construction market.

Vision: United Dominion's vision — A global industrial enterprise consisting of market-leader businesses that manufacture proprietary engineered products for customers worldwide.

Vision '99 Strategies:

Increase profitability through strategic acquisitions.

Pursue international growth markets.

Improve margins through intensive operating focus.

Capitalize on natural synergies of guiding products mosaic.

Accelerate internal development of engineered products.

842. United Parcel Service of America Inc.

55 Glenlake Pkwy. NE
Atlanta, GA 30328
Phone: (404) 828-6000
Web: http://www.ups.com

United Parcel Service of America Inc., a private enterprise, is the world's largest package delivery service — offering both ground and air express delivery services.

Slogan: "The Package Delivery Company More Companies Count On."

The Future: UPS is not just in the delivery business, but in the customer satisfaction business, and customer needs will continue to be the company's driving force. The highest priorities for UPS over the next five years will be to deploy technology that will allow UPS to continue introducing new services, to provide customers with comprehensive information about their shipments, and to provide training so all employees will clearly understand UPS services, the technologies that made them possible, and be able to communicate that information to the customers.

Environment: On the ground and in the air, for United Parcel Service efficiency and resource conservation are synonymous.

Quieting the Skies: Even before Congress passed the Noise and Capacity Act of 1990, which calls for airlines to meet strict noise regulations by the end of 1999, UPS made a multi-billion dollar investment to make its jet freighter fleet as quiet as possible, and the quietest in the air express industry.

843. United States Surgical Corp.

150 Glover Ave.
Norwalk, CT 06856
Phone: (203) 845-1000

Web: http://www.ussurg.com/public/Home-Page.html

United States Surgical Corp. (NYSE; USS) provides medical supplies.

Our Principles and Beliefs: Our customers, and those who benefit from our products, are the driving forces behind everything we do.

Our primary measure of success is customer satisfaction.

We will always act with a sense of urgency and function with a minimum of bureaucracy.

We are dedicated to using our technology to provide superior medical care at the lowest possible cost.

We believe in free enterprise and that the market drives successful businesses.

We believe, above all, that outstanding committed people with a dedication to excellence are the key ingredients of success.

We are a public company with a primary responsibility to our shareholders. We believe adherence to these principles will translate into long-term growth for our shareholders.

844. United Stationers Inc.

2200 East Golf Rd.
Des Plaines, IL 60016
Phone: (847) 699-5000

United Stationers Inc. (NASDAQ; USTR) is a wholesale distributor of office equipment and supplies.

If I Were the Customer ...: At United Stationers, we have two important customers:

Our dealers: Helping dealers be successful is our main goal. Staying aware of their needs, exceeding their expectations, and continually asking ourselves, "If I were the customer ..." will help us discover what we can do to make them even more successful.

Our employees: The talent and ingenuity of our employees will provide our dealers with the superior service they deserve. Working together in an environment which fosters involvement, creativity, trust mutual respect, fairness, integrity, and fun, we will achieve success for our people, our dealers, and our company.

845. United Technologies Corp.
United Technologies Bldg.
One Financial Plaza
Hartford, CT 06101
Phone: (203) 728-7000

United Technologies Corp. (NYSE; UTX) conducts its businesses principally through its operational units: Otis (elevators, escalators, and service), Carrier (heating, ventilating, air conditioning, and refrigeration equipment and service), UT Automotive (automotive components and systems), Pratt & Whitney (engines, service, and space propulsion), Sikorsky (helicopters and parts), and Hamilton Standard (engine controls, environmental systems, propellers, and other flight systems). The company also conducts business through the United Technologies Research Center.

Slogan: Carrier — "Custom Made Indoor Weather."

Statement: In a world that depends on innovation and new ideas, UTC generates them, nurtures them with research and development, and markets them globally. Our major businesses all founded their industries and truly changed the world on the strength of new ideas. Today, those businesses remain recognized leaders across the globe.

The first UTC lesson and rule for international markets is to be first to enter.

The second lesson and rule is constancy of purpose supported by sound strategies, long term goals, and experienced management teams.

Beyond our commitments to kaizen and cost reduction, to technology and innovation, and to globalization, which underpin our shareowner value agenda, we are determined to achieve world leadership in corporate responsibility. The latter includes environmental impacts and remediation, health and safety for our employees and users of our products, recruiting and managing a diverse workforce, and performing to the highest standards of ethics and compliance with laws and regulations in all jurisdictions in which we operate.

We learned early that decentralization works, but only when it meets requirements. Competence in decentralized management teams is an obvious and essential pre-condition. Long years of service is equally an essential pre-condition, to provide opportunity for strategy consensus and value consensus, the only ways a decentralized global organization works effectively together. And our management philosophy is to provide the information and feedback that permit prudent substitution of after-the-fact reviews for before-the-fact approvals, a key requirement in making and keeping organizations responsive and effective.

846. United Van Lines
One United Dr.
Fenton, MO 63026
Phone: (314) 326-3100

United Van Lines, one of the largest moving companies in the world, is a subsidiary of UniGroup Inc., a private holding company which leases and finances trucks and sells insurance.

Service Pledge: Our goal is to develop and maintain permanent relationships with our customers by providing outstanding service, move after move, with no exceptions. We pledge to find a way to get the job done to the customer's satisfaction, no matter how great the challenge; to stand behind every service commitment; and to employ friendly, skilled knowledgeable people who, in the event of a problem, will do whatever is necessary to make things right … right away. In short, we are dedicated to proving, through our performance, that United is the very best professional mover in the world, in the eyes of our most demanding critics — our customers.

Our Guiding Values and Principles:
As a worldwide leader in providing household goods transportation and related services, United Van Lines has built its reputation upon the accomplishments of it people at all levels of the organization. The members of the United family — agents, van operators, and Headquarters employees — all share certain key values and principles:

An appreciation of the individual's rights, responsibilities, beliefs, sensitivities, and needs.

An obsession for turning in the best possible performance on every job ... in every department ... for every customer ... every day.

A recognition that our only product is "service" — and that our product's acceptance depends solely upon the quality each of us invests in it.

An acknowledgment that risk-taking, supported by reason, is a force of unlimited potential.

A commitment to "success," as measured by financial profitability coupled with the uncompromising integrity expected of a responsible, responsive, corporate citizen.

An obligation to be an active, positive force in the world around us — the market we serve, the communities in which we live and work, the industry of which we are part.

An understanding that, regardless of our roles with the United family, we are all partners in the process of shaping tomorrow through today's accomplishments and careful planning for the future.

847. United Water Resources Inc.
200 Old Hook Rd.
Harrington Park, NJ 07640
Phone: (201) 784-9434

United Water Resources Inc. (NYSE; UWR) is a water services company.

Mission: United Water Resources seeks to be the premier water services company in the United States. "Premier" designation is never ours to claim or to own: We earn it only through the eyes of our customers, our employees, our shareholders, and the communities where we operate. And every day we must earn it all over again.

We will provide our customers with services and products that consistently meet or surpass their expectations, and whose quality and value distinguish us in every market.

For our employees, we will provide an environment of trust and teamwork, that inspires them to do their best, challenges them to find creative and innovative ways to meet objectives, rewards them for exceptional achievement, and fosters personal growth and satisfaction.

We will provide our shareholders with a superior return on their investment by responsibly managing our assets and capturing growth opportunities.

We will work as partners with the communities where we operate.

We will treat all people with dignity and respect, and live up to the highest standards of integrity and ethical conduct. And we accept a special responsibility to understand and protect our natural resources.

848. Universal Foods Corp.
433 E. Michigan St.
P.O. Box 737
Milwaukee, WI 53202
Phone: (414) 271-6755

Universal Foods Corp. (NYSE; UFC) is a family of ingredient companies. The Corporation is divided operationally by division: Flavor, color, dehydrated products, Red Star bioproducts, and Red Star yeast and products. Registered trademarks or brand names include Quick Rise, Red Star, Rogers Foods, Universal Flavors, Universal Foods, and Warner-Jenkinson.

Statement: Universal Foods uses technology to develop and deliver high-performance ingredients and systems for foods and other applications, giving distinction to customers' products worldwide. Our areas of technical expertise include flavors, colors, dehydrated vegetables, yeast products, and flavor enhancers and other bioproducts. The company's divisions maintain significant market shares in their respective businesses.

Going forward, we remain focused on a strategy to leverage our process expertise and applications know-how to move into more advanced and sophisticated product categories. We target our technical strengths to match customer needs, partnering with them to develop innovative products that capitalize on consumer trends.

849. Unocal Corp.
2141 Rosecrans Ave.
Suite 4000
El Segundo, CA 90245
Phone: (310) 726-7600
Web: http://www.unocal.com

Unocal Corp. (NYSE; UCL) produces and markets petroleum products and chemical fertilizers.

Our Mission: Unocal produces and sells a broad array of essential energy resources, petroleum products, chemical fertilizers, and specialty minerals that help improve the quality of life for people around the world. Our primary mission is to maximize — ethically and responsibly — the long-term returns to the owners of the company, our stockholders.

Our Vision: To be recognized leaders in creating value by identifying, developing, and producing crude oil, natural gas, and geothermal energy resources.

To manufacture, transport and market high-quality petroleum and chemical products safely and efficiently.

To combine the strengths of a large company with the speed and agility of a small business.

To achieve excellence in all staff functions, providing cost-effective, value-added services to company operations.

To be innovators, who find creative and cost-effective ways to produce new energy resources, develop needed technologies, and protect the environment.

850. UNUM Corp.
2211 Congress St.
Portland, ME 04122
Phone: (207) 770-2211
Web: http://www.unum.com

UNUM Corp. (NYSE; UNM) provides group long term disability insurance and is a leader among special risk insurers. UNUM is also a provider of employee benefits and individual disability insurance. The company also markets long term care and retirement income products.

Slogan: "We See Farther."

Mission: Our mission is: To relieve clients of insurable financial risk. We protect clients from financial hardships that result from retirement, death, sickness, and from disability or other casualty events.

Vision: Vision: We will achieve leadership in our businesses. Leadership does not necessarily mean a dominant market share. Rather, we will achieve leadership in areas which are meaningful and important to our business and the market, e.g., profitability, quality, reputation.

We will focus our business on specialty, risk-relieving products for which we can establish and sustain profitable position. Development of these products will be driven by the needs of customers, in both domestic and international markets.

Values: We take pride in ourselves and the organization's leadership position; we value and respect people; we value customers; we value communication.

851. U.S. Bancorp
111 S.W. 5th Ave.
Portland, OR 97204
Phone: (503) 275-6111
Web: http://www.usbank.com

U.S. Bancorp (NASDAQ; USBC) is in the banking and financial services industry, providing service to customers in the western United States and other selected markets.

Mission: To maximize the long-term value of our shareholders' investment by being widely recognized as a premier provider of financial services in the western United States and other selected markets.

852. U.S. Home Corp.
1800 West Loop South
P.O. Box 2863
Houston, TX 77252
Phone: (713) 877-2311
Web: http://www.ushome.com

U.S. Home Corp. (NYSE; UH) is a leading home builder in the United States.

Slogan: "Now the Fun Begins."

Statement: In order for U.S. Home Corporation to continue to succeed, we must first and foremost be adept at recognizing opportunities.

Today and in the future, the cornerstone of success for homebuilders is in knowing what and where to build — a challenge we are uniquely equipped to meet at U.S. Home.

853. U.S. Long Distance
9311 San Pedro
Suite 300
San Antonio, TX 78216
Phone: (210) 525-9009
Web: http://www.usld.com

U.S. Long Distance (NASDAQ; USLD) is in the telecommunications industry, providing customers with products and services.

Mission Statement: To provide innovative telecommunications products and services that enhance the value of our company for our customers, employees, shareholders, and communities.

Company Vision: Our vision is to capitalize on our ability to manage change

while pursuing strategic opportunities. We will continue to grow internally and through acquisitions in new and existing niche markets. We are a dynamic, evolving company which encourages innovation and teamwork.

854. U.S. Robotics Inc.
8100 McCormick Blvd.
Skokie, IL 60076
Phone (847) 982-5010
Web: http://www.usr.com

U.S. Robotics Inc. is an information access company, making modems and other data communications equipment. The company has been acquired by 3Com Corp. (NASDAQ; COMS).

Slogan: "U.S. Robotics is about ... results, people, access, performance, commitment."

Statement: Our business is to provide access to information. In every aspect of our operations, our people enable us to achieve a high level of performance that can be demonstrated by our financial results. And we have a strong commitment to continuing our growth.

Our objective is to be the world's best information access company. We intend to be a leader in all segments of the market and to be recognized for the quality of our operations and our ability to meet customers' needs.

855. U S West Inc.
7800 E. Orchard Rd.
Englewood, CO 80111
Phone: (303) 793-6500
Web: http://www.uswest.com

U S West Inc. was formed in 1983 as the result of a consent decree between the U.S. Department of Justice and AT&T. The company is one of the regional holding companies providing local telephone service in the United States. The company covers 14 western states and is involved in local telephone service, cellular service, paging, cable service, the publication of telephone directories, communications networks and systems, and financial services. In late 1995, U S West's common stock was divided into two separate entities: U S West Communications Group (NYSE; USWCV) and U S West Media Group (NYSE; UMG).

Vision: By the year 2000, U S West will be the finest company in the world connecting people with their world.

Mission: U S West will be a leading provider of integrated communications, entertainment, and information services over wired broadband and wireless networks in selected local markets worldwide.

856. USA Waste Services Inc.
1001 Fannin
Suite 4000
Houston, TX 77002
Phone: (713) 512-6200

USA Waste Services Inc. (NYSE; UW) is a non-hazardous solid waste services company with collection, landfill, transfer, and recycling operations nationwide.

Slogan: "Performance According to Plan."

Our Plan: Our clear vision of where we were going and how we would get there has served us well over the last four years. Today, more than two dozen acquisitions later, we are no less committed to the tenets that have been the bedrock of our performance: The right people, sharing a common vision, employing proven strategies to build the business.

857. USF&G Corp.
100 Light St.
Baltimore, MD 21202
Phone: (410) 547-3000
Web: http://www.usfg.com

USF&F Corp. (NYSE; FG) is involved in property and casualty insurance, life insurance, and financial services. Its subsidiaries include the United States Fidelity and Guarantee Company, USF&G Financial Services Corp., Thomas Jefferson Life Insurance Co, Fidelity and Guaranty Life Insurance Co., F&G International Insurance Ltd., F&G Re Inc., and Automated Products Inc.

Vision: We aspire to build a company with a strong character of integrity and ethical conduct dedicated to providing very competitive, innovative, high quality insurance products and services to our customers.

We will secure a leadership position in our served markets and earn a superior return for our shareowners by adhering to four fundamental precepts of strategy:

(1) Create a performance driven culture and work environment conducive to the development and growth of our employees which enables them to exercise competitively superior skills.

(2) Compete only in attractive markets and businesses where we have the financial capability and market opportunity to attain a leadership position and earn an acceptable return.

(3) Build market-driven, highly focused businesses that provide value-added, differentiated products and services to our customers.

(4) Organize in a manner that best leverages people, capital, and technology.

858. UST Inc.
100 West Putnam Ave.
Greenwich, CT 06830
Phone: (203) 661-1100
Web: http://www.shareholder.com/ust

UST Inc. (NYSE; UST) is a holding company for its four wholly-owned subsidiaries: United States Tobacco Company, International Wine & Spirits Ltd., UST Enterprises Inc., and UST International Inc. The company is a producer and marketer of smokeless tobacco products, which include Copenhagen and Skoal. Other consumer products include premium wines.

Positioned for the Future: With our

two greatest assets — superior products and talented, resourceful employees — we will continue to capitalize on opportunities, and we will do so as a responsible corporate citizen, supporting and strengthening the communities in which we live and do business. And as always, our goal will be to maximize stockholder value.

Our Objectives:

(1) Expand the market for our moist smokeless tobacco products.

(2) Increase the profitability of our wine operations.

(3) Expand our sales internationally.

(4) Continue to build upon and maximize the potential of our other businesses.

859. Valspar Corp.

1101 Third St. S.
P.O. Box 1461
Minneapolis, MN 55415
Phone: (612) 332-7371
Web: http://www.valspar.com

Valspar Corp. (NYSE; VAL) is a producer, distributor, and marketer of paints and coatings.

Statement: Valspar's mission is to be the recognized leader in the coatings industry.

860. Value Health Inc.

22 Waterville Rd.
Avon, CT 06001
Phone: (860) 678-3400
Web: http://www.vh.com

Value Health Inc. (NYSE; VH) is a provider of specialty managed care benefit programs and health care information services. Value Health's specialty managed care benefit programs include prescription drugs, mental health and substance abuse, and workers' compensation. Value Health's health care information services include clinically based precertification and claims review, provider profiling, claims cost analysis, evaluation and management of health benefit providers, health policy and management consulting, and disease management program development.

Slogan: "Bringing Science to the Art of Managed Care ... Disease by Disease."

Statement: We were founded in 1987 with the objective — expressed in our tag line — of "bringing science to the art of managed care." By that phrase we meant that we wanted to focus on identifying and reducing medically inappropriate care, rather than aiming just at provider discounts or reduced hospital days. We determined that we had to focus on clinical issues, and that required organizing managed care around the same specialty categories that health care itself had developed — for example, mental health care. So, the business of "specialty managed care" was born.

861. Vanguard Cellular Systems Inc.

2002 Pisgah Church Rd.
Suite 300
Greensboro, NC 27455
Phone: (910) 282-3690
Web: http://www.cellone.net

Vanguard Cellular Systems Inc. (NASDAQ; VCELA) is a wireless telecommunications company.

Our Vision: To build one of the nation's leading wireless telecommunications companies by providing products and services of such premium quality, convenience and value that we delight our customers by consistently meeting or exceeding their expectations while, at all times, living up to the highest standards of professionalism, integrity, humility, and community service.

862. Varian Associates Inc.

3050 Hansen Way
Palo Alto, CA 94304
Phone: (415) 493-4000
Web: http://www.varian.com

Varian Associates Inc. (NYSE; VAR) is a diversified electronics company that designs, manufactures, and markets high technology systems and components.

Slogan: "Growth Through Innovation."

Statement: For a high-technology company, new product innovation is the driving force behind growth. While Varian has always been known for its technical creativity, the operational excellence efficiencies implemented during recent years have positioned the company to achieve not just growth, but profitable growth.

863. Varlen Corp.

55 Shuman Blvd.
P.O. Box 3089
Naperville, IL 60566
Phone: (630) 420-0400

Varlen Corp. (NASDAQ; VRLN) provides transportation industries, petroleum refineries, and life science research laboratories with engineered industrial products designed for specialized applications.

Slogan: "Manufacturer of Precision Engineered Products."

Mission: Varlen's primary objective is to increase the long-term value of its shareowners' investment. This will be achieved by building upon our employees' creativity and their commitment to serving customers better and more efficiently than our competitors do in the markets where Varlen chooses to compete.

Varlen will invest resources in selected industrial markets where it has, or can obtain, a leadership position; we will redeploy resources from markets where we cannot. We will continue to enhance our global presence. Varlen's engineered products for the niche markets in which it participates are characterized by differentiable process technology employed in their manufacture and/or superior performance attributes. Our dedication to continuous improvement will be unrelenting.

864. VELCRO USA Inc.

406 Brown Ave.
Manchester, NH 03108

Phone: (603) 669-4892
Web: http://www.velcro.com

VELCRO USA Inc., a division of VELCRO Industries N.V. (NASDAQ; VELCF), manufactures and markets hook and loop fasteners used in homes, at work, in automobiles and refrigerators, on athletic gear and blood pressure cuffs, in computers and on industrial lift belts. The VELCRO brand hook and loop fasteners are named for the French words "velour" and "crochet."

Slogan: "The VELCRO Advantage."

Mission Statement: We, the employees of VELCRO USA Inc., are committed to the continuing success of our company in an increasingly competitive world.

We will continue to improve every aspect of our business, providing superior cost-effective products and services which exceed our customers' expectations.

We will encourage individual achievement within an atmosphere of teamwork.

We will conduct our business honestly, ethically, and safely.

865. Ventritex Inc.

701 E. Evelyn Ave.
Sunnyvale, CA 94086
Phone: (408) 738-4883

Ventritex Inc. (NASDAQ; VNTX) develops, manufactures, and markets implantable defibrillators and related products for the treatment of ventricular tachycardia and ventricular fibrillation, forms of abnormal heart rhythms. The company has entered into an agreement to merge with Pacesetter Inc., a subsidiary of St. Jude Medical Inc., subject to approval.

Statement: Through an ongoing commitment to product superiority, Ventritex has established a reputation as an innovator in implantable defibrillator systems and is developing product advances that will continue to improve tachyarrhythmia therapy.

Looking to the Future: Ventritex's proven success in introducing product advancements in implantable defibrillator therapy has strongly positioned the company to meet future opportunities and challenges in this dynamic market. By working in close partnership with a large base of cardiac electrophysiologists, the company plans to continue providing innovative products that respond to evolving patient and physician needs in implantable defibrillator therapy.

866. Vertex Pharmaceuticals Inc.
40 Allston St.
Cambridge, MA 02139
Phone: (617) 576-3111
Web: http://www.vpharm.com

Vertex Pharmaceuticals Inc. (NASDAQ; VRTX) is a drug discovery and development company that has pioneered the application of structure-based drug design to design orally deliverable, small molecule drugs.

Statement: The company's strategy is to participate in major pharmaceutical markets by designing small molecule therapeutics for life threatening and chronic diseases.

Our goal is to create alliances with major pharmaceutical companies based on shared expertise and strategic commitment, so that together we can successfully take drug candidates to market.

867. VF Corp.
1047 N. Park Rd.
Wyomissing, PA 19610
Phone: (610) 378-1151
Web: http://www.vfc.com

VF Corp. (NYSE; VFC) is an apparel company. Products include jeans, knitwear, playwear, nighttime and intimate apparel, and specialty apparel. Brand names include Lee, Wrangler, Jantzen, Vanity Fair, Barbizon and Healthtex.

Slogan: Lee — "The Brand That Fits."

Mission Statement: VF is a diversified apparel company whose mission is to provide above average shareholder returns by being the industry leader in marketing and servicing basic fashion apparel needs while maintaining conservative financial strategies.

868. VIACOM Inc.
1515 Broadway
New York, NY 10036
Phone: (212) 258-6000
Web: http://www.viacom.com

VIACOM Inc. (AMEX; VIA) is a diversified entertainment and publishing company with operations in four segments: Networks and broadcasting; entertainment; video and music/theme parks; and publishing.

Our Strategy: Our vision remains clear and simple: To be the leading software-driven media company by creating incomparable content, and then molding that content into powerful brands and franchises for global distribution, while remaining fiscally responsible. This overriding mission will continue to define our future, as we capitalize on our leadership positions and on the robust growth prospects of our businesses domestically and in overseas markets.

869. Viking Office Products Inc.
879 W. 190th
10th Fl.
Gardena, CA 90248
Phone: (310) 225-4500
Web: http://www.vikingop.com

Viking Office Products (NASDAQ; VKNG) is a direct marketer, via catalog, of office products to small and medium-sized businesses.

Mission Statement: Viking sells office products to small and medium sized businesses nationwide through innovative, aggressive direct marketing catalogs and programs.

To be successful and grow our company, while each of us advance our careers and benefit our families, we are committed to the following:

1. That every customer large or small, receive our best, honest, and personal service.

2. That each of our efforts results in so impressing our customers that they want to buy from us again.

3. That we provide quality business products at significant savings while generating acceptable profits for our company.

4. That we strive to provide, "next day delivery' to all our customers nationwide.

5. That Viking grow at a healthy rate, producing exceptional results through effective and aggressive marketing, intelligent cost control and involved results-oriented management.

6. That each employee take responsibility for maintaining our business and for recognizing needed changes to "fix" that which is not acceptable.

7. That Viking be recognized by its employees, customers, and suppliers, for excellence, integrity, and market leadership.

870. Vons Companies Inc.
618 Michillinda Ave.
Arcadia, CA 91007
Phone: (818) 821-7000
Parent's Web: http://www.safeway.com

Vons Companies Inc., a subsidiary of Safeway Inc. (NYSE; SWY), is a large, full-service supermarket chain in Southern California. The company operates stores under the names Vons and Pavilions. The company also operates the Jerseymaid Dairies Division in addition to warehouse and distribution facilities and a bakery.

Slogan: "Vons Is Value."

Statement: Our success and satisfaction is derived from meeting our commitment to our associates, our customers, and the communities we serve.

871. Vulcan Materials Co.
One Metroplex Dr.
Birmingham, AL 35209
Phone: (205) 877-3000
Web: http://www.vulcanmat.com

Vulcan Materials Co. (NYSE; VMC) is principally engaged in the production, distribution, and sale of construction materials and industrial and specialty chemicals. The company is a major producer of construction aggregates.

Mission: Vulcan Materials Company is an international producer of industrial materials and commodities that are essential to the standard of living of advanced and developed societies.

Our mission is to provide quality products and service that consistently meet our customers' expectations; to be responsible stewards with respect to the safety and environmental impart of our operations and products; and to earn superior returns for our shareholders.

872. Wabash National Corp.
1000 Sagamore Pkwy. South.
Lafayette, IN 47905
Phone: (317) 448-1591
Web: http://www.nlci.com/wabash

Wabash National Corp. (NYSE; WNC) designs, manufactures, and markets truck trailers, as well as parts and related equipment. The company also manufactures "RoadRailer," a patented bimodal technology that permit a vehicle to run both over the highway and directly on railroad lines.

Slogan: "The Growth Company."

Philosophy: We recognize that without a profit there are no jobs.

Wabash National Corporation will create and maintain an environment that our people are proud to support and enjoy working within because we recognize that people are our most valuable asset.

We will maintain the highest degree of credibility and integrity with our associates, customers, and suppliers.

We will make "WNC" recognized as the quality standard of the industry.

We are committed to the most rapid growth rate which can be achieved without compromise to our people of product.

Wabash National Corporation will be the industry leader in innovation.

Business Strategy: The company's business strategy is to follow an integrated approach to engineering, manufacturing, and marketing which emphasizes flexibility in product design and operations while preserving a low cost structure. Wabash has sought to identify and produce proprietary products in the trucking and bimodal industries which offer added value to customers and, therefore, generate higher profit margins than those associated with standard trailers. The company has developed its leasing business and expects to continue each development. The company also intends to expand its distribution of aftermarket parts and strengthen its existing dealer network in order to more effectively distribute its products.

873. Wachovia Corp.
100 N. Main St.
Winston-Salem, NC 27150
Phone: (910) 770-5000
Web: http://www.wachovia.com

Wachovia Corp. (NYSE; WB) is a bank holding company in the Southeast United States.

Mission and Objectives: Basic Mission: To serve in an exceptional manner the interests of shareholders, customers, employees, and the public, by pursuing progressive business strategies, by practicing sound financial principles, by providing superior service, and by being an exemplary corporate citizen.

874. Wackenhut Corp.
4200 Wackenhut Dr.
Palm Beach Gardens, FL 33410
Phone: (561) 622-5656

Wackenhut Corp. (NYSE; WAK) is a diversified, international provider of security-related services to governmental agencies and industrial and commercial organizations. The company's security business includes physical protection, information security, and investigations. Other business interests include facility management, food service, education and training, and fire prevention and emergency services.

Corporate Vision: By the year 2000, the Wackenhut Corporation will be recognized throughout the world as a uniquely diversified, superior performing and profitable protective and support services company.

875. Wal-Mart Stores Inc.
702 SW 8th St.
Bentonville, AR 72716
Phone: (501) 273-4000
Web: http://www.wal-mart.com

Wal-Mart Stores Inc. (NYSE; WMT) is a major retailer. The company services customers domestically and in Puerto Rico, primarily through the operation of Wal-Mart stores (discount department stores), Sam's Clubs (warehouse membership clubs), and Wal-Mart Supercenters (combination full-line supermarket and discount department stores).

Slogans: "Always." "Watch for Falling Prices." "'Watch for Falling Prices' Isn't Just a Slogan It's a Commitment to Our Customers."

Statement: Each Wal-Mart, Supercenter, and Sam's Club is planned for the people who shop there. That merchandising philosophy is the foundation on which Wal-Mart was built and continues to grow. At Wal-Mart, merchandising is more than a process of stocking products customers buy. Very simply, throughout the Wal-Mart organization, we believe that our job is to buy for our customers, not just sell to them.

876. Walgreen Co.
200 Wilmot Rd.
Deerfield, IL 60015

Phone: (847) 940-2500
Web: http://www.walgreens.com

Walgreen Co. (NYSE; WAG) operates a chain of drugstores.

Slogan: "The Pharmacy America Trusts."

Shareholder Value: We believe in long-term shareholder value: Our employees should be encouraged to own Walgreen stock and participate in our company's future.

Individual shareholders are as important to Walgreen's financial stability as institutions with large holdings.

We will communicate to all shareholders not only financial results, but also a clear vision of our goals and plans.

We will offer shareholders a fair return long-term by reinvesting profits in expansion and technology which offer opportunity to our people and better service to our customers.

877. Walt Disney Co.

500 S. Buena Vista St.
Burbank, CA 91521
Phone: (818) 560-1000
Web: http://www.disney.com

Walt Disney Co. (NYSE; DIS) is a diversified entertainment organization. The company has several segments: creative (motion pictures, home video, and original television programming), broadcasting (ABC Inc.), theme parks and resorts, and consumer products.

Statement: The Disney culture, and maintaining it, is still my number one priority. Equally important is maintaining the autonomous ABC news culture: Serving the broadest possible public interest, being willing to stand for the values of a free press, pursuing the news aggressively, reporting it without fear or favor, and being guided by an unbiased commitment to fairness and honesty and tough-mindedness, all the while resisting the pressure to pull punches, homogenize the product and avoid all controversy — and doing all this with the same high standards of

excellence we pursue in all of our divisions.

878. Wausau Paper Mills Co.

One Clark's Island
P.O. Box 1408
Wausau, WI 54402
Phone: (715) 845-5266
Web: http://www.wausaupapers.com

Wausau Paper Mills Co. (NASDAQ; WSAU) produces and markets specialty paper and related products.

Mission: Wausau Paper Mills Company markets and produces quality specialty paper and converted products to provide value to our customers, employees, and shareholders.

Strategic Intent: Wausau Paper Mills Company is THE benchmark for the markets we serve.

Vision Statement: Wausau Papers will be recognized by our customers as the preferred supplier of quality paper products and services in the markets we serve.

This will be accomplished through a commitment to a continuous quality improvement process that includes:

Consistently meeting or exceeding internal and external customer expectations.

Recognizing our responsibilities to the community, environment, employees, and shareholders.

879. WD-40 Co.

1061 Cudahy Place
San Diego, CA 92110
Phone: (619) 275-1400

WD-40 Co. (NASDAQ; WDFC) produces one product: WD-40. WD-40 is a chemical-petroleum based maintenance product consumed by end-users in homes, factories, garages, farms, and offices throughout the world. It stops squeaks, protects metal, loosens rusted parts and frees sticky mechanisms.

Corporate Objectives: Management is dedicated to the objectives of increasing corporate earnings and dividends by winning the end-users' brand loyalty for our company's only product, WD-40. The company would consider adding another product if it is determined that the company can make a decisive contribution to that product's growth in the area of marketing-distribution. The product would, of course, have to have an attractive profit potential.

While our company is technically a manufacturer, it is really a marketer. Such being the case, it is organized to focus intensive management attention on the critical success area of: Sales policies; marketing plan formulation; and implementation of marketing plan.

880. Weatherford Enterra Inc.
1360 Post Oak Blvd.
Suite 1000
P.O. Box 27608
Houston, TX 77227
Phone: (713) 439-9400

Weatherford Enterra Inc. (NYSE; WII) provides oilfield services and equipment.

Statement of Values: Weatherford Enterra will achieve financial success by providing quality products and services that ensure unparalleled customer satisfaction. We will accomplish this through individuals working as a team in a highly accountable organization. This environment will demand intensity and integrity and encourage individual and group excellence.

881. Wendy's International Inc.
4288 W. Dublin-Granville Rd.
Dublin, OH 43017
Phone: (614) 764-3100
Web: http://www.wendys.com

Wendy's International Inc. (NYSE; WEN) is a major fast-food, hamburger restaurant chain in the U.S., ranked behind McDonald's and Burger King.

Slogans: "Hot 'n' Juicy." "Wendy's Has the Taste." "Ain't No Reason." "Wendy's Kind of People." "Where's the Beef?" "Wendy's, the Best Burger in the Business." "Choose Fresh, Choose Wendy's." "Only Wendy's." "Our Hamburgers Are the Best in the Business, or I Wouldn't Have Named the Place After My Daughter." "Fresh Taste Best."

Mission Statement: Deliver Total Quality.

Vision Statement: To be the customer's restaurant of choice, the employer of choice, and the franchiser of choice.

882. Western Atlas Inc.
360 North Crescent Dr.
Beverly Hills, CA 90210
Phone: (310) 888-2500
Web: http://www.westatlas.com

Western Atlas Inc. (NYSE; WAI) has two primary business segments — oilfield information and industrial automation.

Statement: Western Atlas' total systems approach to manufacturing projects has proven to be a successful business strategy in an industry which historically has had difficulty adjusting its asset base to changing market environments. Concentration on design and engineering, innovative uses of technology, project management, and outsourcing of nonproprietary asset-intensive processes formed the basis for the company's constant reengineering of its activities in this area. Looking at the total process, rather than at a single machine or tool, has resulted in a solutions orientation that has given the manufacturing systems operations of Western Atlas their competitive advantage in the market.

883. Western Digital Corp.
8105 Irvine Center Dr.
Irvine, CA 92718
Phone: (714) 932-5000
Web: http://www.wdc.com

Western Digital Corp. (NYSE; WDC) designs and manufactures high quality hard disk drives, semiconductors, and board level products for the personal computer industry. The company markets these products to leading systems manufacturers and selected resellers.

Vision: Western Digital will be the global quality leader in its products, services, technologies, and business conduct. We will have world-class employees, long-term partnerships with our customers, suppliers, and communities and will deliver superior financial returns to our shareholders.

Mission: Western Digital's mission is to satisfy our customers' requirements by providing world-class computing products and services. We will accomplish this mission through investments in people and technologies that generate sustained profitability.

884. Western Resources Inc.
818 Kansas Ave.
Topeka, KS 66612
Phone: (913) 575-6300
Web: http://www.wstnres.com

Western Resources Inc. (NYSE; WR) provides gas and electric services.

Statement: Our objective is clear. Adding value to the company and to your investment is our goal, while we position ourselves as a leader of energy, security, and related products and services.

885. WestPoint Stevens Inc.
507 West 10th St.
P.O. Box 71
West Point, GA 31833
Phone: (706) 645-4000

WestPoint Stevens Inc. (NASDAQ; WPSN) is a leading producer of bed and bath fashions, including sheets, pillowcases, comforters, blankets, bedspreads, towels, and accessories. The company is also a leading domestic manufacturer of knitted apparel fabrics.

Statement: Our strategies are based on enhancing our dominant brand and li-

censed product offerings, continuing to drive down production and operating costs at every level, and strengthening our focus on growing sales, earnings, and market share.

Our long-term goals remain the same: To increase sales and earnings through three well-defined business strategies:

First, we are positioning WestPoint Stevens as a consumer products company utilizing our branded and licensed products as the comprehensive resource of choice for our customers. We already offer one of the broadest product lines in our industry to virtually every channel of distribution, and we are working with our customers on innovative new consumer products such as deep-pocket sheets and wrinkle-free bedding.

Second, we will continue to strengthen our competitive position by improving efficiencies and lowering costs at every level of our organization.

Third, we will focus on opportunities to increase sales, margins, and earnings. By introducing new products and increasing emphasis on higher-margin products, we are working to improve the profitability of our product mix. Outsourcing of selected products and components will add to profitability.

886. Westvaco Corp.
299 Park Ave.
New York, NY 10171
Phone: (212) 688-5000

Westvaco Corp. (NYSE; W) is a supplier of printing paper.

Mission Statement: The mission of Westvaco fine papers division is to be the preferred supplier in the markets for high quality printing paper.

887. Weyerhaeuser Co.
33663 Weyerhaeuser Way
Federal Way, WA 98003
Phone: (253) 924-2345
Web: http://www.weyerhaeuser.com

Weyerhaeuser Co. (NYSE; WY) operates in the forest/paper products industry.
Our Vision: The best forest products company in the world.

888. Whirlpool Corp.

2000 N. M-63
Benton Harbor, MI 49022
Phone: (616) 926-5000
Web: http://www.whirlpool.com

Whirlpool Corp. (NYSE; WHR) is a manufacturer and marketer of major home appliances.
Slogan: "Making Your World a Little Easier."
Statement: We expect to continue to reap solid profitability from North America and Latin America by proceeding on the fundamental path we've taken in those regions for some time: To greater operating efficiency.

889. White Castle System Inc.

555 West Goodale St.
Columbus, OH 43215
Phone: (614) 228-5781

White Castle System Inc., a private, family-held company, is a fast-food hamburger restaurant chain. The company also sells cooked and frozen White Castle's products to supermarkets for home freezers.
Motto: "The Taste Some People Won't Live Without!"
Pledge: Serving the finest products, for the least cost, in the cleanest surroundings, with the most courteous personnel.

890. Whitman Corp.

III Crossroads of Commerce
3501 Algonquin Rd.
Rolling Meadows, IL 60008
Phone: (847) 818-5000

Whitman Corp. (NYSE; WH) is engaged in three distinct businesses: Pepsi-Cola and other non-alcoholic beverage products (Pepsi General is a franchise for the distribution of Pepsi-Cola products), Midas Automotive services, and Hussmann refrigeration systems and equipment.
Slogan: Midas — "Auto System Expects."
Our Financial Goal: Whitman's primary long-term goal is to provide superior total return to shareholders. To help assure we will meet this goal, Whitman has adopted a set of financial objectives to measure its operating performance. As we meet these objectives, we should outperform the S&P 500 in total return.

891. Whittaker Corp.

1955 N. Surveyor Ave.
Simi Valley, CA 93063
Phone: (805) 526-5700
Web: http://www.whittaker.com

Whittaker Corp. (NYSE; WKR) is in the aerospace/defense industry.
Corporate Mission: Our strategic focus is to be a solutions-based, market-driven business that outperforms competitors through continuous value creation; to be a leader in all markets in which we choose to compete.

892. Whole Foods Market

601 N. Lamar #300
Austin, TX 78746
Phone: (512) 477-5566
Web: http://www.wholefoods.com/wf.html

Whole Foods Market (NASDAQ; WFMI) operates grocery stores featuring fine foods.
Mission Statement: Whole Foods Market is a dynamic leader in the quality food business. We aim to set the standards of excellence for grocers. We are building a business in which quality permeates all aspects of our company. Quality is a state of mind at Whole Food Market.

We recognize that our success reaches far beyond the company by contributing to the quality of life renaissance occurring here on earth. We are willing to share our successes and failures, our hopes and fears, and our joys and sorrows with others in the quality food business. Moreover, we have a responsibility to encourage more people to join us in the quality food business, to adopt higher standards of excellence, and generally to contribute wherever and whenever it makes sense to the quality of life renaissance. The future we will experience tomorrow is created one step at a time today.

The success of our business is measured by customer satisfaction, team member happiness, return on capital investment, improvement in the quality of the environment, and local and larger community support.

Our ability to instill a clear sense of interdependence among our various shareholders is interconnected with our desire and efforts to communicate more often, more openly, and more compassionately. Better communication equals better understanding and more trust.

893. Willamette Industries Inc.

3800 First Interstate Tower
1300 S.W. Fifth Ave.
Portland, OR 97201
Phone: (503) 227-5581

Willamette Industries Inc. (NYSE; WLL) produces forest and paper products.

Statement: For Willamette Industries, flexibility results from a decentralized organizational structure and a management style that promotes growth in shareholder value. Flexibility means developing new products and processes to meet customer needs. It means finding new or underutilized sources of raw material. It means expanding in geographic regions where markets are robust and raw materials more readily available. It means a vertically-integrated structure that makes efficient use of raw materials, allow Willamette to add

value to the resource and the company's basic products.

894. Williams Companies Inc.

One Williams Center
P.O. Box 2400
Tulsa, OK 74172
Phone: (918) 588-2000
Web: http://www.twc.com/twc

Williams Companies Inc. (NYSE; WMB) is in the following businesses: Natural gas pipelines (Northwest Pipeline; Williams Natural Gas; Transcontinental Gas Pipe Line; Texas Gas Transmission; Kern River Gas Transmission), natural gas gathering and processing (Williams Field Services Group, energy services (Williams Energy Services), Liquids pipeline/ethanol production (Williams Pipe Line; Williams Energy Ventures), and telecommunications/technology (WilTel; WilTech Group).

Goal: Consistently provide superior, sustainable returns for our shareholders and maintain performance in the top quartile of comparable businesses.

895. Winn-Dixie Stores Inc.

5050 Edgewood Ct.
P.O. Box B
Jacksonville, FL 32254
Phone: (904) 783-5000

Winn-Dixie Stores Inc. (NYSE; WIN) operates a chain of grocery stores.

Slogans: "America's Supermarket." "The Beef People."

Mission Statement: To innovate and implement better and more efficient ways of meeting the changing needs of our customers.

To employ customer-oriented associates and provide them with the opportunity for training and promotion, while offering pay, benefits and working conditions equal to or better than those generally available in the food industry in our trade area.

To deal fairly with customers, associates

and suppliers in order to merit their continuing patronage and support.

To support civic and charitable efforts for the betterment of the communities in which we live and work.

To operate a financially sound business by energetically increasing sales and controlling expenses, for the purpose of earning a reasonable return for all who have an interest in the growth of our company.

We want to thank all Winn-Dixie associates for their hard work and dedication. By fulfilling the above commitment, we will ensure our future growth and profitability. Our company also thanks our customers, suppliers and shareholders for their continuing patronage and support.

896. Winnebago Industries Inc.

P.O. Box 152
Forest City, IA 50436
Phone: (515) 582-3535

Winnebago Industries Inc. (NYSE; WGO) manufactures and markets RV products.

Mission Statement: Winnebago Industries Inc. is a profit-oriented company which manufactures and markets high-value, quality leisure products.

Secondary mission includes financial management, brand licensing, OEM parts/sales and satellite courier services.

Those activities do not exclude the possibility that Winnebago will participate in other endeavors, providing these endeavors are either synergistic to the primary and secondary missions defined above or represent activities that can be financially justified.

In all cases, the company will meet its defined missions through the proper and effective utilization of capital, processes, and people.

Long-Range Planning: Long-range corporate planning will continue to emphasize consistent improvement in growth and earnings.

Relative to the long-range business, Winnebago will constantly seek areas of opportunity that are synergistic to our current capabilities and resources, in order to offset the cyclical nature of the RV industry.

Our long-term financial objective is to minimize any year-to-year fluctuations in earnings and to constantly improve profits over the previous year.

Corporate Goals: As a corporation, the company conducts its business in accordance with accepted ethical consideration and legal rules and regulations.

In addition, the company will continue to strive to maintain the following goals:

1. The company will position itself primarily as a high-volume, high-quality manufacturer of leisure products and will expand into the commercial vehicle market.

2. The company will operate on a sound financial basis by maintaining a strong financial position and will maintain its industry leadership as measured by market share and return on investment by effectively utilizing its assets to develop new products and services and creative market innovations.

3. The company will develop RV products that will continue to gain a greater share of the market, based on a marketing plan which responds to pricing for affordability, demographics, and psychlographics which adjust to shifts in consumer demand.

4. The company will consider new business opportunities which will contribute to growth and also counter the cycles of the RV business.

5. The company will improve the processes and practices which bring a product from concept to market in order to reduce costs and increase quality.

6. The company will continue to support the concept of profit centers.

7. The company will expand and improve human resource capabilities through training and higher education opportunities, and improved management and team building, so that the optimum potential of

Winnebago employees is attained to perpetuate the enterprise and fulfill its mission.

8. The company will continue to promote the development of exclusive Winnebago and Itasca dealerships through the formation of strategies and plans specifically designed to encourage this exclusivity.

897. Wisconsin Central Transportation Corp.
6250 N. River Rd.
Suite 9000
Rosemont, IL 60018
Phone: (847) 318-4600

Wisconsin Central Transportation Corp. (NASDAQ; WCLY) is a regional railroad company. The company's principal subsidiaries are Wisconsin Central Ltd., Fox Valley & Western Ltd., and Algoma Central Railroad Inc. The company also holds a 30% equity interest in Tranz Rail Limited (New Zealand). Additionally, the company holds a 32% equity interest in North and South Railways Limited (Great Britain).

The Wisconsin Central Pledge: To offer superior transportation consisting of more frequent, dependable train service, at competitive prices, with proper equipment, accomplished by customer-minded employees.

898. Wisconsin Power & Light Co.
222 Washington Ave.
Madison, WI 53703
Phone: (414) 221-2345

Wisconsin Power & Light Co. (private sub.) is an electric utility company.

Vision Statement: The power to shape the future.

Corporate Values Statement: WPL Holding Inc. places the highest value on those partnerships that will move the corporation safely and successfully forward into the future:

We value our partnership with customers and are driven to meet the service standards they demand.

We value our partnership with employees and offer them a continued relationship based on their contribution to the strategic direction and success of the corporation.

We value our partnership with shareowners and strive to create wealth for them.

We value the integrity and dignity of our corporation and that of our partners and pledge to conduct our business consistent with the values we hold.

899. Wisconsin Public Service Corp.
700 North Adams St.
P.O. Box 19001
Green Bay, WI 54307
Phone: (414) 433-1466
Web: http://www.wpsr.com

Wisconsin Public Service Corp. is a wholly-owned subsidiary of WPS Resources Corporation (NYSE; WPS). The company is a regulated electric and gas utility which services Northeastern Wisconsin and an adjacent portion of Upper Michigan.

Our Mission: Provide customers with the best value in energy and related services.

Our Vision: People creating the world's premier energy company.

900. WMX Technologies Inc.
3003 Butterfield Rd.
Oak Brook, IL 60521
Phone: (708) 572-8800
Web: http://www.wmx.com

WMX Technologies Inc. (NYSE; WMX) is in the environmental/waste industry.

Mission Statement: The mission of WMX Technologies Inc. (formerly Waste Management Inc.) is to be the acknowledged worldwide leader in providing comprehensive environmental waste management and related services of the highest quality to industry, government, and consumers using state-of-the-art systems responsive to customer need, sound environmental policy, and the highest standard of corporate citizenship.

In fulfilling this mission, we shall provide a rewarding work environment for our people, cooperate with all relevant government agencies, and promote a spirit of partnership with the communities and enterprises we serve as we strive to be a responsive neighbor, while increasing shareholder value.

901. Wolohan Lumber Co.
1740 Midland Rd.
P.O. Box 3235
Saginaw, MI 48605
Phone: (517) 793-4532

Wolohan Lumber Co. (NASDAQ; WLHN) is a building supply retailer.

Company Creed: Purpose: Our purpose is to make the customer Number One, in our plans and in our actions. Our challenge is to provide the best value in products, service, quality, and price that addresses our customers' needs. By making our customer Number One, they in turn will make Wolohan Lumber Co. Number One.

902. Wolverine World Wide Inc.
9341 Courtland Dr.
Rockford, MI 49351
Phone: (616) 866-5500

Wolverine World Wide Inc. (NYSE; WWW) manufactures and markets internationally recognized footwear brands: Tru-Stitch, Bates, Wolverine, Hush Puppies, Coleman, and Caterpillar.

Mission: Our mission is to provide superior value in comfortable casual and functional footwear for men, women, and children throughout the world.

903. WorldCom Inc.
515 East Amite St.
Jackson, MS 39201
Phone: (601) 360-8600
Web: http://www.wcom.com

WorldCom Inc. (NASDAQ; WCOM) is a global telecommunications company.

Slogan: "One Company, One Source."

Goal: Our goal is to build a new kind of communications company. One that behaves very differently from the monopolies that have developed over the past hundred years. One that can move quickly to meet the changing needs of the business marketplace — by building the right facilities, using the right technologies and offering the right services. One that can leverage the unique assets of the combined companies. One that can utilize advanced expertise and industry leadership in delivering services through Internet-based technologies. That's the kind of business we're building, and in doing so, we believe that we are as well positioned as anyone to lead the industry through the changes ahead.

904. WPP Group PLC
27 Farm St.
London, England W1X 6RD
Phone (0171) 408-2204

WPP Group PLC (NASDAQ; WPPGY) is active in media advertising (J. Walter Thompson; Ogilvy & Mather Worldwide; Conquest; Cole & Weber), market research (Milward Brown International; MRB Group; Research International), public relations (Hill & Knowlton; Ogilvy Adams & Rinehart; Carl Byoir & Associates Inc.), and specialist communications.

What We're About: To develop and manage talent; to apply that talent, through the world, for the benefit of clients; to do so in partnership; to do so with profit.

Statement: WPP's central objective continues to be the provision of outstanding service to clients. As client needs and opportunities change, so do the Group's resources.

After some years of debate about the value of fully-integrated marketing services, client interest is now turned quite rapidly into real demand; and the Group and its companies are extremely well-placed — perhaps uniquely so — to meet it.

Accordingly, a greater proportion of our business is now being conducted by collaboration between different disciplines within the Group. The importance of these new partnerships is most clearly apparent in the acquisition of new business. To nourish this trend, the Group has developed a programme of cross-company initiatives which already include training; incentive schemes; information technology and practice development.

905. Xerox Corp.
800 Long Ridge Rd.
P.O. Box 1600
Stamford, CT 06904
Phone: (203) 968-3000
Web: http://www.xerox.com

Xerox Corp. (NYSE; XRX) manufactures and markets office supplies and equipment.

Slogans: "The Document Company." "Creating Productivity Through the Document."

Statement: We continue to focus on two key objectives: Productivity and growth. Our productivity initiatives are paying off. Our most significant challenge and opportunity is to realize the full potential of our direct sales force and to continue to build effective indirect channels of distribution.

I am confident about our future. Our strategic direction is clear. Our markets are attractive. Our plans to capitalize on these markets are sound. All Xerox people — among the best in the world — are on a single-minded crusade to add value to our customers by helping them become more productive. We know that if we do

well, we will deliver value to our shareholders.

The document is a complex, evolving tool that people use and reuse. Our strategy is to add value to the document across its entire life cycle: Input (receipt and capture), management (archiving, retrieval, construction, summarization, abstraction, authorization, authentication, accounting and work flow) and output (electronic distribution, printing, viewing and use). We provide customer solutions for the complete document cycle drawing upon hardware, software and service offerings that will work in or between networked enterprises.

906. Xilinx Inc.
2100 Login Dr.
San Jose, CA 95124
Phone: (408) 559-7778
Web: http://www.xilinx.com

Xilinx Inc. (NASDAQ; XLNX) designs, develops, and markets (complementary metal-oxide-silicon) programmable logic devices and related development system software. Xilinx products are standard integrated circuits that are programmed by Xilinx customers (electronic equipment manufacturers in the computer peripherals, telecommunications, industrial control and instrumentation, and military markets) to perform desired logic operations.

Slogans: "The Programmable Logic Company." "The Logic Solution for Technology Leaders."

Strategies: Our first strategy is to continue to reduce prices aggressively, commensurate with our ability to lower manufacturing costs.

Our second strategy is to introduce innovative, new product architectures that target new markets as well as high-volume, low-cost applications.

Our third strategy is to continue the enhancement of our software, which reduces prices for our customers by improving silicon utilization and performance.

907. Xircom Inc.
2300 Corporate Center Dr.
Thousand Oaks, CA 91320
Phone: (805) 376-9300
Web: http://www.xircom.com

Xircom Inc. (NASDAQ; XIRC) is a producer of advanced networking products. Xircom designs, manufactures and markets a family of network adapters for connecting portable personal computers to local area networks.

Slogan: "The Mobile Networking Experts."

Challenges: Xircom's challenges are largely those faced by all high technology companies: The pace of change in technology continues to quicken, making product life cycles even shorter. We meet this challenge with more research and development spending, process redesigns to eliminate time-wasting steps, and parallel activities in engineering, certification, and manufacturing.

In addition, our success has attracted imitators. As mobile networking has come to the forefront, a number of companies with desktop networking experience have introduced PC Card products. Thus, the market has become more competitive. We believe our focus on mobile networking solutions and our track record for introducing highly innovative products will allow us to continue to leverage our strengths and maintain a leading market position.

Vision: Our vision and focus will drive further innovations that reinforce Xircom's position as the preferred supplier of mobile networking solutions — and as the Mobile Networking Experts.

908. XOMA Corp.
2910 Seventh St.
Berkeley, CA 94710
Phone: (510) 644-1170

XOMA Corp. (NASDAQ; XOMA) is a biotechnology and pharmaceutical company engaged in the development of products for the treatment of infectious and immune system diseases and other serious disorders.

XOMA's Strengths: Focused pipeline in broad market segments; significant patent position for rBPI compounds; developed infrastructure; experienced management team.

XOMA's Approach: The company is building a portfolio of products based on rBPI, a novel human protein with bactericidal and endotoxin/heparin neutralizing activities.

XOMA is developing therapeutic products for the treatment of major complications due to infectious diseases, traumatic injury and surgery.

Goals: Our goal is to support those product candidates already well advanced in the development process, while maximizing our resources by reducing early-stage R&D and consolidating administrative functions.

909. Zenith Electronics Corp.
1000 Milwaukee Ave.
Glenview, IL 60025
Phone: (847) 391-7000
Web: http://www.zenith.com/home.html

Zenith Electronics Corp. (NYSE; ZE) is a leader in engineering, manufacturing and marketing consumer electronics, color picture tube, cable TV, and network communications products.

Mission: To enhance the entertainment experience by developing, manufacturing, and distributing a broad range of products for the delivery of video entertainment.

Vision: To profitably grow our presence in consumer electronics and network systems by exceeding the value expectations of our customers — delivering unparalleled performance in quality, product capability, cost and responsiveness.

910. ZOLL Medical Corp.
32 Second Ave.
Burlington, MA 01803
Phone: (617) 229-0020

ZOLL Medical Corp. (NASDAQ; ZOLL) designs, manufactures, and markets an integrated line of proprietary, non-invasive cardiac resuscitation devices and disposable electrodes. The company's products are used for the emergency treatment of cardiac arrest victims both inside and outside the hospital.

Statement: We intend to focus increased attention on the substantial opportunities in all segments of the pre-hospital market. Opportunities for our products with basic emergency services, the fastest growing defibrillator market segment, are yet to be fully exploited.

911. Zoom Telephonics Inc.
207 South St.
Boston, MA 02111
Phone: (617) 423-1072
Web: http://www.zoomtel.com

Zoom Telephonics Inc. (NASDAQ; ZOOM) manufactures and markets fax modems.

Mission Statement: For every high-volume segment of the PC fax modem market:

Have a product.

Provide the highest value, as measured by performance per dollar.

912. Zurn Industries Inc.
1 Zurn Pl.
Erie, PA 16514
Phone: (814) 452-2111

Zurn Industries Inc. (NYSE; ZRN) operates in two industry segments: Water control and power systems.

Statement: Zurn is pursuing an aggressive strategy to build shareholder value through profitable growth of core businesses at home and abroad.

INDEX

References are to entry numbers.